PATHWAYS THROUGH
JEWISH
HISTORY

PATHWAYS THROUGH JEWISH HISTORY

Revised Edition

by
RUTH SAMUELS

picture editor
SOL SCHARFSTEIN

KTAV PUBLISHING HOUSE, INC.

Design and art supervision by EZEKIEL SCHLOSS

Library of Congress Catalog Card No. 66-29105

Manufactured in the United States of America

TABLE OF CONTENTS

INTRODUCTION

The history of the Jewish people is unique. It is a saga of high adventure, deep tragedy, and events both joyful and awesome. Above all, it is the story of a people inspired by a great code of laws to survive through the ages with inner dignity. Many historians have called this survival miraculous, for the Jews have always been a minority—the threats to their continuance at times seemingly insurmountable.

The Jews are deeply aware of their history, for it represents not only a record of events but also their spiritual and cultural past, which shaped their way of life. Each generation has contributed to it. Our generation will add its own "peculiar treasure."

No Jew walks alone, for he is accompanied through the course of his days by the memory of the deeds and words of the great men and women who have gone before him. Every Sabbath, in synagogues throughout the world, Jews read a portion of the Torah and a chapter from the writings of the Prophets. On festival, memorial and holy days, the teachings of the Prophets and the deeds of the great leaders are recalled and the sufferings of the Children of Israel are reflected upon. It is a living page—ever new, ever wondrous, ever inspiring.

Great nations have risen, reigned and fallen, but the Jewish people, armed with their code of laws and steadfast in their beliefs, have emerged ever triumphant from wars, destruction and persecution. The history of the Jews reflects the events, ideas and ideals that have contributed significantly to the shaping of civilization.

Glossary of Hebrew Terminology and Names

The glossary is arranged by chapters with words usually appearing in the order they appear in the chapter. Words or names appearing in more than one chapter are generally not repeated in the list unless they are very essential to the later chapter. Casual items are not included.

Sounds are transliterated as phonetically as possible. The system makes no claim to scholarly consistency as its aim is first and foremost ease for the student. Therefore sounds may be represented in various ways depending upon how they appear to the English reader. The transliteration is based on the *Sfardit* as current in some American Hebrew schools and Hebrew speaking camps and does not necessarily adhere strictly to Hebrew enunciation in Israel.

ACKNOWLEDGMENTS

A book spanning so long a period of time and covering so much factual material requires the cooperation of many people. We are indebted to all those whose assistance has made this book possible, but especially to Isaiah Berger, who checked the overall accuracy of the material within the framework of its educational perspectives; Gertrude Hirshler and Deborah Karp, for their help in the editing of the text; Gertrude Pashin, secretary of the project; Jay Stern for compiling the Glossary of Hebrew terminology and names; and Edith Tarcov, without whose inspiration, literary contribution and tireless efforts this volume would never have come into being.

BEGINNINGS

ABRAHAM, FIRST OF ALL HEBREWS

The first great figure to appear on the stage of Jewish history is Abraham. Many centuries ago (about 1900 B.C.E.), according to the Bible, Abraham and his family left their native city of Ur, and wandered westward in search of new land on which to settle. Because they crossed the River Euphrates, people called them *Hebrews (Ivrim, those who came from the other side)*, a name which has stayed with the Jews to the present day. With Abraham, Jewish history began—a history that in the course of its development, has been deeply interwoven with world civilization and profoundly influenced it.

The city of Ur, Abraham's birthplace, was in Mesopotamia. About the time of Abraham, a Babylonian ruler in Mesopotamia, Hammurabi, drew up his famous code of laws. These wise and humane laws provided protection against injustice for all men. Hammurabi's code was the first of its kind in history and marked a great step forward for civilization.

THE FERTILE LANDS OF MESOPOTAMIA

Mesopotamia was a fertile land and attracted many wandering peoples. Various ethnic groups, such as Akkadians, Amorites, Sumerians conquered it and settled there. In some sources they are re-

This stele was discovered in the ancient city of Susa and is inscribed in cuneiform script with the laws of Hammurabi.

ferred to under general names such as Babylonians and Chaldeans. The two mighty rivers of Mesopotamia, the Tigris and Euphrates, flooded their banks each spring, bringing rich minerals to the soil. When the flood waters receded, planting would begin on the vast plain that lay between the two rivers.

Here in this fertile land a great civilization had developed, perhaps the earliest known to man. Its chief city, Ur, was a short distance from the

Excavation site of a temple in the ancient city of Ur.

Euphrates. Modern archeologists, excavating at the site of this ancient city, have unearthed many of its wonders. Ur sparkled with lush gardens and ornate palaces, and also with temples dedicated to the many gods of the land. It was a thriving market center, visited by merchants from near and far. From Ur caravans traveled to many distant points, for the purpose of exchanging goods. Ur also had its share of artists and scientists. The astronomers of Ur were among the first to seek to fathom the mysteries of the stars. From high towers, they studied the heavens each night. The poets and musicians of Ur set the legends of old to new music and the artisans fashioned handsome stone jars and other useful ornamental objects.

THE ANCIENT ORIENTAL WORLD
AND NEIGHBORING EUROPE
BEFORE THE RISE OF THE GREEKS
Scale

Notice that the Persian Gulf extended 150 to 160 miles further north than at present, making Babylonia much smaller than it is today

Statuette of the Babylonian goddess, Ningal, from Ur.

ABRAHAM'S LONG JOURNEY TO THE PROMISED LAND

Such was Abraham's city, generally known as Ur of the Chaldees. The people who lived there worshipped many different gods. They fashioned images of their gods from stone and clay and to these idols they directed their prayers and brought their sacrifices. Abraham, however, believed that there could be only *one* God, a God Who was invisible and Who was ruler over the entire universe. This great truth became increasingly clearer to him as he journeyed westward, away from Ur of the Chaldees.

As we trace Abraham's journey on the map, we see that he came first to Haran, a flourishing city in the kingdom of Mari. His father and brothers settled there, but Abraham moved on. We are told

A drawing of the Babylonian god, Bel—a form of Baal. Bel was one of the great triad of gods. Anu presided "over the heavens above"; Bel over "earth and air"; and Ea over "the waters beneath." Bel was a sun-god with power over nature.

how Abraham worshipped the one invisible God, and how God promised Abraham the land of Canaan as a homeland for him and for all his descendants. With his wife Sarah, his servants, his household goods and his cattle, Abraham pressed on to the Promised Land. His journey covered six hundred miles, through the rich lands that bordered the great Arabian desert; from Ur near the Persian Gulf, up to Haran and on to Canaan.

Following this route carefully on the map, we can clearly see that it forms a crescent, whence comes the name "Fertile Crescent," by which this area is often called, to contrast it with the barren desert on which it borders. Within this Fertile Crescent also lies the land of Egypt. In Egypt, the River Nile, like the Tigris and Euphrates, floods its banks each spring, enriching the land around it. In

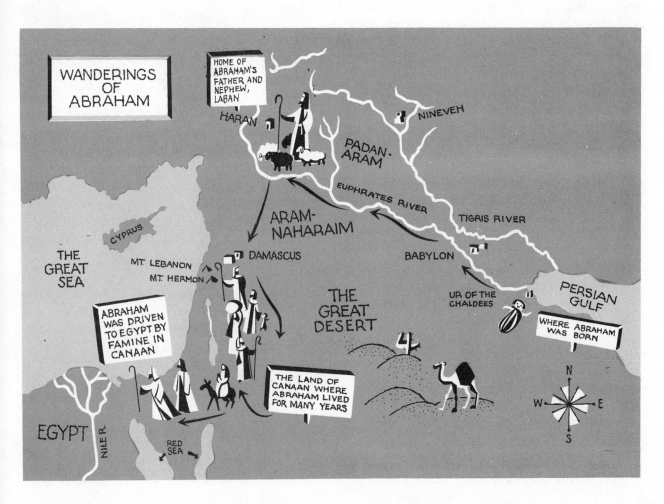

WANDERINGS OF ABRAHAM

HOME OF ABRAHAM'S FATHER AND NEPHEW, LABAN

HARAN

NINEVEH

PADAN-ARAM

EUPHRATES RIVER

TIGRIS RIVER

ARAM-NAHARAIM

THE GREAT SEA

CYPRUS

MT. LEBANON
MT. HERMON

DAMASCUS

BABYLON

UR OF THE CHALDEES

PERSIAN GULF

ABRAHAM WAS DRIVEN TO EGYPT BY FAMINE IN CANAAN

THE GREAT DESERT

WHERE ABRAHAM WAS BORN

THE LAND OF CANAAN WHERE ABRAHAM LIVED FOR MANY YEARS

EGYPT

NILE R.

RED SEA

N
W   E
S

the days of Abraham, Egypt was a highly developed, powerful land, and neighboring people often took refuge within its borders when famine threatened. Later, during a great famine in the land of Canaan, Abraham was to take his family and his herds and journey to Egypt, seeking shelter for a time on the well-watered grazing grounds of this land.

ABRAHAM SETTLES IN CANAAN

Canaan was a sparsely populated land. The Canaanites had settled on the plains, where they cultivated their barley fields, fig trees and date palms, and tended their cattle and sheep. Some of their towns were strongly fortified with walls and towers, so that people could take refuge from the frequent attacks of the desert nomads, who stormed across the River Jordan to steal cattle and raid storehouses. Because of the excavations of modern times, we know how one of these ancient cities, Shechem, looked. It had huge walls and turrets sixty feet high. In its protected center stood the palace of its king, or ruler.

Abraham settled in the hills of Canaan, where he was less exposed to attacks and where the land seemed less desirable to the Canaanites. At Mamre, near Hebron, he pitched his black goatskin tents. Beautiful terebinth trees lent their shade to the little settlement and the hillsides provided pasture for the flocks. Here Abraham raised his son and heir, Isaac; and here, eventually, he bought a piece of land from Ephron the Hittite, to bury his beloved wife, Sarah, in the cave of Machpelah.

The Bible relates that before Abraham died, "in a good old age and full of years," he had arranged for Isaac's marriage. He sent to faraway Haran for his son's wife, for he wanted him to marry from among his own people. Jacob, the son of Isaac, also sought a wife from among his distant kinsmen. After spending many years in the service of his uncle, Laban, Jacob married Laban's two daughters, Rachel and Leah, who, together with their handmaids, bore him twelve sons.

ABRAHAM, ISAAC AND JACOB, THE THREE PATRIARCHS

Thus did the three patriarchs, Abraham, Isaac

and Jacob, establish themselves in the land of Canaan. One of Jacob's contributions to his people was a new name for them. We are told that as he was returning to Canaan after serving his uncle Laban, Jacob met a man while crossing the river Jabbok. After wrestling with Jacob, the man revealed himself as an angel, a messenger of God. He gave Jacob the by-name of "Israel," which means "he who struggled with God." Henceforth, Jacob's children were called the Children of Israel.

THE CHILDREN OF ISRAEL JOURNEY TO EGYPT

A time of famine came to Canaan, and the thoughts of Jacob-Israel turned longingly to the fertile land of the Nile. Joseph, the son of Jacob, was now living in Egypt, where he had risen from servitude to a position of great power, second in

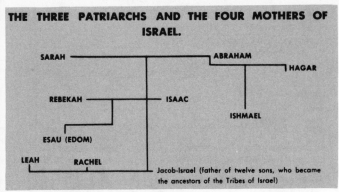

THE THREE PATRIARCHS AND THE FOUR MOTHERS OF ISRAEL.

SARAH —————— ABRAHAM
└ HAGAR

REBEKAH —————— ISAAC
ISHMAEL

ESAU (EDOM)

LEAH   RACHEL

Jacob-Israel (father of twelve sons, who became the ancestors of the Tribes of Israel)

command only to the Pharoah. At Joseph's invitation, Jacob brought his family and flocks into Egypt.

As we have seen earlier, it was customary in times of famine for groups of herdsmen from Canaan and Syria to seek refuge in Egypt. Such groups would come to the borders of Egypt and apply to the officer in charge for permission to enter the land for a temporary stay. From ancient Egyptian paintings, we can picture with fair accuracy what Jacob and his family must have looked like when they came to Egypt at the time of the famine; how they were dressed and what they brought with them. They were garbed in beautifully woven striped garments and cloaks; the feet of the women were encased in small boots, while the men wore sandals. Donkeys, sheep and cattle, spears, shepherds' crooks and even musical instruments were brought along in the caravan. We even know how the men wore their beards, and that the women kept their hair in place with bands across their foreheads.

We can also imagine their rejoicing when they reached the land of Goshen, the fertile country within the northeast Delta of the Nile nearest to Palestine. The Pharaoh of Egypt, desiring to honor

An Egyptian tomb painting of a group of Semites.

the father of Joseph, had assigned this land to the Israelites. Goshen was good grazing land, and there for many years the Israelites lived in peace, tending their flocks and enjoying the respect of their neighbors.

RULERS OF EGYPT

Modern historians believe that these events occurred during the time of the Hyksos. The Hyksos were a warlike tribe from Syria, who swept into Egypt about 1500 B.C.E. They conquered and subjugated the native people and for the first time mighty Egypt had a foreign Pharaoh on its throne. The Hyksos Pharoahs ruled for a period of about one-hundred and twenty years. Joseph was probably a minister under one of these powerful foreign rulers.

SLAVES OF PHARAOH

Eventually the Hyksos were defeated, and Egyptian Pharaohs once more ruled over the land. However, the new Pharaohs, as the Bible tells us, "did not know Joseph." No longer were the Israelites respected as the privileged descendants of a noble ancestor. Like many other peoples within the borders of Egypt, they became enslaved. Egypt was a growing empire and the new Pharaohs had great need for slaves to build their new cities, magnificent palaces and mammoth pyramids in which the mummified bodies of Egypt's royal dead were enshrined. The enormous stones for these pyramids had to be transported by human labor, for machines were few and primitive. Thousands of slaves, both men and women, were drafted for this backbreaking work.

The power of the Pharaohs extended beyond the Egyptian borders. Syria and Canaan were subject dominions, forced to pay tribute to Egypt. From Canaan, Egyptian traders brought home the famed purple dyes and precious cloth for which that land was famous. Egyptian soldiers were stationed as far away from their native borders as the foot of the Lebanon mountains.

As time passed Egypt's power was faced with new threats. Other great empires were rising, and the Pharaohs were forced to use ingenious strategy to retain their position. Treaties of peace were made

Head of Amenhotep IV (1369-1353 B.C.E.)

Hittite stone carvings.

with neighboring lands and strengthened by royal marriages. One such marriage was that of Pharaoh Amenhotep IV to the Mitanni princess Nefertiti. The Mitanni were a people noted for their great warriors and skilled horsemen. From the Mitanni, the Egyptians learned the arts of horse-breeding, grooming and racing. However, the Mitanni were later conquered by the Hittites, and Egypt found herself challenged by a new and powerful adversary.

The Hittites, whose territory extended to the northeastern border of Egypt, had established a strong empire, with its center in Asia Minor.

Mitannean cylinder seal.

Rameses II, then Pharaoh of Egypt, waged a successful war against the Hittites, concluded a favorable treaty and further cemented friendly relations by marrying a Hittite princess.

Rameses II was a Pharaoh with big plans and an ego to match. He seems to have been driven by an unceasing ambition to make his name immortal. Determined that all posterity should remember him and marvel at his works, he even had his initials engraved upon buildings erected centuries before his time. His ambition has been fulfilled to some extent, for modern scientists still marvel at the energy of this busy Pharaoh.

Under the driving ambition of Rameses, the whips of the Egyptian slave drivers cracked down even harder on the backs of the slaves. The unfortunate Israelites were set to making bricks, digging and building. If they dropped from exhaustion, the sting of the overseer's whips soon reminded them that there was no time for rest.

The Israelites proved a handy source of slave labor for Rameses, for he had chosen the Nile Delta as the place where he would erect new cities. This included the land of Goshen, to which the Israelites had come with such rejoicing so many years before. Now the glittering cities of the Pharaoh began to rise on the land where the flocks of the Israelites had grazed. Under the relentless whips of the overseers, the Israelite slaves built the two great store cities, Pithom and

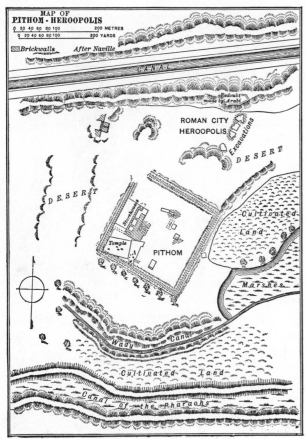

Map of Pithom and the surrounding area. This ancient map was dicovered in 1883.

Ramses. Here were housed the Pharaoh's treasures and grain.

Wherever people are enslaved, there are always stirrings of revolt. The bodies of men can be lashed but the whips cannot penetrate to the spirit. So it was with the Israelites. Their hands were busy hauling, building, fashioning, while their hearts longed and hoped for a day of deliverance.

Rameses was not unaware of the spirit of rebellion. He greatly feared an uprising among the slaves and took many cruel precautions against it. One day a decree was issued that all male children born to the Israelites must be killed. In this merciless way, Rameses hoped to keep the Israelites from growing in numbers.

THE BOY MOSES

Soon after this decree was issued, a male child was born to Jochebed, an Israelite woman, and her husband Amram, of the tribe of Levi. Little did

this humble couple dream that the name of their son was destined to be known throughout the ages as one of the greatest leaders in all history. Desperate to save their baby, they put him into a basket and set him afloat among the bulrushes of the Nile. The Bible tells us how he was found by the Egyptian princess while she and her handmaidens were bathing at the river. Miriam, his sister, watching nearby, saw her brother rescued by the princess. Miriam carried the glad tidings to her mother, and later it was arranged that Jochebed would go to the palace and act as the baby's nurse.

Growing up in the palace, surrounded by every luxury, the Israelite boy rescued by the princess was spared the fate of becoming a slave. The princess gave him the name which was to become one of the most illustrious names in history. She called him Moses.

The boy Moses was given all the advantages enjoyed by sons of royalty. He learned to read, and to write in hieroglyphs on the fine papyrus which the Egyptians had learned to make from the leaves of the native papyrus plant and which has given us our own word "paper."

As Moses grew to manhood, he came to realize that his people were not as fortunate as he. On every hand, he saw the Israelite slaves brutally driven and mistreated. Then occurred an event which brought his luxurious life in the palace to

This scene of brick laying in ancient Egypt was found painted on a tomb at Thebes, Egypt.

Bust of Merneptah.

an abrupt end and sent him fleeing for his life into the wilderness. One day Moses was outraged to see a cruel overseer mercilessly beating an Israelite slave. Moses killed the overseer, and to escape the retribution of the Egyptians, fled to Midian in the rugged Sinai region. There he became a shepherd, living with a Kenite priest named Jethro. Moses married Jethro's daughter, Zipporah, who bore him two sons.

MOSES, FIGHTER FOR FREEDOM

We can only surmise what would have been the fate of the Israelites in Egypt had Moses chosen to stay in Midian, living out his new life in safety and peace. It is such decisions that change the course of history. The Bible relates that in the rugged mountains of Sinai, Moses, a man reared in a palace among a people who worshipped many different gods and idols, had an inspiring experience. To him, through a vision of a Burning Bush that was not consumed, the power and truth of the one God of his fathers were revealed. From that time forward, Moses was a man dedicated to one great task—that of leading his people to freedom.

It was not an easy thing that Moses had chosen to do. The Bible tells us of the obstacles placed in his path by the Pharaoh who, according to some historians, was Merneptah, son of Rameses, who now sat on the throne of Egypt. Again and again Moses, with his brother Aaron, stood before him, pleading for the Israelites' release. Pharaoh, full of confidence and power, turned a deaf ear to the pleas of Moses.

But the burning sense of purpose that drove Moses on through failure after failure was more than a match for Pharaoh's stubbornness. While the overseers lashed their weary bodies, Moses stirred the flagging spirits of the Israelites with the

message of freedom. He spoke to them of their God, telling them they could not serve Him in slavery. He explained to them how much better their lives could be away from Egypt. He filled their despairing hearts with hope. The Israelites listened, and dared to dream of liberty and deliverance.

THE GREAT EXODUS

Egypt had to be stricken by ten disastrous plagues before Pharaoh, fearing the wrath of the God whom Moses and his people worshipped, finally consented to release the Israelites from their bondage and allow them to leave the land. Knowing full well that kings do not always keep their promises, Moses urged the Israelites to comply with the request of the Pharaoh and leave at once. We are told that a multitude of about six hundred thousand men together with women and children left Egypt on that memorable night of the Exodus. That event has been told and retold in song and story and it is not difficult for us, even centuries later, to picture the scene. Mothers hastily rounded up their children and gathered up belongings. Surely, many tears must have been shed over cherished possessions that had to be left behind, for there was neither time nor place for extra baggage on this hasty desperate flight into a future that was uncertain and hazardous. Food, of course, they had to have, but even so, there was barely time to bake the bread they would need. The bread was so hurriedly baked that there was no time for the dough to rise. This was the origin of the custom of eating unleavened bread (*matzot*) on the feast of Pass-

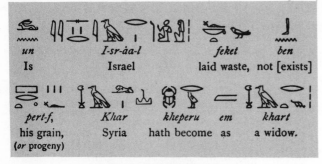

un	I-sr-âa-l	feket	ben
Is	Israel	laid waste,	not [exists]

pert-f,	Khar	kheperu	em	khart
his grain, (or progeny)	Syria	hath become	as	a widow.

Earliest mention of Israel.

The Egyptian text of two lines of Merneptah's stele, a transliteration and a translation. After the word "Israel," note the figures of a man, a woman, and three straight lines.

over (*Pesah*)—a commemoration of the victory won for freedom so many centuries ago.

So the great march out of Egypt began, with families gathered together, each with its own tribe, twelve tribes in all. Moses did not dare lead them by the established route, which was dangerously near the border forts where Egyptian soldiers might have attempted to prevent their escape. The great throng of people, young and old, carrying

In 1896, the archeologist Flinders Petrie discovered this stele of Merneptah.

A tomb painting of an Egyptian war chariot.

their meager belongings, marched slowly eastward, to avoid the border posts. Then their march was halted suddenly by an obstacle that seemed so great as to be insurmountable. Silent and disheartened they stood, the light of hope slowly fading from their eyes as they gazed at the vast expanse of water that appeared before them. They had come to the end of dry land, to the shores of the "Sea of Reeds" (*Yam Suf*), the Suez arm of the Red Sea.

Those who looked back uncertainly in the direction of their former homes were greeted by another sight that chilled their already sinking hearts. Bearing down upon them from the rear was a horde of Egyptian soldiers. Regretting his decision to free the Israelite slaves, Pharaoh was determined to overtake them. With the sea before them and the charioteers and horsemen of the cruel Pharaoh closing in from behind, the Children of Israel were trapped.

Then, miraculously, a strong easterly wind arose. It drove back the ebbing waters of the sea, making a path of dry land. Quietly, but with joyful hearts, the throng followed Moses to the opposite shore. In fierce pursuit, Pharaoh's soldiers also took the dry path through the "Sea of Reeds," but the wind had turned and the tide of the sea was changing. Back rushed the waters, engulfing the chariots and drowning the soldiers.

An Egyptian brick with the imprint of the seal of Rameses II.

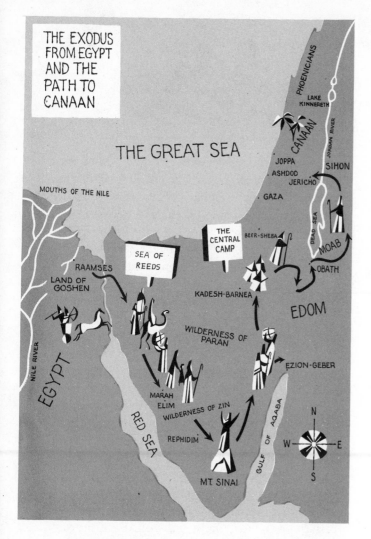

THE EXODUS FROM EGYPT AND THE PATH TO CANAAN

THE GREAT SEA

PHOENICIANS
LAKE KINNERETH
CANAAN
JORDAN RIVER
JOPPA
ASHDOD
JERICHO
SIHON
GAZA
MOUTHS OF THE NILE
BEER-SHEBA
THE CENTRAL CAMP
DEAD SEA
MOAB
OBATH
SEA OF REEDS
RAAMSES
LAND OF GOSHEN
KADESH-BARNEA
EDOM
WILDERNESS OF PARAN
NILE RIVER
EGYPT
EZION-GEBER
MARAH
ELIM
WILDERNESS OF ZIN
GULF OF AQABA
RED SEA
REPHIDIM
MT. SINAI
N W E S

THE WAY TO SINAI AND ON THROUGH THE WILDERNESS

The story of the Exodus is one of the great sagas of all time. Every year, all over the world, Jews commemorate this event by the festival of Passover. For the Israelites at that time, however, the Exodus was only the beginning of a great struggle to establish themselves as a nation—a struggle that was to cover many years of wandering and hardships. Under the inspired leadership of Moses, and with their great ideal of the one God ever foremost in their minds, the Israelites set forth to find the remembered land of their fathers.

To trace the road of the Israelites, one need only follow the water holes and oases of the Sinai desert to the region of Mount Sinai. Since 3000 B.C.E. workmen and miners had traveled this road up to Egypt's ancient copper mines. For many centuries, these mines had not been used. Then the ambitious Rameses II sent his gangs of laborers there to start operating the mines again. Centuries later the Kings of Israel were to send their own workers to mine for copper again.

When the Israelites reached Mount Sinai, Moses ordered them to pitch their tents. This region was well known to him from the past, when he had stayed there with Jethro, the priest. He knew that here the Israelites would be able to rest for a time and graze their flocks. Here, too, would occur the most important moment in the history of the Israelites.

THE TEN COMMANDMENTS

After the camp had been made, Moses ascended the mountain. For days, he was hidden from the people. Then, the Bible tells us, amidst thunder and lightning so that the very mountains shook, the divine voice was reverberating throughout proclaiming the Ten Commandments. When at last they sighted their great leader slowly descending from the heights they gathered in a body at the foot of Mount Sinai to await his return.

Moses brought down from the mountain the Ten Commandments, carved upon two tablets of stone.

Never would Israel forget the day when these

The Bible tells us of the great rejoicing, the ecstatic gratitude that overwhelmed the Israelites when they found themselves safely across the sea. Moses improvised a poem of praise to the Lord. The women also danced joyously to the music of their timbrels and sang a song composed by Miriam, Moses' sister.

Ahead of them lay untold dangers and unreckoned days of weary wandering, but on this great day there was but one song in the hearts of the Israelites—a song of gratitude for their newly-won freedom.

Today the landscape of the Red Sea region is much changed. Close to the "Sea of Reeds" the Suez Canal has been built, but the world still remembers the miracle by which the Israelites were able to pass through the sea on a path of dry land.

A photograph of Mount Sinai. It was on top of this mountain that Moses received the Decalogue.

Moses instructed the people, under the guidance of Bezalel and Oholiab, to construct the Tabernacle. The Tabernacle was the sanctuary in which the Israelites and their priests worshipped God. It was constructed in such a way as to be easily portable. The Tabernacle was inside the Tent of Meeting, a large tent with a strong wooden frame. There was an outer court, supported by pillars and separated from the inner court by curtains. In the inner court stood the actual Tabernacle, which was again divided by a curtain or veil into the Holy Place, where the priests would offer sacrifices on the altar, and the Holy of Holies, which contained the Ark of the Covenant with the Tablets of the Law. The Holy of Holies symbolized the mysterious presence of God among men. The sanctuary was to be a constant reminder to the Israelites of their allegiance and dedication to the service of God.

Moses consecrated Aaron and his sons for the priesthood, anointing their heads with oil in a sacred ceremony. Forever after, Aaron, his sons and their descendants, were to be the priests

ten great laws were proclaimed, for they were to become the basis of all the laws of the Hebrews and the moral core of our great civilization. To this day, the world honors the principles set down in the Ten Commandments. This glorious event is commemorated by the Jewish people annually on the Festival of Shavout.

The Ten Commandments sealed a covenant on the rocky heights of Mount Sinai, between the young nation of Israel and the one God. No other nation had a code of laws so just and humane. The Israelites now truly abandoned the ways of Egypt and dedicated themselves to live by this lofty code.

The *Torah,* as our Bible is called, contains a vivid description of the Ark of the Covenant in which the two holy tablets of the Law were kept. It was a precious, portable shrine made of acacia wood, with handles for carrying it from place to place. Atop the Ark were two angels called cherubim. The Ark and the holy objects used for the service in the Tabernacle all had been fashioned by Bezalel, a pious craftsman and artist.

Moses bringing down the Decalogue. From the Sarajevo Haggadah.

11

A picture of the reconstruction of the Tabernacle.

(*Cohanim*), of Israel. To this day the *Cohanim* perform special duties in the synagogue service.

The duties of the priests were many and varied. They offered the sacrifices for the people and raised their voices in prayer. Bezalel and Oholiab fashioned the prescribed priestly garb. For Aaron, the High Priest, they fashioned the breastplate bearing the *Turim*, the four rows of twelve precious stones, each stone symbolizing one of the tribes of Israel. These garments were worn by the High Priest when he stood before God in prayer.

Each week, the Israelites devoted an entire day, the Sabbath, to rest and prayer. This wise and humane decree introduced an idea completely new to the world. No other people had a day of rest at that time.

The observance of the laws of the Ten Commandments and the religious rituals as laid down in the Torah began with the Israelites at Sinai. When they broke camp and continued their wanderings, they carried with them through the wilderness and on into Canaan the collapsible Tabernacle, the Tent of Meeting and the Ark of the Covenant which housed the Tablets of the Law.

Many of the Israelites in that great wandering horde were sincerely dedicated to their new ideals. The memory of the Exodus and the courage of their leaders, Moses, Aaron and Miriam, was ever before them, inspiring them to renewed faith and purpose. It is not difficult to picture them as they sat around their desert campfires at night beneath the stars, retelling the story of their flight from Egypt, and marveling anew at their miraculous escape.

However, history has no record of any people or nation which was not plagued by some discord and discontent. The Hebrews were no exception. There were many who complained and grumbled. It was inevitable that some fearful souls would yearn for the old ways, the old comforts. Life in Egypt where food had been plentiful and pastures rich seemed,

A reconstruction of the regalia of the Cohanim.

A carving of the Ten Commandments from a Torah Ark.

Fragments from the Nash papyrus, the oldest known Hebrew manuscript containing the Decalogue and the Shema. It was discovered in Egypt and dates from the late Maccabean period.

to some, infinitely preferable to the rugged life in the desert where food was scarce and the grazing land was parched by the sun. Many were the bitter reproaches heaped on the head of Moses when hunger, thirst and raiding enemies threatened.

The story of the "manna from heaven" has become so well known that these words have been adopted by many languages as a figure of speech. Even today the nomads of the Sinai desert eat a food they call manna, a sugary substance that forms on the branches of the tamarisk tree. When the wandering Israelites found the manna, they hailed it as a miracle. Indeed it seemed to them to be the "bread of Heaven."

APPROACHING THE PROMISED LAND

At long last the Israelites drew close to the Promised Land. Moses wisely gave the order for the march to halt, for he wanted time to gauge the power of the many tribes of Canaan and to map his strategy for their conquest by his people. Scouts were sent across the border, among them Caleb and Joshua, Moses' own able young assistants. The scouts were ordered to find out all they could about the condition of the land, the numbers of armed troops and the strength of the fortifications. The scouts returned from this mission with conflicting reports. Some of them spoke in glow-

ing terms of the fertility of the land, bringing back luscious fruits as proof. Others spoke in more somber terms of strong, well-armed soldiers and well-fortified cities.

Moses, realizing that the Israelites still lacked the faith and courage necessary for a successful invasion, led them back into the desert, where they were to wander for a period of forty years.

The Torah records the many difficulties the Israelites encountered during this time of wandering. Hunger and thirst stalked their path. Hostile desert tribes were a constant danger, harassing the people by day, and terrifying and robbing them by night. At times the Ten Commandments must have seemed an impossibly lofty code by which to live. That the Israelites retained this code as a way of life, through hardships which are almost impossible to imagine today, is a fact which has awed and amazed historians throughout the ages. Only a man such as Moses, with his unflagging devotion to a great cause and a magnificent gift for leadership, could have so inspired a people under such stress. Moses patiently taught and explained the new laws and encouraged their observance. Jethro, the Kenite priest and father-in-law of Moses, who had visited with the Israelites on their journey, advised Moses to appoint judges, who were to assist him in the difficult task of governing and advising the people.

Perhaps the very hardships proved a blessing in disguise, toughening the Israelites and uniting them as no swift victory or life of ease could ever have done. Necessity is ever the mother of invention, and the Israelites learned many new skills. They learned to hunt, to make their own clothing and to defend themselves against raiding nomadic tribes. They learned to make their own black goatskin tents for shelter, as some of their ancient ancestors had done.

At the end of forty years of desert life, an entire new generation had grown to adulthood. Few remained of the generation who had known the chains of Egyptian slavery. The new generation had lived no other life than that of the desert and had known no other gods but the one God, no other laws but the Ten Commandments and the laws of the Torah. They were toughened by hardship and united by a common purpose.

Two Tablets of the Law found in the caves of Bet Shearim, Israel. These carvings date back almost two thousand years.

JOSHUA SUCCEEDS MOSES

Moses, the great teacher, had grown old. The time had come to choose a leader to take his place after he had gone. Moses' choice fell on Joshua, a man loved and respected by the people and devoted to the laws of Sinai—a man, too, with a gift for military strategy. Into Joshua's capable hands Moses placed the task of invading Canaan.

Moses knew that he would not live to enter the Promised Land. After he had blessed and consecrated Joshua for his new responsibilities, Moses felt his work was done. From atop Mount Nebo Moses bade his people farewell. Then the old man gazed out over the rich and fertile land which stretched for miles beyond the mountain. In the distance shimmered the waters of the Salt Sea. Below the mountains of Judah, the River Jordan wound like a broad silver ribbon. To the north rose Mount Hermon with its crown of snow. In the

west, possibly, Moses might have caught the faint glimmer of blue that marked the Mediterranean.

Thus, with the knowledge that his people were on their way to the Promised Land, blessed with an able leader and fortified in spirit by their great laws, Moses rested on Mount Nebo. There, soon after, he died. Great was the mourning of the Children of Israel at the loss of their great leader. Moses had been teacher, father and prophet to his people. There would be other great leaders in the years to come, but that unique and special era in their history through which Moses had guided them enshrined him in the hearts of Jews for all time.

The Five Books of Moses, which we call the Torah, end with the account of Moses' death. Every year on *Simhat Torah,* the festival of the "Joy of the Torah," the week-by-week reading of the Torah comes to a close and begins anew. Every year on Simhat Torah, Jews throughout the world listen once more to the words of the closing passage:

A clay tablet written in Babylonian cuneiform by the terrified Egyptian governor, who begs the Pharaoh for help, saying: "The Khabiru (Hebrews) are taking the cities of the king. No ruler remains to the king, my lord; all are lost." The king of Egypt to whom he wrote thus was Ikhnaton, at a time when the Egyptian Empire in Asia was falling to pieces. This letter is one of a group of three hundred such cuneiform letters found in one of the rooms of Ikhnaton's palace at Tell el-Amarna (or Amarna) and called the Amarna Letters, the oldest body of international correspondence in the world. We find in them the earliest mention of the Hebrews.

And Joshua the son of Nun was full of the spirit of wisdom; for Moses had laid his hands upon him; and the Children of Israel hearkened unto him, and did as the Lord commanded Moses. And there has not arisen a prophet since in Israel like unto Moses, whom the Lord knew face to face; in all the signs and wonders which the Lord sent him to do in the land of Egypt, to Pharaoh, and to all his servants, and to all his land; and in all the great might and awesome power which Moses wrought in the sight of all Israel.

Deut. 34:9-12

An aerial view of the Jordan River as it snakes its way across the land of Israel.

GLOSSARY OF HEBREW TERMINOLOGY AND NAMES

Levi	Leyvee	לֵוִי	Abraham	Avraham	אַבְרָהָם
Miriam	Miryahm	מִרְיָם	Hebrews	Ivrim	עִבְרִים
Jethro	Yitroh	יִתְרוֹ	Ur of the Chaldees	Oor Kahs-deem	אוּר כַּשְׂדִּים
Zipporah	Tzipohrah	צִפּוֹרָה	Haran	Ḥaran	חָרָן
Sinai	Seenahy	סִינַי	Sarah	Sahrah	שָׂרָה
Unleavened bread	Matzot	מַצּוֹת	Canaan	Kenah-ahn	כְּנַעַן
Passover	Pesaḥ	פֶּסַח	Hebron	Ḥevron	חֶבְרוֹן
Red Sea	Yam Soof	יַם סוּף	Machpelah	Maḥpelah	מַכְפֵּלָה
The Ten Command-ments	Aseret Hadibrot	עֲשֶׂרֶת הַדִּבְּרוֹת	Jacob	Yah-akohv	יַעֲקֹב
			Isaac	Yitzḥak	יִצְחָק
Torah	Torah	תּוֹרָה	Israel	Yisrah-eyl	יִשְׂרָאֵל
Priests	Kohan-eem	כֹּהֲנִים	Egypt	Mitzrah-yeem	מִצְרַיִם
Bezalel	Betzaleyl	בְּצַלְאֵל	Pharaoh	Paroh	פַּרְעֹה
Manna	Mahn	מָן	Joseph	Yohseyf	יוֹסֵף
Caleb	Kahleyv	כָּלֵב	Goshen	Gohshen	גֹּשֶׁן
Joshua	Yhohshoo-ah	יְהוֹשֻׁעַ	Moses	Mohsheh	מֹשֶׁה
			Jochebed	Yoḥeved	יוֹכֶבֶד
			Amram	Ahmrahm	עַמְרָם

CONQUEST OF CANAAN

THE INVASION BEGINS

When Joshua deemed the time right for entering the Promised Land, he sent his officers through the great throng of Israelites encamped near the River Jordan. The officers instructed the people to prepare themselves for the crossing. When they saw the Ark of the Covenant being carried across the river by the priests, they broke camp and followed.

Some of the tribes had already pitched their tents before reaching the Jordan. The tribes of Manasseh, Gad and Reuben had settled in the territory of Gilead, east of the Jordan. Gilead, a sparsely populated land of grazing grounds, watered by the river Jabbok, had been easily taken by the Israelites.

NEW NEIGHBORS

The peoples of Aram, Ammon and Moab became the new neighbors of the Israelite tribes of Manasseh, Gad and Reuben. The future would see many skirmishes and wars between Israel and these neighbors, but at that time Gilead was at peace. After pitching their tents, the men of Manasseh, Gad and Reuben took up their arms and joined the rest of Israel in the task of conquest.

A stele of an ancient Moabite king standing between two gods. It dates from the twelfth and eleventh century B.C.E.

The peoples of Canaan—the Canaanites, Jebusites and Hittites—lived on farms and in fortified towns and cities. The houses of the city dwellers. were of stone and many of the cities were surrounded by strong walls and watchtowers. The tools these people used and their weapons of war were much more advanced than those of the Israelites. Their spears were tipped with iron. Iron was then a new metal, not yet widely used. Some of the people even boasted chariots, drawn by fine, swift horses. The desert people, on the other hand, used simple spears, bows and arrows. Undaunted by the superior weapons and strong defensive position of his opponents, Joshua made his plans. He was a clever strategist and an excellent general. His men were daring and tough, trained to obey his every command. Under their respected and beloved commander who had been appointed by the great Moses himself, all the twelve tribes of Israel formed a closely-knit army, united and strong. Proudly and confidently they voiced their motto: *Hazak Ve'ematz!* (Be strong and of good courage).

NEW CONQUESTS

Employing a series of brilliant moves and surprise attacks, Joshua began his campaign. The first city to fall was Jericho. The story of how the walls of Jericho came tumbling down has been told and retold through the ages. Modern archeologists have unearthed the ruins of the ancient city of Jericho.

Lakhish, Bethel, and other fortified cities were taken by the invading Israelites. Joshua used the method of ambush very effectively. One wing of his army would mislead the Canaanites by pretending to flee. As the enemy followed in pursuit, Joshua closed in on them with the other wing.

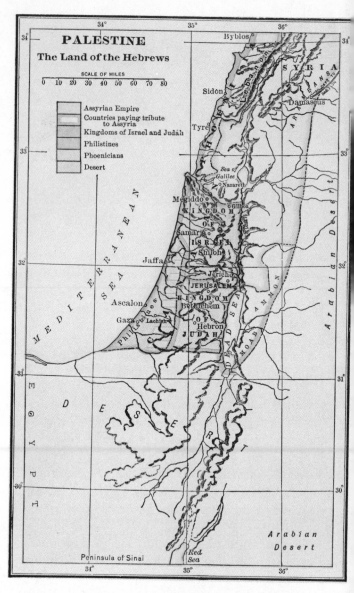

This mound contains some of the remains of the ancient city of Jericho. Much excavating is being done at the site.

Then the wing in mock flight turned back and the enemy would find themselves encircled.

Many of the Canaanites were panic-stricken at the onslaught of these determined invaders. Some of the Canaanite princes and some Canaanite towns made friendly pacts with Israel to avoid battle and bloodshed. The people of Gibeon, fearing Israel's strength, presented themselves before Joshua and, pretending that they had come from a far-off country, offered their friendship to the conquerors.

THE PEOPLE OF ISRAEL SETTLE IN CANAAN

As the conquest of Canaan proceeded, Joshua began to distribute the land among the Israelites, assigning a portion to each tribe, except to the consecrated tribe of Levi to whom were alloted forty-eight special cities in the territories of the different tribes. The Levites, and the priests or *Cohanim* (who were also of the tribe of Levi), received a special assignment—that of tending the laws of Israel and the sanctuary which Joshua had established in Shiloh, where the Holy Ark and the Tabernacle were kept. It was to Shiloh that the people made their pilgrimages, bringing their sacrifices and praying there together.

The sanctuary in Shiloh was tended by Aaron's son Elazar and grandson, Phinehas, assisted by the Levites. Other Levites traveled through the land, making the people familiar with the Ten Commandments and instructing them in the worship of the one God. Out of each harvest, the people of Israel set aside a portion for the priests and Levites, for these men were dedicated solely to their sacred tasks and had neither land nor flocks of their own.

Establishing themselves in their assigned territory was not too difficult for some of the tribes, but others needed the help of all the men of Israel to conquer their portion. As in the days of Abraham, the sparsely populated, mountainous terrain was always easier to conquer than the fertile plains. On the plains there were many strong, walled cities, which offered fierce resistance to the invaders.

Some of the fortified cities would not be captured for a long time to come. Among these were the cities along the fertile coast of the Mediterranean, where the Philistines had recently settled,

and also Jerusalem, the Jebusite fortress in the rocky mountains of Judah.

THE ASSEMBLY AT SHECHEM

The gravest threat facing the Israelites, however, was not the superiority of enemy weapons nor even the strong walls around enemy cities. It was a threat far more difficult to avoid and overcome, a threat to the very foundations of the faith of Israel. The Israelites now found themselves mingling with peoples who worshipped idols. The people of Canaan fashioned idols of stone in many grotesque forms. To these graven images they prayed and offered sacrifices. Having no knowledge of the one invisible God, they worshipped animals, stones, and trees, believing that these things represented the gods who ruled over their lives.

Fearing that his people would fall into the idol-

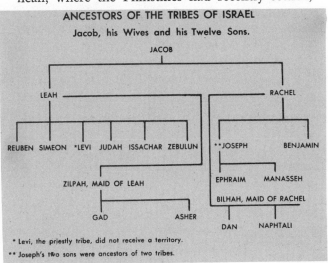

ANCESTORS OF THE TRIBES OF ISRAEL
Jacob, his Wives and his Twelve Sons.

* Levi, the priestly tribe, did not receive a territory.
** Joseph's two sons were ancestors of two tribes.

atrous ways of these pagan tribes, Joshua, now an old man and knowing that his death was near, called the twelve tribes together for a great assembly at Shechem, near Shiloh. Gathered together before their leader, the people listened as Joshua impressed upon them the importance of remaining united and faithfully following the laws of the one God. Joshua was wise enough to know that many of the Israelites would be attracted by the ways of their neighbors. He commanded them to make

A pottery figurine, probably an idol, found in Ashdod, Israel.

their choice between the idols of Canaan and the God of Israel. The people made a solemn promise to Joshua that they would put away all the idols and hold steadfast to the Ten Commandments. With almost one voice they cried: "The Lord our God will we serve, and His voice will we obey." Thus the Israelites renewed their covenant with the one God, and returned to their homes with fresh courage, rededicated to their own way of life.

An Israelite altar unearthed at Meggido.

GLOSSARY OF HEBREW TERMINOLOGY
AND NAMES

Jordan	Yardeyn	יַרְדֵּן
Manasseh	Menahsheh	מְנַשֶּׁה
Gad	Gahd	גָּד
Reuben	Re-ooveyn	רְאוּבֵן
Gilead	Gilahd	גִּלְעָד
Be strong and of good courage	Hazak Ve-emahtz	חֲזַק וֶאֱמָץ
Jericho	Yreeḥoh	יְרִיחוֹ
Lakhish	Laḥeesh	לָכִישׁ
Bethel	Beyt Eyl	בֵּית אֵל
Gibeon	Geevohn	גִּבְעוֹן
Shiloh	Sheeloh	שִׁילֹה
Aaron	Aharohn	אַהֲרֹן
Levites	Levee-yeem	לְוִיִּם
Elazar	Elahzahr	אֶלְעָזָר
Phinehas	Pinḥas	פִּנְחָס
Shechem	Sh'ḥem	שְׁכֶם

Chapter III

A YOUNG DEMOCRACY:
THE ERA OF THE JUDGES

THE LIFE OF THE NEW SETTLERS

The findings of modern archeology indicate that the Israelites in Canaan truly valued their hard-won freedom, and during the first two centuries they followed a democratic way of life. Among the Israelites there was no wealthy class of lords and princes such as the Canaanite people had. The Canaanite nobles lived in fine stone houses, and used beautifully adorned vessels, cosmetics and expensive linens. Serfs and slaves lived in hovels of clay, serving this wealthy class and performing all the heavy labor, tilling the fields and tending the sheep and cattle.

The Israelites had no such rich and idle class, nor a servant class living in hovels. They all tilled their own fields, baked their own bread and wove their own cloth. They tended their own cattle and sheep and guarded their own possessions. Their houses were built simply of sun-baked bricks.

The laws of Sinai protected the people, for under these just laws there could be no serfs or cruel masters. To make sure of this, the law provided that an Israelite who had become enslaved through debt regained his freedom after serving six years. One out of every seven years was declared a Sabbatical Year (*Shemitah*) when the earth was given a rest and whatever was in the field was shared by the poor. Debts were cancelled during

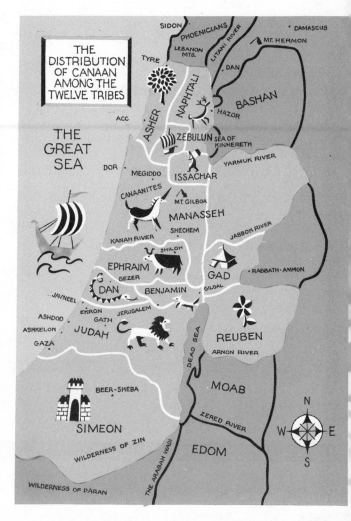

that year. Every fiftieth year was declared a special year called the Jubilee year (*Yovel*). During this special year all debts were cancelled or settled. Each piece of land that had been forfeited by someone through hardship, drought or illness was returned to its rightful owner. Everyone could start life anew. Thus the wise laws of Sinai insured freedom and dignity for all.

THE JUDGES OF ISRAEL

The Israelites were guided and advised by men and women called Judges. Among the Judges of Israel were warriors, priests and seers. The first Judges were chosen to act as military leaders, for whom the Israelites had great need. Farms were frequently raided by warlike neighbors and towns were besieged by strong armies. After peace had been regained, the Judges often continued to lead the people or "judge" them as the Israelites called it. The Judges dealt with problems of government and the settlement of private disputes. Some of the Judges were widely esteemed for wisdom and the people came to them from far and near with their problems. Judges also gave advice in legal matters, personal problems or difficulties involving the entire community.

One of the most difficult tasks facing the Judges was that of keeping the twelve tribes of Israel united as a strong people with a common purpose Now that the tribes had settled into separate groups, each on its own apportioned land, there was a tendency among the people to neglect the great ideal which had made them such a close-knit unit during their time of wandering. The tribes in the north, sharing the same rocky land, the same enemies and problems, were one close unit. Another unit was formed by the tribes around the great central plain of Jezreel (Esdraelon). The tribes in the southern region formed yet another unit, as did the tribes that settled across the Jordan in Gilead. These various groups were not always in close contact with one another.

Whenever there was no Judge whose strong voice represented a central authority for all Israel, some of the tribes would fall away from the tradition of the laws of Sinai. They would no longer make pilgrimages to the Tabernacle at Shiloh, but

An ivory inlay from Khorsabad, Syria, of the Canaanite goddess Astarte, eighth to seventh century B.C.E.

would take sacrifices to the shrines of the Canaanites and lay their offerings before the idols. The Israelites learned much from the Canaanites about weaving, building, and fashioning beautiful pottery and more advanced tools; but unfortunately they also learned from them the ways of idolatry.

The most popular idols of Canaan were Baal and Astarte (or Ishtar.) Baal, a male idol often represented as half-man, half-bull, was all-powerful in the eyes of the Canaanites. Astarte was a goddess of fertility and love. The Canaanites regarded their gods as cruel, wild spirits who must be appeased with acts of cruelty and savagery to match their own.

The Judges tore down many of the heathen altars and condemned those Israelites who turned away from their own God. The faith of Israel faced a threatening challenge which the Judges had to meet constantly by patiently appealing to the people to abide by their own commandments and laws, which were on a much higher level than those of the heathen amidst whom they lived.

THE JUDGES AT THE HELM

The Bible tells us of twelve Judges in Israel,

though little is known about the first three. The first Judge mentioned is Othniel, a younger brother of Caleb, who had been a companion to Joshua on the scouting expedition into Canaan. Othniel, of the tribe of Judah, was an able warrior who led Israel in a war against King Kushan-Rishataim of Aram and drove him out of the land. Ehud, the second Judge, fought and defeated Moab. Shamgar, the third Judge, was the first to drive back the Philistines.

THE CANAANITES THREATEN ISRAEL'S FREEDOM

The Israelites were fiercely determined to hold the land they had won after so many years of hardship. No longer half-starved desert nomads, they had now become farmers, shepherds, artisans and city dwellers. Their new way of life, however, was beset with dangers from all sides. Canaanite soldiers often raided Israelite farms and storehouses. Farmers had to hide their harvests, traders feared for their goods, and roads became unsafe for traveling.

Though the Israelites fought off the continuing attacks bravely, their efforts were futile against the armed might of Jabin, a king of the Canaanites. The soldiers of Jabin, commanded by his general, Sisera, were well-trained and equipped with heavy iron chariots and weapons. For twenty years these marauders terrorized the Israelites. Another Joshua was sorely needed to rally the people against the might of King Jabin.

DEBORAH, LEADER AND JUDGE

In the hill country of Ephraim lived the wise woman Deborah, the wife of Lapidoth. People came from far and near to consult Deborah, for she was a great Judge in Israel. Deborah "held court" near her home at a place between Ramah and Bethel. Here she would sit beneath a palm tree and the people would come and present her with their problems.

Many of the people asked Deborah her opinion of the idols of the Canaanites, and she explained the difference between the ugly little stone images and the power of the one invisible God. Sorrowfully this wise Judge listened to the laments of her people for the loved ones they had lost during enemy attacks. She was outraged and angered by their stories of plundered harvests, stolen grain and fruits, and the hunger that resulted.

Deborah resolved that King Jabin must be defeated. When the time was ripe, she gathered her allies. Summoning Barak, an able warrior of the tribe of Naphtali, she ordered him to commandeer every available Israelite soldier and prepare these men to make a mass attack. Warriors of the tribes of Zebulun and Naphtali answered the call to battle. Then, inspired by the words of Deborah, more soldiers came—from the tribes of Ephraim, Benjamin and Issachar. Deborah and Barak decided upon a very clever strategy by which to outwit the superior numbers and weapons of the enemy. Together, the great Judge and Barak led the warriors of Israel up the sides of Mount Tabor, a mountain that rises over the great plain of Jezreel near the river Kishon.

Confident of an easy victory over this small army equipped with inferior weapons, the mighty King Jabin and his general, Sisera, assembled their heavily armed troops and their iron chariots and waited beneath Mount Tabor for the Israelites to strike.

Shouting their battle cry, the Israelite warriors swooped down from the mountain upon the

---

JUDGES

The Twelve Judges of Israel whose histories are told in the Book of Judges: *

OTHNIEL	DEBORAH	JAIR	ELON
EHUD	GIDEON	JEPHTHAH	ABDON
SHAMGAR	TOLA	IBZAN	SAMSON

* The lives of the later Judges, Eli and Samuel, are told in the Book of Samuel, I.

Mount Tabor raises its peak 1300 feet into the misty clouds. It was here that the armies of Deborah came down to attack and defeat the Canaanites under Sisera.

Canaanites. In the midst of the battle the skies above seemed to open and rain poured down. The river Kishon, normally a peaceful stream, became a raging torrent, rolling and rushing across the plain. The heavy iron wheels of the enemy's chariots were mired in thick, slippery mud. The horses shied wildly, frightened by the storm and the noise of battle. Weighed down by their heavy wet armor, the Canaanite solders were no match for the lightly-armed Israelites, who seemed to be everywhere at once with lightning speed, cutting down the enemy right and left with their spears and sling shots.

The Canaanites, much to their own surprise, were routed: they fled in utter confusion. Sisera, the fierce general, sought refuge in the tent of Jael, a Kenite woman, begging her for water to quench his thirst. Jael gave the great warrior a dry cloak, and some milk to drink, then stood guard at the door of the tent. Unaware that Jael and her husband, Heber, were secret allies of the Israelites, Sisera thought himself safe and fell into a deep sleep. And while he slept, Jael slew him.

THE SONG OF DEBORAH

Great was the rejoicing of the Israelites when they learned that Sisera was dead and that the fierce Canaanite warriors had fled in confusion. Deborah, the prophetess who had so fearlessly led her people, sang a song of praise to the Lord.

The Song of Deborah was to be well remembered by the future warriors of Israel. Many of them would be inspired by her courage, even as they fought on the same spot where the Canaanites had been so completely defeated. On the fruitful plain of Jezreel many bitter battles were to be fought by Israelite warriors yet unborn.

With the Israelite victory at Mount Tabor, the power of the Canaanites came to an end. The successful conquest of this troublesome enemy gave the Israelites a much firmer hold on their new land and established them far more securely in their new life. Peace had come to the Promised Land—at least for a time.

A Canaanite victory celebration on an ivory plaque. The ruler sits on his throne as a court musician plays a lyre. Behind the musician is a warrior leading two prisoners and an armored chariot.

NEW FOES—THE MIDIANITES

In the decades of peace that followed the victory over King Jabin, the ties that had drawn the tribes of Israel so closely together began to loosen once again. Each tribe was concerned mainly with its own needs. Many Israelites had followed the Canaanites in the worship of Baal and Astarte, at altars and shrines on the hills beneath tall trees. The worship of the heathen gods did not require the Israelites to live up to lofty ideals, and many of them became cruel and heedless of their neighbors.

Such was the state of the people of Israel when a new threat to their security arose. Out of the East, from across the Jordan came the warriors of the Midianites, greedily searching for new grazing grounds and plunder. These desert nomads, warlike and strong, came riding on camels capable of living without water for long periods of time. Borne by these swift ships of the desert, the ruthless Midianites bore down swiftly on the land of Canaan, shattering the peaceful existence of the Israelites.

THE DAYS OF GIDEON

Once more there arose a new leader from the ranks of Israel to meet the challenge to freedom. That leader was Gideon, a farmer and warrior from Ophrah. Gideon, a Judge among the people of the tribe of Manasseh, had spoken out boldly and frequently against idol worship. Angrily tearing down the shrines of Baal, he aroused the people and inspired them to follow him, to return to the observance of their own laws and the worship of the one God.

Gideon soon became known throughout the land for his qualities of leadership. When he called for the toughest and most courageous warriors of Israel to battle the Midianites, the response was immediate. Thousands came, but Gideon chose only three hundred of the most stalwart and God fearing warriors for a surprise raid.

In the dead silence of night the Israelite warriors stealthily approached the camp of the sleep-

Gideon's fountain.

ing Midianites. Gideon's small army was equipped with odd weapons—burning torches, jars and pitchers. At a given signal, they held their torches high, shattering the jars and pitchers at the same time in one tremendous crash. The noise was deafening and, to add to the confusion, some of the Israelites blew their rams' horns, shouting, "For God and for Gideon!"

The Midianites were terrified. They tumbled from their tents and fled into the night. The Israelites pursued them and drove them out of the land. Gideon's clever ruse had succeeded and a decisive battle was won by a mere three hundred men. Never again did the Midianites attack Israel.

Gideon, a valiant warrior, and a brilliant strategist, was also a clever political leader. In his effort to defeat the Midianites he succeeded in uniting the tribes of Israel once again.

So great was the confidence of the people in Gideon and so sincere their love for him that the elders of the tribes asked him to be their king. To this request Gideon answered, "I shall not rule over you, neither shall my son rule over you. Only the Lord shall rule over you."

Gideon served as Judge in Israel for many peaceful years and died a very old man.

ABIMELECH WANTS TO BE KING

Gideon's determination that neither he nor his descendants should rule over Israel was not shared by his son, Abimelech. Abimelech, a vain and ambitious young man, devised a cunning scheme for gaining power over the people. He came to the men in his mother's native town of Shechem with the false report that all his brothers were ambitious and each wanted to become king of Israel. It would be better, he suggested to the men of Shechem, to have one strong ruler than to risk a civil war between brothers. The men were impressed by Abimelech's words and decided to make him king. This accomplished, Abimelech then convinced the men of Shechem that it was their duty to slay all the members of the house of Gideon. Only the youngest brother, Jotham, escaped.

Despite his ruthless schemes, Abimelech came to an ignoble end. His own followers, the men of

Shechem, turned against him and a civil war ensued, ending with Abimelech's death in battle at Thebez.

After Gideon, Israel was judged for twenty-three years by Tola, of the tribe of Issachar. Tola was succeeded by Jair of Gilead, who fought the attacking Ammonites and acted as Judge in Israel for twenty-two years.

JEPHTHAH OF GILEAD

Now in Gilead there arose a new Judge named Jephthah, a fierce warrior. At first, Jephthah tried to negotiate peacefully with the prince of Ammon, but to no avail. The Ammonites were bent on annexing Gilead to their territory and were greedy for the tribute they intended to exact from the tribes of Reuben, Gad and Manasseh. They crossed the Jordan and threatened also the security of Judah and the other tribes.

War was inevitable. Jephthah, a man of humble origin who was well acquainted with Gilead's rough mountain terrain, proved a capable military leader. After a bloody campaign, he drove the Ammonites from Gilead. After peace had been established, Jephthah continued to be Judge in Israel.

Jephthah was followed by Ibzan of Bethlehem, who judged for seven years. Ibzan was succeeded by Elon of the tribe of Zebulun who judged for ten years; after him came Abdon of the tribe of Ephraim, who ruled for eight years.

THE PHILISTINES, DANGEROUS NEIGHBORS

A time of great peril had come upon the Israelites. Their most formidable enemy, the Philistines, were on the march.

The Philistines had come from far away. Their long trek had led them originally through Crete, across the Aegean Sea by ship and through Asia Minor on foot and by oxcart. These invaders left a trail of pillage and bloodshed in their wake and their ambitious plan of conquest included even the plunder of mighty Egypt.

In two bloody battles, the Egyptian army under Rameses III defeated the Philistine attack on Egypt's border fortifications. One of these was a naval battle at the mouth of the River Nile, where

A stone relief from Thebes shows a group of Philistine prisoners of Rameses III. In hieroglyphics the Philistines were called *"peles et."* The name Palestine was derived from this word.

the Egyptian fleet destroyed the enemies' ships and prevented their landing. The other battle took place on land, where Egypt's well-trained charioteers won the victory. Reliefs in the Egyptian temple of Medinet-Habu, near ancient Thebes, still tell a vivid story of the land battles between the Egyptians and the Philistines and portray the participants. The Egyptians were smaller of stature and appear slight in comparison to the tall, helmeted Philistines. The reliefs show the many Philistines who were taken prisoner and the inscriptions relate Egypt's pride in this great victory.

THE PHILISTINES SETTLE IN CANAAN

The Philistines marched into Canaan victoriously, for the people were helpless before their bold conquest. They invaded and claimed the rich coastal cities and established five powerful city-states—Ashkelon, Ashdod, Ekron, Gaza and Gath. Each of these five cities in the southern part of the

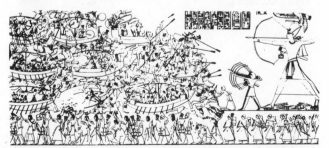

Drawing from an Egyptian stone relief pictures the naval engagement between the ships of Rameses III and the Philistines.

fertile coastal plain was ruled by an independent prince, but all five were strongly united allies in peace and in war. The Philistines then attempted to subject the land of Israel to their power and force the entire people to submit to their yoke. They succeeded in driving the tribe of Dan out of its territory. The people of Dan were forced to move on and settle in the far north of the land.

SAMSON, THE MAN OF STRENGTH

At the time of Samson, the last of the Judges,

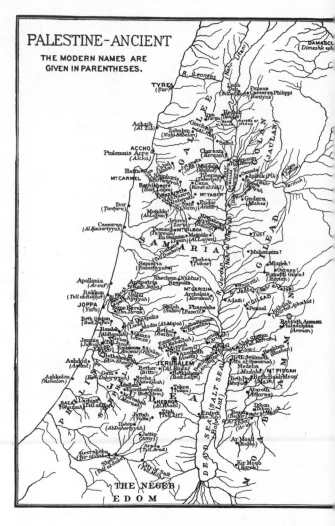

A pottery figurine, probably an idol, found in Ashdod, Israel.

Israel desperately tried to hold off the Philistines. Samson's great physical strength was known and admired both by the Philistines and the Israelites. The story of how this fearless hero was finally brought down by the trickery and deceit of his Philistine sweetheart, Delilah, has been made famous in the world's music and literature. During a Philistine festival, Samson, blinded and made captive, was exhibited at Gaza. Sightless and alone, he exerted the last of his remaining strength to bring down a great Philistine temple, destroying many of his captors and perishing under the crashing pillars himself.

GLOSSARY OF HEBREW TERMINOLOGY
AND NAMES

Mount Tabor	Hahr Tahvohr	הַר תָּבוֹר	Israelites	B'nai Yisrah-eyl	בְּנֵי יִשְׂרָאֵל
Kishon	Keeshohn	קִישׁוֹן	Sabbatical Year	Shmeetah	שְׁמִיטָה
Sisera	Seesrah	סִיסְרָא	Jubilee year	Yohveyl	יוֹבֵל
Jael	Yah-eyl	יָעֵל	Judges	Shohfteem	שׁוֹפְטִים
Megiddo	Mgeedoh	מְגִדּוֹ	Jezreel (Es-draelon)	Yizre-el	יִזְרְעֵאל
Gideon	Geedohn	גִּדְעוֹן	Baal	Bah-ahl	בַּעַל
Abimelech	Aveemeleḥ	אֲבִימֶלֶךְ	Astarte (Ish-tar)	Ahshtohret	עַשְׁתֹּרֶת
Thebez	Teyveytz	תֵּבֵץ	Othniel	Awtnee-eyl	עָתְנִיאֵל
Tola	Tohlah	תּוֹלָע	Ehud	Eyhood	אֵהוּד
Jair	Yah-eer	יָאִיר	Moab	Moh-ahv	מוֹאָב
Jephthah	Yiftaḥ	יִפְתָּח	Shamgar	Shahmgahr	שַׁמְגַּר
Judah	Yhoodah	יְהוּדָה	Philistines	Plishteem	פְּלִשְׁתִּים
Ibzan	Ivtzahn	אִבְצָן	Jabin	Yahveen	יָבִין
Bethlehem	Beyt Leḥem	בֵּית לֶחֶם	Ephraim	Efrahyeem	אֶפְרַיִם
Elon	Eylohn	אֵלֹן	Deborah	Dvohrah	דְּבוֹרָה
Abdon	Ahvdohn	עַבְדּוֹן	Lapidoth	Lahpeedot	לַפִּידוֹת
Ashkelon	Ahshklohn	אַשְׁקְלוֹן	Ramah	Rahmah	רָמָה
Ashdod	Ahshdohd	אַשְׁדּוֹד	Barak	Bahrahk	בָּרָק
Ekron	Ekrohn	עֶקְרוֹן	Naphtali	Nahftahlee	נַפְתָּלִי
Gaza	Ahzah	עַזָּה	Zebulun	Zvooloon	זְבֻלוּן
Gath	Gaht	גַּת	Benjamin	Binyahmeen	בִּנְיָמִין
Dan	Dahn	דָּן	Issachar	Yisaḥar	יִשָּׂשכָר
Samson	Shimshohn	שִׁמְשׁוֹן			
Delilah	Dleelah	דְּלִילָה			

SAMUEL AND THE FIRST KING OF ISRAEL

ELI, THE KIND PRIEST

After the time of Samson, the sanctuary at Shiloh was kept by the priest Eli, assisted by his sons, Hophni and Phinehas. Eli also performed the duties of Judge and the people presented their disputes and problems to him.

Eli noted that time and time again there would come to the sanctuary at Shiloh a woman called Hannah, the wife of Elkanah of the hill country of Ephraim. Hannah would pray earnestly but silently, and her behavior seemed strange. However, when the kind old priest learned that Hannah had been praying for the birth of a son, he comforted her and told her to be of good faith, that God would answer her prayer. Soon thereafter a son was born to Hannah. She called the child Samuel (probably from the Hebrew *Shama El,* God heard).

As soon as Samuel was old enough to leave home, the grateful Hannah brought him to Shiloh to present him to Eli. She requested that Eli make the boy his assistant in the service of the God of Israel. The old priest was delighted to grant Hannah's request and Samuel proved an apt and eager pupil.

Young Samuel was a great joy to Eli, easing some of the bitter disappointment he felt over his own sons, Hophni and Phinehas. These two priests employed their high positions merely to fill their own purses and further their own selfish pleasure. Eli was very pleased with Samuel, for here was a young man who was truly worthy to be a future leader and Judge of Israel, even though he was not a Cohen, a descendent of the priestly family of Aaron. Eli instructed Samuel in the ways of the Law and the faith of Israel. As the years passed, the son of Hannah became well known to the people for his knowledge and great wisdom, and in time he was revered as a man of divine inspiration, a Judge and a prophet in Israel.

THE FATEFUL BATTLE OF APHEK

As the years passed, the Philistines, Israel's dreaded foes, had grown increasingly powerful. They were determined to make themselves the overlords of Israel and they frequently attacked the towns and villages of the land. At last, the Philistine and Israelite armies met on the plain of Aphek in open warfare and a bloody battle was

Archeologists have unearthed the stone relief of the Holy Ark in the ancient synagogue in Capernaum.

fought. The Israelites suffered heavy losses from the very beginning. They retreated to their camp to take counsel for they felt that they were faced with certain defeat. In desperation, the elders of the tribes went to Eli.

"Let us carry the Holy Ark into battle," they pleaded. "It will inspire us to victory."

With the Holy Ark in their midst, the Israelites fought a brave fight, but the superior arms and training of the Philistines proved to be overwhelming. Scores of Israelite soldiers perished in the battle before the entire army of Israel was defeated and put to flight. Among those who perished were Eli's two sons, Hophni and Phinehas. The Holy Ark of the Covenant, with the Tablets of the Law, was captured by the enemy.

An Israelite warrior, running from the battlefield, carried the disastrous news to Eli. The old priest, overwhelmed by shock and grief, died instantly.

DARK DAYS UNDER THE PHILISTINES

In this time of bleak despair for Israel, Samuel took the reins of leadership. In the years that followed, Samuel the seer proved himself an ex-cellent Judge, keenly aware of the needs of the people, wise and just in his decisions and advice.

The Philistines had now succeeded in becoming masters in the land. They destroyed the sanctuary at Shiloh, and the priests and Levites scattered to different parts of the country. Samuel returned to his home in Ramah in the hill country of Ephraim and there the people came to him for counsel.

Samuel's task of keeping alive the faith of Israel was not an easy one in those dark days. Fear and discouragement lay like a heavy yoke upon the people. They were forced to pay heavy tribute to the Philistines. They were not permitted to carry weapons and even their pickaxes and ploughshares had to be sharpened in the forges of the overlords. All Israelites were forbidden to use iron, the precious new metal, for it was to be forged only in the cities of the Philistines. Many of the Israelites turned away from their God in bitterness and began to worship Baal and Astarte, the gods of their conquerors.

THE HOLY ARK FINDS A SHELTER

However, in the midst of utter despair and defeat, the Israelites won a victory of sorts. The Philistines returned to them their most precious possession, the Ark of the Covenant. The enemies of Israel, superstitious and fearful of this sacred symbol, believed the Ark was bringing them illness and misfortune, and therefore carried it back

The Ark in the Land of the Philistines. Copy from the fresco in the synagogue at Dura-Europos, 3rd century, C. E.
Yale University Art Gallery

into Israelite territory. The men of Kiriath-Jearim, in the border country between Judah and Benjamin, bore the Ark up into the hills. There the faithful priests, Abinadab and his son Eleazar, watched over it, waiting hopefully for a time when a new sanctuary could be established.

Without a central sanctuary and under the harassment of their cruel overlords, it was inevitable that the tribes of Israel should be less united than ever. Indeed, civil strife occurred, weakening Israel still further.

SAMUEL THE JUDGE

Despite the military victory scored at Mizpah, Samuel, the wise Judge and priest, realized that his efforts at Ramah alone, were not sufficient to unite the scattered Israelites. Like the priests and Levites of earlier times, he began traveling through the land, encouraging the people everywhere to hold fast to their faith. Samuel taught the laws of the Torah and reminded the people of the courageous sacrifices their ancestors had made to gain this new land. He advised them to hold fast to their land, for he believed that Israel would eventually shake off the Philistine yoke. He knew, however, that a period of preparation was needed first, a time in which Israel could regain its unity and strength.

NEW VOICES—THE MEN WHO FOLLOWED SAMUEL

On his travels, Samuel attracted many followers, men who were inspired by his words and who, like himself, felt called upon to talk to the people about God and hope. These men would sing and play the harp, telling the stories of Israel's past. As time passed, some of these more inspired followers of Samuel began to form little bands of their own. These men were called prophets. Traveling through the land, they sang the praises of God, explained the meaning of the laws of the Torah, and fought idol-worship wherever they found it.

From the very first, these early prophets had a profound influence on Israel. In every town people looked forward to their coming and listened to them eagerly. The prophets brought new ideas to the people, which the people discussed among themselves. Stimulated to renewed interest in their past and in their faith, the Israelites once more believed fervently in their own laws and tradition.

THE PEOPLE WANT A KING

When Samuel grew old, the elders of the tribes became fearful of the future. Who would be Judge after Samuel? Who would be so wise and strong that all the tribes, without exception, would follow him? A cry went up for Samuel to establish a strong central authority over Israel. The people would have to stand united, with forceful leadership, to rid themselves of Philistine tyranny.

SAMUEL GIVES ADVICE

Samuel was deeply troubled when the elders of the tribes came to him and asked him to select a king to rule over them. The wise old Judge was well-versed in the laws of Israel and knew the needs of a free society. He tried to dissuade the elders, for he knew that under a king the people would lose a great deal of that precious freedom. The leaders of Israel had always been chosen by the people, from among the people. There were no nobles from which to choose a king, for everyone was of equal rank. Everyone had a voice in the councils of Israel and no Judge and leader was immune to rebuke and criticism.

Samuel realized that life under a king would be different in many ways. The people would have to maintain a grand style of living for the king at all times. A king would require a royal palace and servants. Hitherto each man had defended the land of his own free will, but with a king a regular army would be needed, with men from each tribe to guard and serve him. Taxes would have to be levied, to meet the civil and military expenses of a kingdom. One by one, Samuel presented these arguments against the establishment of a kingdom —but the elders refused to be discouraged. The people had set their hearts on having a king. Reluctantly Samuel bowed to their wishes.

SAUL, THE FIRST KING OF ISRAEL

Samuel chose the first king of Israel with great wisdom and much diplomacy. Because of the competition and rivalry among the more powerful tribes, Samuel turned to the smaller, poorer tribe of Benjamin for his selection. This tribe had recently been ravaged by a civil war and in its weakened state offered no competition to any other tribe. By choosing a man from the tribe of Benjamin, Samuel wisely avoided the danger of setting the great rival tribes against one another. The man chosen by Samuel was Saul, a dignified, handsome young man, who was respected by all, and a valiant fighter.

The Bible relates how Saul had left home to go in search of his father's runaway donkeys. Traveling through Zuph, he stopped to ask the advice of Samuel the seer, who was speaking there to the people. Samuel took Saul into the hills of Zuph, where he told the young man that instead of the donkeys which he had gone out to seek, he had found a crown.

Samuel anointed Saul by pouring precious oil on his head and blessing him. Saul, the anointed, was now a special person, set apart from all others, consecrated to the service of Israel and dedicated to sacred tasks. Many nations to this day follow the ceremony of anointing a new ruler.

The Biblical account further relates that when Saul left Samuel to begin his journey home he met a band of prophets on the way. As Saul listened to their singing he felt that the spirit of God had descended on him. Uplifted and inspired, he joined the prophets in their songs. The people who saw this were astonished, for they had known Saul as a serious young man but one not greatly concerned with spiritual matters.

"Is Saul also among the prophets?" they cried in amazement.

A Canaanite jar.

SAUL PROVES HIMSELF

Saul was soon to prove himself a forceful leader. The Ammonites, Israel's old enemies, were still smarting from their defeat by Jephthah, the Israelite Judge. Now that Israel was weakened by the yoke of the Philistines, the Ammonites saw their chance to recapture the territory of Gilead. They besieged the city of Jabesh-Gilead. Their king was a cruel, revengeful monarch. As the price of a peace treaty he demanded that the people of Jabesh-Gilead submit to having their right eye put out, branding them forever with the shame of defeat. In their distress, the people of Jabesh sent messengers across the River Jordan, pleading for help. Saul's anger and sympathy were aroused by this threat of the Ammonites and he sent the messengers back to their tribe with a promise of assistance.

Saul sent his messengers from Gibeah throughout the land, asking the men of all the tribes to unite at once to help the city of Jabesh-Gilead. The men of Israel responded and under Saul's capable leadership, Israel attacked the Ammonites, who were already besieging the city. Saul's great hordes of warriors fell upon the Ammonites and sent them fleeing in confusion. Saul drove all the Ammonites out of Gilead. The people of Jabesh rejoiced, loudly praising the triumph of Saul, their new leader.

Saul's victory served a double purpose. It not only vanquished an enemy, but reunited the tribes of Israel as well. Together, they marched to Gilgal to offer sacrifices and prayers of thanksgiving to God. There, led by Samuel, the people proclaimed Saul their king.

THE NEW KING'S TASKS

Saul, the first king of Israel, returned to his home in Gibeah. Now the people of all Israel came to Gibeah seeking judgement and advice from him. However Saul found little quiet and peace for judging and counseling. Most of his energies were required for the far more arduous task of winning battles.

During the years of Israel's decline, the border lands had been left without defenders, making

The stone remains of Saul's ancient fortress at Gibeah.

them easy prey to raids by hostile neighbors. King Saul and his men were called upon to strengthen and defend these borders. In quick succession they drove back the Amalekites, the Moabites and the Edomites.

Modern archeologists have excavated Saul's home in Gibeah. From their discoveries, we know that this first king of Israel does not fit the concept which most of us have of the monarchs of old. He did not live in a sumptuous palace, surrounded by pomp and luxury. His dwelling was strongly fortified, but simple—the house of a ruler who lived in the manner of a well-to-do farmer and warrior of those times. Saul indulged in none of the extravagances of the princes of neighboring countries. He did not wear splendid robes, did not sit upon silken cushions, did not eat exotic foods and did not sleep on richly bedecked bedsteads. King Saul sat on a rough stone bench, drank and ate from simple vessels and wore plain garments. His court was made up of warriors, and his own sons were valiant fighters, going with him into battle whenever he defended the land. Jonathan, the best-known of Saul's sons, was not only a brave young warrior but a fine and daring strategist as well.

THE PHILISTINES FEAR THE LOSS OF THEIR VASSAL

The Philistines had viewed the military successes of Israel's new king with more than a little alarm. Fearing that the newly-united tribes would rise against them, the Philistines massed an army near Gibeah, on a rocky height. Saul made ready for battle and the Israelite warriors gathered at Gibeah.

Prince Jonathan, taking the initiative, planned a daring and effective strategy. Accompanied only by his armor-bearer, he climbed a narrow pass to a height above the place where the Philistine army was camped. Hidden from sight, Jonathan and his armor-bearer began to hurl down rocks and javelins upon the Philistines. Thinking that they were surrounded by a whole army of Israelites, the Philistine soldiers were panic-stricken. They began to fight one another, then fled in confusion. The noise of this upheaval reached Saul and his warriors. They pursued the fleeing Philistines and defeated them so thoroughly that they withdrew from Israel and returned to the borders of their own city-states.

The future, however, was not to be free from encounters with this ambitious and determined enemy. The Philistines still considered themselves the overlords of Israel and would not give up their power without a bitter struggle. No doubt they regarded Saul and his warriors as rebel upstarts who had no right to defy the Philistine authority. Again and again Saul was to meet them in battle.

SAMUEL'S DISAPPOINTMENT

Saul had met Israel's dire need for a courageous and clever military leader; but Samuel was disappointed in the new king. Saul's spiritual values did not always meet the high standards set by the laws of the *Torah.* Saul defended his actions by telling Samuel that he had sacrificed much of the booty of war to the Lord. But Samuel answered

Dagon, a Philistine god.

The name is derived from his physical form which is in the shape of a fish. "Dag" means fish.

that God prefers obedience to sacrifices upon an altar.

The rift widened between Samuel the spiritual leader and Saul, the warrior king. In Samuel's last years he refused to see the king, and predicted that none of Saul's sons would succeed him. A new and different man would be king of Israel, said the old seer—a man who would be more concerned with the spiritual life of his people than Saul.

A TROUBLED KING

Samuel's rejection lay heavily on the mind of King Saul. He became deeply troubled, suffering sleepless nights and days of anguish during which he scarcely spoke to those around him.

Samuel, the aged seer, began to look about secretly for a new king. His choice fell on David, a shepherd, the youngest son of Jesse of Bethlehem, a farmer of the tribe of Judah. Samuel anointed David in secret and proclaimed him the next king of Israel. At the time the young shepherd hardly realized the importance of the ceremony in which he had taken part.

THE SWEET SINGER OF ISRAEL

Soon after his anointment, David was brought to the court of Saul to play his harp and sing his songs for the troubled king. The men around Saul had heard of the outstanding musical talent of this young shepherd of Bethlehem whom the people later called "the sweet singer of Israel."

David's songs were like healing balm to the oppressed spirit of the king. Again and again Saul commanded David to come to his court. The king took a great fancy to the young singer and later gave David his daughter Michal in marriage. The deep friendship between David and Jonathan, son of Saul, has become a classic in the literature of the world.

DAVID THE WARRIOR

David, the "sweet singer," proved himself as capable in battle as he was with his harp and song. He slew Goliath, the giant of the Philistine army who had terrified the Israelite camp. Up and down the land went the stories of David's valiant

The pool of Gibeon. Here (II Samuel 2:8-17,) a group of David's men defeated a band of soldiers fighting for Saul's son, Ishbosheth.

deeds. "Saul has slain his thousands," the people sang, "but David his ten thousands!" From this, however, David was to learn a bitter lesson: it is always dangerous for a man to become more popular than his king.

Saul became suspicious and jealous of David. The music of David's harp grated on his ears and his suspicion extended even to Jonathan, his own son, because he was David's friend. The king began to plot to destroy this popular young hero.

Jonathan learned of his father's plans and warned David, urging him to flee. David, accompanied by his most trusted warriors, fled into the mountains of Judah. King Saul tracked him down and David realized that he would be safe nowhere in Israel. He was forced to seek refuge abroad in the enemy land of the Philistines. There, for sixteen months, he and his men were given shelter at Ziklag, by King Achish of Gath, who was no doubt secretly elated at this sign of disunity in the land of Israel. Though they were the guests of the enemy king, David and his men were closely watched by the Philistines, who did not trust these aliens in their midst.

SAUL'S LAST BATTLE

The Philistine army, encouraged by news of King Saul's decline, prepared again for all-out attack. Their ranks were greatly fortified by many fierce mercenaries. The Philistines advanced to the plain of Jezreel. At the foot of Mount Gilboa a bloody battle took place, close to the very spot where Barak and Deborah had once put the Canaanites to rout. There was no glorious victory this time, for the morose and troubled Saul was no longer a man to inspire courage and enthusiasm in his warriors. The Israelites were overwhelmed by the onslaught of the Philistines with their iron chariots and superior weapons.

The battle at Mount Gilboa was a disastrous defeat for Israel. Many thousands were slain, among them the sons of Saul, including the valiant Jonathan. King Saul, dreading the fate of being taken captive, died by his own sword.

The enemies carried the bodies of Saul and his sons in triumph to their temple at Beth Shan, where they exhibited them on the temple walls. The loyal men of Jabesh-Gilead, remembering now how Saul had so bravely defended them long ago, removed the bodies in the dark of night to save them from further shame. In a quiet, secluded place they laid their dead king and his sons to rest.

DAVID MOURNS SAUL AND JONATHAN

There was room in David's heart for no other emotion but grief when he learned that his king and his beloved friend Jonathan were dead. David composed a song of mourning, one of the great poems of the Bible, extolling the courage of the two great warriors and lamenting their fall in battle.

A fourteenth century stele found at Beth Shan.

36

GLOSSARY OF HEBREW TERMINOLOGY
AND NAMES

English	Pronunciation	Hebrew	English	Pronunciation	Hebrew
Zuph	Tsoof	צוּף	Eli	Eylee	עֵלִי
Jabesh-Gilead	Yahveysh Gilahd	יָבֵשׁ גִּלְעָד	Hophni	Ḥawfnee	חָפְנִי
			Phinehas	Pinḥas	פִּנְחָס
Gibeah	Geevah	גִּבְעָה	Hannah	Ḥahnah	חַנָּה
Jonathan	Yohnahtahn	יוֹנָתָן	Elkanah	Elkahnah	אֶלְקָנָה
David	Dahveed	דָּוִד	Samuel	Shmoo-eyl	שְׁמוּאֵל
Jesse	Yeeshai	יִשַׁי	Aphek	Ahfeyk	אֲפֵק
Michal	Meeḥal	מִיכַל	Abinadab	Ahveenahdahv	אֲבִינָדָב
Ziklag	Tzeeklahg	צִיקְלַג	Eleazar	Elahzahr	אֶלְעָזָר
Achish	Aḥeesh	אָכִישׁ	Kiriath-Jearim	Kiryaht Y'ahreem	קִרְיַת יְעָרִים
Gilboa	Gilboh-ah	גִּלְבֹּעַ			
Beth Shan	Beyt Shahn	בֵּית שָׁן, בֵּית שְׁאָן	Saul	Shah-ool	שָׁאוּל

THE HOUSE OF DAVID

A NEW ERA FOR ISRAEL

The time that followed the death of Saul was difficult and unhappy for the Israelites. The Philistine tyranny weighed heavily upon them. Taxes of tribute were high and the presence of Philistine soldiers stationed throughout the land was a constant reminder of Israel's bitter defeat. Civil strife again disrupted the tribes, for they could not agree on who was to be king in Israel.

Abner, one of Saul's generals, proclaimed Ishbosheth (also called Eshbaal), the last surviving son of Saul, as King. The tribe of Judah refused to accept Ishbosheth as their king and upheld David as their rightful ruler. David ruled in Hebron, the capital of Judah. The luckless Ishbosheth, who proved a weak monarch, was slain by his own men after a brief rule of two years. After Ishbosheth's death the tribes unanimously accepted David as their king.

THE ULTIMATE TRIUMPH

David, now king over all Israel, scarcely had time to take stock of the new situation before the Philistines, eager to prevent Israel from uniting, marched into the territory of Judah. David hastily assembled all available fighting men. The enemy was forced to fight in the Judean hills, a territory well known to David and his soldiers.

The Philistines now found themselves opposed by a brilliant strategist to whom they themselves had unwittingly taught many of the arts of war. David had learned much from the Philistine warriors. With the assistance of his brilliant general, Joab, he forced battle after battle upon the enemy on his own home grounds. David gave the Philistines no peace, attacking them ferociously each time they attempted to rest. With these relentless tactics, he drove the Philistines out of Israel's territory and pursued them into their own land.

The Philistine city of Gath fell to the Israelites. Soon thereafter the war was over and the battle-weary Philistine army began to dissolve. The Philistine mercenaries, ever ready to follow the winner, came over to the side of Israel and found employment with David's army. The crushing power of the Philistines was broken and the heavy yoke was lifted from the people of Israel.

DAVID MAKES ISRAEL SAFE

David now turned to other tasks. The neighboring nations had taken advantage of Israel's weakened state. The Arameans had invaded the border villages of the north. The Israelite territory of Gilead, west of the Jordan, had easily fallen to Ammon, Moab and Amalek. David began an intensive border campaign to regain all lost territory and fortify the border towns against invaders.

THE CONQUEST OF JUDEA

In the midst of the Judean hills there still remained a fortified city which, since the days of Joshua, had resisted all Israel's efforts of conquest. This was the city of Jerusalem, the ancient stronghold of the Jebusites. So successfully had the Jebusites defended their city that Jerusalem was known among the Israelites as practically an unconquerable city. David, determined to forge a strong, united Israel, now laid plans for the capture of Jerusalem.

Joab, David's able general, found a chink in Jerusalem's invincible armor. He learned of a secret passage—a natural tunnel that led through the rocky mountains into the center of the city. Through this tunnel Joab led the Israelite soldiers and took the Jebusites by surprise. Thus did Jerusalem become an Israelite city.

ISRAEL, A GROWING NATION

Within the span of a few years the status of Israel had changed radically. Before the reign of David the nation had been torn by disunity, oppressed by its powerful foes, the Philistines, and threatened and harassed on all frontiers by ruthless, hostile neighbors. Now Israel was fast becoming a power to be reckoned with and respected —a nation ruled by a wise and able king, with the important city of Jerusalem as its capital. Under the reign of David, peace had been won at last and Israel blossomed and grew in its new prosperity.

THE CITY OF DAVID

The tribes of Israel were now firmly united. Jerusalem became the seat of a central government which dealt with issues confronting the nation. In Jerusalem, too, was the residence of King David and the sanctuary in which the Holy Ark rested. On the festivals, throngs of joyous Israelites made the journey to Jerusalem to participate in the services at the sanctuary.

The High Priest was assisted during the services and sacrifices by priests and Levites, who sang songs of praise and psalms. King David contributed his own great talents to the writing of psalms. The Psalms of David have taken an important place in the world's literature.

David playing the harp. From a medieval Jewish manuscript.

RULING A YOUNG KINGDOM

Through an extensive network of civil servants, King David kept in touch with all parts of the land. These representatives, stationed throughout the nation, assisted the people in their affairs, collected taxes for the king and kept him well informed on conditions in the various Israelite territories. At the head of the civil service system were the chancellor and the scribe (*sofer*). The sofer was the writer of chronicles and keeper of the records. Some historians believe that David's sofer and chronicler was the prophet Nathan.

Although David appointed many judges and officials, a great number of people still came to the king directly for advice and judgement. The world outside Israel also found its way to the holy city, for messengers came to Jerusalem bearing tributes from territories which David had conquered. Other monarchs, indicating their respect for a rising nation, sent their ambassadors to seek the favor of the great King David. With these

A modern view of the village of Tyre.

ambassadors David negotiated military pacts and trade agreements.

NEW ALLIES

David established a close alliance with Hiram, the Phoenician king of Tyre, Israel's neighbor in the northwest on the Mediterranean coast. The Phoenicians were prosperous traders, seafarers, skillful architects and craftsmen. These craftsmen fashioned handsome glass and metal wares and colored their cloth a beautiful purple. The Phoenicians of Tyre had discovered the secret of making a particularly beautiful purple dye and Tyrian purple became famous throughout the ancient world. Phoenician architects were sent to many parts of the ancient world including Egypt and Mesopotamia.

It was their traders, however, who brought the greatest renown to Phoenicia. These daring sailors traveled far and wide with their wares, founding settlements as their trading centers in many distant lands. One such center was Carthage, later to become a strong foe of Rome.

Now that David was in control of territory from the foothills of the Lebanon to the Gulf of Aqaba, he had much to offer to the Phoenicians. The

Traditional tomb of Hiram, King of Tyre.

Modern Hebrew	Old Hebrew	Phoenician	Early Greek	Later Greek	Latin	English
א			A	A	A	A
ב			S ٩	ß	B	B
ג			٦	٢	C G	C.G
ד			Δ	Δ	D	D
ה			∃	Ł	E	E
ו			Y	Y	F V	F.V.U
ז			I	I	...	Z
ח			B	B	H	E.H
ט			⊗	⊗	...	TH.PH
י			٤	ş	I	I
כ			k	k	...	K.KH
ל			٨	L ٨	L	L
מ			M	M	M	M
נ			Ч	N	N	N
ס			⊞	⊞	X	X
ע			o	o	O	O
פ			٦	Γ	P	P
צ			٢	M	...	S
ק			φ	φ	Q	Q
ר			٩	P	R	R
ש			₹	₹	S	S
ת			X	T	T	T

Table showing how the Hebrew and Phonecian letters passed through Greek and Latin forms to their present English form.

Phoenicians were desirous of using the great caravan routes connecting Tyre with Egypt, Mesopotamia and Arabia, and also eager to exchange their own wares for the valuable iron and copper from Israel's mines in the southern desert. David, in turn, ever on the alert for ways to further the advancement of his nation, was anxious for Israel to learn some of the Phoenician skills, especially in building, craftsmanship and commerce.

David made an important trade pact with Hiram, king of Tyre, and in this exchange received something of great value—wood from the magnificent cedars that grew in the forests of Lebanon. With this beautiful and fragrant wood, and with the help of Phoenician architects, David built his palace in Jerusalem.

A THRIVING NATION

The land of Israel had become a thriving nation, with a splendid capital city of which any people might have been proud and a king to whom even the mightiest monarchs paid homage. The Israel-

A mighty cedar of Lebanon.

ites were prospering. Farmers and shepherds, no longer forced to take up arms against marauding bands, were able to devote themselves fully to the raising of crops and the tending of their sheep and cattle.

At harvest time, the farmers would bring their grain, flax, grapes, figs, dates and honey to the market place in the city. The shepherds would bring their wool, their leather and meat. The potters, weavers, dyers, smiths and leather workers from the cities traded their wares. The market place was the common meeting place, where traders would come to exhibit foreign goods. The caravans of foreign merchants traveled on the roads of the Land of Israel, bringing spices, fine woods, pottery, cloth and jewels from countries near and far.

It was truly a time of peace and plenty.

NATHAN, THE PROPHET, UPBRAIDS THE KING

In addition to Saul's daughter, Michal, David had other wives, as was the custom in the Near East. Among his wives was Bathsheba, who had been the wife of Uriah, an army captain. David had ordered Uriah into combat, where he was slain. The king then married the captain's beautiful widow.

This act of human weakness unbecoming a king of Israel aroused the ire of the prophet Nathan. The prophets of Israel represented the moral conscience of the people and they were dedicated to defend and uphold the principles of justice. As spokesmen of right against might the prophets were dauntless and fearlessly criticized the kings whenever their actions were not in keeping with the high ethical stardards of Israel's laws. Accordingly, the prophet Nathan rebuked King David, making him aware of the seriousness of his deed. Although David realized that he had done wrong and repented his transgression, Bathsheba remained his favorite wife and her son Solomon became his favorite son.

THE REBELLIOUS PRINCES

When David grew old he found it difficult to decide which of his sons was to succeed him as king, for Israel had not yet produced a ruling

The traditional tomb of Absalom, son of David.

dynasty with a continuing line of kings. The House of David was destined to become such a dynasty, but now King David was faced with dissension and discord in the naming of his successor.

Several of David's sons were casting hopeful eyes at the crown. Amnon, the eldest, expected to be chosen. Absalom, the third son, a handsome young soldier-prince with many loyal followers, had similar expectations. Absalom was ambitious for the crown regardless of cost. He schemed to have his brother Amnon killed, and fomented a revolt against his father the king. Absalom's followers proclaimed him king in Hebron.

Joab, David's trusted old general, went out with an army to subdue the rebellion. The king begged Joab to spare Absalom's life but circumstances decreed otherwise. Absalom was defeated in battle and forced to flee before Joab's soldiers. As he escaped, his long hair, of which he was so proud, caught in the branches of a tree, halting his flight. He was then captured and slain by Joab. When the news of Absalom's death was brought to King David, the old father was grief-stricken.

"O my son Absalom," he cried. "Would I had died for thee, O Absalom my son, my son!"

Absalom's revolt was followed by that of Prince Adonijah, the fourth of David's sons. Adonijah's revolt spread like wildfire and attracted many important men. Even the faithful old general, Joab, commander of David's army, lent his support to it, as did Abiathar, the priest.

DAVID MAKES A CHOICE

David realized he must waste no time proclaiming his choice. Summoning Nathan, the prophet, he bade him anoint the true heir—the gentle, wise Prince Solomon, son of Bathsheba. Nathan the prophet, Zadok the priest and Benaiah, captain of the king's guard, supported Solomon, the king's choice. Solomon was anointed by the priest Zadok and proclaimed king. The rams' horns sounded and the people shouted, "Long live King Solomon!"

King David's work was done. His had been a reign of glory and triumph, during which Israel had risen from a scattered, disunited people, torn by civil strife, to become a strong, prosperous nation. David's last act for Israel, that of appointing a worthy successor to carry on the difficult tasks of government and leadership, had been accomplished. The young shepherd had marched a long and victorious way from the hills of Bethlehem. He had become king over all Israel, respected and admired by monarchs throughout the ancient world and deeply loved by his own people. The

The tomb of King David atop Mount Zion.

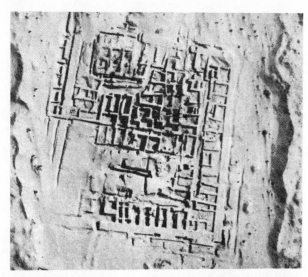

An aerial view of the ruins of Ezion-Geber. King Solomon's smelter was located in the large building at the upper left.

brave warrior had fought a good fight. When he died, all of Israel mourned "the sweet singer of Israel."

A KING OF PEACE

Solomon took over the reigns of government with efficiency. He took careful stock of Israel's assets, his father's accomplishments and the possibilities at hand. He completed the fortifications and building projects which David had begun and furthered the trade alliances with other nations. Solomon was a king of peace, whose riches and wisdom were to become fabled through the ages. Under his rule, Israel experienced an era of prosperity and glory—a time of peace and progress.

THE KINGDOM GROWS WEALTHY

The friendly alliance between David and King Hiram of Tyre proved a rich inheritance for Solomon, who became a close friend of the Phoenician monarch. Both kings were aware of the importance of Ezion-Geber, Israel's new port on the Red Sea, and both were desirous of enlarging it. Ezion-Geber, could open the sea route to India for the Phoenician traders, eliminating the necessity of their taking the more costly and often dangerous land route through Mesopotamia. With Hiram's assistance, Solomon turned to the task of building a navy for the land of Israel. Soon Phoeni-

cian and Israelite traders were traveling together, exchanging their wares for the rich offerings of far-flung lands.

To the seaports of the ancient world the Phoenicians carried the cedar wood of the Lebanon, and linens and other fine woven cloth. The Israelites exported their most valuable new product, the copper from the mines of the Negev in the southern desert. This copper was the main source of their new wealth.

The people of Canaan, especially the Phoenicians, had long been accomplished in the weaving and dyeing of cloth, and in the days of Solomon these industries flourished in Israel. Modern archeologists have found dyeing vats from that period in the old cities of Hebron and Kiriath-Sepher, where dyeing plants were operated.

From their allies, the Phoenicians, the Israelites learned to trade, to build ships, and to produce the beautiful Tyrian purple. Many other colors were also manufactured in Israel's dye plants: red, from the roots of flowers, and yellow from the saffron and pomegranate plants.

Exquisite linens were woven in Israel's textile centers. Herbs and flowers furnished some of the ingredients for cosmetics which apparently were in

The entrance to the copper mines at King Solomon's smelter.

43

great demand by the feminine population even in those ancient times. Rouge was made from chalks; ointment, eye-shadow and henna hair dyes were concocted and exported. In exchange for these exports, the traders of the two nations brought back many new and exotic things to intrigue and delight the senses of Israel and enrich their tables. Cinnamon from India—spices, balsam and myrrh from Arabia. From balsam and the essence of flowers, incense and perfumes were made.

Israel's greatest source of wealth were the rich mines in the southern desert. Here iron was mined and smelted and the precious copper refined on the spot. In recent years these famous mines of King Solomon have been excavated and experts have marveled at the construction of the refineries at Ezion-Geber. More than two thousand years ago, Solomon's engineers discovered how to harness the power of the strong north and south winds that blow over the desert.

One section of the ruins of King Solomon's stables at Meggido.

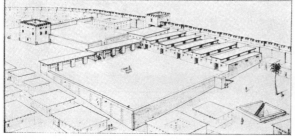

A reconstruction of the stables.

This same principle is still used in the modern Bessemer method of making steel to work the drafts and bellows of the huge furnaces. Solomon's refineries must have been in constant operation, for copper from Ezion-Geber was exported to all parts of the ancient world, making Israel a major trading power.

King Solomon took great delight in horses, and he imported many beautiful steeds from Egypt for his fine stables. These horses were used by Solomon's well-equipped army. Solomon himself rode about in great splendor, escorted by a personal guard armed with golden shields and flashing armor. From all over the ancient world people came to marvel at the glory of Solomon's court, over which he presided on an ivory throne overlaid with pure gold.

The fame of the beautiful city of Jerusalem spread throughout the ancient world. Solomon was a hospitable king and the great and near-great from Israel and from many lands came to see the marvels of the Holy City. Jerusalem's markets attracted many visitors, for they offered a fascinating array of wares that dazzled the eyes of sightseers and intrigued their curiosity. On display were objects of silver, gold and copper, fashioned by skillful smiths, fine pottery, leather, cloth, and spices and precious jewels from distant countries. To accommodate the many visitors to Jerusalem, Solomon had improved Israel's roads, and many inns were built to provide shelter for the travelers and their animals.

Through the efforts of Solomon's fine merchant marine, the Israelites now had contact with the peoples of southern Asia and Africa and came to know their wares and ways.

SOLOMON, THE BUILDER

Now Solomon turned to the one project which would demand his greatest effort, the one most dear to his heart and the hearts of all his peoples—the building of the Holy Temple (Bet Hamikdash), on Mount Zion. Until now, Israel had worshipped God in simple sanctuaries that housed the Holy Ark. Solomon wanted a more fitting House of God—a magnificent temple that would be the grandest house in all Jerusalem, indeed in all the

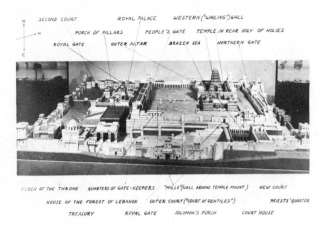

SECOND COURT — ROYAL PALACE — WESTERN ("WAILING") WALL
PORCH OF PILLARS — PEOPLE'S GATE — TEMPLE IN REAR — HOLY OF HOLIES
ROYAL GATE — OUTER ALTAR — BRAZEN SEA — NORTHERN GATE

PORCH OF THE THRONE — QUARTERS OF GATE-KEEPERS — "MILLO" (WALL AROUND TEMPLE MOUNT) — NEW COURT
HOUSE OF THE FOREST OF LEBANON — OUTER COURT ("COURT OF GENTILES") — PRIESTS' QUARTER
TREASURY — ROYAL GATE — SOLOMON'S PORCH — COURT HOUSE

Model of King Solomon's Temple and palace.

An aerial view of the old city of Jerusalem.

land of Israel.

From his close friend and ally, King Hiram of Tyre, Solomon received the cedar wood of Lebanon for the building of the Temple. Solomon paid for this precious wood with the products of Israel—grain and oil, olives and figs—and with copper from the mines of Ezion-Geber.

Solomon had chosen the most gifted architects to design the Temple, for of all his many building projects—palaces, cities and fortifications—the Holy Temple claimed his highest ambition and his deepest interest.

The Temple was built of stone and precious wood, with great pillars and spacious inner courts, with special places appointed for the various rites of the services. The interior was paneled with cedar wood. Gold, newly brought to the land of Israel from other countries in exchange for copper and olive oil, was lavishly used to make Solomon's temple a dazzling sight to behold. This precious metal was used in its pure form for numerous and varied adornments, and in fashioning the ceremonial instruments—the lavers, bowls and the great seven-branched Menorah. Architects and

builders, artists and goldsmiths, all worked mightily to give of their best to this great project. Not one iron tool was used in the building of the Temple, for iron was a metal associated with violence and war—while the Temple was the House of God, Who wanted all men to live in peace.

When the great work was completed, Jerusalem was thronged with jubilant people. Many had come merely to marvel, but many others had come to rejoice and rededicate themselves to their faith.

One can imagine the hush that fell on the crowds as the priest carried the Holy Ark to the inner shrine, the Holy of Holies, in the inner court of the Temple. The outer courts were crowded with worshippers. Priests offered prayers and sacrifices on the altars, and Levites sang psalms and played their instruments. It was a day both festive and solemn for Jerusalem when the glorious symbol of Israel's ancient faith, the Temple of Solomon, was dedicated to the service of one God.

Jerusalem in hieroglyphic script (Egyptian), about 2375 B.C.E.

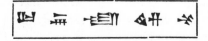

Jerusalem in cuneiform script (Assyrian), about 1350 B.C.E.

A reconstruction of the bronze Altar of the Holy Temple.

45

PEOPLE FROM NEAR AND FAR COME TO JERUSALEM

Of all the attractions which drew visitors to Jerusalem, the Temple was by far the most outstanding. Its solemn grandeur lent an air of sanctity to the city, and the faithful of Israel came from every corner of the land to worship in the splendid edifice. These people came from Dan in the north, at the foot of Mount Hermon where the River Jordan begins its rise, and from Beer-Sheba in the south, in the torrid land of the Negev. From every direction people poured into the holy city of Jerusalem. They brought their wares for trading to the busy markets: they presented their problems and disputes to the judges at the king's court and they left their sacrifices and offerings and said their prayers of thanksgiving and supplication at the Temple.

SOLOMON AND THE QUEEN OF SHEBA

Israel's seafaring men had brought back to their homeland many reports of the riches of Arabia and the beauty of the Arabian queen. Finally the Queen of Sheba herself journeyed from her far-distant empire to visit King Solomon's court. One can well imagine the festive atmosphere of ancient Jerusalem during that exciting time. The Queen of Sheba, for all her feminine charm, was also a

A reconstruction of King Solomon's house in the Forest of Lebanon.

clever diplomat and businesswoman, and it is most likely that at some time during the feasting and festivities the lovely lady took the opportunity to reaffirm her country's trade pact with Israel. The story of King Solomon and the beautiful Queen of Sheba is among the most fascinating episodes of antiquity.

King Solomon had a huge household with many wives. In the manner of the great monarchs of his time, Solomon kept a luxurious harem, a palace where these wives lived. Many of them were foreign princesses, whom he had married in order to cement treaties with foreign kings. There was an Egyptian princess in Solomon's harem and a princess from Phoenicia. The foreign princesses often brought with them from their native lands their own priests and their idols. It may be that Solomon, in spite of his sound judgement and great wisdom, dismissed these idols as the harmless toys of foolish women, little realizing the danger they presented to the very foundations of his country.

DISCONTENT GROWS IN A WEALTHY LAND

Along with new, advanced methods in industry, the foreigners who came to Solomon's court also introduced their own superstitions and the gods they worshipped. Some of the Israelites at court adopted these foreign habits and customs.

Meantime, a change was taking place in Israel's old way of life. Scores of unskilled laborers were needed for Solomon's many projects, and for work in his mines. Great masses of Israelites became

Ruins of the temple of the moon god in Marib, ancient capital of Sheba in South Arabia.

poor laborers, while only a few of the people grew rich. These latter became merchants, artisans, designers and builders, chroniclers and officials in the civil service, or officers in the king's army.

For the first time in Israel's history the people were distinctly divided into two classes—the rich and the poor; the esteemed and respected on the one hand and the lowly on the other.

Every citizen paid tribute to the king in some way. Taxes were levied on the wealthy for highway construction, for building projects and for the maintenance of the civil service and the king's soldiers and servants. The poor who could not pay taxes had to contribute their services to the king as laborers or soldiers. The warning of Samuel the seer, which had gone unheeded by the people of Israel so long ago, now seemed to echo across the years. The people had chosen to be ruled by a king, and the people were paying a heavy price, both in property and in freedom, for their choice.

Some of the lands which David had conquered became restless under Solomon's rule. They were confident that were they to revolt, Solomon would not march against them as his father had done. One by one, the outlying territories began to break away. Hadad, the prince of Edom, regained part of his old territory. In the north, Rezon, the king of the wealthy city-state of Damascus, revolted and regained independence for his people. In days to come, Damascus would again prove a bitter and formidable enemy of the people of Israel.

The seeds of rebellion were being sown among Solomon's own people as well. Jeroboam, of the tribe of Ephraim, a young officer in the king's army, led a group of rebel Israelites from the north. The northern tribes had become discontented, chafing under their heavy burden of taxes and forced labor. They felt that they had not benefited from Solomon's rule. Jeroboam's revolt did not measure up to his ambitions, however, for although he had hoped that it would succeed well enough to make him king, his plan was discovered and thwarted. Jeroboam fled the country and found asylum in Egypt at the court of the Pharaoh Shishak. There he bided his time, keeping a close eye on events in Israel from afar. Meanwhile, his followers in

the north kept the peace, waiting for the day when Jeroboam would return and renew the rebellion.

Wise and wealthy Solomon was reaping a golden harvest, but the seeds of discontent were sprouting uncomfortably close to the throne. There were many among his nobles at court who disapproved of the king's tolerance toward the priests and servants of his foreign wives who prayed to their own idols and offered sacrifices to them under Solomon's own roof.

Throughout the land there were many who longed for the simpler ways of days gone by. David's old soldier companions, who had fought with him to win new land for Israel, watched with alarm as some of these lands were lost. Apparently Solomon believed that it was better to rule only

PALESTINE
in the time of
DAVID AND SOLOMON

An aerial view of the ruins of Meggido.

those who wanted to be ruled, for his policy continued to be one of peace. He chose to make his country prosperous through commerce and friendship with his neighbors rather than by repeated war and conquest. In the eyes of many Israelites, Solomon was a king who valued wealth and pomp far too highly, at a price they grew increasingly reluctant to pay.

King Solomon died after a rule of forty years. The combined rule of the two great kings, David and Solomon, had covered a span of eighty years which had seen Israel grow into an important, wealthy nation. Now Solomon, the king who had made the name of Israel known throughtout the ancient world, was dead. His passing was mourned by many. Rebohoam, the son whom he had named as his successor, was acclaimed king. Yet the throne which Solomon's son ascended was resting on shaky foundations. There were many who wondered uneasily how long Israel's peace and unity would endure and how successful its newest ruler would be.

GLOSSARY OF HEBREW TERMINOLOGY AND NAMES

Zadok	Tzahdohk	צָדוֹק	Ishbosheth	Eesh-Bohshet	אִישׁ בֹּשֶׁת
Ezion-Geber	Etzyohn Gever	עֶצְיוֹן גֶּבֶר	Joab	Yoh-ahv	יוֹאָב
Hiram	Ḥeerahm	חִירָם	Ammon	Ahmohn	עַמּוֹן
Negev	Negev	נֶגֶב	Amalek	Ahmah-leyk	עֲמָלֵק
Mount Zion	Hahr Tzeeyohn	הַר צִיּוֹן	Jerusalem	Yrooshahlah-yeem	יְרוּשָׁלַיִם
Holy Temple	Beyt Ha-mikdahsh	בֵּית הַמִּקְדָּשׁ	Scribe	Sohfeyr	סוֹפֵר
Candelabrum	Mnorah	מְנוֹרָה	Tyre	Tzohr	צוֹר
Beer-Sheba	B'eyr Shevah	בְּאֵר שֶׁבַע	Lebanon	L'vahnohn	לְבָנוֹן
Queen of Sheba	Malkat Shvah	מַלְכַּת שְׁבָא	Aqaba	Ahkahvah	עֲקָבָה
			Uriah	Ooreeyah	אוּרִיָה
Hadad	Hah-dahd	הֲדַד	Nathan	Nahtahn	נָתָן
Edom	Edohm	אֱדוֹם	Bathsheba	Baht-shevah	בַּת שֶׁבַע
Rezon	Rzohn	רְצוֹן	Solomon	Shloh-moh	שְׁלֹמֹה
Damascus	Dahmesek	דְּמֶשֶׂק	Amnon	Ahm-nohn	אַמְנוֹן
Jeroboam	Yahrahvahm	יָרְבְעָם	Absalom	Ahv-shalohm	אַבְשָׁלוֹם
Shishak	Sheeshahk	שִׁישַׁק	Adonijah	Adohneeyahoo	אֲדֹנִיָהוּ
Rehoboam	Rḥahvahm	רְחַבְעָם	Abiathar	Evyahtahr	אֶבְיָתָר

REVOLT AND DIVISION:
THE KINGDOMS OF ISRAEL AND JUDAH

REVOLT AT SHECHEM

Rehoboam, Solomon's son and successor, lacked the great abilities of his father and grandfather, but he was a prince of the House of David and the tribe of Judah followed him loyally. Not so the northern tribes, however, who were reluctant to pledge themselves to the new ruler until he would lighten their burdens of taxes and forced labor and promise to respect their rights. King Rehoboam received warning from the tribes in the north that they would not be his loyal subjects unless he met their demands. Rehoboam, reared in his father's luxurious palace and not endowed with great qualities of leadership, was more concerned about his own glory and pleasures than about the welfare of his people.

The elders of the northern tribes did not go to Jerusalem to pay homage to the new king: instead, they asked Rehoboam to come to an assembly at Shechem in the territory of Ephraim. Accompanied by a group of his personal friends and some of his father's old advisors, the young king journeyed to Shechem.

When the leaders of the northern tribes asked the young king at Shechem to give them assurance that he would lighten their taxes and ease their burdens, Rehoboam kept them waiting three days for his answer. Solomon's old advisors, experienced in the ways of government, strongly urged Rehoboam to grant the requests of the people, pointing out to him that the loyalty of the northern tribes was an important asset to the kingdom. Rehoboam, confident of his power as master of all Israel and encouraged by his haughty young friends, refused to make the concessions. Instead, he informed the northern tribes arrogantly that he would demand even higher taxes and more labor services than his father required.

The men of the north were not meek, and were not ready to accept oppression from absolute monarchs. These northern subjects of the Israelite king believed that the king ruled to serve and lead his people and not to oppress them. Rehoboam's arrogance angered and offended the people of the northern tribes and they broke out in open revolt. Only the tribes of Judah and Benjamin upheld the young monarch. The other ten tribes chose a new

PALESTINE
as divided between
JUDAH AND ISRAEL

much of Judah's power had been lost and a great deal of its influence weakened. The empire created by David and Solomon no longer existed, and many former allies had abandoned the House of David. The Phoenicians, who had been responsible for much of the old Israel's wealth and excellent trade connections, now terminated their trade pact.

Judah suffered another great blow when Shishak, Pharaoh of Egypt, attacked the kingdom in the fifth year of Rehoboam's reign. The advance of Shishak's armies was swift and unexpected. One after another Judah's fortresses fell to the Egyptians and Jerusalem was taken without a struggle. Shishak spared the Holy City the horror of

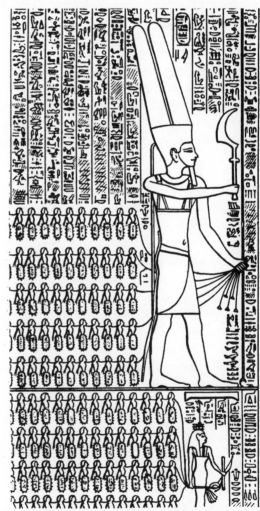

Pharaoh Shishak immortalized his victory over King Rehoboam in a relief on the wall of the great temple in Karnak. In his hand can be seen the ropes by which he leads the captives from the conquered city of Judah. Each of the captives represents a city in Judah.

leader—Jeroboam, the veteran rebel of the northern tribe of Ephraim, who had returned from Egypt. Egypt was now ruled by the ambitious Pharoah, Shishak, of a new dynasty. Shishak, having learned of Solomon's death, was delighted at the prospect of disunity in Israel and had encouraged Jeroboam to return home.

Taking advantage of the crisis at Shechem, Jeroboam headed the revolt against Rehoboam. The situation became so threatening that Rehoboam and his advisors fled back to Jerusalem.

TWO KINGDOMS

The fateful assembly at Shechem resulted in the division of the flourishing kingdom of David and Solomon into two separate smaller kingdoms: the northern kingdom of Israel, under Jeroboam; and the southern kingdom of Judah, under Rehoboam.

Throughout the reigns of Rehoboam and Jeroboam, there was war between Israel and Judah. Each kingdom fortified the frontier. Judah reinforced many of its fortresses—but in spite of this, destruction but ransacked Judah's treasury and marched back to Egypt laden with booty. Among the prizes were many of the golden vessels from the Temple and the famous golden shields which Solomon's guards had worn so proudly. Judah was impoverished when the Egyptians withdrew.

JEROBOAM ABANDONS JERUSALEM

The people of the northern kingdom of Israel still looked to Jerusalem as their sacred city. On festival days they journeyed to the Holy City, to join the people of Judah in prayers, sacrifices and holiday processions. Jeroboam, ambitious to be recognized as head of a new royal line entirely separate from Judah, looked with misgivings upon the devotion of his subjects to the Temple. He feared that this bond between the two kingdoms would eventually serve to unite them again.

The lessons Jeroboam had learned during his enforced sojourn in Egypt were still fresh in his mind. The Egyptian Pharoahs, with the help of the nobles and priests, kept their people submissive by encouraging them to worship animal idols in order to arouse their superstitions and fears. A people filled with fear and superstition is much more easily controlled than one of free, independent individuals who think for themselves. Remembering the ways of Egypt's rulers, Jeroboam had altars and shrines erected in Bethel and Dan, to entice his people to offer prayers and sacrifices in their own land rather than in Jerusalem. In open violation of the Ten Commandments he placed in the shrines the images of golden calves, proclaiming them to represent the God of Israel.

This seal belongs to the period of Jeroboam and was found at Meggido. The line above the lion reads "Shema." The line underneath reads "Seal of Jeroboam."

Jeroboam's purpose in introducing idol worship to Israel was twofold. He hoped that it would not only strengthen his power over his own people, but that it would also serve further to cement his bond with Egypt.

There were many in Israel who blindly obeyed Jeroboam's commands to worship the golden calf. These people gave up their pilgrimages to Jerusalem and journeyed instead to the shrines at Bethel and Dan, scarcely realizing that by so doing they were abandoning their ideal of the one invisible God.

The thoughtful and faithful of Israel were bitterly disappointed in their king and fervently hoped for a time when things would change. Weakened as they were by civil war and weary of bloodshed, there was little to do now but bide their time.

THE VOICES OF THE PROPHETS

Although it seemed that this dark night of disunity would spell the final decline for Israel, the first faint signs of a new dawn were appearing on the horizon. Strong new voices could be heard among the people of Israel and Judah—often in humble places, in caves and on mountainsides— by the roadside or at the city gates. These were the voices of the prophets, explaining how the ways of man should serve the ways of God. Some of these prophets were sons of rich, noble families —others came from the farms or from simple mountain huts. Their backgrounds were many and varied—but their message was one and the same. As one voice, these courageous and inspired men spoke out fearlessly against injustice, idol worship, and the oppression of the poor by the rich.

The prophets traveled from place to place, caring for neither wealth nor physical comfort. Often they would travel in groups, singing and praying together to the accompaniment of their own music. Wherever the prophets went, the people gathered to listen, to pray, and to renew their faith.

ASSYRIA, A GROWING GIANT

During these unhappy years in Israel's history, a great new power had begun to assert itself in Mesopotamia. This was the kingdom of Assyria, whose powerful armies were marching out of the Assyrian capital of Nineveh to conquer the nations from the Mediterranean to the Euphrates, from Egypt to Lebanon. The prophets of Israel warned the people about the threat of these new enemies, cruel masters who showed little mercy to those they conquered, and would suppress their worship of the one God.

JUDAH, A SMALL NATION

Israel, the northern kingdom, was more severely affected by the struggle between Assyrian idol worship and the faith in the one invisible God than was the smaller country of Judah, which was more remote from the paths of trade and war. Few of the people of Judah were rich, for the nation had lost its wealth, but in times of peace life went on much as it had before. The people continued in their old pursuits of farming, cattle breeding, crafts and trading. Each year, on the three pilgrim festivals of *Sukkot, Passover,* and *Shavuot,* people from all over Judah made pilgrimages to their beloved Temple of Mount Zion in Jerusalem. They also came to the courts of the king to seek justice in legal disputes.

Much of the outer splendor of Jerusalem was gone, but its market places were still crowded and

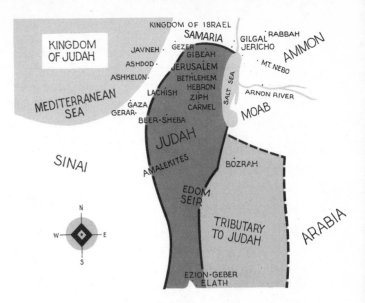

busy. Here the farmers and shepherds exchanged their cattle, grain, olive oil and honey for the textiles and leather, the vessels and tools, spices and goods from other lands which were to be had in the city. The people of Judah were proud of their famous capital, high in the mountains, with its fortifications and palaces, its markets and fine buildings. They were proud, too, that they were still ruled by the same dynasty which had given them such great kings as David and Solomon. Until the very end, Judah was ruled by an uninterrupted line of kings of the House of David.

An Assyrian army marching through a wooded region.

Pilgrims to Mt. Zion are greeted by the sound of the shofar as they ascend the mountain on an annual Passover pilgrimage. Note the curved ram's horn, typical in Oriental Jewish communities.

GLOSSARY OF HEBREW TERMINOLOGY AND NAMES

Rehoboam	Rḥahvahm	רְחַבְעָם
Jeroboam	Yahrahvahm	יָרָבְעָם
Israel	Yisrah-eyl	יִשְׂרָאֵל
Judah	Yhoodah	יְהוּדָה
Assyria	Ahshoor	אַשּׁוּר
Nineveh	Neen-vey	נִינְוֵה
Bethel	Beyt Eyl	בֵּית אֵל
Dan	Dahn	דָּן
Sukkot	Sookoht	סֻכּוֹת
Passover	Pesaḥ	פֶּסַח
Shavuot	Shahvoo-oht	שָׁבוּעוֹת

THE NEW KINGDOM OF ISRAEL: BATTLEGROUND OF CONFLICTING LAWS AND GODS

TURMOIL IN ISRAEL

As opposed to the kingdom of Judah, the northern kingdom of Israel was ruled by nine separate dynasties. Like Jeroboam, many of Israel's kings had once been officers in the army and had revolted against their predecessors. Many of these rulers continued to encourage the people to worship the idols at the shrines established by Jeroboam. The new kingdom was a constant battleground between two ways of life: the way of the Law and the God of Israel against the ways of idol worship. Many people from Israel still made their pilgrimages to the Temple in Jerusalem.

Within decades following Jeroboam's death, five different kings ruled over Israel. Jeroboam's son, Nadab, was assassinated and succeeded by Baasha. Baasha's son, Elah, was assassinated by his general, Zimri. Zimri ruled for only seven days. When he discovered that Omri, another of Elah's generals, was approaching with an army to claim the throne for himself, Zimri burned the royal palace and perished in the flames.

THE REIGN OF KING OMRI

King Omri, an able general, established order in Israel. He defeated the Moabites and made them Israel's vassals. The famous Moabite Stone which was discovered by archeologists in 1868 records how Moab was enslaved by the House of Omri and

The Moabite Stone.

made to pay tribute to Israel. Abandoning Israel's old capital of Tirzah, Omri built a beautiful new capital — Samaria. Samaria became an important city, well fortified and strategically located in the central hills of Ephraim. From Samaria new trade routes developed — to the south and, most important, to Phoenicia in the north.

Omri reverted to the tradition of King Solomon and traded with the Phoenicians. He fortified Israel and brought peace and prosperity to the land. For the first time since its beginning, the new Israel was secure among its neighbors and free of bloodshed and bickering among the generals who were ambitious to gain the throne. In the House of

The stone tower of Jezebel in Jezreel.

Omri, Israel at last had a strong ruling dynasty. So famous did Omri become that Assyrian records refer to Israel as the "Land of the House of Omri."

But, although he was shrewd in battle and wise in the ways of commerce, King Omri was not deeply aware of the spiritual needs and ideals of the people, and the Bible describes him as having done evil "in the eyes of the Lord."

AHAB AND JEZEBEL

When Omri died, Ahab became king. Evidently, intent on cementing his pact with Phoenicia, Ahab married the Phoenician princess, Jezebel. Jezebel brought her idols and priests to her new home as the wives of King Solomon had done. Strongly influenced by Jezebel, his vain and haughty wife, King Ahab set up shrines to Baal, the most popular Phoenician idol. Jezebel scorned the traditions of Israel and looked with contempt upon its democratic laws and its worship of one invisible God. She had little understanding for the importance of equal justice toward rich and poor alike and had no interest in the people's welfare. In her own country, the people were oppressed by the rich nobles, who had complete authority and power.

Jezebel, with her priests of Baal, set about teaching the Phoenician way of life to the people of Israel, persecuting any who defied her. Many of the prophets were killed at her command. Many

others escaped, however, for the people protected them. Obadiah, Ahab's own household steward, saved over one hundred prophets in the mountain caves of Ephraim near Samaria, secretly supplying them with food.

Not many people had the courage to criticize Ahab and Jezebel openly. There was one, however, who would not be silenced. This was the prophet Elijah. Boldly and passionately Elijah spoke for the poor who, according to the laws of Israel, were to be afforded protection from cruelty and unjust taxes. Elijah warned Ahab that he must uphold these laws and serve the one God.

ELIJAH FIGHTS FOR JUSTICE

Elijah had come across the Jordan from Gilead, where he had lived the simple life of a shepherd. Now he traveled through the kingdom of Israel, preaching justice and truth. Many things which he saw shocked and dismayed him — the glitter and luxury of life among the nobles of Samaria and the many shrines they had erected to the idol

Excavating the ruins of Ahab's magnificent palace at Samaria. He ruled Israel from 876-853 B.C.E.

Baal. Elijah spoke out fearlessly against the rich, powerful priests of Baal. He fought their influence, upholding and defending the ancient traditions and faith of the people of Israel.

Wherever he journeyed, he comforted the poor, healed the sick and encouraged the people to serve God. In many places he destroyed the shrines of Baal. From all sides, Elijah heard shocking stories of King Ahab's cruelties. One of the saddest of these stories was the story of Naboth, who had dared defy the king.

Naboth had owned a beautiful vineyard near the king's palace. Despite the king's threats, Naboth had refused to surrender this vineyard, for it had been in his family for generations. The ruthless Jezebel arranged to have Naboth falsely accused of sacrilege and treason. Naboth suffered the punishment customarily inflicted on those who committed this crime—he was stoned to death.

Elijah was outraged. He went to see King Ahab and boldly took him to task, prophesying the destruction of the House of Omri as a dynasty which had become unfit to rule. Struck with remorse at Elijah's words, King Ahab mourned, fasted and asked God's forgiveness. Unfortunately, his repentance and good intentions were no match for the influence of the imperious Queen Jezebel.

Elijah was greatly loved by the people of Israel. Stories of his bravery, his compassion, his helpfulness to the poor and sick, were told through the length and breadth of the land. In time, he was to become a symbol of the spirit of freedom. Tradition tells us that Elijah would appear to announce the coming of the Messiah. Each year on the Seder night, when we celebrate our deliverance from Egypt, we remember Elijah, the symbol of the spirit of freedom.

AHAB'S ALLIANCES

King Ahab failed to uphold the laws and religion of Israel and never won the love and confidence of its people. But he was successful in his military campaigns and in establishing friendly relations with Israel's neighbors. Like all the rulers of the Middle East, Ahab kept a wary eye on the growth of the Assyrian empire; he was well aware that its armies were advancing closer and closer to his country. Realizing the importance of obtaining allies against these powerful conquerors, Ahab gave his daughter Athaliah in marriage to Jehoram, crown prince of Judah, thus strengthening Israel's bond with that country. When Ahab became involved in a war with Aram, Judah's army aided in winning the victory. Ahab captured Ben-Hadad, king of the Aramean city-state of Damascus, but wisely gave him his freedom in exchange for a strong trade agreement and military alliance.

King Ahab's pacts with Judah, Aram, Phoenicia and Moab were well-timed, for the Assyrian armies commanded by King Shalmaneser III were bearing down upon the River Jordan. Ahab and his allies met them in battle at Karkar. The coalition resisted valiantly and in the end the Assyrian hosts departed. The allies could now breathe more easily, but their triumph was short lived. Ahab, aided by his friend and ally, Jehoshaphat of Judah, besieged Ramoth-Gilead, then an Aramean city. But soon after, King Ahab died from wounds received in this battle.

Ahab was succeeded by his son, Ahaziah, but this unfortunate king soon fell ill and died. He was followed by his brother Joram, the last king of the House of Omri.

An ivory carving of King Hazael of Damascus. The carving was found at Arlon Tash in Syria.

JEHU'S REBELLION — END OF THE HOUSE OF OMRI

Jehu, one of the king's officers, led a rebellion

The black obelisk was set up by Shalmanesser III in his palace at Nimrud. It is inscribed with the story of his battles.

against King Joram. Jehu was supported by the prophet Elisha, the disciple of Elijah, who was carrying on the work of his teacher now that the beloved prophet was dead. Elisha was confident that Jehu, once he became king, would abolish idol worship in Israel and support the laws of the land. Jehu's revolt, a bloody one, was successful. In it, Queen Jezebel perished, and with her all the members of the House of Omri. Jehu now ascended the throne of Israel.

ATHALIAH USURPS THE THRONE OF JUDAH

This revolt against the House of Omri brought grave consequences to Judah. King Ahaziah was killed in ambush on his journey home from Samaria, where he had been visiting his cousins of the House of Omri. Ahaziah's mother, the unscrupulous and ambitious Queen Athaliah, was a true daughter of Jezebel and Ahab. When Athaliah learned of her son's death, she saw her chance to become queen of Judah. Ordering all the princes of the House of David killed, no matter how closely they were related to her, she became queen and ruled Judah tyrannically and ruthlessly.

One prince had escaped the cruel queen's henchmen: Joash, her small grandson. He had been saved by his aunt Jehosheba and his uncle, the high priest Jehoiadah. For seven years Jehoiadah and Jehosheba kept Joash hidden in their home. When the time was thought ripe for revolt, Jehoiadah

brought the prince before the elders of Judah and Joash was anointed king. This brought to an end the tyrannical rule of Athaliah, and peace was established in Judah once more.

ISRAEL IN THE DAYS OF KING JEHU

Jehu, the new king of Israel, was the first ruler to forbid idol worship in the northern kingdom. At last the people could worship their God and observe His laws openly. However, King Jehu was not successful in his foreign relations. To ward off an invasion by Damascus, he sent tribute to King Shalmaneser of Assyria and asked for his protection. In spite of his plea, Damascus marched against Israel and Jehu was defeated. Thus Israel became a tribute-paying vassal of Damascus.

MORE WARS WITH DAMASCUS

In the days of King Jehoahaz, son of Jehu, the kingdom of Israel suffered severely under the yoke of the Arameans of Damascus and struggled for many years to free itself. King Jehoash, son of Jehoahaz, fought Aram three times and finally was victorious. Now it was the Arameans of Damascus who paid tribute to Israel.

ISRAEL'S WEALTH

A time of prosperity began for Israel. Samaria, its capital, was a flourishing city. The reign of King Jeroboam II, son of Jehoash, saw foreign merchants coming once more to Israel's markets. New trade pacts were signed with the Phoenicians of

A section of the black obelisk of Shalmanesser III is devoted to Jehu. This scene is copied from the obelisk, and shows Jehu paying tribute to the victorious Shalmanesser.

A stone carving of two Arameans.

Tyre and wealth flowed into the kingdom.

Unfortunately, Israel's new prosperity was limited to the nobles and merchants, who failed to remember that the poor were their brothers. Workers in the city were underpaid, and the rich farmers and cattle breeders dealt unfairly with their help. The builders exploited their masons. The shepherds, laborers and small farmers paid high taxes and dwelt in hovels, while their rich masters lived in luxury and idleness.

King Jeroboam II, like other rulers before him, restored the material wealth and power to Israel but had no understanding for the inner needs of the people. He did not observe the laws of Moses, and he encouraged his people to adopt the ways of their foreign neighbors of Damascus and Tyre. His judges decided in favor of the rich, and his priests were more favorably disposed toward the costly offerings of the wealthy than to the humble sacrifices of the poor. The kingdom of Jeroboam appeared strong and powerful, but it was a nation of inner weakness and injustice.

AMOS SPEAKS FOR JUSTICE

Now another strong voice arose in the land, crying out against the men of power who forced the greater part of the people to endure poverty and injustice. Amos, a shepherd from Tekoa, spoke boldly and openly in the city of Samaria, declaring that the sacrifices made by the rich on the altar at Bethel were meaningless as long as the donors did not act justly.

Although Amos was a simple man, he possessed a great knowledge of the political problems of his day. He warned that all the wealth of Samaria would be useless against the threat of Assyria unless the kingdom of Israel would be united and strong, and he declared that only by keeping the laws of Moses could the nation regain this unity and strength.

The wealthy class of Israel were annoyed by this prophet in crude shepherd's garb who warned of doom at a time of prosperity. They asked Amos to leave Samaria, but Amos was not so easily silenced. He continued to speak out fearlessly, telling the rich that God would be more pleased by acts of justice than by costly offerings.

In the days of Amos, another, younger prophet began to speak in Israel. This was the prophet Hosea, who was to witness not only the prosperity of Israel under Jeroboam II, but also a time of unhappy changes. The death of Jeroboam was followed by a quick succession of kings and a time of greed, murder and decay which was to hasten the destruction of the kingdom.

HOSEA'S WARNINGS

Like Amos, Hosea possessed both spiritual and political vision; he foresaw Assyria's invasion of Israel and warned the people to arm themselves morally against the coming time of danger.

Each year, on the Sabbath before The Day of Atonement, *Yom Kippur,* Hosea's words are recited in synagogues throughout the world—words that inspire the people of Israel to repent and return to their God and His laws: "Return, O Israel, to the Lord thy God . . ." (Hosea 14:2-10).

REBELLIONS IN ISRAEL

Israel's brief period of wealth and security ended with the death of Jeroboam II. His son, Zechariah, faced with still another rebellion, reigned only for a short time. He was followed by Shallum who reigned one month, after which Menahem, a general, seized the throne and became king. Menahem's reign, too, was a time of trouble and uncertainty.

ASSYRIA, THE CONQUEROR NATION

Assyria had conquered all of Babylonia and its mighty armies were drawing ever closer to Israel. In the light of this common threat, Israel, Judah, Aram and Tyre drew closer to one another. These lands along the Mediterranean coast clearly understood their difficult strategic position, for they represented the bulwark between the new Assyrian empire and the older power of Egypt. It was inevitable that Assyria would try to conquer Egypt, her strongest rival, and thus gain possession of the riches of the Nile and the gateway to Africa. Egypt, too, was aware of this danger and attempted to persuade the smaller nations to unite with her against Assyria. King Menahem of Israel was faced with a difficult decision: which of the two giants would prove a faithful ally—or, rather, which would be the less ruthless overlord? Menahem made his choice—and sent his tribute to Assyria.

A new king now sat on the Assyrian throne— Pul, who became known as Tiglath-Pileser III. He was a soldier who had risen from the ranks. He and his sons were cruel kings, a ruthless and ambitious dynasty, dedicated only to conquest. Constantly on the march, they invaded one land after another and subjected the helpless people to their tyrannical rule.

REBELLIONS AND PREPARATIONS FOR WAR

Another revolt took place in troubled Israel. Menahem's son, Pekahiah, perished in the rebellion and Pekah, one of the soldiers who had led the uprising, became king. Pekah, the new king, joined the alliance of small nations along the Mediterranean who planned to meet Tiglath-Pileser in battle. Israel had allied herself with the Edomites, the Philistine city-states, the Phoenicians and the Arameans in a desperate effort to ward off Assyria.

Israel approached Ahaz, king of Judah, who was already a vassal of Assyria, asking him to join the coalition. Ahaz firmly refused, for he did not believe Assyria could be defeated. He chose to stay out of the war, but the allies, bent on winning his

PALESTINE
At the time of the
ASSYRIAN CONQUEST

Tipshah

Hamath

Tadmur

ASSYRIA

Zidon
Zarephath
Tyre
Accho
PHENICIA
Dan
Kadesh
Damascus

Aphek
Jabesh Gilead
Dor
Samaria
Shechem
Ramoth Gilead
ISRAEL
GILEAD
AMMON
Shiloh
Joppa
Bethel
Rabboth Ammon
Heshbon
Ashkelon
Jerusalem
Medeba
MOAB
Gaza
PHILISTINES
Bethlehem
JUDAH
Hebron
Ar Moab
Beer-sheba
Kir Moab

EDOM
Sila

A stone portrait of Tiglath-Pileser III from Nimrud.

A seal which belonged to an official of Ahaz, King of Judah. It reads, "Ushna, servant of Ahaz."

distant countries far from their homelands. Scattered in a strange land and broken in spirit, the conquered nations offered no threat of revolt to their captors.

The Ten Tribes who made up the kingdom of Israel were deported to distant provinces in the vast Assyrian empire, and people from another land conquered by Assyria were brought to the hills of Ephraim and the city of Samaria to replace the deported Israelites.

The northern kingdom of Israel was no more; its glory had vanished—its people were gone. Those few who had escaped to Judah told tales of suffering and defeat. They now realized that the warnings of Amos and Hosea had indeed been prophetic.

support, marched against Jerusalem to force Ahaz to change his mind. Ahaz, caught in a serious predicament, asked for Assyria's help in ridding Judah of the invaders.

Judah remained at peace but the allies who attempted to withstand Assyria fared badly. The Assyrians had already begun their march to Egypt. They took Damascus and carried King Rezin and many of his nobles into captivity. The people of Israel were filled with despair and heavy forebodings of doom about the future.

At this dark moment, Israel again was torn by revolt. King Hoshea, a rebel who had taken Pekah's throne, ruled over the remnant of what had once been wealthy Israel. He hoped for an opportunity to shake off the Assyrian yoke and win back Israel's northern lands. When King Tiglath-Pileser of Assyria died, Hoshea made an alliance with Egypt and refused to pay further tribute to Assyria.

THE FALL OF THE NORTHERN KINGDOM

Shalmaneser V, the new Assyrian king, would tolerate no rebellion. He invaded Israel at once, and laid siege to Samaria, her capital. Samaria had been wisely planned and well-fortified by King Omri, however, and for three years its valiant defenders withstood the Assyrian invaders. Shalmaneser died during the siege, but his successor, King Sargon II, continued the campaign. Samaria finally was forced to surrender and fell to Sargon II in the first year of his reign.

Assyria dealt ruthlessly with conquered nations. The subject peoples would be deported to

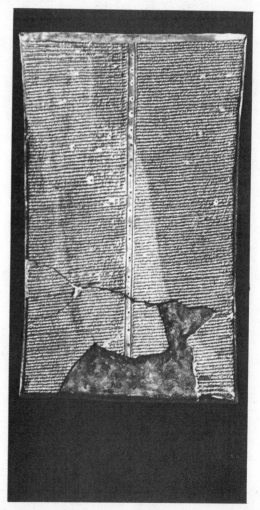

A stone tablet with the victory inscription of Sargon II over Israel. "I besieged Samaria and carried off 27,290 of its people as booty."

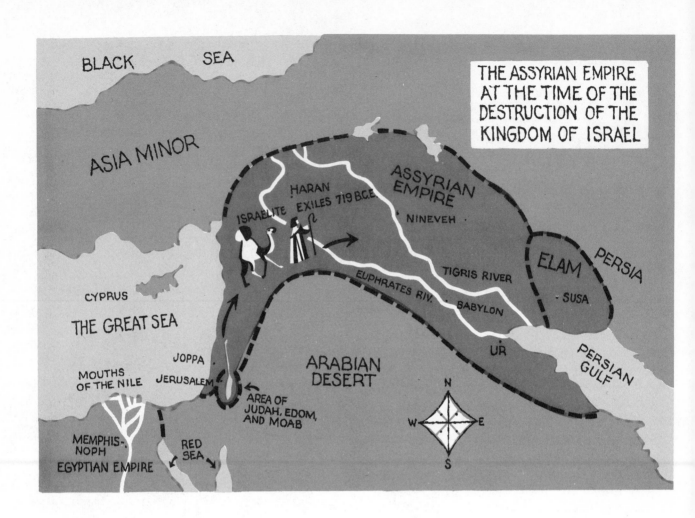

BLACK SEA

ASIA MINOR

THE ASSYRIAN EMPIRE AT THE TIME OF THE DESTRUCTION OF THE KINGDOM OF ISRAEL

ASSYRIAN EMPIRE

HARAN
ISRAELITE EXILES 719 BCE
NINEVEH

ELAM

PERSIA

CYPRUS

THE GREAT SEA

TIGRIS RIVER
EUPHRATES RIV.
BABYLON
SUSA

UR

PERSIAN GULF

JOPPA
MOUTHS OF THE NILE
JERUSALEM
ARABIAN DESERT
AREA OF JUDAH, EDOM, AND MOAB

N
W   E
S

MEMPHIS-NOPH
EGYPTIAN EMPIRE
RED SEA

GLOSSARY OF HEBREW TERMINOLOGY
AND NAMES

Jehu	Yeyhoo	יֵהוּא	Nadab	Nahdahv	נָדָב
Elisha	Eleeshah	אֱלִישָׁע	Baasha	Bahshah	בַּעְשָׁא
Joash	Yoh-ahsh	יוֹאָשׁ	Elah	Eylah	אֵלָה
Jehosheba	Yhoh-shevah	יְהוֹשֶׁבַע	Zimri	Zimree	זִמְרִי
Jehoiadah	Yhoh-yadah	יְהוֹיָדָע	Omri	Awmree	עָמְרִי
Jehoahaz	Yhoh-aḥaz	יְהוֹאָחָז	Moab	Moh-ahv	מוֹאָב
Jehoash	Yhoh-ahsh	יְהוֹאָשׁ	Tirzah	Tirtzah	תִּרְצָה
Amos	Ah-mohs	עָמוֹס	Samaria	Shohmrohn	שֹׁמְרוֹן
Hosea (Prophet)	Hoh-sheyah	הוֹשֵׁעַ	Ahab	Aḥahv	אַחְאָב
			Jezebel	Eezevel	אִיזֶבֶל
Day of Atonement	Yohm Keepoor	יוֹם כִּפּוּר	Obadiah	Ohvadyahoo	עֹבַדְיָהוּ
			Elijah	Eyleeyahoo	אֵלִיָּהוּ
Zechariah	Zḥaryah	זְכַרְיָה	Naboth	Nahvot	נָבוֹת
Shallum	Shahloom	שַׁלֻּם	Messiah	Mahshee-aḥ	מָשִׁיחַ
Menahem	Menaḥem	מְנַחֵם	Athaliah	Ahtahlyah	עֲתַלְיָה
Tiglath-Pileser	Tiglaht-Pilesser	תִּגְלַת פִּלְאֶסֶר	Jehoram	Yhorahm	יְהוֹרָם
Pekahiah	Pkaḥyah	פְּקַחְיָה	Ben-Hadad	Ben-Hahdahd	בֶּן־הֲדַד
Pekah	Pekaḥ	פֶּקַח	Shalmaneser	Shahlmahn-essser	שַׁלְמַנְאֶסֶר
Ahaz	Aḥahz	אָחָז			
Rezin	R'tzeen	רְצִין	Jehoshaphat	Yhohshah-phaht	יְהוֹשָׁפָט
Hoshea (King)	Hoh-sheyah	הוֹשֵׁעַ	Ahaziah	Aḥazyahoo	אֲחַזְיָהוּ
Sargon	Sargohn	סַרְגוֹן	Joram	Yorahm	יוֹרָם

JUDAH, STRONGHOLD OF FAITH

A reconstruction of the fortified city of Lakhish.

The little kingdom of Judah had lived rather peacefully for many years. Since it was remote from the routes of the great caravans, it did not seek important trade and military pacts and most of its kings had tried to avoid war. The splendor of Solomon's days was gone, but the real glory still remained—the Temple on Mount Zion in Jerusalem. Here the people of Judah brought their offerings and celebrated their festivals. Jerusalem's marketplaces were still busy and in the courts of law judges heard complaints and settled disputes.

ISAIAH, STATESMAN AND MAN OF GOD

When King Ahaz of Judah had been faced with a difficult choice—either to appease Assyria or to join forces with the other small nations against her—he had turned for advice to a man of great brilliance and wisdom. This man was the prophet Isaiah who had counseled both the father of Ahaz, King Jotham, and his grandfather, King Uzziah. Isaiah was a well-educated man, born of a noble family. He had a wide knowledge of Judah's political problems. Isaiah advised King Ahaz

Seal of Jotham, son of King Uzziah.

The grave of King Uzziah is marked by this engraved stone tablet.

not to join the alliance against Assyria, for he was positive that the allies would be no match for the mighty Assyrian war machine. King Ahaz followed Isaiah' advice and refused the allies' request that he join them.

AHAZ APPEASES ASSYRIA

Soon after this came the news that the alliance had been defeated. All Judah mourned the destruction of Israel and the plight of the Ten Tribes lost in captivity in far-off Assyria. King Ahaz, frightened lest Judah share the same fate, tried in every way to win the favor of the Assyrians. He began

A drawing from a relief in the palace at Khorsabad pictures King Sargon and his vizier.

to follow the Assyrian ways of life and worship, even installing idols in the Temple. Isaiah, who had advised neutrality, not submission, was bitterly disappointed in Ahaz and criticized him severely. He foresaw that the king's policy could bring nothing but disaster to Judah.

ISAIAH AND MICAH, PROPHETS OF PEACE IN DAYS OF DARKNESS

Foreseeing the destruction of Judah, Isaiah wrote prophecies of great comfort and compassion during these dark days. Inspired by visions of hope and longing for the happiness of all mankind, this great prophet also wrote of the day when all peo-

The Isaiah Scroll—one of the Scrolls discovered in a cave above the Dead Sea.

ples would live together in harmony, serving the one God—the God of peace.

Today, high on a marble wall opposite the United Nations Building in New York City, are engraved these words of Isaiah—an ancient prophecy of peace for the peoples of all the world to read and ponder:

They shall beat their swords into ploughshares, and their spears into pruning hooks: nation shall not lift up sword against nation, neither shall they learn war any more.   (Isaiah 2:4)

Another prophet who spoke in those days was Micah, a young man of humble birth from the

65

small village of Moresheth-Gath in the Judean hills. Micah grieved for Samaria and wept for the sufferings of the people of Israel. He warned the people of Judah not to forsake their laws. As Amos had done before him. Micah reminded the people that God wanted more of them than sacrificial offerings.

"What does the Lord require of thee," cried Micah, "save to do justice and to love mercy and to walk humbly with thy God!"

The prophet Isaiah and his younger contemporary Micah both shared the same ideals of faith and peace. Their voices were heard throughout Judah and while the people often seemed indifferent, the inspiring words of these two great prophets left a deep impression.

KING HEZEKIAH'S REFORMS

King Ahaz was succeeded by his son Hezekiah. Heeding Isaiah's warnings, Hezekiah rid Judah of the idols his father had installed and strengthened the nation by upholding its laws and traditions. The memory of the fall of the Kingdom of Israel was ever present in Hezekiah's thoughts.

Unrest was breaking out among the countries

The Hebrew inscription found in the tunnel of Siloam.
Text of the Siloam inscription: "The tunnel [is completed]. And this is the story of the boring through: While yet they plied the pick, each toward his fellow, and while yet there were three cubits to be bored through, there was heard the voice of one calling to another, for there was a crevice in the rock on the right hand. And on the day of the boring through, the stone-cutters struck, each to meet his fellow, pick upon pick; and the waters flowed from the source to the pool for a thousand and two hundred cubits, and a hundred cubits was the height of the rock above the heads of the stone-cutters."

Underground tunnel leading to the pool of Siloam.

which had been conquered by the Assyrians. Hezekiah joined the general spirit of revolt and refused to pay further tribute to Assyria. In the Philistine city of Ashdod and in other places, the people revolted and defied the rule of the Assyrian governors. Egypt, still independent and anxious to strengthen herself further, encouraged these revolts. Secret envoys were sent out of Egypt to the rebellious states, seeking alliances. Egyptian envoys came to Jerusalem and secret conferences were held. Envoys from the Babylonian king in far-off Mesopotamia also came to seek Hezekiah's aid against the hated Assyrian giant. Egypt and Babylonia had already allied themselves against Assyria.

Pool of Siloam in the old city of Jerusalem.

Quietly and efficiently, Hezekiah prepared Judah for revolt. He devised a major engineering project to increase the city's water supply. The waters of the River Gihon were diverted into a reservoir, called the Pool of Siloam, and an underground tunnel was constructed to bring this water into the city. In this way, Hezekiah made sure that the city should not suffer from a shortage of water in case of a siege.

In the year 1880, two boys playing in this ancient reservoir, which by then had long gone dry, accidentally discovered a secret passageway, half-filled with water. When archeologists explored the passageway they found Hebrew inscriptions deep inside, dating from the days of Hezekiah. The inscriptions relate how two crews of Hezekiah's workmen met at this point when the tunnel was completed. One crew had dug from Siloam, the other from Jerusalem.

ASSYRIA FIGHTS REBELLION

After the death of King Sargon of Assyria, the rebellious allies hoped to strike. However, King Sargon's successor, King Sennacherib, had learned that rebellion was brewing, and he went forth with a mighty army to crush the revolt. Hezekiah's preparations had been made just in time, for King Sennacherib invaded Judah, storming its fortresses and smashing great holes in their walls with his battering rams. The approach of the invading army and its engines of siege must have been a terrifying sight. Each engine carried a mighty battering ram and a crew of archers who shot their arrows into the towns of Judea from a distance. The archers were accompanied by their own shield-bearers, ready to storm the walls when the time came. These ancient siege-engines were akin to the tanks of today—formidable machines, capable of crush-

A relief of an Assyrian battering ram making a breach in a fortress wall.

A relief of the siege of Lakhish by the troops of Sennacherib.

ing whatever stood in their path. To this day the ruins of the ancient walls of the fortress of Lakhish show the scars of these Assyrian war machines.

AN UNUSUAL ALLY

Sennacherib laid siege to Jerusalem. Guided by King Hezekiah and the prophet Isaiah, the people of the city bore up bravely, but as the siege wore on, food became so scarce in the city that surrender seemed inevitable.

Then an unexpected ally came to the rescue of the beleaguered city. The plague, that dread disease of ancient times, providentially struck the Assyrian camp. Thousands of Assyrian soldiers perished in the epidemic and were buried in hastily-dug mass graves. These graves have been excavated by modern archeologists and the skeletons found there bear witness to the fate of the Assyrian attackers. His army sadly diminished, Sennacherib withdrew from Jerusalem.

The prophet Isaiah mourned for the ravaged land of Judah. Towns and cities were burned or lay in ruin. Yet, even in the midst of the ruins there were prayers of thanksgiving, for the people had survived the Assyrian onslaught. Before them now lay the great task of rebuilding their ravaged land. In haste they set to work, rebuilding their towns, replanting their fields, and tending their vineyards again.

JUDAH IS SAFE ONCE MORE

Sennacherib had returned to Nineveh, where all his energies were now required to defend his empire. Rebellions had broken out close to his

Castle of Sennacherib at Mosul, Iraq.

suffered the same fate as his father. He was assassinated. He was succeeded by his son, Esar-Haddon, who was forced to engage in continuous fighting to maintain his power. Revolt threatened everywhere, even at home in the lands of the River Tigris where the Medes and Babylonians rebelled. The great Assyrian empire seemed to be about to crumble.

With the Assyrian armies fighting far away, Judah breathed more easily. Yet the events of the past were not forgotten. The people lived under the constant threat of a new Assyrian invasion. When Hezekiah died, his son King Manasseh submitted completely to Assyrian rule, even reinstating idol worship to appease the foreign overlords.

THE REIGNS OF MANASSEH AND AMON

The aging prophet, Isaiah, whose voice for so many years had been heard in Judah, now foresaw its destruction and fall and again he warned of the consequences of abandoning the ancient laws. But

This six-sided cylinder of baked clay contains descriptions of the battles of Sennacherib. It records the invasion of Palestine and the siege of Jerusalem.

Victory monument of King Esarhaddon. He is leading two captive kings on a leash attached to hooks which pass through their lips.

capital, in Mesopotamia itself. Sennacherib finally

the words of the old man went unheeded.

King Manasseh was an obedient vassal. The country was impoverished by the high taxes he collected for the Assyrian masters. Foreign idols stood in the Temple of God and corruption reigned among the nobles of Judah, even reaching into the lives of the Levites and priests. After Isaiah died, and his voice was no longer a comforting and inspiring force, many of the Judeans turned to the Assyrian idols.

Despite Manasseh's submissive obedience, Assyrian officials began to doubt his loyalty. They summoned him to Nineveh to punish him. In exile he suffered great indignities. When he returned to Jerusalem he had changed completely. The post-Biblical writings known as Apocrypha have preserved a prayer which Manasseh said. It is the prayer of a man filled with great remorse.

Manasseh's son, King Amon, continued his father's policy, paying heavy tribute to Assyria and worshipping the idols of the alien overlord. Amon was most unpopular and was assassinated after a reign of only two years.

ASSYRIA CONQUERS EGYPT

In the days of King Manasseh and King Amon of Judah, Assyria was ruled by King Ashurbanipal, son of King Esar-Haddon. Ashurbanipal accomplished the dream of many an Assyrian ruler before him—he conquered Egypt. Ashurbanipal's armies took No-Amon and Thebes, the two splendid Egyptian temple cities on the upper Nile. These cities, the pride of Egypt, were plundered and burned by the Assyrian soldiers. Beautiful Thebes was destroyed. Many people were taken captive and great quantities of gold, silver and precious stones were carried back to Nineveh.

ASHURBANIPAL TURNS TO PEACE

After he had vanquished Egypt, a great change came over Ashurbanipal. He lost interest in war and devoted himself to cultural projects. He founded a vast library, where many great works of art and many historical documents were collected. To express his zest for adventure, without engaging in war and bloodshed, he became an accomplished big game hunter. At last Assyria seemed to have had its fill of conquest.

THE DECLINE OF ASSYRIA

More and more new threats of rebellion plagued the successors of Ashurbanipal. While Assyria was busy keeping its many rebellious vassals in check,

An Assyrian stele showing King Ashurbanipal carrying upon his head a basket filled with gifts.

An Assyrian relief showing the troops of Ashurbanipal battling the Elamites.

the empire was suddenly invaded by the Scythians, a people from the Black Sea region. Wild and fearless riders, they came on horseback, plundering and looting wherever they went. Hordes of these Scythian horsemen raced through Assyria's territories, and throughout the entire Fertile Crescent. Using the roads along the Mediterranean, they ravaged the coastal cities. Judah, farther inland, was spared. The Scythians rode on to the borders of Egypt but the Egyptians persuaded them to turn back by offering gifts and tribute. Laden with booty, the Scythians returned home, leaving the peoples of the Fertile Crescent with memories of violence and plunder.

A GREAT REFORMER

While the Scythian hordes swept through ancient empires, a new king had come to the throne of Judah. Josiah, the son of Amon, was a very different man from his father. Josiah heeded the words of the prophet Zephaniah, who had criticized the corruption that prevailed in Judah in the days of King Amon. The new king rid the land of the idols and corrupt officials and returned to the laws of Israel and the worship of one God. Josiah had all the idols destroyed and the Temple thoroughly cleansed.

A LONG LOST BOOK INSPIRES THE PEOPLE WITH NEW COURAGE

During the process of cleansing the Temple, a

A Scythian bowl.

A Hebrew letter written on a potsherd, era of King Josiah. In the letter the writer complains to the royal governor that his cloak has been confiscated, and asks for its return.

great discovery was made. A scroll was found which had lain forgotten and unused for generations. When the priests examined the scroll they found it to be the Book of Deuteronomy—the last of the Five Books of Moses. It summarized and explained the Ten Commandments and all the laws of Israel. Hilkiah, the high priest who had discovered the book, and Huldah, a prophetess, encouraged the king to study this long-lost book and to read from it to all the people of Judah. Standing before a large assembly, Josiah read from the Book of Deuteronomy, as the people, young and old, stood listening in awe to the ancient words.

All over Judah priests assembled the people and read to them from the book. The people became familiar with their laws, their history and traditions. They discussed the stories of Abraham, Isaac and Jacob, the first Patriarchs. They exclaimed over the great Exodus from Egypt and Israel's wanderings in the desert and recalled later events up to their own time. Most important of all, the Book of Deuteronomy taught the people the meaning of their laws. Strengthened by this new knowledge, the people of Judah regained faith and

One of 20,000 clay tablets taken from the library of King Ashurbanipal.

dignity.

Such was the state of Judah when Assyria was dealt its final blow. Two prophets in Judah, Nahum and Zephaniah, had prophesied that the destruction of Assyria was at hand. King Josiah had heard and believed these prophecies. Now they

A Babylonian tablet called the "Gladd Chronicle." It tells about the conquest of Nineveh by the armies of Nabopolassar.

were to come true. After the death of King Ashurbanipal, the Medes and Babylonians attacked Assyria from both the north and south. Assyria was faced with defeat. The armies of the victorious allies met at Ashur and marched on together to Nineveh, the once invincible Assyrian capital. A bloody and desperate battle was fought at Nineveh after which the city finally fell and was completely destroyed by the victors. Mighty Nineveh was leveled to the ground.

THE FATEFUL BATTLE OF MEGIDDO

In its final days, Assyria turned for help to

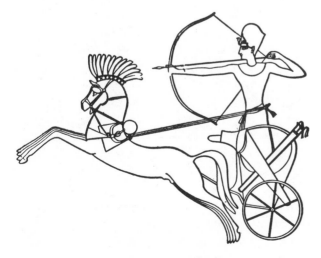

An Egyptian war chariot.

71

A relief from Carchemish showing two heavily armed soldiers.

joined the Assyrian forces in Mesopotamia to fight for the city of Haran. But here the Medes and Babylonians were victorious, defeating Assyria and her Egyptian ally. Necoh suffered another serious defeat by the new powers in a battle at Carchemish. Bitterly disappointed, the Pharaoh withdrew from Mesopotamia and his army retreated through the lands which they had so recently conquered.

THE NEW BABYLONIAN EMPIRE

The Medes and the Babylonians divided the Assyrian empire between themselves. The Medes took the territories of the north and the northeast; the Babylonians those of the south and southwest —the lands of the Fertile Crescent.

By the time the conquest of Assyria had been completed, Nabopolassar, the victorious Babylonian king, was a very old man, no longer able to lead military campaigns. He sent his son, crown prince Nebuchadnezzar, to take possession of Assyria's former lands.

In Judah, a sad time had followed the death of King Josiah. After the defeat at Megiddo, Judah had become a vassal of Egypt under Pharaoh Necoh, a harsh master, who forced Judah into utter submission. The reign of Josiah's son, Jehoahaz, lasted less than a year. He was taken captive to Egypt and died in exile. Necoh then appointed Jehoahaz' brother, Jehoiakim, as king of Judah. Jehoiakim was an obedient vassal. He installed Egypt's gods in Judah, followed Egypt's laws and

Egypt, its old enemy and rival. Egypt's Pharaoh, Necoh, prepared to take his army to Mesopotamia to aid Assyria, the dying giant. It was Necoh's hope that, after victory, he would be given a fair share of Assyria's lands. Confident that his armies could pass freely through the lands which lay between him and the Assyrian forces, the ambitious Egyptian ruler began his march. But King Josiah had no intention of allowing Egyptian soldiers to march unmolested through Judah, nor did he wish to see Assyria assisted.

Josiah summoned Judah's small army to halt the Egyptians. Although the Egyptian soldiers were superior both in numbers and arms, Josiah hoped that the high morale of his own soldiers would bring Judah victory.

Josiah's army met the Egyptians at Megiddo, the gate to the plain of Jezreel and the site of many battles in the past. It was a bloody, desperate battle and Judah suffered a disastrous defeat. Josiah, the courageous king, perished at Megiddo with many of his brave men. Pharaoh Necoh now considered Judah his own vassal, to be yielded to him along with other concessions after the campaign was victoriously concluded.

After Judah's defeat, Pharaoh Necoh's armies

Seal of Eliahim, a servant in the court of King Jehoiachin.

72

paid heavy tribute.

Like a bone between two huge ferocious dogs, Judah found itself a small, weak nation with Egypt on one side and the advancing armies of Nebuchadnezzar on the other. Fortunately for Judah, prince Nebuchadnezzar interrupted his victorious march to the east when he received news of his aged father's death, returning to Babylon to receive homage as the new king. Thus little Judah was granted a brief time of peace.

Egypt now sought to undermine the power of Babylonia by encouraging its new vassals to revolt. King Jehoiakim of Judah, encouraged by the Egyptian Pharaoh's promise of assistance in case of a Babylonian attack, refused to pay tribute to Nebuchadnezzar. King Nebuchadnezzar promptly sent an army to Judah, but the little country stood firm under King Jehoiachin, who was only eighteen years old when he succeeded his father, Jehoiakim.

JUDAH INVADED

Nebuchadnezzar himself finally took command of his troops, destroyed many cities of Judah and marched up to the gates of Jerusalem. The promised Egyptian assistance never materialized and Nebuchadnezzar took Jerusalem, carrying young King Jehoiachin and many important families into captivity.

THE FIRST EXILES IN BABYLON

Judah's attempt to cast off the Babylonian yoke had only made matters worse. King Jehoiachin was now exiled in Babylon along with many of his country's craftsmen, musicians, soldiers and nobles. Zedekiah, an uncle of Jehoiachin, one of Josiah's sons, had ascended Judah's throne.

King Zedekiah faced the same problem which had confronted his predecessors—should he rebel and shake off bondage or should he allow Judah to remain the vassal of Babylonia?

Most of the king's advisors favored rebellion, confident that Babylonia was not interested in further expansion. This confidence was strengthened by news reaching Judah that the captives in Babylon were being well treated. Unlike the Israelite captives in Assyria, the exiles in Babylonia were not dispersed over various vassal lands, nor were

An Assyrian relief showing Jewish prisoners of war playing lyres.

they persecuted. Many of the exiles had found useful employment and sent letters and messages home to their friends and relatives reporting how well they were faring. Encouraged by these stories, the members of Judah's war party urged King Zedekiah to revolt.

JEREMIAH, ADVOCATE OF PEACE

Zedekiah had another advisor who urged him to cease all thought of revolt and devote himself solely to insuring Judah's peace and welfare. This advisor was the aged prophet, Jeremiah. Jeremiah was born in Anathoth, a small village near Jerusalem. The son of a wealthy family of priests, Jeremiah had been given a good education by his parents. Before he received the call to prophecy he had lived the life of a studious young man. In the Book of Jeremiah he relates that he considered himself "a mere child," too young to go forth and proclaim his visions. But the call to prophecy proved stronger than his misgivings and Jeremiah, then still a very young man, went forth to Jerusalem to declare the word of God. Now, in the days of Zedekiah, Jeremiah was an old man. He had lived through the good years of Josiah's reign, the fall of Jehoahaz, the exiling of Jehoiachin and the devastation of Judah.

Jeremiah's political awareness was as keen as his spiritual faith was deep. He deeply distrusted Egypt, for he had seen how she had mistreated Judah and selfishly encouraged alliances between small states so that they might act as a buffer between Egypt and Babylon.

In the days of Jehoiakim, Jeremiah had gone to the Temple of Jerusalem and prophesied that the House of God would be destroyed if the people did not willingly bear the yoke of Babylon. The people had been shocked by what seemed to them disloyalty and Jeremiah became very unpopular. He was finally arrested and thrown into prison. After his release the prophet retired to his native town, Anathoth, with his loyal disciple Baruch, to whom he dictated his visions.

A tablet from the period of Nebuchadnezzar which dates and mentions the fall and sack of Jerusalem.

JEREMIAH IN DISGRACE

Baruch journeyed to Jerusalem with the purpose of bringing the words of the prophet to the king's attention. Jehoiakim refused to listen and scornfully burned the scrolls containing Jeremiah's message. Undaunted, Jeremiah continued to dictate his visions to his faithful disciple.

In the days of Zedekiah, Jeremiah returned to Jerusalem to plead for the peace and unity of Judah and its people.

For ten years Judah had been wavering between two choices—open revolt against Babylonia or peaceful acceptance of vassaldom. Zedekiah and his allies were about to decide in favor of revolt. Again the courageous Jeremiah raised his voice against this plan.

The people listened to the aged prophet when he appeared among them. He warned them that Judah was far too small and weak a nation to challenge the mighty empire of Babylonia. He begged them to preserve what freedom remained and comforted them by predicting that some day the captives would return from Babylon and Judah would be rebuilt.

The words of Jeremiah reached the exiles in Babylon by letter and messenger and gave them courage. There were those in Judah who laughed mockingly at Jeremiah but many others, heeding his warnings, paid their tribute willingly and supported the king in his refusal to rebel.

Meanwhile, the Pharaohs of Egypt continued to support all efforts at revolt against Babylonia and sought allies for a last stand against the new empire.

When Judah's neighbors approached Zedekiah to form an alliance against Babylonia he veered back to the side of the war party and began preparing his country for a long siege. Fortifications were strengthened, food and arms were stored and all able-bodied men were trained for defense.

In despair over these preparations for another war, the prophet Jeremiah renewed his warnings. Zedekiah, never a strong personality, turned a deaf ear to Jeremiah's words, and obeyed his other advisors. Jeremiah was denounced as unpatriotic and again cast into prison.

An alliance was formed between Judah, Edom, Moab, Ammon and the Phoenician cities of Tyre and Sidon. Pharaoh Apries of Egypt assured the allies of his support.

In the ninth year of his reign, after a long period of indecision, Zedekiah, the last king of Judah, revolted against Nebuchadnezzar of Babylonia. The year was 588 B.C.E.

JUDAH IS INVADED AGAIN

King Nebuchadnezzar dealt swiftly with the rebellion. His army of charioteers, infantry and cavalry far outnumbered the combined forces of the allies. One by one, the fortresses and cities of Judah fell to the Babylonian king. The fortresses of Lakhish and Azekah put up valiant resistance but

A wall of stone blocks, the remains of the city walls of Jerusalem.

finally capitulated.

The Babylonian tidal wave rolled on to Jerusalem, the last fortified city of Judah. No help came from Judah's allies for they were busy defending their own cities. Pharaoh Apries not only failed to keep his promise of assistance but treacherously attacked his own allies, the coastal cities of Tyre and Sidon. The siege of Jerusalem was briefly interrupted while Nebuchadnezzar marched off to do battle with the Egyptian army. The Egyptians evaded him by retreating to their newly-won Phoenician ports. The Babylonian armies marched back into Judah and laid siege to Jerusalem once again.

The people of Jerusalem valiantly defended their city against the battering rams, spears and firebrands of the enemy. For eighteen long months the walls around the city withstood the attack, but on the ninth day of Ab in the year 586 B.C.E., Jerusalem fell.

The Babylonians destroyed the Temple and set fire to the rest of the city. Grief and horror swept through the population. Many fled the burning city by night into the rocky Judean hills.

King Nebuchadnezzar entered Jerusalem in the morning, while his soldiers continued the destruction and plundering. King Zedekiah was taken captive. He was forced to witness the death of his children. Then he was blinded and put in chains. Nearly all of the people of Judah were deported to Babylonia. By the end of the year 586 B.C.E. the land of Judah was desolate. Its farms and vineyards lay barren. Its towns and cities were in ruins.

With the fall of the kingdom of Judah, four hundred years of rule by the House of David came to an end.

GEDALIAH, GOVERNOR OF JUDAH

Only a small community was left in Judah. Among those remaining was Gedaliah, the son of Ahikam. Gedaliah, a just man and a friend and protector of the prophet Jeremiah, was appointed governor of Judah by King Nebuchadnezzar.

In spite of Gedaliah's valiant attempts to rebuild Jerusalem and reunite the people, his rule was destined to be short-lived. He was assassinated by Ishmael, a prince of the House of David.

THE FALL OF THE KINGDOM OF JUDAH

Many more Judeans were transported to Babylonia in punishment of this violent act of rebellion, for King Nebuchadnezzar wanted obedient sub-

A copy of an Assyrian relief showing plunder being removed from a defeated city.

75

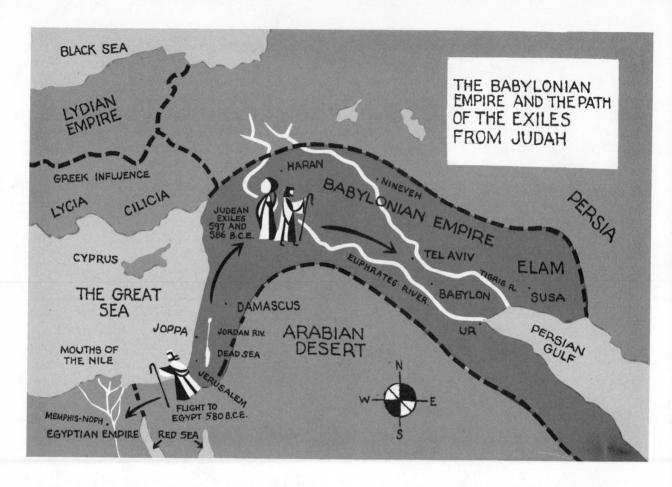

THE BABYLONIAN EMPIRE AND THE PATH OF THE EXILES FROM JUDAH

jects and was determined to stamp out any sign of revolt.

One of the deportation centers was at Ramah near the tomb of Rachel, beloved wife of the Patriarch Jacob. The prophet Jeremiah wrote these mournful words to describe the spirit of the refugees as they passed the tomb on their way to exile:

Rachel, is weeping for her children . . .
(Jeremiah 31:14)

Only a very few of the people remaining in Judah escaped the new deportations. Some fled to the mountains and stayed in hiding; others managed to escape to Egypt. Jeremiah and his disciple Baruch were compelled to flee with these latter refugees.

LIFE IN BABYLONIA

Some of the Judean exiles in Babylonia had

Foot; turned around in 2			
Donkey			
Bird; turned over with feet to the right			
Fish			
Star			
Ox; turned over in 2			
Sun or Day			
Grain; top of stalk turned over			

Early Babylonian signs showing their pictorial origin.

This list of eight signs shows clearly the pictures from which the signs came. The oldest form is in column 1; column 2 shows the departure from the picture and the appearance of the signs as the lines began to become wedges. In column 3 are the later forms, consisting only of wedges and showing no resemblance to the original picture.

KINGS OF ISRAEL AND JUDAH

KINGS BEFORE DIVISION OF KINGDOM

1040–1017 B.C.E. SAUL
1010–977 B.C.E. DAVID
977–937 B.C.E. SOLOMON

ISH-BOSHETH
about 1017–1010 B.C.E.
(ruled only over part of Israel)

THE NORTHERN KINGDOM OF ISRAEL

THE KINGDOM OF JUDAH

ruled by the House of David

937–722 B.C.E.

937–915 B.C.E. 1. JEROBOAM
915–914 B.C.E. 2. NADAB
914–890 B.C.E. 3. BAASA (BAASHA)
890–889 B.C.E. 4. ELAH
889 B.C.E. 5. ZIMRI
889–875 B.C.E. 6. OMRI
875–853 B.C.E. 7. AHAB
853–852 B.C.E. 8. AHAZIAH
852–842 B.C.E. 9. JEHORAM (JORAM)
842–815 B.C.E. 10. JEHU
815–798 B.C.E. 11. JEHOAHAZ
798–782 B.C.E. 12. JEHOASH
782–741 B.C.E. 13. JEROBOAM II
741 B.C.E. 14. ZECHARIAH
741 B.C.E. 15. SHALLUM
741–737 B.C.E. 16. MENAHEM
737–736 B.C.E. 17. PEKAHIAH
736–734 B.C.E. 18. PEKAH
734–722 B.C.E. 19. HOSHEA
722 B.C.E. The Assyrians destroy Samaria and lead the Ten Tribes, the people of Israel, into captivity.

937–586 B.C.E.

937–920 B.C.E. 1. REHOBOAM
920–917 B.C.E. 2. ABIJAH (ABIJAM)
917–876 B.C.E. 3. ASA
876–851 B.C.E. 4. JEHOSHAPHAT
851–843 B.C.E. 5. JEHORAM (JORAM)
843–842 B.C.E. 6. AHAZIAH
842–836 B.C.E. 7. ATHALIAH (WIFE OF JEHORAM)
836–796 B.C.E. 8. JOASH
796–767 B.C.E. 9. AMAZIAH
767–737 B.C.E. 10. UZZIAH (AZARIAH)
737–735 B.C.E. 11. JOTHAM
735–720 B.C.E. 12. AHAZ
720–692 B.C.E. 13. HEZEKIAH
692–641 B.C.E. 14. MANASSEH
641–639 B.C.E. 15. AMON
639–608 B.C.E. 16. JOSIAH
608 B.C.E. 17. JEHOAHAZ (Shallum)
608–597 B.C.E. 18. JEHOIAKIM (ELIAKIM)
597 B.C.E. 19. JEHOIACHIN (JECONIAH)
597–586 B.C.E. 20. ZEDEKIAH (MATTANIAH)
586 B.C.E. End of the Kingdom of Judah. The Babylonian Exile.

All dates are approximate

---

been sent to agricultural districts to labor on the farms of the conquerors and many were taken to the great city of Babylon. It is not difficult to imagine the homesickness and the bitter sorrow which must have filled the hearts of the exiles as they walked by the rivers of Babylon. The fame of Judah's musicians and singers had spread far and wide and the Babylonians often asked the captives to sing them the songs of Zion. From the depths of their despair the exiles sang new songs, rising from the glorious memories of desperate struggles of the past and the stark tragedy of the present:

By the rivers of Babylon
There we sat down, yea, we wept,
When we remembered Zion.
Upon the willows in the midst thereof
We hanged our harps.
For there they that led us captive
Asked of us words of song,
And our tormentors asked of us mirth:
'Sing us of the songs of Zion.'
How shall we sing the Lord's song
In a foreign land?
If I forget thee, O Jerusalem,

Let my right hand forget her cunning
Let my tongue cleave to the roof of my mouth
If I remember thee not: If I set not Jerusalem
Above my chiefest joy.

(Psalm 137)

A painting of the main thoroughfare of Babylon showing the famous Ishtar Gates.

The exiles built a new life in Babylonia. Some continued to be farmers, others went to work on the irrigation and canal-digging projects which turned dry stretches of clay into fertile land. Most of the exiles, however, settled in the great cities of Babylonia such as Babylon and Tel Abib. The common bond of exile drew the Judeans closely together. Many who had been farmers and shepherds in Judah now became craftsmen and traders so that they could live in the cities close to their friends and kinsmen.

From the many Babylonian records unearthed by modern archeologists, we know that life in the Babylonian cities was on a high level of civiliza-tion. Among the records were found the books of a Jewish firm of Babylonian traders, Murashu and Sons, of the city of Nippur. These books were pre-served in large clay jars much like those which held the Dead Sea Scrolls, written six hundred years later. Judging from the record books, Mura-shu and Sons was apparently known throughout Babylonia.

Babylonia's most splendid city was its capital, Babylon. Babylon was graced with beautiful tem-ples and palaces, great squares and gardens and well laid-out streets. The houses of the rich were of stone, sumptuous and ornate, containing luxurious furnishings and adorned with murals and mosaics. Even the gates of the city were decorated with mo-saics. In the center of all this magnificence rose the famous Tower of Babylon, one of the great wonders of the ancient world.

However, not all Babylonians lived a life of luxury. The poor and oppressed were great in number and often were enslaved, to be bartered like wares. There was no year of Jubilee to liberate them. The women of Babylonia had few rights and their status was much inferior to that of the men. They were not held in respect as were the women in the families of Judah.

In the midst of these strange and foreign ways, the exiles held fast to their own traditions. They kept to themselves in their own communities, ob-serving their Sabbath, their own holidays and their own religious laws. There was no High Priest in exile to perform the ancient rites of prayer; no more sacrifices were offered and no pilgrimages made to a central shrine. Each community con-ducted its own services in its own house of prayer. As their ancestors had done before them, carrying the symbols of their faith wherever they wandered, so the Judeans had carried their most sacred pos-sessions into exile. Precious Scrolls of the Law had been rescued from the destruction of the cities and from these scrolls the priests read portions from their ancient laws and history, deriving there-from much comfort for their present tragic state and more hope for a joyous future. Levites sang the old melodies, the psalms. Prophets spoke of God and gave renewed courage to the people.

Thus did the exiles from Judah, in idolatrous

Babylon, keep alive their faith and their traditions. Yet always, lying beneath the surface of their new life in a strange land, there was the dream of returning home one day to Judah and their beloved Mount Zion.

NEW LEADERS IN BABYLON

New leaders arose among the Jewish communities of Babylonia, to inspire and comfort the people. Some of these leaders were poets who sang of the bitterness of exile and of the longing for home. Others devoted themselves to the task of recording the history of Judah and Israel and the time of exile. One of the outstanding leaders of that time was the prophet Ezekiel.

Ezekiel was a man of the priesthood who had come into exile from Jerusalem. Remembering the ravaged battlefields of Judah, Ezekiel likened them dramatically to a desolate valley of dry bones. God, he declared, would breathe life into these dry bones, and the desolate valley would be transformed into a place of new life. Restored, the people would return to their own land. To achieve this restoration, the prophet asserted, each man would have to accept responsibility for his own acts and his own soul. The Jews of Babylonia listened to Ezekiel and took heart.

While the new prophet spoke to the exiles of new hope, the power of Babylonia began to wane. The kings and nobles became indolent as a result of their life of wealth and luxury. They cared nothing about new conquests and were seemingly content to rest on their laurels, recording the empire's former achievements. The vast historical archives at Babylon were filled with these records.

In spite of Babylonia's weakening power, many years were to pass before the great empire was brought to its knees. The Pharaohs of Egypt had failed to realize their dreams of reconquering their former possessions. The once powerful Phoenicians were now concerned only with furthering their commerce. Their merchants traveled all over the Babylonian empire, to the shores of the Black Sea and as far as India. Phoenician colonists had founded trading posts far away on the African coast of the Mediterranian. Like the Babylonians, the Phoencian priests of Tyre were busy making records of past history and filling the official

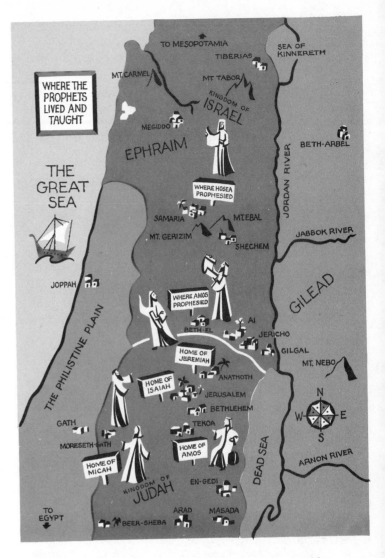

archives. The lust for conquest had spent itself among the nations of the Fertile Crescent and Babylonia had nothing to fear from them.

While the Babylonian rulers and nobles grew complacent, admiring their jewels and arranging feasts to honor their gods, the spirited young nation of Persia was on the march to the west, in the mountains of Iran. The Persians had been vassals of the Medes but under the leadership of the young Persian king, Cyrus, they gained their independence. Cyrus, the son of a Persian prince and a Median princess, was a brilliant and ambitious general.

The rumble of Persian conquest grew louder and the rulers of the uneasy nations formed a strong alliance against young Cyrus. King Croesus

79

of Lydia, famed far and wide for his enormous wealth; King Nabonidus of Babylonia; and Pharaoh Amasis II of Egypt joined forces to halt and destroy the advancing Persians. Cyrus defeated and captured King Croesus and took Lydia. Then he marched on to challenge the armies of Belshazzar, crown prince of Babylonia.

Belshazzar, son of Nabonidus, was a wasteful and irresponsible ruler, given to pleasure and extravagant revels. Neither Belshazzar nor his father pursued the tolerant policy of their predecessors. They forced all the people, including the Jews, to worship the idols of Babylonia. But frivolous though he was, Belshazzar was aware of the threat from the advancing Persians. The Bible records that during one of his feasts, Belshazzar summoned Daniel, a Jewish seer, to interpret strange signs which had appeared on the wall of his palace. The king's most learned advisors had been unable to decipher this "handwriting on the wall," but Daniel explained that it foretold the destruction of Babylonia and the death of Belshazzar. And indeed, soon after Daniel's dire predictions, Belshazzar was murdered.

CYRUS, THE TOLERANT CONQUEROR

The armies of Babylonia were routed in defeat by the disciplined, well-organized troops of King Cyrus. The Babylonians awaited with dread the plunder and devastation which they believed would inevitably follow. Cyrus, however, was unlike the conquerors of old. He entered the Babylonian cap-

Tomb of King Cyrus.

ital with a minimum of harm to life and property. The entire ancient world marveled at the peaceful way in which this new lord took over the rule of the mighty Babylonian empire.

King Cyrus proved to be an efficient administrator and a monarch of great tolerance. He put an end to waste and extravagance and granted religious freedom to all, believing that a nation flourished best under such conditions. The lot of the poor was greatly improved; they were housed and fed, while the pleasure-seeking nobles were re-

Inscribed cylinder which records the capture of Babylon by Cyrus. It tells how "without battle and without fighting Marduk (God of Babylon) made him (Cyrus) enter into his city of Babylon; he spared Babylon tribulation, and Nabonidus the (Chaldean) king, who feared him not, he delivered into his hand." Nabonidus, the Chaldean king of Babylon, was not in favor with the priests, and they assisted in delivering the city to Cyrus.

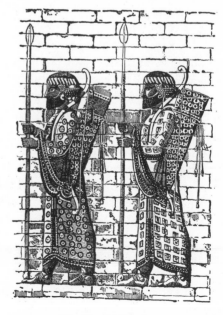

Persian soldiers.

Relief of Ahura-Mazda, the supreme god of the Persians.

From the Biblical Book of Ezra we learn that about 42,000 Jews from all over Babylonia joined in the exodus to Judah. Their long and difficult journey took them through the lands of the Fertile Crescent, retracing Abraham's trek of ancient days. Young and old, inspired and courageous, the band of exiles set forth. As they journeyed, they sang the ancient psalms and composed new songs of their own. After a journey of five months they reached Jerusalem.

During fifty years of exile and during the long trek back to the homeland, those who remembered Jerusalem had sung its praises. The young people had listened in awe to the stories of the land of Israel with its mountains and valleys, its lush vineyards and lovely cities. Time had dealt harshly with the beloved homeland—its beauty and splendor now existed only in the memories of the old.

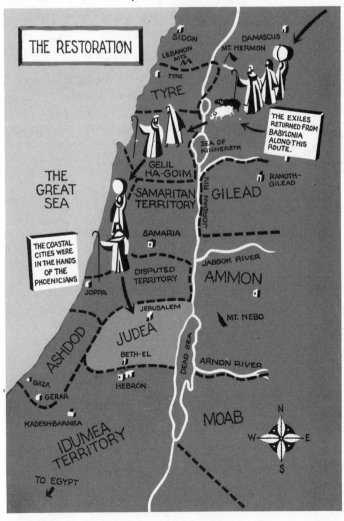

quired to give up their excessive feasting and revelry. Many of the peoples of Babylonia regarded Cyrus as their liberator. Under his rule, Persia became a great nation.

THE EXILES ARE PERMITTED TO RETURN HOME —538 B.C.E.

The conquest of Babylonia by the Persians was a great boon for the Jewish exiles. King Cyrus was sympathetic to them and soon issued a decree permitting them to return to Jerusalem and restore their Temple. Great was the rejoicing among the Jewish communities. Scores of the exiles sold their fields and their cattle, their shops and houses and prepared to make the long-dreamed-of journey back to their homeland. But there were many others, who after having lived in Babylon for fifty years, decided to remain there.

The land lay barren. Fields and vineyards were deserted; villages and towns were in ruins. Jerusalem was a city of desolation. The magnificent Temple of Solomon was destroyed, and grass was growing on its crumbling walls.

The pioneers from Babylonia wasted no time lamenting the past. All their energy was needed now for rebuilding. On the site of the Temple they erected an altar for the worship of God. They plowed the barren fields and tended the cattle they had brought with them. The returned exiles were joyfully assisted in their labors by the few Jews who had escaped deportation and had re-mained in Judah. These refugees had been living in great poverty in the Judean hills where they had fled for safety.

The head of the community was Zerubbabel, a prince of the House of David and grandson of King Jehoiachin. Zerubbabel had led the returning pioneers back to their land and was appointed governor by King Cyrus. The priest Joshua, son of an ancient priestly family, assisted Zerubbabel in his task.

The Second Commonwealth, founded by the returning Babylonian exiles, was called Judea.

BOOKS OF THE BIBLE — THE TANAKH

I. THE PENTATEUCH — THE TORAH
The Five Books of Moses

1.	Genesis	— Bereshit
2.	Exodus	— Shemot
3.	Leviticus	— Vayikra
4.	Numbers	— Bamidbar
5.	Deuteronomy	— Devarim

II. THE PROPHETS — NEVI'IM

a. Early Prophets — Nevi'im Rishonim

1.	Joshua	— Yehoshua
2.	Judges	— Shofetim
3.	Samuel, I	— Shemuel, Aleph
	Samuel, II	— Shemuel, Bet
4.	Kings, I	— Melakhim, Aleph
	Kings, II	— Melakhim, Bet

b. Later Prophets — Nevi'im Aharonim
The Three Major Prophets:

Isaiah	— Yeshayah
Jeremiah	— Yirmeyah
Ezekiel	— Yehezkel

The Twelve (Minor) Prophets —

Hosea	— Hoshea
Joel	— Yoel
Amos	— Amos
Obadiah	— Ovadyah
Jonah	— Yonah
Micah	— Mikha
Nahum	— Nahum
Habakkuk	— Habakkuk
Zephaniah	— Zephanyah
Haggai	— Haggai
Zechariah	— Zekhariah
Malachi	— Malakhi

III. THE HAGIOGRAPHA — KETUBIM
(Sacred Writings)

a. The Three Poetical Books —

Psalms	— Tehillim
Proverbs	— Mishle
Job	— Iyob

b. The Five Scrolls — The Megillot

Song of Songs	— Shir Hashirim
Ruth	— Rut
Lamentations	— Ekhah
Ecclesiastes	— Kohelet
Esther	— Esther

c. The Historical Books

Daniel	— Daniel
Ezra	— Ezra
Nehemiah	— Nehemyah
Chronicles, I	— Divre Hayamim, Aleph
Chronicles, II	— Divre Hayamim, Bet

GLOSSARY OF HEBREW TERMINOLOGY AND NAMES

Jehoahaz	Yhoh-ahaz	יְהוֹאָחָז	Isaiah	Y'shayahoo	יְשַׁעְיָהוּ
Jehoiakim	Yhoh-yahkeem	יְהוֹיָקִים	Ahaz	Ahahz	אָחָז
Jehoiachin	Yhoh-yaheen	יְהוֹיָכִין	Jotham	Yohtahm	יוֹתָם
Zedekiah	Tzidkeeyahoo	צִדְקִיָּהוּ	Uzziah	Ooziyahoo	עֻזִּיָּהוּ
Jeremiah	Yirmyahoo	יִרְמְיָהוּ	Micah	Meehah	מִיכָה
Anathoth	Ahnahtoht	עֲנָתוֹת	Moresheth-Gath	Mohreshet-Gaht	מוֹרֶשֶׁת־גַּת
Baruch	Bahrooh	בָּרוּךְ	Hezekiah	Hizkeeyahoo	חִזְקִיָּהוּ
Lakhish	Laheesh	לָכִישׁ	Gihon	Geehohn	גִּיחוֹן
Azekah	Ahzeykah	עֲזֵקָה	Siloam	Sheeloh-ah	שִׁילֹחַ
Ab	Ahv	אָב	Sennacherib	Sahnheyreev	סַנְחֵרִיב
Gedaliah	Gdahlyahoo	גְּדַלְיָהוּ	Esar-Haddon	Eysahr-hahdohn	אֵסַר־חַדֹּן
Ahikam	Aheekahm	אֲחִיקָם	Manasseh	Mnahsheh	מְנַשֶּׁה
Ishmael	Yishmah-eyl	יִשְׁמָעֵאל	Amon	Ahmohn	אָמוֹן
Rachel	Raheyl	רָחֵל	Josiah	Yohsheeyahoo	יֹאשִׁיָּהוּ
Zion	Tzeeyohn	צִיּוֹן	Zephaniah	Tzefahnyah	צְפַנְיָה
Tel Abib	Teyl Ahveev	תֵּל אָבִיב	Hilkiah	Hilkeeyahoo	חִלְקִיָּהוּ
Dead Sea Scrolls	Mgeeloht Yahm Ha-melah	מְגִלּוֹת יַם הַמֶּלַח	Deuteronomy	Dvahreem	דְּבָרִים
			Necoh	Nhoh	נְכוֹ
Ezekiel	Yhezkeyl	יְחֶזְקֵאל	Megiddo	Mgeedoh	מְגִדּוֹ
Cyrus	Kohresh	כּוֹרֶשׁ	Carchemish	Kahrkmeesh	כַּרְכְּמִישׁ
Belshazzar	Beylshahtzar	בֵּלְשַׁאצַּר	Nebuchad-nezzar	Nvoohahd-netzahr	נְבְכַדְנֶאצַר
Daniel	Dahnee-eyl	דָּנִיֵּאל			
Ezra	Ezrah	עֶזְרָא			
Zerubabel	Zroobahvel	זְרֻבָּבֶל			

JUDEA, THE SECOND COMMONWEALTH

THE SAMARITANS

At the time of Assyria's conquest a small number of Jews had succeeded in remaining in the northern kingdom of Israel. They had intermarried with the people whom the Assyrians had settled in the territory around Samaria. Their descendants were called Samaritans. The Samaritans considered themselves Israelites, but they had accepted some of the customs of other nations. When they learned of the exiles' return, the Samaritans, eager to become a part of the new commonwealth, offered their assistance in its rebuilding.

The newly returned pioneers thoughtfully considered this offer but declined it. Throughout the years of exile the Jews had jealously guarded their ancient traditions and their own way of life. They greatly feared that if they included the Samaritans in their future plans these strangers might introduce idolatrous ways and even bring idols into the new Temple.

The Samaritans were bitterly offended by the Jews' refusal of their assistance. They subsequently built a temple of their own on Mount Gerizim and worshipped in their own territory. Thenceforth the two peoples were enemies.

The Samaritans now sought to hinder the Jews from completing their Temple in Jerusalem by writing letters of false accusation to Persia. In these letters, the Samaritans claimed that the Jews were planning to revolt and asked King Cambyses II,

Mosaic in an ancient Samaritan synagogue, showing the Greek influence.

Trypylon relief at Persepolis showing King Darius I and Xerxes. Xerxes is standing behind the throne.

son of Cyrus, to order a halt to the reconstruction of the Temple. The rebuilding of the Temple was temporarily halted.

In their bleak despair the Judeans turned to their prophets. The prophets bade them be of good faith, foretelling that the building of the Temple would be resumed soon—even in their own day. For several years no further work was done on the Temple, for the Jews dared not defy the order of the Persian king. During these years the prophets Haggai and Zechariah were a source of great help and strength to the community.

Cylinder seal with the name of Darius in three languages—Persian, Assyrian and Scythian.

Upon the succession of King Darius, the Jews sent letters of petition to the new king and the young Darius considered their case. During this process the old decree of King Cyrus was found and the Jews were declared innocent of the charge brought against them. Darius sent messengers to encourage the building of the Temple and the pioneers eagerly returned to the completion of their great project.

Unfortunately, the Samaritans were not the only enemies of the Jews. Edomites, Moabites and Ammonites attacked the poorly-armed settlers. Raiding parties seized their meager harvests and attacked their houses in the city. The ancient fortifications of Jerusalem had tumbled down and offered no protection against raiders.

Relief showing Darius I seated on his throne surrounded by attendants.

THE JEWS REBUILD THE TEMPLE

Despite these harassments the Jews toiled on. They worked night and day, living in poor huts and sparing time from the building only to provide the barest necessities of food and clothing for themselves. They who had enjoyed the wealth and plenty of Babylonia now lived in privation so that they might know the deeper joys of the spirit.

In comparison to the magnificent Temple of Solomon the new Temple was simple indeed. However, the Levites sang the same sacred old melodies and the priests offered the same prayers and sacrifices as they had in the First Temple. Again, the people came and assembled in the courts to worship.

A TIME OF TROUBLE

The task of reconstructing the Temple completed, the people could now turn to the rebuilding of the land. As time passed, however, the community became disorganized. The building of the Temple had been a great common purpose, uniting the Judeans and inspiring them to a supreme effort. Now that the Temple was finished, a period of laxness set in. Many found it difficult to withstand the influence of the foreign ways of their pagan neighbors. Some Jews had accepted the customs of Moab, Ammon, Edom and Samaria and many Jewish men had married foreign women. These wives brought their own gods with them into their new homes and taught their children to worship them.

Judea was poor—even the priests and Levites found themselves without means and were obliged to leave the Temple to earn their own livelihood, so that the Temple suffered from neglect.

Meanwhile, the Jews in Babylonia had not forgotten their brothers who had returned to Judea. They rejoiced at the news of the Temple's completion and sent letters of encouragement and gifts of money to the pioneers. But the news from Judea was disheartening.

EZRA THE SCRIBE

Among those in Babylonia who were distressed

Reputed Tomb of Ezra the Scribe.

A modern-day sofer assembling a Torah. Here we see him sewing the sheets of parchment to the wooden rollers.

by the news of Judea's troubled state was Ezra, a learned Jew of priestly descent. Ezra, a dedicated teacher, had many disciples whom he instructed in the Torah. He was highly skilled in the art of writing Scrolls of the Law, as were his disciples. Men who engaged in writing of Scrolls of the Law were known as scribes and Ezra has become known in Jewish history as Ezra the Scribe (*Ezra Hasofer*).

When Ezra applied to King Artaxerxes for permission to go to Jerusalem with his disciples his request was granted. The king and the Jewish community of Babylonia generously gave Ezra many gifts for the Temple and also the supplies he needed for the long journey. Approximately fifteen hundred Jews, eager to return to their homeland accompanied Ezra to Judea. They arrived in Jerusalem in the summer of 458 B.C.E. and were warmly welcomed by the people of Judea who had gone forth to meet this new group of pioneers.

Ezra began his task without delay. He traveled through the land visiting and teaching, but he was saddened and disturbed to find among most of the people a lack of knowledge of the Torah. There also were other conditions that troubled Ezra. The few people who had become rich in Judea were following the example set by their foreign neighbors, and exploited the poor without mercy. In order to gain a new foothold in the land, the Judeans had compromised some of their most cherished values.

Ezra persisted in his task of teaching the people and winning them back to the ways of the Torah. Patiently, he reasoned with them, reminding them of their great struggle to regain their homeland and their high purpose in doing so. A great many people were deeply impressed by Ezra's words and promised to give up the heathen ways which were undermining their character. Then Ezra was compelled to make a harsh rule. He asked all the men who had married foreign women to end their marriages and send their wives back to their native lands. It was a stern measure but Ezra felt that only in this way could Judea rid itself of idol worship and foreign influence. As he witnessed the many sad partings between husbands and wives, Ezra was moved to compassion—but the future of Judea was at stake and he steeled himself to think only of this one goal.

NEHEMIAH

The next major task was to fortify Jerusalem against the hostile bands of raiders by rebuilding the city's walls. This act, however, would create suspicion of the Judeans and they would be accused of planning revolt.

Help came when Nehemiah, a Babylonian Jew,

Hebrew coin dating back to the 4th century B. C. E., the period of Ezra the Scribe. The coin is inscribed Y H D (in ancient Hebrew script) which stands for Yehud. Yehud was the Persian name of the Jewish satrapy during this period.

was appointed governor of Judea. Nehemiah had been the trusted cupbearer of the Persian king, Artaxerxes I, in Shushan. Like Ezra, Nehemiah had been distressed by the stories of the trouble in Judea and had asked permission to return to Jerusalem.

The two great leaders, Ezra and Nehemiah, combined their efforts to restore the commonwealth of Judea. Ezra was Judea's spiritual guide; Nehemiah, the governor, was its political leader. Inspired by Nehemiah, the people set about rebuilding the walls of Jerusalem with great enthusiasm.

"Come," they said, "let us go and rebuild the walls of Jerusalem. Let us end our shame. We shall work in the daytime and stand watch during the night."

The walls and fortifications were completed in just fifty-two days. The men of Judea defended the walls fiercely and the raiders soon began to think twice before they attacked. The lion of Judah was rising from its defeat and standing brave and proud again to do battle for its rights.

Nehemiah was well versed in Jewish law and with the help of Ezra he laid the foundations of the new Jewish commonwealth. The Torah was the constitution, the fundamental law of Judea. Ezra and his disciples, traveling among the people, instructed them in the laws and saw to it that the Jews should live by their own laws and not by those of their heathen neighbors or of Persia.

Nehemiah set an excellent example for Judea's merchants and landowners by dedicating himself completely to the rebuilding of the land and the welfare of the people. He reinstated the old law of the Seventh Sabbatical Year, in which the land would lie fallow. He also proclaimed that every fiftieth year would be a year of Jubilee. In this year all debts would be forgiven and all lands that had been lost through hardship would return to the original owners. The old tax of a tenth of the harvest as well as the leave offerings were reinstated for the benefit of the priests and Levites who tended the Temple. These taxes made it possible for the Temple service to continue uninterrupted.

The new commonwealth of Judea began to thrive. Farmers and shepherds harvested in peace

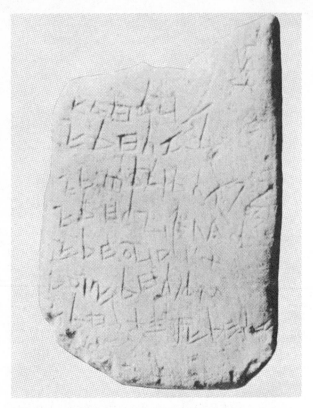

The Gezer Calendar Stone discovered by R. Macalister in 1908. This tenth century, B.C.E., limestone plaque is inscribed with a planting schedule of the ancient Palestine farmer.

taining to the observance of the Sabbath and the festivals. No work was to be done in the city on the Sabbath and the gates of Jerusalem would be closed to commerce and, as in the days of old, the Jewish festivals would be celebrated again all over Judea. On the pilgrim festivals and the High Holy Days all who were able would come to Jerusalem to celebrate and worship at the Temple.

That first Sukkot was a memorable day for the people of Judea and a day of profound significance for generations of Jews yet unborn.

Ezra and his disciples, the Scribes, continued their travels through the land. They carried the Scrolls of the Law with them and taught not only the judges of the courts but every person who would come to learn. During this time a new script was developed. This was the Hebrew script much as we know it today. Many Jews learned to read and write and with the help of the explanations of Ezra and the Scribes they became familiar with the words

As in ancient days, Jews all over the world celebrate the holiday of Sukkot by blessing the *lulav* and *etrog*.

and took their oil and wool, their fruits and grain to the market in Jerusalem. Traders came again from the neighboring countries to sell their wares in the city.

THE SPIRITUAL REVIVAL

Ezra and Nehemiah had fought a good fight. Together they had fulfilled the task of effecting a political reconstruction and spiritual rejuvenation in the land. On the day before the Festival of Sukkot, in the year 445 B.C.E., hundreds of Judeans made their way to Jerusalem to celebrate this pilgrim festival. They assembled in the ancient City of David and built their tabernacles.

On the day before the festival Ezra called for a great assembly. The people gathered to hear the proclamations of their two great leaders. Nehemiah and the priests and Levites of the Temple stood before the assembled Judeans while Ezra read to them from the Torah. He proclaimed again the just and merciful laws of Israel and the rules per-of the Torah. Thus did the Jews come to be a people of students, occupying themselves diligently with the study of the Law.

The example of Judea was followed throughout the Jewish communities of Egypt and Persia. Hebrew was again spoken, read and written, slowly replacing the Aramaic tongue of Babylonia and Persia which many Jews had adopted.

Ezra and the Scribes revived the Oral Tradition. The Oral Tradition, an unwritten code, consisted of the interpretation of the laws of the written Torah as handed down by the Elders, Prophets and Scribes since the times of Moses and Joshua. After the time of Ezra, the Oral Tradition continued to be passed down from generation to generation by word of mouth. In this process many new interpretations were added, since each generation applied the Torah to its own times and its own particular problems. This process culminated many centuries later in the written constitution of these interpretations into the collections of the *Mishnah* and *Talmud*.

THE SYNAGOGUE

The re-esablishment of the community by Ezra and Nehemiah was followed by an era of peace for Judea. Towns and villages were rebuilt; land was

Ruins of the ancient synagogue at Capernaum.

tilled and cultivated. Many towns built their own small market places and houses of prayer. In these houses of prayer the priests and Scribes taught the Torah and instructed the people how to observe the festivals. Here the people met to celebrate the Sabbath and holidays, to conduct their meetings and discuss their community problems. Here judges held court, and here marriages were celebrated. These houses of worship and learning, these centers of community life, became what we now refer to as synagogues. In the course of centuries, especially after the Second Temple, the synagogue became the heart of every Jewish community — a place where the stranger could seek shelter, the poor would receive alms and where those with problems or disputes could come for counsel.

THE BIBLE IS COMPILED

The Scribes collected and carefully examined all the holy writings which had been composed since the completion of the Five Books of Moses, to determine which of these was worthy of inclusion in the great collection of holy books which eventually became known as the Bible. The Bible was to be

Origin and development of the Hebrew square alphabet.

89

"The Book of Books," and its content was to be the most important body of writings. Doubtlessly, some of the scriptures known in the days of the Scribes were lost, while others became part of different, later collections, outside the Bible. The best known of these later collections are called the Apocrypha and the Pseudepigrapha. The group of learned Scribes that interpreted the Laws of the Torah were known as *Anshe Kenesset HaGedolah,* the Men of the Great Assembly.

THE STORY OF ESTHER AND THE FESTIVAL OF PURIM

Persia's control over Judea was rather mild and though still a vassal of Persia, Judea was left to govern itself. The Jews of Babylonia also fared well during most of the period of Persian rule. The story of Esther, however, relates an incident which was not typical of those times. Haman, first minister to King Ahasuerus of Persia, devised a scheme to have all the Jews in Persia killed. This plan was foiled by the wise Jew Mordecai and his cousin, Queen Esther, the wife of Ahasuerus. Ahasuerus is usually identified with Xerxes or Artaxerxes. The festival of *Purim* ("Feast of Lots" after the lots by which Haman wanted to set the date for the mass killing) commemorates the rescue of the Persian Jews by Esther, the brave and beautiful queen.

Traditional tomb of Esther and Mordecai.

An Aramaic scroll written by the Jews of Elephantine to Bagoas, Persian governor of Judea. In the letter they ask for permission to rebuild their synagogue.

JEWISH SETTLEMENTS OUTSIDE JUDEA

The Jewish communities kept in close touch with Judea. Jews from many lands sent gifts to Jerusalem and Jews everywhere paid the annual Temple tax.

The little country of Judea did not afford all of its sons the opportunities they sought. Many Judeans were enticed by stories of the great cities of other lands and left their small country to settle in the Jewish communities of Egypt and Babylonia.

Among the Jewish colonies outside Judea was Elephantine, also known as Yeb, on an island in the Nile near Aswan. Elephantine was a fortress city, a military colony which had been settled by Jews as far back as the Babylonian conquest of Egypt. Archeologists excavating in Elephantine have found papyrus scrolls, dating from about 410 B.C.E., bearing letters written in Aramaic by this Jewish community to Bagoas, then Persian governor of Judea. The letters ask permission to rebuild the Jewish temple there and assistance in doing so.

GLOSSARY OF HEBREW TERMINOLOGY AND NAMES

Samaritans	Shohmrohneem	שׁוֹמְרוֹנִים
Mount Geri-zim	Hahr Gree-zeem	הַר גְּרִיזִים
Haggai	Ḥahgai	חַגַּי
Zechariah	Zḥaryah	זְכַרְיָה
Darius	Dahryahvesh	דָּרְיָוֶשׁ
Ezra the Scribe	Ezrah Ha-sohfeyr	עֶזְרָא הַסּוֹפֵר
Nehemiah	Nḥemyah	נְחֶמְיָה
Artaxerxes	Artaḥshahshtah	אַרְתַּחְשַׁשְׁתָּא
Seventh Sab-batical Year	Shnaht Shmeetah	שְׁנַת שְׁמִיטָה
Jubilee	Yohveyl	יוֹבֵל
Elders	Zkeyneem	זְקֵנִים
Prophets	Nvee-eem	נְבִיאִים
Mishnah	Mishnah	מִשְׁנָה
Talmud	Tahlmood	תַּלְמוּד
Synagogue	Beyt Knesset	בֵּית כְּנֶסֶת
Bible	Tanaḥ	תַּנַ"ךְ
Men of the Great Assembly	Anshey Knes-set Hagdoh-lah	אַנְשֵׁי כְּנֶסֶת הַגְּדוֹלָה
Esther	Esteyr	אֶסְתֵּר
Purim	Pooreem	פּוּרִים
Haman	Hahmahn	הָמָן
Ahasueros	Aḥashveyrohsh	אֲחַשְׁוֵרשׁ

THE PERIOD OF GREEK RULE

THE POWER OF ATHENS

While the Persians had been making conquests and extending their empire, an advanced form of civilization, with its center at Athens, was being developed in Greece. The wealth and culture of the Greek city-states and the Greek islands were the envy of the ancient world. The Persians, deciding this was a prize too rich to ignore, set out to conquer Greece.

Over a period of fifty-one years, Persia fought many bitter battles both on land and at sea in an attempt to conquer Greece. In the end the Persians failed.

Bust of Alexander the Great.

THE CONQUERING MACEDONIANS AND ALEXANDER THE GREAT

Persia finally was forced to withdraw from Greece but now both nations faced a new threat—the Macedonians from the rugged country on Greece's northern borders.

Under King Philip, the Macedonians invaded the lands of the Hellespont and conquered Greece. When his son, Alexander the Great, became king of the Macedonians, he determined to bring the culture of Greece to the lands of the East.

Alexander's plans of conquest were vast and

Mosaic found at Pompeii records the battle at Issus between the Macedonians and the Persians. Alexander the Great, bareheaded (at left), charges the bodyguard surrounding the Persian King Darius III.

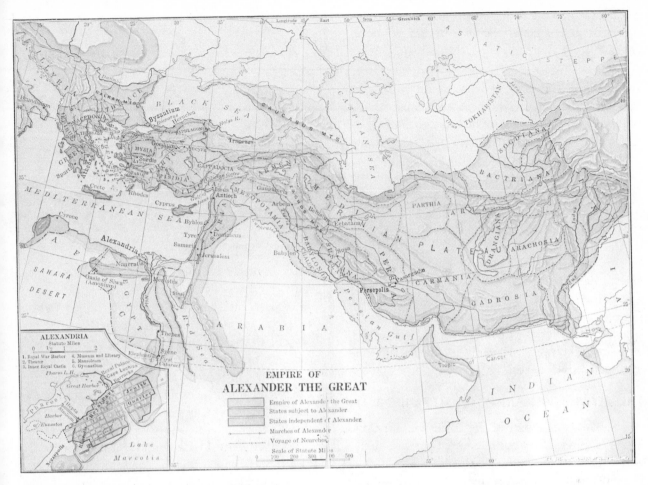

EMPIRE OF
ALEXANDER THE GREAT

Empire of Alexander the Great
States subject to Alexander
States independent of Alexander
Marches of Alexander
Voyage of Nearchos
Scale of Statute Miles

ALEXANDRIA
Statute Miles

1. Royal War Harbor   4. Museum and Library
2. Theater   5. Mausoleum
3. Inner Royal Castle 6. Gymnasium
Pharos L. H.

elaborate. He was familiar with the life of Persia and included that country in his scheme of conquest. He succeeded in conquering all the lands of Persia from the Aegean Sea to the Black Sea and the borders of India, and from the Taurus Mountains to the land of Egypt. When Alexander reached the little land of Judea he showed himself to be kindly disposed toward its people, for he had been told that the Jews had a remarkable civilization of their own, and he loved and respected culture and scholarship.

Legend relates that when Alexander came to Jerusalem he was met at the city gates by Jaddua the High Priest. Seeing Jaddua attired in his priestly robes, Alexander, deeply moved, bowed before him. He told the Jews who welcomed him that he had once dreamed of a stately priest like Jaddua who had prophesied his victory over the Persian Empire. Jewish legends also tell how the people of Judea, in turn, admired this young conqueror for

his tolerance and his talents.

Alexander founded many cities in the territories he conquered. The most famous of these cities was in Egypt and was named Alexandria, in honor of

Alexander the Great being greeted by the High Priest Jaddua. From a fourteenth century French picture.

93

the great conqueror. Built on the Nile delta, Alexandria became a great trading port and center of Greek culture. True to his youthful dreams, Alexander now proceeded to introduce Grecian culture and the Greek way of life wherever his conquests took him. Alexandria, the new metropolis on the Nile, was to bear witness to the fulfillment of Alexander's dreams long after his death. This great city was to become a monument to the mighty conqueror whom history has given the title "Alexander the Great."

However, Alexander's new empire was destined to be short-lived, for the young ruler died of a fever when he was only thirty-three years old. His three most powerful generals conspired against his heirs and brutally murdered Alexander's family. One, Antigonus, took over the rule of Macedonia and Greece. Another, Seleucus, and his descendants, ruled the territories which had once been under Babylonia. The third, Ptolemy I, and his descendants, ruled over Egypt.

THE JEWISH COMMUNITY OF ALEXANDRIA

Judea became a part of the Ptolemaic kingdom and was to remain so for a hundred years. A flourishing Jewish community developed in Alexandria, the most important city of the Ptolemaic kingdom. Jewish settlers had helped in the building of the city and Alexander had granted them the same rights and privileges he had given the Greek citi-

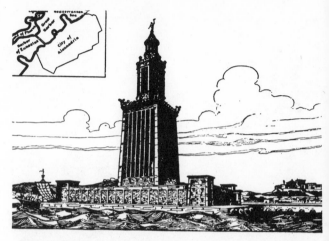

A reconstruction of the famous lighthouse in the harbor of Alexandria.

zens. Attracted by the many opportunities which the city offered, Jews flocked to Alexandria from other parts of Egypt and from the rugged Judean hills. In this city on the Nile the Jews found not only new opportunities but a new way of life as well. As time passed, Alexandria became increasingly Greek in appearance. King Ptolemy I erected a marvelous lighthouse three-hundred feet high at the city's busy port. It was a famous landmark and was regarded as one of the Seven Wonders of the World. Ptolemy I also founded in Alexandria a great library which became the center of the city's many cultural activities. Both Ptolemy I and Ptolemy II not only developed trade but also protected and furthered the arts and sciences. Indeed, under the rule of the Ptolemies, Alexandria became the most important Greek cultural center outside of Greece.

Although the Jews of Alexandria practiced

ALEXANDRIA

Map of Alexandria showing the extensive Jewish quarter.

Ancient wall painting shows King Ptolomy I sacrificing to the gods.

94

Bust of Ptolemy

Under the second ruler of the Ptolemaic line, Ptolemy Philadelphus, the Bible was first translated into Greek. We are told that Ptolemy II, with his great library at Alexandria, possessed all the great books of the world—except the Five Books of Moses. He sent a request to the High Priest at Jerusalem, asking for a copy of these books and for permission to have them translated into Greek. When the books arrived the king invited seventy Jewish sages to Alexandria and set each sage to work by himself on the translation. The seventy sages had no contact with one another. Yet, when their work was finished, all seventy translations were identical. We do not know whether this story is fact or legend, but this first Greek translation of the Bible came to be known as the Septuagint, meaning the translation "by the Seventy."

The Septuagint created a stir among scholars, and laymen alike. By that time Greek had become

their own religion and conducted their own communal life in their synagogue they were attracted to the ways of the Greeks. They adopted the Greek language and many Jews took part in Greek sports and philosophical debates. For centuries the Jews of Alexandria had to wrestle with one of the gravest problems confronting Jews of their time—Greek civilization versus the Jewish way of life.

THE SEPTUAGINT

The Ptolemies were kind to the Jews, and for more than a hundred years Judea was at peace under the protection of Egypt. The Ptolemies did not demand unreasonable taxes and seldom interfered with the Judean government.

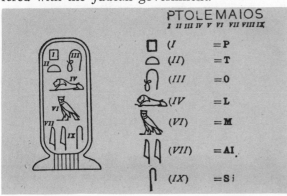

Oval containing the name "Ptolemy" in hieroglyphics.

A page from the Septuagint, Exodus XIX.

the official language throughout the ancient world. Jews who knew Greek but no longer knew Hebrew were now able to read their own Holy Scriptures. In addition, the Septuagint translation also enabled

95

Ptolemy II decreeing the liberation of Jewish captives and authorizing the translation of the Bible into Greek. From an eleventh century manuscript.

non-Jews to read the Bible. Thus the entire ancient world became acquainted with the history and ideas of the people of the little land of Judea.

JUDEA IN THE DAYS OF THE PTOLEMIES

In Judea itself, the people continued to live peacefully, abiding by the laws of the Torah as explained by the High Priest and the Great Assembly of the Scribes. The Torah was not a secret book to be read only by scholars. It was the law and the way of life for the entire Jewish people. Beginning with the days of Ezra the Scribe, the Torah was studied by many Jews—farmers and shepherds, merchants and artisans. Unlike the great masses of people in the ancient world, the Jews were able to read and write. The Scribes, teachers and scholars who made up the Great Assembly, represented many different groups and classes of population.

The Great Assembly, known also as the Great Synagogue, interpreted the laws of the Torah. As time passed, many new interpretations of the Torah had to be made because of constantly changing conditions. The Great Assembly also served as a training ground for those who would go forth to teach in the synagogues of Judea's communities.

The most prominent and beloved high priest during the Ptolemaic period was Simon the Just. Simon devoted himself to the service in the Temple and worked with the Great Assembly to further the welfare of the people. However, a new struggle for power among the rulers of the empire founded by Alexander was soon to put an end to the time of peace and freedom which Judea enjoyed in the days of Simon the Just.

THE SELEUCID RULERS

The Seleucid kings of Syria fought to win the lands of Palestine from the Ptolemies of Egypt. After many battles the Syrian king Antiochus III defeated Ptolemy V of Egypt in 198 B.C.E. This final victory placed Judea under the intolerant rule of the Seleucid kings.

Syrian kings placed their own sympathizers in all positions of power in Judea's government in order to force their own customs on the Jews. The Seleucid kings were Greeks and, like the Ptolemies of Egypt, they promoted and spread Greek culture. Greek ideas and the Greek way of life had become very fashionable among many of the wealthy nobles of Judea. The Jews who admired and followed Greek civilization became known as the Hellenists.

The Rosetta Stone. In 1799 a French engineer, Boussard, discovered a basalt slab at Rosetta, Egypt. It contained an inscription in two languages, Greek and Egyptian; and in three alphabets, Greek, Egyptian (Demotic) and Egyptian hieroglyphics.

Greek inscription (before the Second Temple) carved on a synagogue column, "Gift of Theodorus, the son of Olympus, for the salvation of his daughter Matrona."

HELLENISM AND JUDAISM

Gradually, the people of Judea divided into two factions: the Hellenists, who had adopted the Greek way of life and Greek religious ideas; and the Hassidim, or "Pious Ones" who were in the majority and who continued to adhere to the laws of the Torah.

The ideas of the Greeks were very different from those of the Jews. The Jews were concerned with the beauty and perfection of man's soul, which could never be represented by statues or pictures. It was the Jewish ideal to live as servants of the one invisible God—to act justly and show mercy and to obey the commandments of the Torah.

The Greeks, on the other hand, prized physical beauty and harmony above all else. The statues of their deities were artistic masterpieces. The Greeks represented their gods and goddesses in the form of human beings and believed that they possessed all the weaknesses and faults of men.

Thus, while the young Jewish men went to the Synagogues to study and learn how best to strive for spiritual perfection, Greek youths went to the stadiums to train their bodies in sports in order to achieve their goal of physical perfection.

The Greeks had schools, too, but the emphasis there was on the realm of nature rather than on the world of the spirit. Many Jews were fascinated by Greek culture. The Greek way of life opened a door to a new world for some affluent and pleasure seeking people of Judea. Many Jews were willing to cast aside their ancient traditions and lose themselves in this new life completely. Throughout the years of Greek domination over the Fertile Crescent,

the Hellenists, who followed the ways of Greece, and the Hassidim, who upheld the ways of Judaism, fought each other bitterly. Once more the fate of Judaism hung in the balance.

Judaism was threatened abroad as well as at home. Many Jews had left their homeland and settled in foreign lands. These Jews were known as the Jews of the Diaspora (Dispersion) and they, too, were exposed to strong Hellenic influences in the cities where they lived.

THE REIGN OF ANTIOCHUS IV

The situation came to a head under the rule of Antiochus IV, son of Antiochus the Great (Antiochus III). This Syrian king had hoped to follow in his father's footsteps and become a great monarch, but his dreams were threatened by a new power rising in the west which was to storm across the ancient world like a ruthless giant.

The Romans, as these conquerors were called, had taken Greece and Macedonia and marched on to Asia Minor. Their ships of war had crossed the Aegean and invaded the western possessions of

Three Greek mythological figures, Orpheus, Eurydice and Hermes.

Syria. Syria could not stop them and the Romans took the lands northwest of the Taurus.

Antiochus IV spared no pains to defend his empire against the growing power of Rome. Proud of his Greek ancestry and determined to unite all the peoples of the ancient world under his rule, he had sought to force his subjects to follow the Greek way of life to the exclusion of all others. Antiochus found supporters in Jerusalem among the Hellenists and used them to exploit Judea. He imposed high taxes on the Judeans to help defray the expense of hiring mercenary soldiers, equipping his vast army and maintaining his splendid court at Antioch, the Syrian capital.

Antiochus greatly disapproved of the stubborn little nation of Judea, whose people insisted on clinging to their own civilization and religion. He began his drive to bring the Jews to terms by deposing their high priest, and selling the office to Jason, a man who had promised to aid the king by raising Judea's taxes. Jason, though a man of

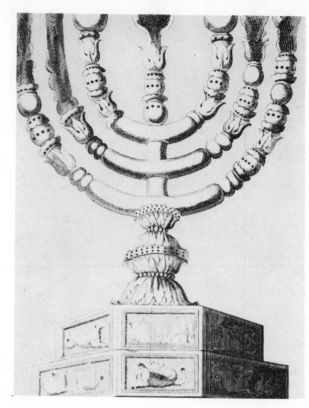

An 18th century German replica of the seven branched Temple menorah.

Statue of Zeus (Jupiter) found at Caesarea. Throughout Judea, Syrian overlords pressed the Jews to worship before such idols at public altars.

priestly descent, was an enthusiastic Hellenist who had lived in Antioch and even changed his name, Joshua, to the Greek name of Jason. Jason made the office of High Priest a mockery, turning the Holy Temple into a shrine for Greek idols, and Greeks came to the Temple Mount to worship them.

Antiochus crowned this humiliation of the Jews by placing a statue of himself in the Temple. As was frequently the custom of the great rulers of those times, Antiochus had declared himself a god.

In time, Antiochus began to mistrust even Jason and deposed him also. In his place the king appointed Menelaus, an even more ruthless and ambitious supporter of Syria. The people of Judea were outraged and ashamed that there should be such scoundrels in their midst.

To satisfy the ever-growing demands of the ambitious king, Menelaus raised Judea's taxes still more. He stole funds and sacred objects from the Temple and spied on the men around him.

Silver coin of Antiochus IV.

ANTIOCHUS OUTLAWS THE JEWISH RELIGION

Eventually, Antiochus outlawed the Jewish religion. It became a serious offense to observe the Jewish laws. The Torah was a forbidden book; the Sabbath, festivals and holy days could no longer be celebrated in public. The dietary laws could no longer be observed officially, and finally circumcision, the very mark of the Jew, was forbidden. The Torah had to be studied in secret. Even quoting from Jewish law meant to endanger one's life.

Antiochus added the Greek word "Epiphanes" ("God made manifest") to his name. Many Judeans, however, would refer to him as Antiochus Epimanes—"Antiochus the Madman." Although Antiochus had proclaimed himself a god and decreed that those who opposed him would die, there were still many brave men and women in Judea who refused to pay him homage at the Greek shrines. Whenever Greek soldiers would enter a village to force obedience, they would find people who would stand up proudly and refuse to bow to the Greek idols. Scores of these courageous rebels were tortured; many were put to death.

Hannah, a Jewish mother, had to witness the deaths of her seven sons who bravely refused to obey the oppressors. Eleazar, an old and respected teacher, was tortured and killed because he refused to eat pork, forbidden by biblical dietary laws. Many of the Hasidim fled into the Judean hills and lived in rocky caves, fugitives in their own land. They waited and prayed for the time of revolt and liberation which they felt was sure to come.

THE RISE OF THE MACCABEES

The first stirrings of rebellion started one day in the small village of Modin, near Jerusalem. On that day Syrian officials and soldiers had come to Modin to collect taxes and to force the people to worship the Greek gods. There was an old priest in the village, a man called Mattathias, of the Hasmonean family. Mattathias, surrounded by his five sons, walked up to the heathen altar. A Jew who collaborated with the Syrians had just bowed to the idols. Mattathias raised his sword high and his voice out loud and clear:

"He who is with God, let him come to me!" he cried, and slew the traitorous idol worshipper.

The old priest's bold act inspired his sons and followers. They fell upon the Greek soldiers and officials and killed them. Only a few escaped.

The long-awaited revolt had begun! News of the incident at Modin spread like wildfire until all Judea was inflamed. Mattathias, his sons and their followers fled to the mountains and joined hands with the Hasidim. A central camp was set up and the rebel's ranks grew by leaps and bounds as new guerrilla fighters joined the revolutionary movement. Syrian transports were harassed on the roads by Judean rebels, and Syrian soldiers no longer could enter villages to collect taxes and force idol worship without being attacked.

Mattathias, the old priest, died soon after the beginning of the revolt but his five sons vigorously took over his leadership. They gave the command to the third son, Judah, who was called Ha-Makkabi —the Hammerer. The letters of his name is said to have stood for the rebels' password and battle cry: *Mi Kamokah Ba'elim, Adonai!* ("Who is like you among the gods, O Lord!"). The men of Judea rallied to the five sons of Mattathias—Judah, Johanan, Simon, Eliezer, and Jonathan—who became known as the "Maccabees."

THE REVOLT OF THE MACCABEES

Conditions in Judea grew steadily worse. Menelaus, the High Priest, had built a new stadium to encourage the young men of Judea to participate in Greek festivals and rituals. He had assisted the Syrians in erecting Greek altars throughout the land, and had burdened Judea with high taxes. He enforced the Syrian law according to which all who observed the laws and religion of Judaism were subject to torture and death.

The Priests and Levites were in despair. They

had left the desecrated Temple and many of them had joined the rebels in the Judean hills. Many of the Jewish Hellenists, who had only wanted to liberalize some of the Jewish laws, were horrified to see what Greek influence had done to their people. They had dreamed of a fused culture that would combine attractive features of both Greece and Israel. Instead, they found themselves forced to worship Greek idols and Antiochus Epiphanes. Many celebrations were held in honor of the god-king and the Hellenist Jews were forced to attend a religious rite for him every month.

Although the revolutionary movement in Judea was growing day by day, Antiochus refused to take it seriously. He felt secure with his highly trained and well-equipped army. He sent two detachments to Judea—one from Samaria and one from Syria—supremely confident that they would quickly annihilate the Jewish rebels.

Judah Maccabee, an able general and a fine strategist, avoided an open attack on the Syrian detachments. Biding his time, he first defeated the force from Samaria and later found an opportunity to ambush the other Syrian force in the narrow pass of Beth-Horon. The Syrians, taken by surprise, were routed. They fled in wild disorder, leaving their weapons and equipment behind—much to the delight of the rebels who had need of such supplies.

Silver shekel from the First Jewish Revolt against Rome, 66-70 B.C.E.

Antiochus sent out a fresh army with orders to crush the rebellion, even at the cost of destroying Judea. The new force came armed to the teeth, certain of victory and numbering forty thousand infantry and seven thousand cavalry.

Judah Maccabee's small army of six thousand untrained men were armed only with equipment they had managed to take from the enemy and with the few weapons that had been made in the crude forges of Judea. But the rebels had two advantages over Syria. First, they knew the Judean territory. Secondly, they were fighting for a prize of untold value—their freedom. They were desperately determined to make a firm stand against the Syrian attacks, no matter what the cost.

Again Judah avoided open battle. Instead, he made a surprise attack at night with three thousand men on the Syrian encampment at Emmaus. Again the Syrians, unable to rally in time, took flight. Syrian losses were heavy and their camp site was in flames. The Jews had won another great victory against overwhelming odds.

A fresh Syrian army was summoned from Idumea but this force also was successfully ambushed and put to rout near Beth-Zur by Judah Maccabee and his men.

Now the Judean roads were free and the triumphant Jews marched over them toward the Temple in Jerusalem. A dismaying sight greeted them on the Temple Mount—for the Temple was defiled by dirt and refuse and desecrated by idolatrous images. Together, the victorious Jews set about cleaning their house of worship. Judah Maccabee and his men were assisted in this task by the priests and by the people of Jerusalem. Joyfully this army of cleaners and polishers worked, and when their work was done they erected a new altar to their one God in order to rededicate themselves to their faith.

Maccabean tombs at Modin.

A very rare menorah of about the ninth century. The triangular trough for the shammash candle shows that this is a Hanukkah menorah.

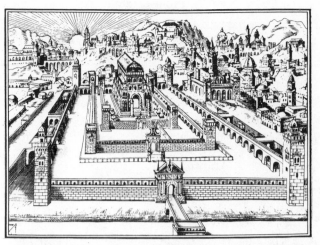

An artist's idea of the Bet Hamikdash, the Temple in Jerusalem. The large area, the Temple Mount, was surrounded by a wall.

On the 25th day of Kislev, 165 B.C.E., three years after its desecration, the Temple was rededicated. The Eternal Light and the golden Menorah were lit once more. The Menorah of those times had only seven branches. It may still be seen today depicted on the reliefs of the Arch of Titus in Rome.

Tradition tells us that the victors found only enough oil in the Temple to keep the Eternal Light burning for one day. Yet the Eternal Light and the golden Menorah burned for eight full days. The eight-branched Menorah of today and the annual eight-day celebration of Hanukkah, the Festival of Lights, commemorate the victory won for freedom by Judah Maccabee and his courageous followers.

GLOSSARY OF HEBREW TERMINOLOGY
AND NAMES

Circumcision	Meelah	מִילָה	Greece	Yahvahn	יָוָן
Hannah	Ḥahnah	חַנָּה	Alexander of Macedon	Ahleksahndros Mookdohn	אֲלֶכְסַנְדְּרוֹס מוּקְדוֹן
Eleazar	Elahzahr	אֶלְעָזָר	Jaddua	Yahdoo-ah	יַדּוּעַ
Modin	Mohdee-een	מוֹדִיעִין	Antigonus	Ahntignohs	אַנְטִיגְנוֹס
Mattathias	Mahtityahoo	מַתִּתְיָהוּ	Seleucus	Slevkoos	סְלֶיְקוֹס
Judah	Yhoodah	יְהוּדָה	Ptolemy	Tahlmai	תַּלְמַי
Maccabee	Mahkahbee	מַכַּבִּי	Septuagint	Targoom Ha-sheeveem	תַּרְגּוּם הַשִּׁבְעִים
Johanan	Yoḥahnahn	יוֹחָנָן			
Simon	Shimohn	שִׁמְעוֹן	Simon the Just	Shimohn Ha-tzadeek	שִׁמְעוֹן הַצַּדִּיק
Eliezer	Elee-ezer	אֶלִיעֶזֶר			
Jonathan	Yhohnahtahn	יְהוֹנָתָן	Hellenists	Mityahvneem	מִתְיַוְּנִים
High Priest	Koheyn Gahdohl	כֹּהֵן גָּדוֹל	Hassidim	Ḥaseedeem	חֲסִידִים
			Diaspora	Golah or Gahloot	גּוֹלָה, גָּלוּת
Beth-Zur	Beyt Tzoor	בֵּית צוּר			
Kislev	Kisleyv	כִּסְלֵו	Antiochus	Ahntyoḥos	אַנְטִיוֹכוֹס
Eternal Light	Neyr Tahmeed	נֵר תָּמִיד	Dietary Laws	Kahshroot	כַּשְׁרוּת
Hanukkah	Ḥahnookah	חֲנֻכָּה			

JUDEA BECOMES AN INDEPENDENT NATION

THE STRUGGLE FOR INDEPENDENCE

Although the Maccabees had won religious freedom for Judea, the country was still under the shadow of the tyrannical rule of Syria. However, in spite of their outnumbered forces and inferior equipment, the Jews continued to fight against the powerful Syrian army with grim determination. The battles were fierce and bloody and claimed the lives of many brave Judeans, among them Judah Maccabee's brother Eliezer. Thinking that he had sighted the Syrian king seated on a great elephant, Eliezer attempted to slay the enemy monarch. But he missed his mark, and succeeded only in wounding the elephant. The huge beast fell to the ground, crushing Eliezer to death beneath it.

Realizing the ever present danger, Judah Maccabee shrewdly decided to gain protection for Judea by making a pact with Rome, a rapidly growing power at that time.

For a time, this pact kept the Syrian kings at bay, for they were fearful of attacking an ally of a power as mighty as Rome. Gradually, however, this fear lessened and Syria again invaded Judea, regaining some of her old strongholds.

DEATH OF JUDAH MACCABEE

Not all the battles were victorious for the Syrians. Judah Maccabee succeeded in defeating a Syrian elephant corps near Beth-Horon. A month later, however, the Syrians returned with a fresh army of twenty-two thousand men. Against this overwhelming force Judah Maccabee pitted his army of eight hundred. Sheer bravery was not enough and the Judeans suffered a grave defeat.

Judea suffered a terrible loss; Judah Maccabee fell in battle. The beloved leader was carried home to Modin by his retreating soldiers and laid to rest beside his father.

Despite the loss of their great warrior leader, the Judeans stubbornly refused to submit to Syrian rule. The Jewish fighters retreated for a time to the old territory of Gilead, to the west of the Jordan. During this retreat Judah Maccabee's brother Johanan was killed in ambush.

Death had now taken all but two of the five brave brothers. Jonathan and Simon Maccabee still lived to carry on the struggle for independence. Jonathan, the new leader of Judea's freedom fighters, set up headquarters in Michmash, where King Saul had once defeated the Philistines.

The people came to regard Jonathan as their High Priest. While the Maccabees, sons of Mattathias the Hasmonean, were indeed of priestly descent, they were all only "ordinary" priests. They could not trace their ancestry back to Zadok, the noble High Priest of Solomon's day. Still the people held the Maccabees in great honor. Many Judeans began coming to Michmash to seek Jonathan's advice and guidance and to ask him to perform the priestly rituals and prayers for them.

SYRIA WEAKENS

Meantime, in Syria, much inner confusion and strife had begun. King Antiochus had died and the Syrian nobles were fighting each other over the

Copper half shekel of Simon Maccabeus.

right to the throne. Each contender, hoping to gain Judea's support, sent an envoy to Jonathan with messages of friendship, gifts and promises of peace.

Demetrius, strongest of the Syrian contenders for the throne, helped Jonathan enter Jerusalem, which was held by Syrian troops. The people of Jerusalem welcomed Jonathan joyfully, acclaiming him as their new High Priest. On the festival of Sukkot, 152 B.C.E., Jonathan performed the services in the Temple for the first time.

However, Demetrius was never to become king of Syria. Tryphon, a ruthless Syrian general, had designs on the throne. Tryphon not only hated Jonathan for supporting Demetrius but was bitterly envious of the Judean leader's popularity. Tryphon devised a treacherous plan to destroy Jonathan. He invited the Judean leader to his palace at Ptolemais on the Mediterranean coast. Jonathan accepted the invitation and went to the palace unarmed, believing the Syrian general to be his friend. Tryphon had his unsuspecting guest ruthlessly murdered. By a series of equally heartless schemes, Tryhon finally succeeded in becoming king of Syria.

SIMON RULES JUDEA

Simon, the last of the Maccabean brothers, succeeded Jonathan as High Priest. He immediately cut all bonds with Tryphon of Syria who had murdered his brother. By then, Syria was greatly

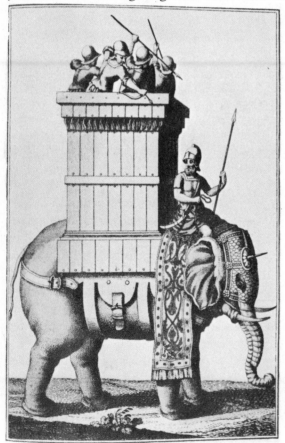

A Syrian war elephant.

Shekel of Simon Maccabeus, second year of Independence, 140-139 B.C.E.

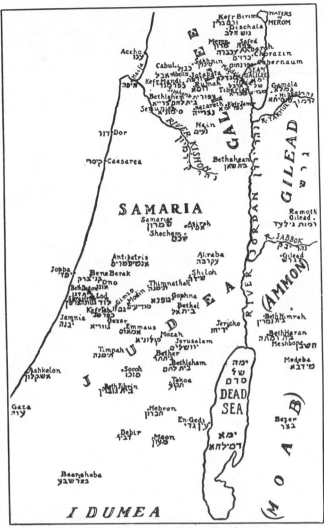

Map of Palestine in the days of the Maccabeans, according to Talmudic sources.

Simon, a wise ruler, brought happiness and prosperity to Judea. Jews came from Babylonia, Egypt and many distant lands to visit Jerusalem and the Temple. Traders came once again with their wares; richly laden caravans wended their way through the land. Simon captured the port of Jaffa on the Mediterranean Sea and greatly increased Judea's commerce.

Like his brother Judah, Simon realized that Rome was a power to be reckoned with. As Judah had done before him, Simon sent a delegation to Rome and a new pact was sealed between Rome and Judea, making them allies.

JOHN HYRCANUS SEEKS CONQUEST

Simon was succeeded at his death by his son, John Hyrcanus. John Hyrcanus was an ambitious man and wanted to extend the borders of Judea by conquering other lands. Taking advantage of the confusion that prevailed in Syria at that time, John Hyrcanus began his conquest. He captured Gaza and other coastal cities. He then attacked the weakened by inner strife. Simon began to expel from Jerusalem the Syrian soldiers who had been stationed there in the fortress of Acra since the days of Antiochus. Garrison by garrison, the Syrians were forced to abandon their stronghold in the ancient City of David, until finally the old fortress was manned entirely by Jewish soldiers. At last Judea was free from the Syrian yoke.

INDEPENDENCE AT LAST

For the first time in centuries, Judea was an independent nation, free of foreign rulers. The people rejoiced. Simon called a gathering of priests and leaders to represent the Judean community. This great assembly proclaimed Simon and his descendants High Priests and rulers of Judea.

A temple in the rock-cut city of Petra, the capital of Nabataea. John Hyrcanus expanded the borders of Israel and conquered Idumea and Nabataea, in Transjordan.

Page from Samaritan Bible. Damascus, 1485.

Samaritans, destroyed their temple on Mount Gerizim and incorporated Samaria into Judea.

After fortifying Judea's borders east of the Jordan to prevent an attack during his absence, John Hyrcanus began a new campaign. Turning south to Edom (Idumea), he conquered and annexed that country as King David had done before him. John Hyrcanus forced the Idumeans to adopt Judaism.

Like his father, John Hyrcanus was both High Priest and head of state. He struck new coins to commemorate his reign. Under his rule, Judea grew prosperous and expanded to the borders of what had once been King Solomon's empire. But many people were dissatisfied with the policies of their new ruler.

THE PHARISEES AND THE SADDUCEES

As a result of the discontent with John Hyrcanus, two opposing parties developed in Judea— the Pharisees and the Sadducees. These parties disagreed not only in politics but also with regard to the interpretation of the Torah.

The Sadducees were originally named after Zadok, the High Priest of Solomon's time. Most of the Sadducees were high-ranking priests, noblemen and wealthy merchants. They supported John Hyrcanus and his stern, literal interpretation of the Torah, often for the benefit of the upper classes. They were opposed by the Pharisees, who took their name from the Hebrew word *Perushim,* meaning "separatists." They were the more democratic spokesmen and were concerned with the welfare of the common people, they therefore advocated a less literal and in many cases a more flexible interpretation of the Law to do justice to existing conditions. At the same time they were dedicated to the preservation of tradition and strict loyalty to the spirit of the Torah.

After the death of John Hyrcanus, his son Aristobulus declared himself first king of Judea. This pleased the Sadducees, for they thought that Judea would now have a royal court, with all the pomp and wealth that went with it. But Aristobulus died after ruling for only one year. He was succeeded by his brother Alexander Jannai. Like his father John Hyrcanus, Alexander Jannai was a worldly man.

The aristocratic Sadducees gave Alexander Jannai their full support. During the twenty-seven years reign of Alexander Jannai, Judea was involved in many military campaigns. The king captured additional coastal cities, and some territories west of the Jordan.

The struggle between the Pharisees and Sadducees grew very bitter during this time. With the help of the king, the Sadducees obtained a majority in the Great Sanhedrin, which was both the law-giving body and Supreme Court of Judea.

THE ORAL TRADITION

The Pharisees and the Sadducees disagreed sharply on the question of the Oral Tradition (Unwritten Law). From time immemorial the Oral Tradition was handed down from generation to generation together with the written Torah. However, since the days of Ezra and the Scribes, the Oral Tradition had developed and grown into a discipline of law and ritual. Generations of Scribes had interpreted the meaning of individual laws of the Torah. More interpretations were needed, and added, to meet the requirements of changing political, economical and social conditions.

The Pharisees believed in the validity of the Oral Tradition. They viewed the Torah as a law to be understood by all the people and to be applied to every phase of daily living. Their scholars constantly worked to expand and to develop the Oral Tradition much as legal scholars in America today

A sofer, or scribe, writing in the traditional way in which scrolls of the Torah and other holy works have been set down since the days of the Second Temple.

interpret and reinterpret the Consitution for the Supreme Court of the United States so that the law of the land may be applied to any question that arises. In addition the Pharisees dealt with questions such as the meaning of life and the relationship between man and God. They were deeply committed to the task of educating the Jewish people.

The Sadducees, by contrast, did not recognize the Oral Tradition. They believed that the Torah was a strict, inflexible code, which could neither be discussed nor tampered with. The Sadducees felt that it was not necessary for the people to understand the laws of the Torah. They thought knowledge of the Law should be reserved for the priesthood.

But most of the people of Judea, believing that the Torah belonged to all Israel and not just to a select few, stood with the Pharisees.

THE PHARISEES BECOME THE MAJORITY PARTY

When Alexander Jannai had grown old and was nearing his death, he realized that the Pharisees were a strong force in Judea. Therefore he advised his wife and successor, Salome Alexandra, to grant the Pharisees a more active part in the affairs of government. Accordingly, Queen Salome appointed a Pharisee, her brother Simon ben Shetah, as the new president to the Sanhedrin. The Queen's choice was a wise one, for Simon ben Shetah was a learned, able man who contributed much to edu-

cation and instituted many good laws.

AN ERA OF PEACE

Queen Salome's reign was an era of peace. She drew many capable honest men into the government and established a fairer balance between the two parties in the Sanhedrin. The Pharisees had always believed that the sacred office of the High Priest should be separated from the kingship, but Alexander Jannai had steadily refused to give in to this demand. Now, in the reign of Queen Salome, this separation was made. While the Queen acted as head of the state, her son Hyrcanus acted as High Priest. Another son, Aristobulus, assisted her in her royal functions.

Pleased by this separation of state and priesthood, the Pharisees loyally supported the Queen. They were now the majority party in the Sanhedrin and used their power well. They saw to it that only fair-dealing, responsible men, familiar with Jewish law and the decisions transmitted in the Oral Tradition should be appointed judges. Guided by their leader, Simon ben Shetah, the Pharisees improved the Judean school system. Many well-trained teachers were sent out into the communities of Judea to teach young people to read and write, and to instruct them in the study of the Torah. At a time when many peoples of the ancient world were illiterate, many of the people of the little country of Judea not only could read and write but were familiar with their religion, their laws, their literature and history. Thus, during the seven years of Salome Alexandra's reign, Judea prospered and flourished.

CIVIL WAR IN JUDEA

After Salome's death her two sons, Aristobulus and Hyrcanus, contended for the crown. Jew fought Jew in a bitter civil war which lasted for five years. Finally, the warring factions turned to Pompey, the Roman general, asking him to arbitrate their dispute. Pompey, who was then waging a victorious campaign in Asia Minor, had just taken Damascus. To this great general came three separate Judean delegations seeking protection and help: one group representing Hyrcanus; another representing Aristobulus; and the third, a delega-

Model of a warship in the maritime museum of Haifa reconstructed from a wall painting in a Jerusalem catacomb.

tion of Pharisees, representing the Judean people. The Pharisees asked Pompey to choose neither of the sons of Salome but to restore rule by the High Priest who would be aided by the Sanhedrin. Pompey, thinking first of what would be best for Rome, decided in favor of Hyrcanus, the weaker contender. Soon after this decision, Pompey's legions overran Judea. The Judean cities were unprepared and were easy prey for the Romans. Jerusalem was besieged for three months, then finally, one Sabbath, fell to the Romans. Thousands of Jews lost their lives and many others were taken captive. Aristobulus was taken prisoner and carried off by Pompey to Rome along with scores of other Jewish captives.

After almost eighty years of independence, Judea was once again under the domination of a foreign power. The Judean coastal cities and Mediterranean ports now became part of the Roman province of Syria. Hyrcanus was reinstated as High Priest but his power was subject to the control of Rome. Antipater, an Idumean, acted as advisor to Hyrcanus. Soon the power of Hyrcanus was further reduced by Rome. Prince Alexander, son of Aristobulus, had escaped while he was being deported to Rome. Gathering together an army, he tried to overthrow the rule of his uncle Hyrcanus. Alexander was soon defeated by Gabinius, Syria's Roman proconsul, and the unfortunate revolt only led to further loss of freedom for Judea. The new Roman province of Palestine was divided into five districts, and Hyrcanus was left governing only the small district of Jerusalem.

TROUBLE IN ROME

Meanwhile, Rome had ceased to be a republic. A bitter struggle broke out between Pompey and Julius Caesar for control of the empire. In order to weaken Pompey's power in Judea, Caesar freed Hyrcanus' brother, Aristobulus, equipped him with an army and encouraged him to start a revolt. But the proposed rebellion did not come off. Aristobulus was poisoned in Rome and his son Alexander was executed by Pompey in Antioch.

Rome was torn in two by the struggle between

Copper coin of Salome Alexandra.

Bust of Pompey.

Bust of Julius Caesar.

Pompey and Caesar. Caesar marched against Pompey and defeated him. Pompey fled to Egypt, where he was murdered by his own men.

A JUDEAN SUPPORTS CAESAR

Caesar now rallied all his might to keep his power in Rome. In Judea he won the support of Hyrcanus and his advisor, Antipater. Antipater was a clever, scheming man. He came from Idumea, where his family had been forced to convert to Judaism in the days of John Hyrcanus' conquest of the Idumeans. Antipater had been the chief advisor of Hyrcanus during the civil war in Judea. Now Antipater rose to great political power. Together with Hyrcanus, he strongly supported the cause of Julius Caesar.

A Jewish army of three thousand men fought with Caesar's legions in his campaign in Egypt. In this campaign, Caesar defeated Ptolemy XII, the husband of Cleopatra. Cleopatra became the ruler of Egypt, now a vassal of Rome.

In gratitude for the help the Jews had given him in Egypt, Caesar reinstated Hyrcanus in both his priestly and secular positions. Hyrcanus was made an *ethnarch,* which means a ruler in the name of Rome. Caesar decreed that the office of ethnarch was to be hereditary in the Hasmonean family. Caesar also rewarded Antipater with the high honor of Roman citizenship.

During the short period he was in power, Julius Caesar considered himself a friend of the Jews and acknowledged them as allies of Rome. In Egypt, he restored to the Jewish residents of Alexandria their old rights of citizenship which they had lost. In Judea, he supported both Hyrcanus and Antipater as leaders of the Jewish community.

ANTIPATER BECOMES FIRST PROCURATOR

Caesar knew nothing about the Judeans' resent-

Portrait coin of Cleopatra.

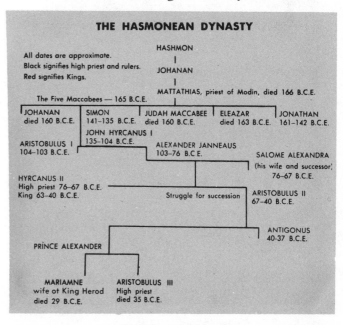

THE HASMONEAN DYNASTY

HASHMON

All dates are approximate.
Black signifies high priest and rulers.
Red signifies Kings.

JOHANAN

MATTATHIAS, priest of Modin, died 166 B.C.E.

The Five Maccabees — 165 B.C.E.

| JOHANAN died 160 B.C.E. | SIMON 141–135 B.C.E. | JUDAH MACCABEE died 160 B.C.E. | ELEAZAR died 163 B.C.E. | JONATHAN 161–142 B.C.E. |

JOHN HYRCANUS I 135–104 B.C.E.

ARISTOBULUS I 104–103 B.C.E.

ALEXANDER JANNEAUS 103–76 B.C.E.

SALOME ALEXANDRA (his wife and successor) 76–67 B.C.E.

HYRCANUS II High priest 76–67 B.C.E. King 63–40 B.C.E.

Struggle for succession

ARISTOBULUS II 67–40 B.C.E.

ANTIGONUS 40-37 B.C.E.

PRINCE ALEXANDER

MARIAMNE wife of King Herod died 29 B.C.E.

ARISTOBULUS III High priest died 35 B.C.E.

ment of Antipater. Many Jews considered Antipater an outsider because he was an Idumean, and the Idumeans had become converted to Judaism only recently. They felt that he could not possibly understand Judea. Many knew how selfish and ambitious he was, and they bitterly resented his rise to power.

Unaware of all this, Caesar appointed Antipater to a most important office. He made him the first Roman procurator in Judea. The procurators were the direct representatives of Rome in the various Roman dominions.

As soon as he became procurator, Antipater appointed his own two sons as governors of Judea's districts. His older son, Phasael, a just and conscientious man, was made governor of Jerusalem. The governorship of Galilee was held by his younger son, a brilliant but ruthlessly ambitious man named Herod.

HEROD BECOMES RULER

While Herod was governor of Galilee, rebels gathered in the Galilean hills to prepare for a re-

King Herod built the city of Caesarea as a seat of government for the Roman procurators. He named it "Caesarea" in honor of Caesar Augustus. All that now remains of this once busy Palestinian deep water port are fragmented stone pillars awash in the Mediterranean Sea.

Relief from a Jewish sarcophagus found in Rome, showing a seven branch menorah.

volt against Rome. These partisans and their leader, Hezekiah, wanted to fight for Jewish independence. Herod discovered their activities and had the partisans arrested; then he ordered that they be executed to the last man.

The news of Herod's cruelty shocked the Great Sanhedrin in Jerusalem. Herod was summoned to appear before the Sanhedrin to stand trial for his action. Accused men usually came before the Sanhedrin dressed in black, as a sign of their humility. Herod, however, entered the court dressed in the purple garments of a prince, and surrounded by his soldiers. The men of the Sanhedrin would have wanted to punish Herod severely, but they had to be lenient with him because he had the strong protection of Hyrcanus, the High Priest. Herod, a man of violent temper, wanted to revenge himself on the Sanhedrin and on the people of Jerusalem for having called him to account. Only his father, Antipater, managed to keep him from storming the city with his soldiers.

Unfortunately for Judea, Caesar, who had been its protector, was murdered in Rome. Caesar's supporters and the last of the Roman republicans fought each other bitterly. Caesar's supporters, Octavian and Marc Antony, won the upper hand in the battle of Philippi.

Marc Antony became the ruler of Asia. Jewish delegations went to see him repeatedly to complain about Herod's cruelty. Marc Antony did not listen, for Herod had already become his personal friend.

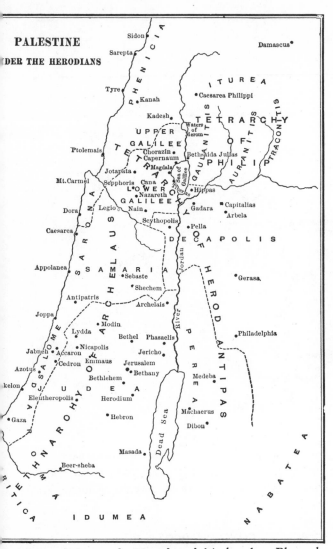

PALESTINE
UNDER THE HERODIANS

Rome drove back the Parthians, but Antigonus continued to rule Judea. Antigonus felt secure in his rule, though Herod's family and his supporters were still encamped outside Jerusalem in the fortress of Masada.

Herod himself was not in Masada. Herod, the clever politician, had sailed for Rome. There he appeared before Marc Antony and Octavian with expensive presents. Herod must have been a man of great personal charm. Despite the difficult situation in Judea, he convinced his Roman friends that he was the only one who could keep Judea under control. He pointed out that he had always been a loyal friend of Rome while Antigonus had treacherously supported the Parthian invasion. Herod made his point with the Romans. He returned home as king of Judea.

HEROD BECOMES KING OF JUDEA

With the help of Roman legions, Herod entered Judea, his new kingdom. He laid siege to Jerusalem, and after five months of fighting, the city surrendered. Herod immediately executed forty-five of Jerusalem's noble citizens, for he wanted no opposition. Antigonus, too, was executed by the Romans.

Herod did not want to rule in Judea by tyranny alone. He wanted to be the true king of the land. While he laid siege to Jerusalem, he had married Mariamne, a Hasmonean princess. By connecting himself with the ancient Hasmonean dynasty he hoped to win the support of the people.

Instead, he made Herod and his brother Phasael *tetrarchs,* or co-rulers, of Judea.

ANTIGONUS OVERTHROWS HEROD

Suddenly the Parthians, who now ruled Babylonia, invaded the Roman province of Palestine. The Parthians found an ally in Antigonus, the last surviving son of Aristobulus. Antigonus gathered all the discontented groups under his leadership. These joined the invaders and took advantage of the fighting to overthrow the rulers of Judea. Hyrcanus was taken captive by the Parthians. Antipater died, and the fighting still continued against his sons. Herod, his brother, and all his supporters, were driven out of Jerusalem. For three years, Antigonus ruled as king of Judea.

Portrait coin of Emperor Marc Antony, 41 B.C.E.

111

The Roman Empire ruled all the lands around the Mediterranean Sea. The Parthians ruled Babylonia to the east.

HEROD'S REIGN OF TERROR

Herod the Idumean proved to be a cruel ruler. He was very ambitious, and he craved splendor and fame. He never really felt secure on the throne of Judea, and he suspected rebellion and danger everywhere. Many people had to pay with their lives because of Herod's fears.

In the early days of his reign, he appointed Aristobulus, Mariamne's younger brother, as High Priest. Aristobulus was popular, and people would cheer him as he passed through the streets. They were happy to see him officiate in the Temple. All this alarmed Herod. Afraid that his well-liked brother-in-law would become the center of a revolt against him, he had Aristobulus murdered.

Herod was also afraid of Hyrcanus, who had returned from Parthian captivity a broken old man. Hyrcanus was falsely accused of plotting a revolt and was executed. Eventually, Herod came to mistrust even Mariamne, his own wife, and he put her to death. Herod lived in fear that a Hasmonean would take the throne from him. He sought to make his position secure by a reign of terror and murder.

HEROD'S ECONOMIC PROSPERITY

Despite his cruelty, history refers to Herod as "Herod the Great." While the Judeans hated and feared Herod, the Romans admired him for bringing wealth to their empire. Herod increased the trade of Judea. Situated between Syria and Egypt, Judea was crossed by the great trade routes that ran east and west. Caravans coming from Arabia and Persia would make their first stop in Judea. Traders even came from distant India. And ships

Copper coin of King Antigonus.

Jerash in the mountains of Gilead, one of the cities of the "League of Ten Cities."

A view of the Talmudic city of Tiberias, named by Herod in honor of Emperor Tiberius.

from Greece and Africa landed at Judea's Mediterranean ports.

Herod gained control of several free cities on the coast of Judea which had been built by Greek and Roman settlers. These cities had been part of a confederation called the *Decapolis,* or "League of Ten Cities." As part of Judea, they brought new wealth to the country. Herod collected high taxes from his people. Some of the money went to Rome, and some for his own Judean projects.

HEROD AS A GREAT BUILDER

Herod delighted in building elaborate structures and he built new cities and named many of them in honor of his Roman friends: Tiberias, in honor of the emperor Tiberius; and the coastal city of Caesarea, in honor of Caesar. He also built amphitheatres and arenas, where gladiators and captives had to fight and wrestle with untamed beasts, as was the custom in the arenas of Rome.

Herod's most ambitious building project was the improvement and enlargement of the Temple. For five hundred years the Temple, built by the returning Babylonian exiles, had served as the Sanctuary. It was a small building of simple de-

sign, which was deteriorating with age. It was not at all like the splendid Temple of Solomon's reign. Herod spared no cost or effort in rebuilding the Temple. Portion by portion, his workmen and architects restored and improved it. Throughout his reign, Herod continued work on the Temple compound. The building was begun in 20 B.C.E. and was only finished after Herod's death in 4 C.E.

Herod's Temple Compound was magnificent. All through the lands of Asia Minor people marveled at its beauty and splendor. Like all of Herod's buildings, it was built in the classic Greek style. Herod raised a strong wall around all the Temple grounds, and above the main gate he placed an eagle, the golden emblem of Rome.

The Jews were deeply offended. How could they allow this warlike emblem to disgrace the peaceful sanctuary of God? One day, while Herod lay ill, the rumor spread that he was dead. At once, a group of Pharisees rushed to the Temple gate and removed the hated Roman emblem. When Herod recovered and heard of this occurrence, he was enraged and had the men put to death.

The beauty of Herod's Temple gave him prestige abroad, but it did not win him the love of his people.

THE TRUE LEADERS OF JUDEA

The people of Judea no longer looked to their king or even their High Priest for leadership, for the High Priest was appointed by Herod, and, after the reign of Herod, by Rome. Instead, they looked for guidance to the scholars and teachers of the

One of the high level aqueducts built by Herod.

Torah, the men of the Great Sanhedrin. Despite the tyranny of Herod and his Roman successors, learning still flourished in Judea. The Oral Tradition helped the people in the difficult problems of everyday life, under the pressure of Roman rule.

The chain of tradition started, according to the *Tractate Aboth* of the *Mishnah,* with Moses who handed it over to Joshua, who in turn handed it over to the Elders. From them it came down to the prophets who handed it over to the Men of the Great Assembly. The latter were the Scribes, and they were the scholars who were the real spiritual leaders of the people. The Great Sanhedrin, the highest religious authority, was usually composed of seventy-one scholars who followed in the footsteps of the sages of the Great Assembly. Jerusalem became the center of Jewish learning. Students and scholars would come from Egypt and Babylonia, from Syria and Persia, to study with the

Warning-Stone from Herod's temple, discovered in 1871, now in the museum at Constantinople. It stood originally at the top of one of the stairs that led to the Court of Israel. The warning, written in large Greek characters, reads as follows: "Let no foreigner enter within the balustrade and embankment about the sanctuary. Whoever is caught makes himself responsible for his death which will follow."

scholars of the Great Sanhedrin and to hear their interpretations of the laws of the Torah.

HOW THE SANHEDRIN FUNCTIONED

The Great Sanhedrin was presided over by two leaders, known as *Zugot,* meaning "pairs." The Zugot consisted of a *Nasi,* which means "Prince" or "Chief," and an *Av Bet Din,* which means "Presiding Judge."

Usually the Nasi would be the more conservative of the two, while the Av Bet Din would lead the opposition. Their discussions were often sharp and brilliant and many of the debates and legal decisions of the Zugot became famous. The most famous of these Zugot or "pairs" of scholars were Hillel and Shammai.

Copper coin of Herod.

HILLEL'S GREATNESS

Hillel was a brilliant young man, who had come to Judea from Babylonia in the days of Hyrcanus. He wanted to study with Shemayah and Abtalion, who were the leaders of the Sanhedrin at that time. Hillel was very poor but he loved learning. In Jerusalem he earned the money to pay for admission to the lectures at the academy by cutting wood and by doing other hard physical labor. But there were times when he could not even earn the small fee he needed.

One cold winter's night when he did not have the admission fee, Hillel lay atop the roof of the schoolhouse where he listened to the lectures until he fell asleep from exhaustion. The next morning, when the academy assembled, the scholars found the hall exceptionally dark. Looking up at the skylight, they found the sleeping Hillel blocking the

Remains of a first century, B.C.E., Herodian building. The style is a mixture of Greek and Roman.

HILLEL AND SHAMMAI

Shammai was a brilliant scholar who came from a wealthy, noble family of Jerusalem. He was stern and conservative. He argued the law with Hillel, who usually took the more lenient, flexible view. Hillel's deep concern was that all the Jews should be able to observe the Law. Shammai, on the other hand, interpreted the law so strictly that not everyone was able to live up to the standards he preached. Shammai was a pious scholar, devoted to preserving the Law and the Jewish way of life.

The famous legalistic debates between Hillel and Shammai caused a great stir in the Jewish communities of their day. Wherever Jews assembled, studied and prayed, the teachings of Hillel and Shammai would be discussed.

sun. Touched by the young man's great devotion to learning, the teachers provided Hillel with a scholarship so that he could attend the lectures without having to do exhausting labor to earn his admission fees.

Hillel became a great scholar. For a short time, he returned to Babylonia to teach. But he was recalled to Jerusalem to join the Great Sanhedrin. His wisdom and learning were recognized by Jewish scholars everywhere.

Once Hillel was asked to tell what he considered the fundamental principle of Judaism. His famous answer was: "What is hateful to you, do not do unto others. All the rest of the Torah is merely an explanation of this rule." Hillel said that the way to the law, and to God, was to love peace and to love mankind. He valued the unity of Israel above all, and warned his students never to set themselves apart from the community of the Jewish people.

So greatly respected was Hillel that the office of Nasi of the Sanhedrin became hereditary in his family.

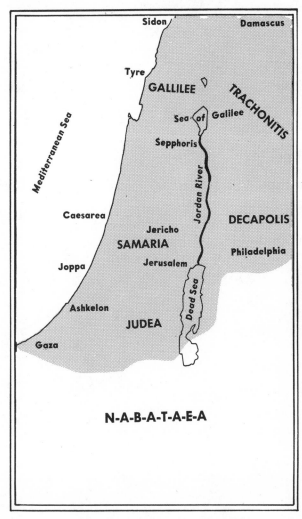

Map of Israel in the time of Hillel.

GLOSSARY OF HEBREW TERMINOLOGY
AND NAMES

Salome	Shlohmtzee-yohn	שְׁלוֹמְצִיּוֹן	Michmash	Miḥmahsh	מִכְמָשׁ
			Hasmoneans	Ḥahshmohnah-eem	חַשְׁמוֹנָאִים
Simon ben Shetah	Shimohn ben Shetaḥ	שִׁמְעוֹן בֶּן שֶׁטַח	Zadok	Tzahdohk	צָדוֹק
Herod	Hohrdohs	הוֹרְדוֹס	Hyrcanus	Hohrknohs	הוֹרְקְנוֹס
Galilee	Gahleel	גָּלִיל	Pharisees	Proosheem	פְּרוּשִׁים
Masada	Mtzahdah	מְצָדָה	Sadducees	Tzedookeem	צְדוֹקִים
Tiberias	Tveryah	טְבֶרְיָה	Aristobulus	Ahreestohvlohs	אֲרִיסְטוֹבְלוֹס
Pairs	Zoogoht	זוּגוֹת	Alexander Jannai	Ahleḥsahndehr Yahnai	אָלֶכְסַנְדֶּר יַנַּאי
Prince	Nahsee	נָשִׂיא	Sanhedrin	Sahnhedreen	סַנְהֶדְרִין
Presiding Judge	Ahv Beyt Deen	אַב בֵּית דִּין	Oral Tradition	Torah Sheb'ahl Peh	תּוֹרָה שֶׁבְּעַל פֶּה
Hillel	Hileyl	הִלֵּל	Written Torah	Torah Shebiḥtahv	תּוֹרָה שֶׁבִּכְתָב
Shammai	Shahmai	שַׁמַּי			
Shemayah	Shmahyah	שְׁמַעְיָה			
Abtalion	Ahvtahlyohn	אַבְטַלְיוֹן			

HEROD'S SUCCESSORS

REVOLT IN JUDEA

After Herod's death, revolt flared up in Judea. The people could not forget Herod's cruelty, and did not want to be ruled by his son Archelaus, who was to succeed him as king. Herod's two other sons, Antipas and Philip, also ignored Archelaus' claim to the throne, for Herod had promised them each a part of his kingdom.

Three delegations from Judea each asked Rome to decide in their favor. The Pharisees wanted all the sons of Herod removed from rule. Antipas and Philip wanted their own claims recognized, and Archelaus wanted to be the sole king of Judea, as his father had been. The Emperor Augustus divided the kingdom among all the three brothers, making each one of them an ethnarch. Philip ruled the district east of Galilee, Antipas ruled Galilee and Perea, and Archelaus ruled Judea, Samaria and Idumea. Philip was just and fair but Archelaus and Antipas followed in their father's footsteps. After a reign of ten years, Archelaus was deposed and replaced by Roman procurators.

JUDEA BECOMES A ROMAN POSSESSION

Judea, with Samaria and Idumea, was now a Roman possession, ruled by Roman procurators.

Relief of Emperor Augustus.

These officials were cruel and ruthless. They collected high taxes, of which they took a good portion for themselves. Garrisons of Roman soldiers were stationed throughout the land.

Most of the Roman procurators cared little about the people they governed. Mostly their only concern was to send treasures and tax money to Rome in order to impress the Roman emperors

117

and further their own careers. Many of them ruthlessly filled their own coffers, and when their term of office was over they went back to Rome rich and powerful.

Judea suffered greatly under the rule of the procurators. Still, the people never gave up the hope of shaking off this burden. They longed to be free, to be ruled once again by a just High Priest and by the Great Sanhedrin. Some still hoped fervently to throw off Roman bondage altogether, and to regain full political independence.

THE SPIRIT OF REBELLION

The spirt of revolt against oppression never died in Judea. The people chafed under Roman rule. When the Emperor Augustus ordered a census to be taken, many were roused to open resistance. It seemed to the Jews an addtional humiliation to be counted like cattle.

In the hills of Galilee, guerilla fighters rallied to Judah, the son of the partisan leader Hezekiah, whom Herod had executed. These rebels wanted to fight Rome at all costs. Despite the obvious military superiority of their enemy, they felt compelled to oppose Rome to show their spirit of independence.

THE PHARISEES OPPOSE REBELLION

The Pharisees and the Great Sanhedrin in Jerusalem opposed this rebellion. They believed in passive resistance marked by constant devotion to Jewish Law. According to the Pharisees,

Roman soldiers in battle dress.

faith, study and a just way of life were the only ways to hasten the coming of freedom and peace. They felt that open rebellion against Rome, like the earlier revolts against Assyria and Babylonia, would end in utter destruction.

THE REBELS FORM A PARTY

The zealous rebels were violently opposed to the pacifism of the Pharisees. They founded their own party, and called themselves the *Zealots*. Many of the more extreme Zealots formed partisan bands in the Galilean hills. They ambushed Roman transports, and they would come down to the villages at night to attack Roman patrols. The Zealots considered themselves the militant guardians of Jewish dignity. They even killed many Jews whom they suspected of treachery and sympathy with Rome. Day and night Roman soldiers patrolled the roads to prevent these acts of rebellion.

Temple of Augustus.

LONGING FOR THE MESSIAH

Those were terrible days for the people under Roman rule. They had to pay exorbitant taxes. Many who were suspected of sabotage against Rome were tortured in Roman prisons. Many people were executed by crucifixion. Many lost all hope that conditions would ever improve. They saw all the suffering, disunity, corruption, and cruelty and wondered when and how it would all end.

The ancient prophets had foretold an era of peace and justice, to be heralded by the coming of the Messiah. According to the prophets, the Messiah or "Anointed One," a descendant of the House of David, would bring a golden age of peace, when mankind would be freed from all its suffering. Many people felt that only the Messiah would be able to end their despair.

THE ESSENES

The yearning for the Messiah led to the formation of sects generally described as *Apocalyptists*. The ideas of the Apocalyptists influenced many religious sects in Judea. The best-known of these sects were the Essenes. The Essenes were dedicated to a life of purity, study and charity. They owned no property as individuals, but held everything in common. It is possible that their manner of living was inspired by the teachings of the prophets of old. The Essenes were not permitted to live in families, and very few women were allowed to join their sect.

Most of the Essenes lived together in secluded communities, following their own strict rules. They were extreme pacifists, totally opposed to war and bloodshed. They ate no meat and lived frugally. Many of them would wander out into the desert

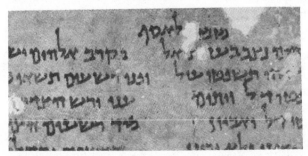

A fragment from one of the Dead Sea Scrolls. Compare Psalm 82: 1-4.

Ancient jars found in caves at Qumran, containing some of the famous Dead Sea Scrolls. These scrolls may have been written by a sect of Essenes living under Roman rule.

for long periods of fasting, meditation, and prayer. They would immerse themselves in ritual baths to symbolize inner purity.

As the Essenes developed their own ways, they veered away from some of the old rituals of Judaism. Many Essenes wandered through the land and preached to the people, and often put forward their own ideas.

The famous Dead Sea Scrolls, which were recently discovered in a cave near the site of En-Gedi, are a rich source of information about the beliefs and rituals of these ancient sects.

THE PREACHER JOHANAN

In the days of Antipas, there was a wandering preacher by the name of Johanan, who was to become known in history as John the Baptist. It is believed that he may have belonged to the Essene sect, or to some other apocalyptic group. He spoke

119

of the coming of a better world, and of the Messiah who would soon appear to bring it about. John led his followers into the Jordan and bathed their heads, in a symbolic act of purification. This act, which resembled the ritual bath of the Essenes, later became known as baptism.

News of this preacher reached Antipas, and he feared that his sermons would stir the people to revolt. Thus, like many other rebels, John the Baptist was arrested and executed.

JESUS OF NAZARETH

Among those who listened to John's sermons and were baptized by him was a young man from Nazareth named Joshua—or Jesus. Jesus had been influenced by his meeting with John the Baptist. Eventually, Jesus also traveled through the land with a band of disciples.

Jesus was familiar with the words of the great sages, and would frequently quote the wise sayings of the Rabbis. But his own teachings differed from those of the Pharisees. Jewish scholars based their opinions on the Oral Tradition, but Jesus did not do only this. He also spoke in his own name and challenged the accepted spiritual authorities. This was a bold thing to do, for even the great prophets of old had not acted so independently. They had humbly introduced their visions with the words: "Thus saith the Lord." But Jesus would say: "*I say unto you.*" This simple introduction overawed his followers and soon it was said among them that their leader was none other than the Messiah himself.

PONTIUS PILATE CRUCIFIES JESUS

In the year 30 C.E., at the time of Passover,

A view overlooking the city of Nazareth.

Stone inscription of the name of Pontius Pilate, found in the ruins of Caesarea.

Jesus went to Jerusalem. During the festivals, when the city would be crowded with pilgrims, Jerusalem was often a hotbed of revolt. To keep the people in check, the Roman procurator, Pontius Pilate, had ordered that Roman soldiers should constantly patrol the thoroughfares and the busy streets of the city. That year in the crowded streets, the disciples of Jesus proclaimed their master as the Messiah. As Jesus attracted more followers the Roman procurator looked upon him with apprehension. Later, Roman soldiers brought Jesus before Pontius Pilate. He was accused of rabble-rousing and of pretending to be the Messiah, the "King of the Jews." Pontius Pilate condemned Jesus to be executed by crucifixion.

THE FOLLOWERS OF JESUS

The followers of Jesus of Nazareth, who was also called the Nazarene, remained together even after the death of their leader. It was whispered among them that the dead Messiah had risen from his grave. Thus the followers of Jesus, those Jews from the Galilean hills who now called themselves Nazarenes, unsuspectingly were the founders of a whole new religion—Christianity.

At the time, the crucifixion of Jesus was but one of the many cruel acts of Pontius Pilate in Judea. So many complaints reached Rome about this ruthless procurator that he was eventually relieved of his post and had to leave Judea.

Copper coin of Agrippa I.

A HASMONEAN BECOMES KING OF JUDEA

A grandson of Herod and Mariamne, named Agrippa, was living in Rome in captivity. Although he was a captive, Agrippa had many friends among the young Romans. After the death of the ethnarch Philip, Gaius Caligula, the new Emperor of Rome, gave Agrippa the small tetrarchy of Galilee to rule.

The Emperor Claudius, who succeeded Caligula soon thereafter, extended Agrippa's kingdom to include all of Galilee and Judea. Once again a descendant of the Maccabees, through his grandmother Mariamne, became king over Judean territories.

CLAUDIUS REIGNS WITH TOLERANCE

Claudius was a tolerant ruler. During his reign the people of Judea again breathed the air of freedom. They could read and think as they pleased without fear of punishment. They could argue and state their own opinions openly.

During the reign of Claudius, the Jews found new friends. Queen Helena, who ruled the little kingdom of Adiabene in northern Mesopotamia

Model of the Temple built by Herod the Great. He started it in 20 B.C.E. but it was not completed until 64 C.E.

and had become a convert to Judaism, came with her retinue to visit Jerusalem. She brought gifts to the Temple and, together with her nobles, offered prayers there. The year in which she visited Jerusalem was a year of famine and the queen donated a large sum of money to help relieve the hunger of Judea's poor.

Like Queen Helena, many non-Jews at this time

Outside the city of Jerusalem, some distance to the north, is a rock-hewn site popularly known as the Tombs of the Kings. It was originally prepared about 60 C.E. as the tomb of Queen Helena of Adiabene. At the entrance of the tomb proper is a movable rolling stone by which the entrance could be closed.

had become interested in the ideas of Judaism. They had learned about Judaism from the Septuagint, the Greek translation of the Bible. Since Greek was the international language throughout the Greek and Roman period, the Septuagint was widely read. Many people converted to Judaism and asked to be allowed to join Jewish communities. The kingdom of Adiabene remained loyal to Judaism and later, in the days of the Jewish war against Rome, sent help to the fighters of Judea.

AGRIPPA I AND II

King Agrippa I reigned over a territory almost as large as that which had been under the scepter of Herod. Unlike his grandfather Herod, Agrippa was a pious Jew, and a fair and just king. Each

Bust of Agrippa, general of Augustus.

Agrippa II ruled only over Philip's old, small northeastern district but although his political power was limited, Agrippa II was a courageous spokesman for his people before the Romans. However, he was unable to prevent new procurators from governing Judea and Galilee with the harshness customary among Roman officials.

Copper coin of Agrippa II, in the eleventh year of his reign.

year on the festival of Sukkot, he would read from the Book of Deuteronomy before the assembled people, as King Josiah had done long ago.

Agrippa was concerned for the safety of Jerusalem. He began the building of a third, strong wall to protect the north side of the city. But this project remained unfinished. After a reign of only three years, he died and his son Agrippa II succeeded him.

GLOSSARY OF HEBREW TERMINOLOGY AND NAMES

Pharisees	Proosheem	פְּרוּשִׁים
Sanhedrin	Sahnhedreen	סַנְהֶדְרִין
Zealots	Kahnah-eem	קַנָּאִים
Messiah	Mahshee-aḥ	מָשִׁיחַ
Essenes	Eeseeyeem	אִסִּיִּים
Dead Sea Scrolls	Mgeeloht Yahm Hamelaḥ	מְגִלּוֹת יַם הַמֶּלַח
En-Gedi	Eyn Gedee	עֵין גֶּדִי
John the Baptist	Yoḥahnahn Hahmahtbeel	יוֹחָנָן הַמַּטְבִּיל
Nazareth	Nahtzeret	נַצֶּרֶת
Jesus	Yeyshoo	יֵשׁוּ

THE JEWISH WAR WITH ROME

THE ZEALOTS RESIST ROME

The Zealots were the most extreme of the Jewish patriots. They hated Rome and all it stood for. They had pledged themselves to resist the power of Rome and they considered every Jew who collaborated with the Romans as their enemy. The Zealots regarded themselves as the successors of the Hasidim and the valiant Maccabees. From their headquarters in the Galilean mountains the Zealots conducted guerrilla warfare against Rome and its sympathizers, ambushing transports of Roman soldiers and tax collectors, and attacking Jewish towns where Roman feasts and games were conducted. Greeks, Romans and Jewish collaborators came to fear the fighting Zealots, whose influence among the Jewish population was steadily growing.

The resistance of the Zealots became a constant problem to the Roman procurators. The procurator Felix captured Eleazar, the leader of the Zealots, and sent him to Rome as a captive. But this act only spurred the Zealots to further rebellion. The Greek and Roman population of Caesarea lived in open enmity with the Zealots. Even the Jews of Jerusalem, led by the men of the Great Sanhedrin, did not approve of their attitude. The men of the Great Sanhedrin advocated a policy of peace. Thus the growing fanaticism of the Zealots became a serious danger to Jewish unity which almost plunged Judea into civil war.

THE REBELLION AGAINST FLORUS

Florus was the last Roman procurator of Judea. When he came to Judea, he was greeted by a rebellious people. But he took no interest in the problems of the Jews. He was ruled only by his own greed and ambition. He increased taxes, which were already high, because he was in constant need of money, ever eager to fill his own pockets. Evenutally, he took a great sum of gold from the Temple treasury.

The Jews were indignant. Their Temple funds had been raised by voluntary taxes that they had imposed on themselves. The fund supported the people's own religious institutions, schools, and charitable work. Despite the high taxes, people still gave this money gladly. But to the poor shepherds and farmers, the small shopkeepers and craftsmen, giving to the Temple fund often meant a great sacrifice. And much of this money came from Jewish communities in distant lands.

The streets of Jerusalem were buzzing with discontent. Some of the people showed their contempt for Florus by a practical joke. They took the baskets that were used for collecting money for the poor, and passed them around on the streets, full of jingling coins, crying "Alms for Florus! Alms for poor, poor Florus!"

Florus was enraged, and sent out his soldiers to punish the pranksters. Many were killed in the streets of Jerusalem, and homes were plundered. Florus was still not satisfied. He ordered reinforcements from Caesarea.

INDEPENDENT JERUSALEM

The people of Jerusalem, led by the Zealots, armed themselves to fight the Romans. They would not passively accept punishment. Men, women, and children helped defend their city. The Romans were unable to hold their fortress in Jerusalem. They gave up the palace, where Florus had lived, and were forced to leave the city. Instead of inflicting cruel punishment, the Romans had to acknowledge defeat.

Soon another Roman army appeared before Jerusalem but this army also was forced to leave the city. Jerusalem was in the hands of the Jews. On their way back to Syria, in the pass of Beth-Horon, the Romans were ambushed by the partisans of Galilee. They were put to flight in a decisive Jewish victory.

In the fall of 66 C.E., Judea began its last brief period of independence. Once more the Jews ruled themselves.

PREPARATIONS FOR WAR

Despite their great joy, the people were aware that Rome would not give up Judea so easily. They knew they would have to go to war with Rome, and so they prepared for a new Roman invasion. They were certain that Galilee would be the first territory invaded, because it was closest to the Roman bases in Syria. Help came from the kingdom

Medieval drawing of Josephus.

of Adiabene, whose nobles had converted to Judaism. This little country sent funds to help Judea prepare for war.

The Jews prepared to make a stand in Galilee under the command of Josephus, a well-educated young man who was related to the Hasmoneans. Josephus had been in Rome, and he knew how to deal with the enemy.

Josephus was well qualified in many ways to command the Jewish troops, but he had one serious shortcoming: he lacked enthusiasm and courage, and did not really believe that the Jews could win. Many were displeased with his leadership. He could not unite the various guerrilla troops, nor could he inspire the fighters of Galilee with confidence. He was even accused of not dealing severely with Rome's sympathizers, and of being unworthy of his position. His chief opponent was the Galilean guerrilla fighter, Yohanan of Giscala, who distrusted him. Many would have preferred Yohanan to Josephus as leader of the Jewish army.

THE ROMANS ATTACK

In the spring of 67 C.E., a Roman army of 60,000 well-equipped soldiers commanded by Vespasian, the greatest general of his day, invaded

Portrait coin of Vespasian, 69-79 B.C.E.

JOSEPHUS SURRENDERS

Josephus gave himself up to the Romans. He was put into chains and brought before the victorious Vespasian. Eager to appear friendly to the Roman cause, Josephus spoke sweet words of flattery and submission. Josephus made the prediction that Vespasian soon would be emperor of Rome. Vespasian was surprised, for Rome was then under the rule of the tyrannical emperor Nero, and Vespasian had no claim to the succession. Still, the prediction set Vespasian thinking, and it made him feel more kindly disposed toward Josephus.

GALILEE IS CONQUERED

The last strongholds in Galilee were held by small partisan bands. These were Mount Tabor, where Deborah and Barak had once defeated the Canaanites, and Giscala, Yohanan's home town. But after the fall of Jotapata, it was clear that Galilee was lost. Mount Tabor surrendered. The few fighters who survived the Roman onslaught made their way to Jerusalem, led by Yohanan of Giscala. The people of Giscala made a brave last stand, to cover up the escape of their valiant fighters. Soon after, Giscala surrendered, and all of Galilee was in the hands of the Romans.

Galilee. Vespasian was already famous for having conquered the Germanic tribes, and for crushing the rebellion of the Britons. Vespasian was aided by his son, the able young general Titus, who brought reinforcements from Egypt. One by one, the fortifications of Galilee fell to Vespasian.

Josephus failed to organize a strong stand against the Romans. The Jewish forces suffered setback after setback. Finally, Josephus and his men were forced to retreat to the fortress of Jotapata. After a siege of two months, Jotapata fell. The forty men who were left in the fortress killed themselves before the Romans entered it. Of all the brave fighters of Jotapata, only Josephus and his armor-bearer survived, and they were taken prisoners by the Romans. They had not joined the others, who preferred death to dishonor.

Portrait coin of Emperor Nero 54-68 B.C.E.

Josephus before Emperor Vespasian, from a twelfth century manuscript.

REVOLT IN ROME

While Vespasian was preparing to besiege Jerusalem, he received news of a revolt in Rome. The emperor Nero had committed suicide, and three contenders, one after another, had seized the throne. All three were murdered within a year. Now the victorious Roman armies proclaimed Vespasian as the next emperor. Leaving his armies under the command of his son Titus, Vespasian left for Rome. In Rome he became emperor, just as the captive Josephus had predicted.

Jerusalem prepared for its last defense. Yet even in the hour of greatest danger, the Zealots fought with other Zealots whom they considered too lenient. Simon Bar Giora, the Zealot leader, fought with Yohanan of Giscala, who had come to help defend the city with his partisan fighters.

Roman coin with portrait of Titus, 79-81 C.E.

TITUS LAYS SIEGE TO JERUSALEM

In the year 70 C.E., Titus laid siege to Jerusalem. He was determined to destroy Jerusalem and the Temple, where the people refused to worship the gods and emperors of Rome.

In these final hours of their resistance, the fighters of Jerusalem were united. Despite hunger and hardship, the defenders held out courageously. Day and night they heard the heavy thud of the Roman battering rams and the terrifying *ballistas*,

which shot hundred-pound boulders into the city. The outer walls of Jerusalem gave way; so did the third, northern wall which King Agrippa had never completed. The Jews were still steadfast. They held the upper city, and their beloved Temple. Many still hoped that some miracle would happen, and the city would be saved.

Brass coin of Vespasian, with inscription "Judaea Capta." Struck in 72 C. E.

On the 17th of Tammuz, conditions in Jerusalem grew worse. For the first time since the days of Judah Maccabee the sacrifices in the Temple had to be discontinued because of heavy fighting in the Temple area. Yet the defenders fought on. Their leaders, Yohanan of Giscala and Simon Bar Giora, gave them courage.

JOSEPHUS AS HISTORIAN

Outside the walls, Titus spurred his soldiers to climb the city's last wall, and so make an end to the bloody siege. Titus had a strange companion in those days: Josephus, the descendant of the Maccabees. From the enemy camp, Josephus, now called Josephus Flavius, after the family of Vespasian and Titus, watched the defeat of his people.

Years later, in Rome, Josephus Flavius was to write the history of the Jewish War. We are indebted to this strange man for an excellent account of the events that led to the fall of Judea, during the last, sad and complicated years. In his history, Josephus claimed that he had foreseen Judea's defeat, and that he felt he could serve his people better as an observer and historian than as a fighter.

Memorial inscription of the 10th Roman Legion, which was stationed at Jerusalem after the city was conquered by Titus in 70 C.E.

and Simon Bar Giora, with many of their brave men, were taken captive.

Josephus reports how he pleaded for the lives of the prisoners. He succeeded in saving some, but many more died. Josephus went into the burning city and rescued many books and Holy Scrolls of the Law, but he could do no more than that. Jerusalem had fallen and with all his influence in Rome, Josephus could not change this tragic fact.

With the fall of Jerusalem, the community of Judea was destroyed. Yohanan of Giscala was imprisoned for life. Simon Bar Giora, with seven hundred brave soldiers, was taken captive to Rome. Many others, men, women, and children, were deported to Rome as slaves.

THE ARCH OF TRIUMPH

When Titus marched home victorious, the Jewish captives were paraded in front of the Roman populace. They were forced to march in the procession into the Roman Forum, carrying the treas-

Arch of Titus.

THE TEMPLE IS DESTROYED

On the ninth of Ab, in the year 70 C.E., on the anniversary of the day Nebuchadnezzar had destroyed the Temple of Solomon, Titus stormed Jerusalem. A Roman soldier climbed the wall and threw a burning torch into the Temple. In moments, the Temple was in flames. Still, many defended its inner courts, which were the last stronghold and the heart of Judean life. Many died in the burning Temple, or took their own lives in despair. Some of the fighters tried to escape from the city, to make a stand in another Judean fortress. But they did not succeed. Yohanan of Giscala

128

A copy of the carving on the Arch of Titus, showing the menorah and other furniture of the Temple being carried in triumph through the streets of Rome.

ures that Titus had taken from Judea.

The Romans had the custom of erecting an arch of triumph whenever a general returned victoriously from a military campaign. The Arch of Titus, commemorating the defeat of Judea, can still be seen in Rome. One of the reliefs on the arch shows the Jewish captives marching in this procession.

JUDEA IS DEFEATED

Judea was destroyed and its people conquered. More than a million people died during the war, and thousands were carried off into exile and slavery. The orchards and fields were destroyed, and the forests were gone. Many cities fell. The Jews lost their independence. Palestine was now governed by a representative of the Roman emperor.

Jewish communities throughout the ancient world mourned for Judea, for Jerusalem, and above all, for the Temple, which had been the spiritual center of their lives.

Many Jews now lived in Rome as captives and slaves. Many of the captives died when forced to fight in the arena against other captives or wild beasts, for the amusement of the people.

Judea was a land of desolation. Of the Temple, only the ruins of the western wall were left. Jews assembled there in prayer, conducting their services, reading from the Torah. Many wept as they stood by the ruined wall. On the Ninth of Ab, *Tishah Be'ab,* Jewish pilgrims would come from many lands, to mourn for their lost Temple.

Despite the loss of their land and their Temple,

The Western Wall in the Old City of Jerusalem is all that remains of the Second Temple.

the Jews, unlike their neighbors, did not adopt the ways of the Romans. They continued to live according to the laws of the Torah. The Torah helped them deal with the problems of their new situation and gave them hope and courage to face the future.

GLOSSARY OF HEBREW TERMINOLOGY
AND NAMES

English	Transliteration	Hebrew
Zealots	Kahnah-eem	קַנָּאִים
Hasidim	Ḥahseedeem	חֲסִידִים
Maccabees	Mahkahbeem	מַכַּבִּים
Eleazar	Elahzahr	אֶלְעָזָר
Josephus	Yohseyf	יוֹסֵף
Yohanan of Giscala	Yoḥahnahn Migoosh Ḥahlahv	יוֹחָנָן מִגּוּשׁ חָלָב
Vespasian	Ispahsyahnohs	אִסְפַּסְיָאנוֹס
Titus	Teetohs	טִיטוֹס
Simon bar Giora	Shimohn bahr Geeyohrah	שִׁמְעוֹן בַּר גִּיוֹרָא
17th of Tammuz	Sheevah Ah-sahr B tah-mooz	שִׁבְעָה עָשָׂר בְּתַמּוּז
9th of Ab	Teeshah B'ahv	תִּשְׁעָה בְּאָב
Western Wall (of the Temple)	Kohtel Hah-ma-ahrahvee	כּוֹתֶל הַמַּעֲרָבִי

THE STRUGGLE FOR SURVIVAL

THE QUESTION OF SURVIVAL

In the days before the siege of Jerusalem, many feared that the Jews would not be able to survive as a people if their country were to be destroyed by the Romans. Without a land, the Jews would no longer be a nation ruled by an independent Sanhedrin. Without the Temple, the center of Jewish life everywhere, how would the Jews keep their identity?

But there were others who believed that the Jews did not need a land or a Temple to be united as a people. They felt that the Torah was a sufficiently strong bond. Among those who held this view was Rabbi Yohanan Ben Zakkai, a scholar who had been a member of the Great Sanhedrin and became a great leader of the Jewish pople.

A PLAN FOR SURVIVAL

Yohanan Ben Zakkai believed that the survival of Judaism depended on the preservation of the Torah in the hearts of the people. Yohanan had devoted his life to the study of the Torah, having been a student of Hillel when he was very young. Now he was an old man. Like most of the Pharisees, he had opposed the war with Rome. Hating bloodshed, he believed in passive resistance, and taught that true dignity would come not from rebellion but only from faithful observance of the Torah.

A menorah carved out on the wall of a tomb in Bet Shearim, in northern Israel, dating from the time of Judah Ha-Nasi. Archeologists began digging here in 1936 and have uncovered a synagogue and hundreds of tombs in the area.

When the Romans laid siege to Jerusalem, Yohanan Ben Zakkai thought of a plan to preserve the tradition of the Torah. He decided to start a school —an academy of Jewish learning—away from Jerusalem where the Torah could be studied and questions of Jewish law could be discussed. In connection with the school, he planned to set up a *Bet Din* or Court of Jewish Law where scholars of the Great Sanhedrin would be given an opportunity to act as teachers and judges. Yohanan Ben Zakkai desperately wanted to accomplish this project before it was too late.

In those days it was impossible to leave Jerusalem. While the city prepared for a Roman invasion under Vespasian, the Zealots watched for any Jew suspected of treason. They were afraid that a traitor might give away the city's secret defenses to the Romans and therefore they allowed no one to leave the city. Nonetheless Yohanan was determined to leave the city so that he could start his school.

According to a tradition, Yohanan had his students spread the news that he, Yohanan, had died. Yohanan then had himself put into a coffin, and his disciples carried him out of the city, under the watchful eyes of the Zealots, presumably to bury him.

An 1825 painting of the synagogue of Rabbi Johanan ben Zakkai. According to tradition it was in this synagogue that Johanan said his last prayer before being smuggled out of the besieged city of Jerusalem.

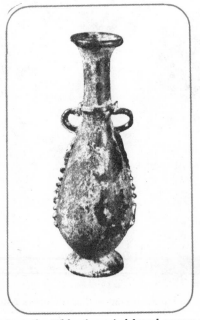

Glass jug from the Mishnaic period found among the tombs at Mount Carmel.

Once he was out of the city, Yohanan Ben Zakkai stepped out of the coffin, very much alive. When the scholars were stopped by the first Roman patrols, Yohanan asked to be brought before their commander, the general Vespasian.

VESPASIAN GRANTS A "SMALL" FAVOR

Vespasian granted the scholar an audience, for he knew that Yohanan had opposed the war. Yohanan predicted that Vespasian would soon become emperor of Rome. Vespasian was very pleased by this prediction and promised to grant any favor that Yohanan might request. This was exactly what Yohanan Ben Zakkai had hoped for. He promptly asked for permission to set up a school in Yavneh, a small town by the seacoast.

Vespasian probably thought that Yohanan would ask for shelter, money or special privileges. But the right to set up a school—this must have seemed like a very small favor to the Roman general. Permission was granted. Little did Vespasian

Ancient "gold glass" with the Ark of the Law, menorot, shofrot and lulavim.

A building thought to be the tomb of Johanan ben Zakkai, near Tiberias on the shore of Lake Kinneret in Israel.

realize that this scholar was establishing much more than a school. He was founding a spiritual armory that would prove stronger than all the military might of the conquerors.

THE SCHOOL AT YAVNEH

Yohanan Ben Zakkai went to work at once setting up a school in Yavneh (also known as Jamnia) to which he immediately invited scholars and students. As soon as his colleagues arrived, he set up the Bet Din. In Yavneh the scholars continued their studies and conducted services in the synagogue with the town's community.

Every morning Rabbi Yohanan himself would open the door of the schoolhouse to his students, and he would be the last to leave at night. Soon the little town of Yavneh became the place where scholars and students assembled, and where justice was pronounced in the Bet Din. Eventually, Yohanan Ben Zakkai formed a Sanhedrin that was modelled after the Great Sanhedrin of Jerusalem, a court of seventy-one scholars who decided on all matters of law and all questions of learning, and on the proper interpretation of the Torah.

The small community of Yavneh watched the fate of Jerusalem with great pain. When the news came that Jerusalem had fallen and the Temple had been destroyed, Yohanan wept and rent his clothes in mourning. Yet he would not allow his disciples to despair. To those who grieved and mourned Rabbi Yohanan spoke words of consolation, quoting to them the teachings of the prophet Hosea—that it is justice and mercy, rather than sacrifice, that God requires of man. He reminded them that there was much to be done. The scholars of Yavneh had to be awake and watchful. The chain of the Torah must not be broken.

THE GREATNESS OF YOHANAN BEN ZAKKAI

Rabban Yohanan Ben Zakkai was the first Nasi, or president, of the Sanhedrin in Yavneh. The teacher of a whole generation of scholars, he was respected for his wisdom, his initiative, and his brilliant decisions. He was also beloved for his humility, his love and respect for everyone. Rabbi Yohanan Ben Zakkai lived simply, devoted to the welfare of his students, to the Jewish community,

Two panels from the mosaic pavement of the fourth century synagogue at Hammat, Tiberias. Tiberias was the seat of the Sanhedrin at this time.

Seat of Moses from the third century synagogue at Chorazin, Israel. This seat of honor was reserved for the rabbi.

YOHANAN ORDAINS NEW RABBIS

Yohanan Ben Zakkai realized that new judges, teachers, and scholars had to be trained and ordained, as had been the practice in the days of the Great Sanhedrin. These scholars would have the title of Rabbi or "master." Yohanan himself had been ordained a "master" by a scholarly teacher, after completing his necessary studies. This long line of properly trained and ordained teachers went back to Moses, who had ordained Israel's first priests and judges, and to his successor, Joshua. Since the days of Moses, the ceremony of the "Laying-on of Hands" had been the symbol of consecration. The rabbis, ordained by Rabbi Yohanan Ben Zakkai, would hand on the Oral Tradition to the next generation. Once ordained, the scholar ceased to be a disciple and became a teacher. These new rabbis were the links in the great, unbroken chain of teachers of the Torah.

Yohanan and those who followed him were called *Tannaim*, meaning "repeaters," "teachers." The period in which they were active is known as the Tannaitic era.

and the study of the Torah. He did not take false pride in his wisdom. He considered that only the study of the Torah made his life a useful one. He did not demand subservience from others. When he walked on the streets of Yavneh, he would be the first to greet whomever he met, young or old, Jew or Gentile.

A reconstruction of the famous synagogue at Kfar Nahum.

A terra cotta oil lamp (Palestine, third century C.E.) showing the columns of the Temple.

YAVNEH BECOMES JUDEA'S SPIRITUAL CAPITAL

The eyes of Jews everywhere were on the town of Yavneh. Despite war and hardship, the people gained courage and inspiration from the teachings of their rabbis.

Most of the rabbis remained in Yavneh after their ordination to join the teachers and scholars of the academy and the judges of the Sanhedrin. Others went out into the communities of Judea, to help teach the people the Torah and the religious observances. Despite the fact that hundreds of thousands of Jews had died in the war against the Romans, there were still Jews living in Judea which was still known as *"Eretz Yisrael,"* the "Land of Israel."

There was no longer a Temple where Jews could worship and sacrifice. The rabbis comforted the people and taught them how to worship in their synagogues.

Slowly the people of Judea rebuilt their homes and cultivated their fields and vineyards again. However, they no longer actually owned their land. The Romans were the real landlords and collected heavy taxes. Formerly, every Jew had given the sum of one shekel as a voluntary contribution to the Temple. Now he had to pay that shekel as an additional poll tax levied on all Jews in the Roman Empire. Despite these new hardships, the Jewish people carried on their life. In their synagogues, they worshipped and studied, held meetings and celebrated their festivals.

Jewish communities in Egypt, Babylonia, Arabia and Rome also looked to Yavneh for guidance. No one enforced the laws and decisions made in Yavneh, but Jewish communities throughout the ancient world voluntarily followed the decisions on the Jewish law that were made at the great Academy of Yavneh.

THE BEGINNING OF CHRISTIANITY

After the death of Jesus of Nazareth, the sect that followed his teachings found a new leader in Saul of Tarsus. Saul was a Jew and a Roman citizen who had come to Jerusalem to study with the Sanhedrin. He was attracted to the beliefs of

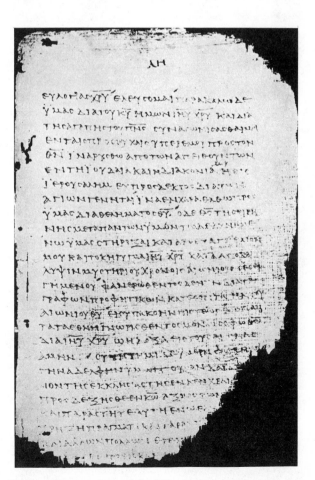

Earliest known manuscript of the letters of Paul—200 C.E.

135

the Nazarenes, and he became a zealous adherent to the new sect. He went into the synagogues of Judea and preached in the name of Jesus, whom he considered the Messiah.

The Jews were not responsive to Saul for they felt there was nothing new in the ethical pronouncements attributed to Jesus. The same ideas had been presented much earlier in the teachings of the prophets Isaiah and Amos, and those of Hillel. They could not accept the Messianic and divine claims of Jesus, for these were contrary to the pure monotheistic ideals of the Jewish faith.

But Saul was determined to spread the new creed. He changed his name from Saul to Paul, and became a missionary to the pagans. He traveled to many lands, and then wrote letters to the new converts, to confirm them in their new beliefs. Later, the teachings of Jesus and his followers, including the writings of Paul, were set down in a collection of books called the *New Testament*. These books began to appear soon after Paul's death, but were not put into their final form until the fourth century. The Christian Bible includes the *New Testament* as well as the Jewish Bible, to which Christians refer as the *"Old Testament."*

Paul was put to death in Rome for having preached a new faith to the pagans, which was strictly forbidden by the Roman authorities. Yet Paul's influence had been very great among the groups in various lands that followed the faith he had preached. These groups established houses of worship which later became known as churches. One such church was soon established in the city of Rome itself. All these small churches felt themselves bound to one another in one large community, the Christian Church. The Nazarenes broke away completely from Jews and Judaism and no longer represented the Jewish tradition as believed and practiced by authentic Jews.

GAMALIEL BECOMES THE NEW NASI

When Yohanan Ben Zakkai retired as Nasi of the Sanhedrin, his place was taken by Gamaliel II, a descendant of Hillel.

Gamaliel applied all his energies to the task of preserving Judaism under the new conditions confronting the Jewish people. He supervised the for-

Rabbi Gamaliel surrounded by his disciples. A painting from the Sarajevo Haggadah.

mulation of many new rituals and prayers, including prayers for the restoration of the Temple.

It was decided in Yavneh that portions of the Torah and the writings of the Prophets should be read in the synagogues every Sabbath, and on the holidays. Shorter sections of the weekly Sabbath portions were to be read on Mondays and on Thursdays, when the farmers would come to the towns for market days. Jews everywhere still follow this custom today. The scholars in Yavneh arranged prayer services for *Sukkot, Pesah,* and *Shavuot.* Now that the Temple was destroyed, the Jews could no longer make pilgramages to Jerusalem, and services had to take place in the local synagogues. Thus the scholars of the Academy, and the new Sanhedrin at Yavneh, had many decisions to make.

GAMALIEL'S CONFLICTS

Gamaliel's great concern for unity among the Jewish scholars made him very intolerant at times. Gamaliel was troubled by the bitter differences of opinion that often occurred in the Sanhedrin. He feared that these differences would eventually destroy the authority of the Sanhedrin. He wanted the Nasi to be the final arbitrator in all differences among the scholars. Many of the scholars who opposed his decisions resented Gamaliel.

One scholar, Rabbi Joshua Ben Hananiah, was worried that the Sanhedrin might lose its democratic character. One year Rabbi Joshua and some of his colleagues disagreed with Gamaliel's calculations of the calendar. Joshua maintained that the Nasi had erred by one day, which would change the date of Yom Kippur. But Gamaliel would not listen to Joshua. He remained firm in his decision. To prove his authority, he ordered Rabbi Joshua to appear before him in his workday clothes on that day. Joshua obeyed. Gamaliel was deeply moved by Joshua's humility. "Happy is the age," Gamaliel said to Joshua, "when great men obey inferior ones."

But their reconciliation did not last. The opposition decided to remove Gamaliel from office.

Traditional tomb of Gamaliel II, at Jamnia.

For several years a very young scholar, who was a descendant of Ezra, served as Nasi. Gamaliel took his dismissal gracefully. He did not withdraw from the Sanhedrin but continued to attend its sessions, although his opinions would never be shared by a majority. He also continued his teaching duties. He sought out his opponents, and apologized to them humbly for his severity. He went to visit Joshua Ben Hanania, and was greatly surprised to discover that the scholar was earning his living by needle-making. Gamaliel, who had been so occupied with his duties as Nasi, had been unaware of the poverty of many of the scholars of Yavneh. In addition to performing their duties at the academy and at the Sanhedrin, many of the Tannaim worked as artisans to earn their livelihood.

Eventually, Gamaliel regained the respect of his

Ancient stone menorah excavated from a synagogue ruin at Tiberias, second century B.C.E.

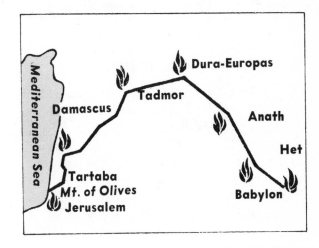

This map shows the points at which signal fires were built to announce the beginning of the new month. Starting at Jerusalem, the message was sent to the cities of Babylonia, so that all Jews would keep the holidays at the same time.

137

colleagues, and he was reinstated as the Nasi of the Sanhedrin of Yavneh. Never again did he, or any other Nasi, attempt to hinder the democratic procedure of the Sanhedrin.

Page from a Hebrew Bible with commentaries. The narrow column at the upper left is the Aramaic translation by Onkeles.

THE BIBLE TAKES FINAL FORM

Under Gamaliel II, the Sanhedrin declared that not all the "sacred" writings composed after the Persian period could definitely be considered part of the Holy Scriptures. Many of these "outside" writings, among them the *Book of the Maccabees*, became known as the *Apocrypha*.

Seven hundred years after the days of Ezra the Scribe, who had begun to collect the books for inclusion in the Holy Scriptures, the Hebrew Bible had taken on the form in which we know it today.

The Septuagint, the old Greek translation of the Bible, no longer seemed adequate. A new Greek translation was made in Palestine by Aquila, a

Hebrew clay stamp used for sealing wine jars, with inscription from Jeremiah. Found in Babylonia, it dates from the second or third century.

convert to Judaism, who was helped in his great undertaking by some of the most learned Tannaim of Yavneh. This was the translation which Jews would use later, in the many faraway communities of the Disperson. Only fragments of this version were preserved.

The most widespread ancient version of the Bible among the Jews is the Aramaic translation attributed to Onkelos, a convert to Judaism, who is sometimes confused with Aquila. The Aramaic version was intended for the masses of Aramaic-speaking Jews in ancient times. However, it continued to exert an influence and it is still printed side by side with the original Hebrew text in modern editions of the Holy Scriptures, and some pious

Greek inscription with menorah, from the Bet Shearim catacombs, third century.

Jews still recite it with the regular weekly portion.

RABBI AKIBA AND THE MISHNAH

One of the greatest of the many scholars and rabbis who taught at Yavneh was Rabbi Akiba. Akiba had once been an ignorant shepherd, eager to acquire a knowledge of the Law. He had fallen in love with Rachel, the daughter of his wealthy master, and they had married. Rachel made many sacrifices to enable her husband to devote himself to study. Rabbi Akiba became the most brilliant scholar of his day. His decisions were concise and clear. He was not only a great scholar, but also a great teacher, and students eagerly flocked to his lectures.

With the help of his colleagues, Rabbi Akiba started on a great project—he began to arrange the many legal decisions of the Oral Tradition into categories and sections. He did not write these decisions down for it was not yet the practice to do so. But Akiba created the classification of Sabbath laws, marriage laws, and the laws of property. His arrangements are called the "Mishnah of Rabbi Akiba."

Akiba had his own school at B'ne B'rak, where he instructed his students. Under the leadership of the academy, many smaller, separate schools were founded around Yavneh.

THE JEWISH COMMUNITY IN THE REST OF PALESTINE

Years of peace followed the war against the Romans, and the Jewish community of Palestine put this period to good use. Under the leadership of the Tannaim of Yavneh, the people organized new ways of communal living. The old Temple tax was replaced by a voluntary contribution for the support of the courts and the academy, and to help the poor and the needy in the land.

The Sanhedrin in Yavneh set up lower courts in all the larger Jewish communities to try simple cases. The more complicated cases were brought before the Bet Din or High Court, at Yavneh.

The synagogues, the schools and the Bet Din centered around each Jewish community. Jewish learning flourished in the land. Almost every Jew could read and write. The level of education in Palestine in those days was higher than that which existed in Europe only a century ago when many of the common people were still illiterate.

Holy tombs in Tiberias, from a 1598 manuscript written in Italy. The large tomb, upper right, is that of Rabbi Akiba. The tomb, upper left, is that of Rabbi Akiba's wife. She is buried in the cave below the tomb. In between and below are tombs of other rabbis.

GLOSSARY OF HEBREW TERMINOLOGY
AND NAMES

Gamaliel	Gahmlee-eyl	גַּמְלִיאֵל	Yohanan Ben Zakkai	Yoḥahnahn ben Zahkai	יוֹחָנָן בֶּן זַכַּי
Shema	Shmah	שְׁמַע	Court of Jewish Law	Beyt Deen	בֵּית דִּין
Eighteen Benedic- tions	Shmohneh Esrey	שְׁמֹנֶה עֶשְׂרֵה	Yavneh (Jamnia)	Yahvneh	יַבְנֶה
Joshua Ben Hanania	Yhohshoo-ah ben Ḥah- nahnyah	יְהוֹשֻׁעַ בֶּן חֲנַנְיָה	Nasi	Nahsee	נָשִׂיא
Apocrypha	Sfahreem Gnoozeem	סְפָרִים גְּנוּזִים	Laying-on-of- hands, or ordination	Smeeḥah	סְמִיכָה
Onkelos	Ohnklohs	אוֹנְקְלוֹס	Tannaim	Tahnah-eem	תַּנָּאִים
Rabbi Akiba	Rahbee Ahkee- vah	רַבִּי עֲקִיבָא	Land of Israel	Eretz Yisrah-eyl	אֶרֶץ יִשְׂרָאֵל
Rachel	Raḥeyl	רָחֵל	New Testa- ment	Breet Haḥah- dahshah	בְּרִית הַחֲדָשָׁה
B'ne B'rak	Bney Vrahk	בְּנֵי בְרָק	Jewish Bible	Tahnaḥ	תַּנַּ"ךְ
			Christians	Nohtzreem	נוֹצְרִים (from נַצְרֶת)

A NEW REBELLION AGAINST ROME

TRAJAN'S MARCH OF CONQUEST

Peace in Judea ended when the Roman emperor Trajan began a new march of conquest. Trajan dreamed of equaling or surpassing Alexander's greatness as a conqueror. His great ambition was to conquer India, the far-off land famous at that time for its riches and its wonders.

He invaded the land of the Parthians, Armenia and Mesopotamia. On his march, he occupied the small kingdom of Adiabene, whose nobles had converted to Judaism and had supported the Jews in their fight against Rome. Like all the conquered lands, Adiabene became a new province of Rome, subject to Roman law.

Under Trajan's rule, revolts were stirring in many parts of the Roman Empire. Jews revolted in Cyprus, in Egypt and in Cyrene. However, these revolts were cruelly suppressed, and resulted only in disappointment and even more hardships.

HADRIAN "REBUILDS" JERUSALEM

Trajan's campaign of conquest ended suddenly when he died on one of his expeditions. His successor, the emperor Hadrian, abandoned Trajan's policy of conquest. The Roman Empire was already huge and unwieldy, and it seemed to Had-

Bust of Emperor Trajan.

Trajan's Column erected in the Roman forum in 113 C.E. It is of Parian marble and stands 100 feet high. Around it winds a spiral band of one hundred and fifty-four relief scenes, passing twenty-two times around the shaft. This band contains twenty-five hundred human figures, and if it could be unrolled it would be over 650 feet long. An examination of one of these reliefs shows us that they are very interesting works of art, wrought with much skill. They record Trajan's great campaigns.

rian too dangerous to add more lands. It was hard enough to keep the many subjected peoples in a state of submissiveness, and rebellion broke out constantly in different parts of the Empire. Roman legions had to put down revolts in many dominions —in Germania, Gaul, and Britain; in Spain, Egypt, Mesopotamia, Parthia and Palestine. There was hardly a province that did not cause Hadrian worry.

Hadrian promised to rebuild Jerusalem. But how disappointed the Jews were when they realized what was happening! Hadrian was not building the Jerusalem of their past, the setting for the Temple of God. Instead, he was building a heathen city, with a circus and arena, and with a temple for the gods of Rome. Hadrian visited the city and

supervised the building projects himself. At the same time he proclaimed new laws that made it hard for the Jews to practice their religion, including a law forbidding circumcision.

BAR KOKHBA LEADS A REVOLT

Judea had been at peace. There was no revolt, even during the stormy days of Trajan's campaign. But now the country seethed with anger and with the spirit of rebellion. Many Jews were impatient to rise against Rome, and to fight once more for their freedom. Even in the academy, where the scholars usually favored peace, rebellion was growing. Rabbi Akiba was among those who wanted to oppose the power of Rome.

At the time of Hadrian's visit to Palestine, Akiba was a very old man. Akiba had heard about a brave young Jew, a man of great magnetism and religious fervor, who was gathering around him those who wanted to fight. His name was Simon Bar Kozeba. Akiba met the young man and was deeply moved by this fiery young patriot. Akiba accompanied him on a journey through the land, speaking to the people, and recruiting a following for him. Akiba renamed him Simon Bar Kokhba, which means "Son of a Star," be-

Engraved stone with name of Emperor Trajan, found in Caesarea.

cause he felt that this young man had extraordinary strength and spirit. Like many other Jews, Akiba came to believe that Bar Kokhba might indeed be the Messiah himself, who had come to restore political independence to the Jewish people.

Hadrian's departure from Palestine to return to Rome was the signal for revolt. The Jewish fighters stationed themselves in caves and valleys of the rugged mountains of their land, ready to strike. Roman soldiers were ambushed and their supplies were taken. Revolt had broken out! Rome sent an army to defeat Bar Kokhba and his men—but the Romans were defeated. Bar Kokhba went from victory to victory, liberating one town after another, and the Roman army was chased into Syria.

A BRIEF PERIOD OF INDEPENDENCE

The victorious Bar Kokhba and his army entered Jerusalem. Everyone rejoiced! Freedom was won, as in the days of the Maccabees. An altar was erected at the site of the Temple in Jerusalem. An uncle of Bar Kokhba, the priest Eleazar, officiated at the services. Bar Kokhba was declared head of the state, to be assisted by Eleazar. Under the leadership of Bar Kokhba, Judea had two short years

Bust of Hadrian.

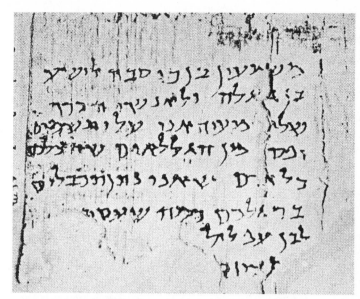

Letter of Simeon Bar Kokhba found in Wadi Murubaat in the Desert of Judah (1952).

of independence.

Bar Kokhba had special coins struck to celebrate Judea's newly won independence. The coins showed the Temple gate with a star above it, on one side, and the name of Bar Kokhba and the date (about 131-132 C.E.) on the other.

ROME STRIKES AGAIN

When Hadrian heard the news of the revolt in Judea, he summoned Severus, his most able general, who was then engaged in a campaign in Britain. Severus appeared in Judea with a powerful army. But in the mountain passes and valleys, Jewish fighters swooped down upon their enemies. The Romans were repeatedly ambushed and beaten, and Severus suffered heavy losses.

Emperor Hadrian now came to Judea to advise Severus. He brought with him new forces and equipment to replace those which had been destroyed, for he felt that Rome could not afford to let the rebellious Jews go unpunished. Hadrian wanted to use Judea as an object lesson for the many other subjugated nations that made up the Roman Empire. In the end, Severus was successful. He destroyed the many strongholds of the Jewish fighters one by one. In the rugged terrain, which his enemies knew so well, he defeated them unit by unit. When he saw that Severus had the situation under control, Hadrian returned to Rome. With Jerusalem in Roman hands, Hadrian felt that he could rely on Severus to finish the campaign successfully.

THE DEFEAT OF BAR KOKHBA

Severus laid siege to the mountain fortress of Betar, southwest of Jerusalem. There Bar Kokhba and his brave fighters made a final stand. The Jewish soldiers fought desperately, and the Romans had heavy losses. But in the end Betar fell. Thirst and starvation had taken a heavy toll of the Jewish defenders. Their water supply had been discovered, and the men in the fortress lived under the most difficult conditions. Bar Kokhba and his fighters died in their last battle, defending Betar.

When Severus reported his victory to the Roman Senate, he omitted the phrase usually used by the generals of Rome: "I and my army are well." The people of Judea had caused him great hardship, and his army was greatly weakened. It was a hard-won victory for Rome.

HADRIAN'S DECREES AGAINST THE JEWS

Bitter days followed Bar Kochba's defeat. Hadrian was determined to stamp out revolt forever in Judea. He realized that the strength of the Jews lay in their religion, in their schools and synagogues, and in their rabbis and teachers. He, therefore, forbade the study of the Torah, and had synagogues and academies officially closed.

Bronze bust of Emperor Septimius Severus.

The Jewish religion was now more proscribed than ever before and was considered illegal by the Roman authorities. Only in secret and under great danger could the Jews observe the laws and customs of Judaism. The rabbis and scholars met in secret places to study and interpret the laws of the Torah, so that they might help the people meet the problems of this difficult period.

The land of Judea was laid waste. Fifty fortresses had been destroyed and a thousand villages lay in ruins. Jerusalem was completely destroyed. As was their custom, the Romans cleared away the ruins of the city and plowed up the ground so that they might use the site to erect a new Roman city. On the soil of Jerusalem the Romans built the city Hadrian had planned. Above the buried ruins of Jerusalem there rose a heathen city, with temples for the worship of Roman gods. The city was named Aelia Capitolina, in honor of the Emperor Aelius Hadrian.

Bar Kokhba coins.

Coin minted to commemorate the founding of Aelia Capitolina.

The new Roman city was out-of-bounds to Jews. No Jew was allowed to live there any longer, or even to enter it. To create a secure Roman province, Rome brought settlers to Palestine from other parts of the empire. The new settlers were loyal, obedient subjects, willing to follow the laws and customs of Rome.

YAVNEH IS CLOSED

The laws against the Jews were ruthlessly enforced. The academy of Yavneh and the Sanhedrin were officially disbanded. The synagogues, schools, and courts throughout the land were closed. Rabbis and teachers were imprisoned or tortured. Many were painfully put to death. Yet these brave men remained faithful to the Torah and many went to their death saying prayers and singing psalms.

RULES TO LIVE BY

In the small town of Lydda an academy had been founded by the Tanna Eliezer ben Hyrcanus, a former student of Yohanan Ben Zakkai and Akiba's teacher. Akiba now met secretly with some of his students and colleagues in a hidden attic in Lydda. These scholars had to determine quickly how the people of Judea should meet the bitter challenge of the new Roman laws. The Rabbis knew that any attempt to follow all the commandments of the Torah at this time would lead to certain death for the whole Jewish community. After serious debate, they determined that, regardless of what other laws and customs they might be forced to abandon, the Jews must adhere steadfastly to three important principles and suffer martyrdom rather than to transgress them: (1)

They were not to worship idols; (2) They were not to shed innocent blood; (3) The preservation of the purity and sanctity of Jewish family life.

THE COURAGEOUS MARTYRS

According to a traditional report, ten great rabbis, including the beloved Rabbi Akiba, died the death of martyrs. The last of these courageous martyrs was Rabbi Judah Ben Babba. Before his imprisonment he had defied Hadrian's law against ordaining rabbis. He had met secretly with the students of the imprisoned Rabbi Akiba, ordained them into the rabbinate, and told them to escape, to hide, or to go abroad, so that they might keep the Jewish tradition alive. Many of these young rabbis went into hiding in the mountain caves of Judea. Others went to Babylonia, where a new academy had been established in the city of Nehardea.

HADRIAN'S FAILURE

Hadrian did not succeed in breaking the continuous tradition of the Torah, the chain that had bound generation to generation throughout Jewish history. The work of the martyred rabbis was carried on by their surviving students, in the moun-

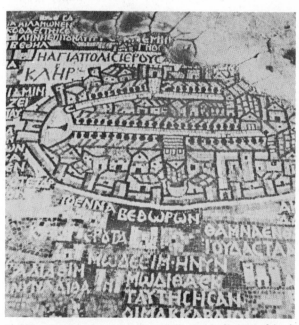

A fifth century mosaic map of Aelia Capitolina, Hadrian's reconstruction of Jerusalem, found in a Greek church in Jordan.

145

Wall painting in the synagogue of Dura Europos in Babylonia, built in the time of Samuel and uncovered by archeologists in 1932.

A Latin inscription in the North African city of Cyrene, telling how the Jews had risen in rebellion against the Roman Empire in the year 115 C.E. Many revolts by courageous Jews of different lands were crushed by the mighty Romans.

tains of Galilee and in distant Babylonia.

On their way to their secret meeting places, the scholars and their disciples would often dress as hunters and carry bows and arrows. This disguise would fool the Roman guards, and the students would be allowed to pass unnoticed. *Lag Ba-Omer,* known as the Scholar's Festival, commemorates the bravery of these students of Akiba, who continued in the study of Torah under the very eyes of Hadrian's soldiers. We still celebrate this day as a holiday every year.

In the days of Hadrian's persecutions, many Jews left Palestine. Some emigrated to Egypt and Babylonia to join friends and relatives there. Many Jews who had been taken captive were sent to Rome as slaves.

PERSECUTION ENDS

Emperor Antoninus Pius, the successor to Hadrian, ended the period of persecution. He allowed the Jews to practice their laws and their religion once again. But he kept in force two important restrictions on their freedom: (1) no Jew was to enter Jerusalem, and (2) restriction of conversion to Judaism.

With the restriction against conversion, the emperor wanted to prevent the further spread of Judaism. Many people had converted to Judaism before the days of Hadrian's persecutions. As the translation of the Jewish Scriptures became more widely known, an increasing number of people became attracted to Judaism. New Jewish communities sprang up throughout the Roman Empire. This period of conversion ended with the new decree. The Jews were strictly forbidden to proselytize.

Rabbi Akiba instructing his pupils. From the Sarajevo Haggadah.

GLOSSARY OF HEBREW TERMINOLOGY
AND NAMES

Bar Kochba	Bahr Koḥvah	בַּר כּוֹכְבָא
Simon Bar Kozeba	Shimohn bahr Kohzeevah	שִׁמְעוֹן בַּר כּוֹזִיבָא
Betar	usually Beytahr	בִּיתֵּר, בֵּית תָּר, בֵּיתָּר
Eliezer ben Hyrcanus	Elee-ezer ben Hohrknohs	אֱלִיעֶזֶר בֶּן הוֹרְקָנוֹס
Judah Ben Babba	Yhoodah ben Bahvah	יְהוּדָה בֶּן בָּבָא
Nehardea	Nhahrd'ah	נְהַרְדְּעָא
Scholar's Festival	Lahg Bah-ohmer	ל״ג בָּעֹמֶר

THE ORIGINS OF THE MISHNAH
AND TALMUD

A CENTER IN GALILEE

With the end of persecutions in Palestine, a new Jewish center was founded in the Galilean town of Usha. Rabbi Judah ben Ilai, a student of Rabbi Akiba, had established an academy there, patterned after the academy in Yavneh. The scholars who studied and taught at Usha were the heirs of the rabbis who had expounded the Law at Yavneh. Gamaliel II had been succeeded as Nasi by his son, Simon. Once again the Nasi acted as the spiritual head of the Jewish community, and was recognized as such by the Roman authorities.

The new Sanhedrin quickly set about reopening the synagogues and schools throughout the land. Jews could again ordain rabbis and teach their children to read and write Hebrew, and acquaint them with their laws and their history. Voluntary taxes could be collected, which would enable the community to support its legal and educational institutions, and to help its poor.

THE TANNAIM

Most of the Tannaim of the period of the Nasi Simon had once been students of Rabbi Akiba. Best known among this generation were Simeon Bar Yohai, Rabbi Meir, and Judah ben Ilai.

Simeon Bar Yohai was a mystic, deeply involved in the hidden meanings of each passage of the Torah. In the revolt against Hadrian, Simeon had been condemned to death for voicing revolutionary ideas, but had managed to escape. For thirteen years he lived hidden in a cave in the Galilean hills. With him were his son and his students, whom he continued to teach even during this difficult time. Later he taught in the Palestinian town of Tekoah.

An old stone building near Lake Kinneret or Tiberias which is supposed to house the tomb of the great sage Rabbi Meir.

A silver coin issued by the revolutionary government of Bar Kokhba. He and his followers set up a Jewish state (132-135 C.E.) which was soon crushed by the Romans.

Simeon Bar Yohai's ideas are believed to have given rise to the mystic writings known as the *Kabalah.* His influence was felt for many centuries. The *Zohar,* which was written a thousand years later by Moses de Leon of Spain, still showed the influence of Simeon Bar Yohai, and in fact is actually attributed to him.

Simeon Bar Yohai captured the imagination and love of many people. On Lag Ba-Omer, which is believed to be the day of his death, pilgrims still visit his grave in Meron, near Safed in Israel, to mark the day with special festivities.

Rabbi Meir continued the work of his master, Rabbi Akiba, in collecting and categorizing the material of the Oral Tradition. Rabbi Meir was a brilliant scholar, with an unusually good memory. He was well versed in Jewish law and in all the biblical writings. A story is told that on one Purim day he came to a synagogue in Galilee and found that there was no *Megillah* from which to read the story of Esther. Rabbi Meir promptly sat down and wrote a complete copy of the scroll, all from memory.

Rabbi Meir was a captivating orator and his

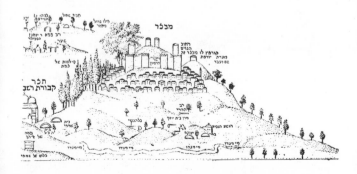

A pictorial view of Safed by Haim Pinie, 1775.

lectures attracted crowds of listeners. Not only students and scholars, but also the great masses of the people enjoyed hearing him. Rabbi Meir was married to Beruriah, a scholar in her own right. She was very highly regarded and many of her observations have been preserved in the Talmud.

Rabbi Judah ben Ilai was Rabbi Meir's brilliant opponent in many legalistic debates. Some of the wise sayings of Meir and Judah ben Ilai have been preserved in a popular section of the Mishnah called the *Pirke Avot,* or *"The Sayings (or Ethics) of the Fathers."*

JUDAH HA-NASI

The literal meaning of the Hebrew word *Nasi* is "prince." It was a very fitting title for the head of the Sanhedrin, for the Nasi had to be a man of learning and fine character whose everyday life would set an example for the people. The Nasi most beloved and best remembered for these qualities was Judah, who became known as Judah Ha-Nasi, which means Judah the Patriarch. Judah had succeeded his father, Simon, and held the office of

Once a year on Lag Ba-Omer, Safed becomes the scene of fervent religious processions. Here we see a spirited group of Jews making the pilgrimage to the Tomb of Simeon Bar Yohai.

Stone tomb in the Bet Shearim catacombs with Hebrew and Aramaic inscriptions. The tomb contains the remains of the daughters of Simon ben Gamaliel and Judah Ha-Nasi.

Nasi for almost fifty years.

Judah was humble, charitable, of noble bearing and spirit, and beloved by all the people who knew him. An outstanding scholar, and codifier, he is referred to as the last of the Tannaim, for with him, the great era of the Tannaim came to an end. Judah is often simply referred to as "Rabbi."

Judah Ha-Nasi set up the Sanhedrin and the academy in Bet She'arim, and later in Sepphoris. He was very eager to unify the scattered Jewish communities throughtout the world. As the Nasi, he had the sole authority to ordain rabbis and judges even for posts in faraway lands.

Judah was greatly concerned about the survival of the Hebrew language. He wanted Hebrew to be a living language, used every day in Jewish homes. But even in the land of Israel, Jews now spoke Aramaic, the language of their neighbors, the non-Jewish peoples of Palestine, Babylonia and Persia. But Judah Ha-Nasi and his household spoke only Hebrew. It was said that Judah's servants spoke a better Hebrew than many scholars. But his love of the Torah and of the Hebrew language went hand in hand with wide cultural interests. He knew many languages. He spoke and read Greek and Latin, and he was learned in many subjects. Judah had many non-Jewish friends including, some say, the Roman emperor Marcus Aurelius.

Judah saw how hard it was for the Jews in Roman Palestine to keep this traditional Sabbatical year, the seventh year in which the land must lie idle by command of the Torah, for the Roman tax collector appeared regularly every year, regardless of whether the Jews had a harvest of not. Judah proposed that in some instances the law against working the land during the Sabbatical Year be eased in order to relieve the people of the constant threat of poverty and debt.

Much activity was going on in Sepphoris. Many students came from Babylonia to study with Judah and his colleagues in Sepphoris. Judah was among the most popular teachers. He used to say: "I have learned much from my teachers; more from my colleagues, but most of all from my students." Judah gave freely of his wealth to needy students and scholars, and to the poor of the land.

RECORDING THE ORAL TRADITION

Judah's whole life was dedicated to one great task: the writing down and editing of the Oral Tradition. Since the days of Ezra and the Scribes, a wealth of decisions, Biblical commentaries and laws had accumulated. Judah Ha-Nasi knew that all of this material was in danger of being lost and forgotten unless it would be arranged, codified, and written down. The Oral Tradition had grown to such a volume that no one could possibly remember all of it. In years past, the scholars had felt that it would be against the spirit of Jewish law to write down the Oral Tradition but now they believed that this step had to be taken if the Torah was to survive. With the assistance of his colleagues and students, Judah set to work on this great task. He

Remains of the entrance to the tomb of Judah Ha-Nasi.

A page of the Talmud with some of the commentaries. The selection is from Baba Kamma, first tractate of the Order Nezikim. The Talmudic passage is in the center island, the lines of Mishnah being followed by the Gemara beginning on the fourteenth line. To the left is the commentary of Rashi, and to the right, that of the Tosafists.

arranged, edited, and wrote down the entire Oral Tradition. This work is called the *Mishnah*. The Mishnah is the first part, and the basis, of the encyclopedia of Jewish law and lore known as the *Talmud.*

In this gigantic task, Judah and his colleagues were aided by the work done by previous scholars. Since the day of Yohanan Ben Zakkai and the academy of Yavneh, efforts had been made to organize some of the vast material of the Oral Tradition.

In the days of the Tannaim, it had been the custom in legal discussions to refer to "the decisions of Hillel," or "the decisions of Shammai," or to the decisions of other scholars. Rabbi Akiba and Rabbi Meir were not content with this personal way of classifying decisions, and proceeded to classify them by the kinds of law to which they referred.

DIVISIONS OF THE MISHNAH

Judah Ha-Nasi codified all the legal commentaries and decisions of the Oral Tradition according to subject matter, cataloguing them into the following six main divisions:

1. *Zeraim* (Seeds): laws concerning agriculture.
2. *Mo'ed* (Festivals): laws pertaining to the observance of the Sabbath, festivals and fast days.
3. *Nashim* (Women): laws concerning marriage and divorce.
4. *Nezikim* (Damages): civil and criminal laws.
5. *Kodashim* (Holy Matters): laws concerning the Temple services, sacrifices, and *Shehitah* (Kosher slaughter).
6. *Tohorot* (Purities): laws of ritual purity and cleanliness.

Each of these divisions in turn is subdivided into Tractates (*Massekhtot*), Chapters (*Perakim*), and Paragraphs (*Mishnayot*).

A great many legal decisions, commentaries, discussions, parables, and stories had come down to the generation of Judah Ha-Nasi but not everything could be included. Many a day and night was spent with his colleagues and with his students, discussing what to include and what to leave out.

HALAKHA AND AGGADAH

The Mishnah is written in the pure beautiful Hebrew Judah Ha-Nasi spoke and loved. It consists mainly of *Halakha* and also includes *Aggadah*. Halakha is the part that deals only with law. It consists of the discussions of the rabbis, and their decisions in particular legal cases. These decisions were always based on passages and laws of the Torah, Aggadah, or Haggadah, which means tale, or story, and consists of selections from the sermons of the Tannaim, and of stories and parables illustrating and explaining the meaning of a Biblical passage, or a point of law.

Many people who found Halakha, the legal part of the Mishnah, too difficult or too dry, loved the Aggadah. It was said among the people that in hard times, "Aggadah refreshes the heart like wine."

A page from the Mishnah Ketubot. The Mishnah is on top of the page. Below to the right is the commentary of Obadiah of Bertinoro, who lived in Italy and then in Jerusalem in the fifteenth century. To the left is the commentary of Yomtov Lipmann Heller of Prague, of the seventeenth century.

WRITINGS OUTSIDE THE MISHNAH

Some of the scholars of Judah Ha-Nasi's day and of the generation following him decided to preserve some parts of the Oral Tradition that had not been included in the Mishnah. This material is known as *Baraitha*. The most famous collection of additions to the Mishnah is called the *Tosephta*.

THE END OF AN ERA

For many years Judah suffered from a painful ailment, but he worked on and devoted himself fully to his task. He also continued with his teachings and his activities at the Sanhedrin. When

A fourth century synagogue mosaic in Tiberias.

for two hundred years thereafter the office of Nasi was held by disciples of the School of Hillel. The emperors of Rome recognized the Nasi as a personage of princely rank, referring to him as the Patriarch. Non-Jews often wondered how it was possible that these men, who had no real legal power to enforce their rulings in the Jewish communities, were respected by all Jews as if they were rulers. The laws and decisions of the *Nesiim* were followed by Jewish communities everywhere, of their own free will. Jews paid a voluntary tax to maintain their schools and their religious and legal institutions. They also contributed freely to the charities for the poor.

The next two hundred years were difficult ones for the Jews in Palestine. The land had never recovered from the ravages of war. Oppressed by heavy Roman taxation, the people had to struggle to make ends meet. Fields lay barren and mountains stayed bare. The Romans had taken from the country what they could, but they had not done anything to replant and restore the ravaged soil. For many decades, Gamaliel III and his successors succeeded in keeping up Palestine's highly developed educational system. The Sanhedrin was still

Judah Ha-Nasi died, he was mourned deeply by his friends, his colleagues and students, and indeed by the whole community of Israel. He was one of those rare men who embodied the spirit of a kind father for an entire people. "Not since Moses," the people said, "has there been a man like Judah, who so combines leadership with Torah." Crowds of people paid the last honors to Judah, as his body was brought to burial at Bet She'arim. It seemed that everyone felt that a great period of Jewish history had come to an end.

With the death of Judah Ha-Nasi the period of the Tannaim had ended. The work of the Tannaim was preserved in the Mishnah, which served as a groundwork of Jewish law for generations to come. Much as the United States Supreme Court now consults the Constitution and its amendments for guidance, the Sanhedrin consulted both the Torah and the Mishnah in its legal decisions.

THE PATRIARCHATE

Judah Ha-Nasi's son, Gamaliel III, presided as Nasi over the academy and the Sanhedrin, and

Part of an Aramaic letter written in Palestine in Talmudic times.

153

At the outer edge of the modern city of Jerusalem are rock-cut burial caves dating back to the first century C.E. Members of the Sanhedrin were buried in these caves.

the center of the community of Israel. The Nasi alone could ordain rabbis, and he alone, with the help of the scholars of the Sanhedrin, could fix the Jewish calendar. He had to see to it that Jews throughout the world would know when to celebrate their festivals.

THE AMORAIM

Outside of Palestine, new academies were rising and flourishing in the faraway land of Babylonia. In the town of Nehardea, two students of Judah Ha-Nasi, Rav and Samuel, started to teach and make independent decisions. They based their work on the Mishnah. The new generations of scholars after Judah Ha-Nasi — both in Palestine and in Babylonia — were called the *Amoraim,* meaning "speakers" or "interpreters." A wealth of new discussions, decisions, stories, and allegories accumulated, both in Galilee and in the new academies of Babylonia. Many of the Babylonian scholars still came to the academy at Tiberias, in Palestine, to study with the masters and judges of the academy and the Sanhedrin.

YOHANAN AND SIMEON

One of the oustanding scholars at Tiberias was Yohanan Bar Nappaha. The son of a poor blacksmith, Yohanan had been one of the disciples of Judah Ha-Nasi. One of the first scholars to establish a method for studying the Mishnah, Yohanan also developed a method for commenting on its sources. He was much admired by Jewish scholars everywhere, and in turn had great respect for the Babylonian scholars and their new academies.

Yohanan was a friendly man who loved to talk to everyone he met. One day, when he visited a public bath, he met a stranger who impressed him very much. This man was of outstanding physical appearance, a strong athletic man, full of vitality. His name was Simeon Ben Lakish. Simeon told Yohanan that he had once been thrown into the arena with Roman gladiators, and had survived. He also had been a trainer of wild animals. Simeon must have talked at length about his many experiences. He even hinted that he had been the head of a band of highwaymen.

Simeon and Yohanan became close friends. Eventually, Yohanan convinced the athletic Simeon to start an entirely new life, to join him, and to study in the academy. Simeon Ben Lakish followed this new road, and in time he became a great rabbi. Many of the brilliant discussions between these two rabbis were to be recorded by later scholars. There is a romantic note to this story. The handsome Simeon married the beautiful sister of Yohanan.

THE RIFT WITH CHRISTIANITY

The period of scholarship in Israel was interrupted by an event which deeply affected Jews everywhere: the Roman Emperor, Constantine, embraced Christianity. Constantine thought that the new force of Christianity could help revive the Roman Empire, which had become weak. After his conversion, Constantine looked with disfavor on Judaism, and tried to undermine it.

Although Judaism was the mother religion from which Christianity had developed, the rift between the two religions was growing greater. Christians no longer considered themselves related to the Jews by religion. For one thing, most of the converts to Christianity had come from other nations and they brought some of the ideas of the

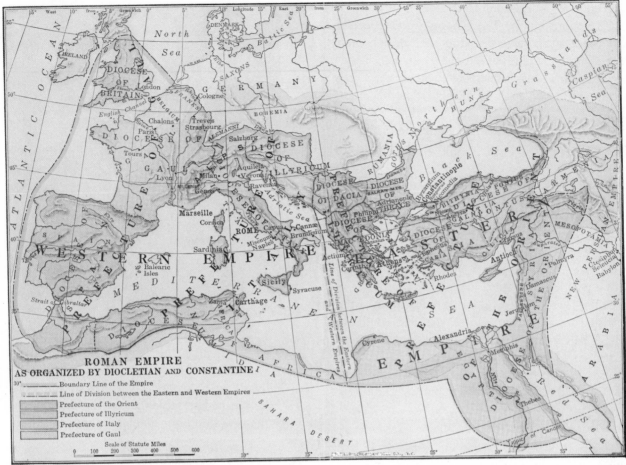

ROMAN EMPIRE
AS ORGANIZED BY DIOCLETIAN AND CONSTANTINE

_____ Boundary Line of the Empire
_ _ _ _ Line of Division between the Eastern and Western Empires
Prefecture of the Orient
Prefecture of Illyricum
Prefecture of Italy
Prefecture of Gaul

Scale of Statute Miles
0   100   200   300   400   500   600

older pagan religions in which they had formerly believed. Christianity's "order of days" was derived from the Persian cult of Zoroaster. The Persians had worshipped their sun god on Sundays, so Sunday became the Sabbath of the new Christian sect. As the years passed, Christianity moved further and further away from Judaism. By the time the Roman Emperor Constantine had converted to the new faith, Christianity had completed its separation from Judaism; it had a church of its own and its own distinct rituals.

Under Constantius II, new restrictions were pronounced for the Jews of the Roman Empire, and a revolt broke out among the Jews of Galilee. The Romans crushed the uprising cruelly. They destroyed Sepphoris and Tiberias, the seats of the academies. Everywhere, Jews had to flee for their lives.

A BRIEF PERIOD OF PEACE

Constantius' successor, Julian the Apostate,

Bust of Emperor Constantine.

155

who rejected Christianity, treated the Jews of Galilee more kindly. The schools were reopened and peace again reigned in the land. Julian even sent a letter to the Nasi, Hillel II, in which he addressed him as his "Venerable Brother, the Patriarch. . . ." In the letter, he told Hillel of his intention to rebuild the Holy Temple. Julian was considering a military campaign against the Parthians, and he hoped for Jewish support. But nothing came of his plan.

Julian's reign was short, and after his death the Roman Empire again was under a Christian emperor. Henceforth, Christianity was the official religion of the Roman Empire. Though the stern measures of Constantius were not reinstated, many restrictive laws were passed which forced the Jews into a position of disadvantage.

Hillel II realized how difficult the position of the Jewish community in Galilee was. He could no longer be certain that the academies and the Sanhedrin could continue to exist, or that his descendants, the men of the School of Hillel, would always be allowed to be Nasi.

HILLEL FIXES THE CALENDAR

Hillel II made an important decision. It had always been the privilege of the Nasi to make known the calendar every year. Messengers would then bring the new calendar to all the Jewish communities. Hillel decided to make a more permanent calendar, which would help to unify Jewish communities everywhere even if the Sanhedrin should cease to be. He made certain calculations and wrote down specific directions, so that Jews would be able to celebrate the holidays in the same manner and at the same time. Henceforth all Jews used Hillel's

Constantine's order to the ruler of Cologne concerning the Jews in the city.

Julian the Apostate.

method to calculate the Jewish calendar and the dates of the festivals.

Hillel II was a great scholar and an able Nasi. His work helped preserve the Jewish tradition long after the community of Galilee no longer existed.

THE GEMARA IS WRITTEN

In the days of Hillel's son, Gamaliel V, and his grandson, Judah IV, the end of the Jewish community in Palestine seemed near. Working under great pressure, the last of the Palestinian Amoraim collected and codified all the important legal discussions, teachings and decisions that had taken place in Palestine since the completion of the Mishnah. This work was called the *Gemara*. The Gemara, together with the Mishnah, make up the Talmud. Thus a complete edition of the Talmud consists of two parts: the Mishnah, which is the foundation, and the Gemara, which is the superstructure.

There are two Talmuds: the Palestinian Talmud and the Babylonian Talmud. Both versions have the same first part—the Mishnah. They differ only in the second part—the Gemara. The Palestinian Gemara, which is shorter, was the work of the Amoraim in Palestine. The Babylonian version was the work of the Amoraim in Babylonia. The Pales-

Before the invention of printing, the preparation of a calendar was a laborious undertaking. This calendar or *luah* of the Hebrew year 5036 (1276 C.E.), was found in a Bible manuscript.

tinian Talmud was completed with the end of the Patriarchate, while the Babylonian Gemara was still to grow.

THE SPLIT IN THE ROMAN EMPIRE

Although the Roman Empire was officially a Christian state, united by one religion, it was torn by strife and disunity from within. In the fourth century the empire split into two states: a western state, Rome; and an eastern state, the new Byzantine Empire. Palestine, including what was once Judea, became part of the Byzantine Empire. Because Byzantium and Rome were constantly at loggerheads, it became impossible for the Jews who lived in the dominions of Rome to send their voluntary taxes to Palestine. The Roman authorities interfered with the sending of this money, because they were afraid that it might fall into the hands of their Byzantine enemies.

THE END OF THE PATRIARCHATE

Deprived of outside financial support, the Nasi, the academy, and the Sanhedrin became impoverished. Just then the Nasi, Gamaliel VI, died,

leaving no sons. The Byzantine emperor, Theodosius II, took this opportunity to abolish the Patriarchate. This was the end of the central Jewish authority in Palestine. Many Jews who felt unable to go on without leadership left Galilee. Under Byzantine rule, Palestine became a Christian country. Restrictive laws continuously made

Bas-relief near the city of Persepolis shows Emperor Valerian (258 C.E.) begging for mercy from Shapur, the victorious Persian king.

the life of the Jews there more difficult. Hiding in their own land like strangers, only a handful of Jews remained in a few remote Galilean villages.

The Patriarchate had come to an end. But the

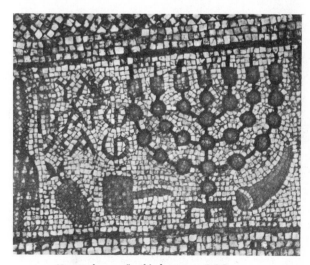

Menorah mosaic, third century B.C.E.

157

Ancient Jewish communities in Asia Minor where Jews migrated during the restrictive period of the Byzantine occupation of Palestine.

history of the Jews and their civilization did not end with the House of Hillel. The Jews had lost their homeland, but not their tradition, which is based on the humane laws of the Torah. Their sense of history and their faith as a people was still a living, growing heritage. But now the spiritual leadership of Jewish communities everywhere passed over to the Jewish community of the land of Babylonia.

GLOSSARY OF HEBREW TERMINOLOGY AND NAMES

Usha	Ooshah	אוּשָׁא
Judah ben Ilai	Yhoodah ben Ilahi	יְהוּדָה בֶּן אֶלְעַאי
Simon	Shimohn	שִׁמְעוֹן
Tannaim	Tahnah-eem	תַּנָּאִים
Simeon Bar Yohai	Shimohn bahr Yoḥai	שִׁמְעוֹן בַּר יוֹחַאי
Meir	Mey-eer	מֵאִיר
Kabalah	Kahbahlah	קַבָּלָה
Zohar	Zohahr	זֹהַר
Meron	Meyrohn	מֵירוֹן
Safed	Tzfaht	צְפָת
Scroll	Mgeelah	מְגִלָּה
Beruriah	Brooryah	בְּרוּרְיָה
Sayings of the Fathers	Pirkey Ahvoht	פִּרְקֵי אָבוֹת
Judah Ha-Nasi	Yhoodah Hah-nahsee	יְהוּדָה הַנָּשִׂיא
Bet She'arim	Beyt Sh'ah-reem	בֵּית שְׁעָרִים
Mishnah	Mishnah	מִשְׁנָה
Talmud	Tahlmood	תַּלְמוּד
Oral Tradition	Torah Sheb'ahl Peh	תוֹרָה שֶׁבְּעַל פֶּה
Seeds	Zrah-eem	זְרָעִים

Festivals	Moh-eyd	מוֹעֵד
Women	Nah-sheem	נָשִׁים
Damages	Nzeekeem	נְזִיקִים
Holy Matters	Kawdahsheem	קָדָשִׁים
Purities	Tawhawroht	טָהֳרוֹת
Tractates	Mahseḥtoht	מַסֶּכְתוֹת
Chapters	Prahkeem	פְּרָקִים
Halakha	Hahlaḥah	הֲלָכָה
Aggadah	Ahgahdah	אַגָּדָה
Baraitha	Bahraitah	בָּרַיְתָא
Tosephta	Tohseftah	תּוֹסֶפְתָּא
Amoraim	Ahmohrah-eem	אֲמוֹרָאִים
Nehardea	Nhahrd'ah	נְהַרְדְּעָא
Rav	Rahv	רַב
Samuel	Shmoo-eyl	שְׁמוּאֵל
Simeon Ben Lakish	Shimohn ben Lahkeesh or Reysh Lahkeesh	שִׁמְעוֹן בֶּן לָקִיש, רֵיש לָקִיש
Calendar	Looaḥ	לוּחַ
Gemara	Gmarah	גְּמָרָא
Palestinian Talmud	Tahlmood Yerooshahl-mee	תַּלְמוּד יְרוּשַׁלְמִי
Babylonian Talmud	Tahlmood Bahvlee	תַּלְמוּד בַּבְלִי

THE NEW SPIRITUAL CENTER IN BABYLONIA

THE HISTORY OF THE JEWISH COMMUNITY IN BABYLONIA

Babylonia was a rich, fertile country situated between the Tigris and Euphrates rivers. Jews had lived there for hundreds of years—as far back as 597 B.C.E., a decade before the fall of the First Temple, when according to tradition, Jehoiachin, the King of Judah, had founded a settlement in the city of Nehardea. This community became the center of Jewish life in Babylonia.

At the time of the Second Temple, more Jews lived in Babylonia than in Judea. The Babylonian community of Jews was rich and prosperous. It contributed generously toward the rebuilding of Palestine. For centuries, Jews in every part of Babylonia voluntarily paid the Temple tax, which was collected in Nehardea and sent to Judea under armed guard.

Some of the Babylonian Jews lived on the great fertile plains and were farmers and cattlemen; others worked in the cities as craftsmen, merchants, bankers and traders. In Babylonia the Jews maintained their own synagogues, their own houses of study and their own courts where Jewish law was observed. Although these institutions were not of the same high caliber as those in Palestine, they

Illustrated Persian manuscript in Hebrew letters. The Persians ruled over Babylonia during the time of the Amoraim and many Jews lived in all parts of the Persian Empire.

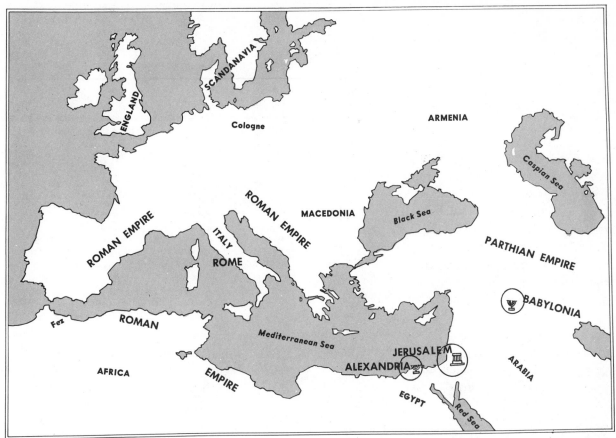

The largest Jewish communities are encircled: the city of Alexandria in Egypt; the land of Israel itself; and the center of Babylon.

never ceased to exist. The Jewish courts, synagogues and schools in Babylonia looked for guidance in the Great Assembly and later to the Great Sanhedrin in Jerusalem.

Like Jews everywhere, the Jews of Babylonia regarded Palestine as the spiritual center of Judaism. Babylonian students, including the great Hillel, flocked to the teachers of the Great Sanhedrin in Jerusalem. Even after the destruction of the Second Temple, Jews from Babylonia continued to study with the Tannaim at Yavneh, Tiberias and Sepphoris.

In Roman times Babylonia was ruled by the Parthians, able warriors who for centuries succeeded in holding off the Roman conquerors. The Parthians were tolerant toward the Jews in their land. Refugees from Judea streamed into the Babylonian provinces of the Parthian Empire, to begin a new life there. Thus the Jewish community in Babylonia grew in both numbers and strength.

THE EXILARCH

The Jewish community in Babylonia was headed by an official known as *Resh Galuta,* meaning "leader of the Exile," or Exilarch. This office was hereditary. The Exilarchs were descendants of King David, tracing their descent back to Jehoiachin, who had been King of Judea at the time of Nebuchadnezzar.

The Exilarch ruled over all the Jewish communities in Babylonia. He collected the taxes assessed by the Babylonians and the taxes which the Jews levied on themselves. In the period of the Second Temple the Exilarch also collected the Temple taxes. Later, when contributions to the academies replaced the Temple tax, the Exilarch collected these also.

161

The Exilarch was the highest authority in the Jewish courts of justice and in all the secular affairs of the Babylonian Jewish community. At the time of the Second Commonwealth in Palestine, he was held in high esteem as the fourth most important man in Babylonia, after the king himself. The Exilarch was a powerful prince. He lived in a beautiful palace in Nehardea and wore splendid royal robes. When he appeared in the streets, a runner would announce his coming. The Jews of Babylonia were proud of their Exilarch and showed him great respect.

Because the community often lacked able leaders and teachers, the Jewish educational and legal institutions in Babylonia eventually deteriorated. But there always were talented young students from Babylonia who went to study at the academies in Palestine. Two of these young Babylonians were among the most gifted of Judah Ha-Nasi's students. They were Abba Arikha (Abba, the Tall), and Samuel. Samuel was an extraordinary young man, learned in many fields. Some called him Yarhina'ah (The Astronomer), because of his great knowledge of astronomy. He was also a physician and treated Judah Ha-Nasi for a painful eye disease. Abba Arikha was an outstanding, devoted Jewish scholar. Later he became known simply as *Rav* (master, rabbi, teacher). "Rav"

Entrance to the underground rock tombs of the Sanhedrin in Jerusalem. Learned rabbis were entombed in stone coffins so that the people might show their respect for them through visits, study and prayer.

was eventually to become the title of all ordained rabbis.

When these young Babylonians returned home to Babylonia, they brought back with them the newly written Mishnah, the great work of their teacher, Judah Ha-Nasi.

RAV AND SAMUEL

Rav was appointed inspector of the markets and of weights and measures throughout the Jewish communities in Babylonia. As Rav journeyed through the land, he saw how slack the spiritual life of the community had become. The young scholar determined to revive the culture of the Jews and improve their educational level. He began to reorganize the system in the schools and synagogues. Eventually, Rav was appointed head of the academy at Nehardea, but he declined this position so that it might be given to his friend, Samuel. Although Samuel was younger than he, Rav knew his friend was a great scholar. Besides, Samuel had been born in Nehardea, knew the customs of the city and its life and was well suited for the post.

Rav left Nehardea and founded a new academy in the city of Sura in a distant part of Babylonia, near the great city of Pumpeditha.

Since Rav was an inspiring teacher and administrator, his new school attracted many scholars and students. The lecture halls were not large enough

Magic bowl with Hebrew inscription found in the ruins of Babylon.

to hold all the people who crowded into them, eager to listen and learn. Soon Rav became a popular and beloved leader among the Jews of Babylonia.

Rav instituted a revolutionary new plan of study, open to anyone who wanted to take advantage of it. Each year during the month of *Adar* (about March) and the month of *Elul* (about September), when the farmers could be spared from their work and when artisans and merchants could take a rest during their slack season, **Rav** would give a special course in Jewish law. These months were called the months of *Kallah* or "Assembly."

During the months of Kallah and during the weeks preceding the holidays, people would stream into Sura from all corners of the surrounding provinces to attend the popular courses at the academy. The Exilarch himself would come to Sura to celebrate the months of Kallah. This was a special delight for the people who cheered their leader enthusiastically as he passed through the streets dressed in his beautiful robes.

A thirst for learning took hold of the Babylonian Jews; throughout the land synagogues and schoolhouses were improved and Jews met in great numbers to study, discuss and learn.

With the help of the Mishnah, Babylonian scholars could apply the laws of the Torah to life in exile. By introducing the Mishnah to their students, Rav and Samuel succeeded in their great purpose—to make the Torah a living guide, a help to the Babylonian Jews in meeting the many problems with which they were faced.

The teachings of the Amoraim of Babylonia, collected in the Babylonian Talmud, have deeply influenced Jewish law in many lands. As the schools in Palestine grew less important, Jews all over the world began to look to the decisions of the Babylonian Amoraim for guidance.

Samuel evolved a sixty-year Jewish calendar, which he published and sent to the scholar Yohanan Bar Nappaha in Palestine. A century later, this calendar was to aid the Patriach Hillel II in devising a new calendar which became the first official calendar for use by Jews everywhere.

Samuel and Rav remained close friends and collaborators throughout their lives. Together, they

Fragment of an ancient manuscript prayerbook showing the "Ahabah Rabah."

made revisions in the *Siddur,* the Jewish prayer book. Rav wrote the beautiful *Alenu* prayer for Rosh Hashanah which is part of our daily prayers to this day. Samuel wrote a shorter version of the *Shemoneh Esreh* (or Amidah) — the Eighteen Benedictions.

Samuel was also a great jurist. One of his most important decisions was that every Jew was to consider himself bound by the laws of the land in which he lived, unless such laws would interfere with the Jewish religion; and that every Jew had the obligation to be a good, responsible citizen of the city and country where he resided.

The last years of Samuel were darkened by trouble. In 226 C.E., the Parthians of Babylonia were overthrown by the Persians. The new Persian rulers were followers of the religion of Zoroastrianism. They believed in a god of light and fire. The religion was named after its founder, Zoroaster. The fanatical priests of Zoroaster wanted to force

Conflict between two Zoroaster deities—Ormuzd (Ahura Mazda), the god of light and wisdom, and Ahriman, the dragon-deity of darkness and evil.

their cult upon all the inhabitants of the lands conquered by the Persian rulers, and a time of persecutions began for the Jews, who were not willing to accept the new religion. Only the intervention of Samuel, who had influence at the Persian court, helped to ease the hardships the Jews were made to suffer during this period.

Samuel died in 257 C.E. Soon thereafter, Nehardea was plundered by Palmyrene invaders, who temporarily interrupted Persian rule. Nehardea never regained its former importance. It was reconstructed, but the centers of Jewish learning were thenceforth at Sura and Pumpeditha.

RABBAH BAR NAHMANI

Many of the great Babylonian Amoraim acted also as rabbis in synagogues. One of the most brilliant among them was Rabbah Bar Nahmani, head of the academy at Sura for twenty-one years. Rabbah Bar Nahmani preached at Sabbath services, expounding the Law, explaining Biblical passages and entertaining the people with stories and homilies. So many students flocked to hear Rabbah

teach, during the months of Kallah, that he was accused of cheating the government of taxes by causing too many people to leave their work twice a year. In the end Rabbah was forced to flee, never to return. He died a victim of the hardships of exile.

RAV ASHI

The troubled Jewish community found a new leader, Rav Ashi, a highly gifted scholar, of a noble and wealthy family. When still a young man, Rav Ashi had been appointed head of the academy of Sura.

The uncertainties of Jewish life under the rule of the new Persians had brought the academy to a state of deterioration. Rav Ashi set to work immediately, erecting new lecture halls, revising the

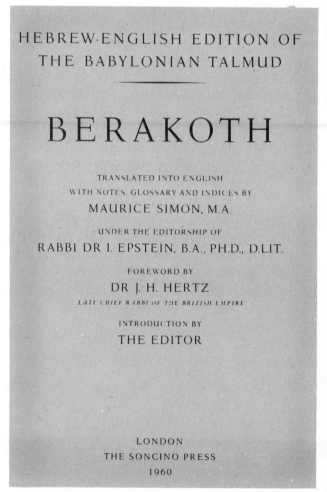

HEBREW-ENGLISH EDITION OF THE BABYLONIAN TALMUD

BERAKOTH

TRANSLATED INTO ENGLISH
WITH NOTES, GLOSSARY AND INDICES BY
MAURICE SIMON, M.A.

UNDER THE EDITORSHIP OF
RABBI DR I. EPSTEIN, B.A., PH.D., D.LIT.

FOREWORD BY
DR J. H. HERTZ
LATE CHIEF RABBI OF THE BRITISH EMPIRE

INTRODUCTION BY
THE EDITOR

LONDON
THE SONCINO PRESS
1960

Title page from the Soncino Hebrew-English Talmud.

164

THE TALMUDIC AGE

SOFERIM (scribes)
Fifth to Third
centuries B.C.E.

The generations of scholars and teachers who carried on the work of EZRA.

ZUGOT (pairs)
Second century
B.C.E. until
about 10 C.E.

The two leaders of the great Sanhedrin who carried on the teachings and interpretations of the Torah after the period of the Soferim. HILLEL and SHAMMAI were the last and most brilliant of the Zugot.

TANNAIM (teachers)
First and Second
centuries C.E.

The scholars and teachers whose works are recorded in the Mishnah.

- 41 GAMALIEL I, Nasi and last president of the Great Sanhedrin.
- 70 JOHANAN BEN ZAKKAI, founder of the academy of Yavneh.
- 80 GAMALIEL II, Nasi and head of the Sanhedrin and of the academy at Yavneh.
- 130 RABBI AKIBA.
- 138 RABBI MEIR and SIMEON BAR YOHAI.
- 165–200 JUDAH HANASI (Judah I), Nasi, head of the Sanhedrin and the academy, compiler of the Mishnah.

AMORAIM (speakers)
Third to Sixth
centuries C.E.
(about 200-499)

The scholars and teachers whose work is recorded in the Gemara.

- 210 GAMALIEL III, son of Judah Hanasi, head of the academy and of the Sanhedrin.
- 219 *ABBA ARIKHA (RAV) and MAR SAMUEL founded the Babylonian Talmud.
- 225 JOHANAN BAR NAPPAHA and SIMEON BEN LAKHISH.
- 259 HILLEL II, Nasi and head of the academy and of the Sanhedrin, introduced the fixed calendar.
- 370 Completion of the Palestinian Talmud.
- 425 GAMALIEL IV, last Nasi. End of Patriarchate.
- 354–427 *ASHI and
- 499 RABINA, compiled the Babylonian Talmud.

SABORAIM (reasoners)
500 until 530 C.E.

The scholars and teachers who completed the editing of the Babylonian Talmud. Until the time of the Gaonate great Babylonian scholars bore the title of SABORA.

This chart refers to only a few of the many Talmudic scholars. Babylonian scholars are marked with an asterisk*.

---

courses of study and making them more meaningful to his listeners. Again the people streamed into Sura during the Kallah months and before the holidays. As of old, the Exilarch could come to honor the throng of students with his presence. Inspired and encouraged, Jews throughout Babylonia again studied the Torah and Mishnah and joyfully participated in a rich and varied community life.

Rav Ashi turned his attention to the perpetuation of the vast material that had been developed by the Amoraim of Babylonia. Just as the teachings in the Mishnah had been passed on as Oral Tradition before they were collected and written down, so had the teachings of the Amoraim of Babylonia been passed on by word of mouth from generation to generation. Seeking to preserve this important body of teachings for the generations to come, Rav Ashi brought all the teachings of the Amoraim into one collection which we know today as the Babylonian Gemara, and which contains all the teachings developed by the Amoraim of Babylonia.

Now Rav Ashi, aided by his students and colleagues, set to work to codify the material of the Babylonian Gemara according to the classifications of the Mishnah, following the groupings devised by Judah Ha-Nasi. During the months of Kallah, many students contributed to this collection their own discussions and decisions, with stories and allegories which they had heard from previous teachers.

For fifty years Rav Ashi presided over the academy of Sura, winning from the Jewish community the title *Rabbana,* our master—an honorary title which was ordinarily conferred only on the Exilarchs.

After Rav Ashi's death a time of persecutions begain again under a cruel Persian king. Rabina, who succeeded Ashi as head of the academy of Sura, seeing the danger to Jewish survival, determined to preserve the teachings of the Babylonian Amoraim. But although he continued the work of editing and codifying, it took another generation of scholars to complete the work. This next generation of scholars, the *Saboraim* (reasoners) did the final reading and editing of the Babylonian Gemara. By the year 530 C.E. the Babylonian Talmud, consisting of the Babylonian Gemara, together with the Mishnah, was completed.

THE BABYLONIAN TALMUD

An immense and many-sided work, the Babylonian Talmud is written mostly in Aramaic, the

Silver plate of King Khosru.

Silver Persian portrait coin of King Khosru I (531-579 C.E.)

everyday language of the Babylonian Jews. The Aramaic of the Talmud is closely related to Hebrew. It is written in Hebrew characters and strikes the modern reader as a dialect of Hebrew.

The Babylonian Talmud was like a pathway leading from the Jewish life of the past towards the future. Generations of Jews were to build their lives and thoughts upon this immense encyclopedic work.

Simultaneously with the Talmud, collections of *Midrashim* appeared. Midrashim are stories and commentaries which illustrate passages from the Bible. When the rabbis preached to the people in the synagogues, they would often retell tales from the Midrashim, and quote the wise commentaries from the Aggadah, the stories and parables found in the Mishnah and the Gemara. The people delighted in these stories and quotations, and parents loved telling them to their children. Aggadah and the Midrash are part of the rich folklore of the Jewish people and have kept growing in volume over the centuries.

At the time when the Talmud was being completed, an unhappy period began in Babylonia—not only for the Jews but for people of all religions. The priests of a new, fanatic cult sought to convert everyone. The Exilarch was executed and many synagogues were closed as were the great academies of Sura and Pumpeditha, not to reopen again for almost fifty years.

KHOSRU I—531-579 C.E.

In 531 C.E. a new Persian king, the tolerant Khosru I, ascended the throne. Under this ruler the academies of Sura and Pumpeditha reopened. From then on, the heads of the great academies were called the *Geonim.* The honorary title

"Gaon" means excellency. By now the Patriarchate in the Land of Israel had come to an end and the Geonim of the Babylonian schools were regarded as the spiritual leaders of all the Jewish communities. In the reopened academies the newly completed Babylonian Talmud was studied and became the basis for further work.

A new productive period of Jewish life began. The Persian Empire, of which Babylonia was part, was at peace. Its people prospered and its cities were filled with beautiful gardens and palaces. Persian poets and painters, architects and sculptors, created many beautiful works. Persian craftsmen fashioned handsome objects of metalwork and made lovely materials of cloth and silk.

After the death of Khosru II, however, Persia went into a decline. Weaker kings struggled bitterly with the Byzantine Empire. Persia was beset by unrest, poverty and high taxes. The unceasing revolt of the Persian nobles caused constant bloodshed.

Meanwhile, in the deserts of Arabia, a new pow-

Byzantine warriors.

er was preparing for conquest—a people driven on by a new religion and a need for fertile land.

GLOSSARY OF HEBREW TERMINOLOGY
AND NAMES

Tigris	Ḥidekel	חִדָּקֶל
Euphrates	Praht	פְּרָת
Fall of the First Temple	Ḥoorbahn Bahyit Reeshohn	חָרְבַּן בַּיִת רִאשׁוֹן
Exilarch	Reysh Gah-lootah	רֵישׁ גָּלוּתָא
Abba, the Tall	Ahba Ahree-ḥah	אַבָּא אֲרִיכָא
Yarhina'ah (The Astronomer)	Yahrḥeena-ah	יַרְחִינָאָה
Teacher	Rahv	רַב
Sura	Soorah	סוּרָא
Pumbeditha	Poombedeetah	פּוּמְבְּדִיתָא
Adar	Ahdahr	אֲדָר
Elul	Elool	אֱלוּל
Months of Assembly	Yahrḥey Ḥah-lah (Kahlah)	יַרְחֵי כַלָּה
Prayer book	Sidoor	סִדּוּר
Alenu	Ahleynoo	עָלֵינוּ
Rabbah Bar Nahmani	Rahbah bar Naḥmahnee	רַבָּה בַּר נַחְמָנִי
Rav Ashi	Rahv Ahshee	רַב אַשִׁי
Rabbana	Rahbahnah	רַבָּנָא
Saboraim	Sahvorah-eem	סָבוֹרָאִים
Midrashim	Midrahsheem	מִדְרָשִׁים
Geonim	G'ohneem	גְּאוֹנִים
Gaon	Gah-ohn	גָּאוֹן

THE JEWS IN ARABIA

In the great desert known as the Arabian peninsula lived the Arabs, a nomadic people divided into many separate Bedouin tribes. Most of them lived in tents, wandering with their herds of cattle and sheep from meagre pasture to meagre pasture, from oasis to oasis, across the vast stretches of desert sand.

There had been Jewish settlements in Arabia as early as 70 C.E., when the Temple was destroyed. Some of the Jews of Arabia had settled on the oases of the northwestern strip of the Arabian peninsula, where they became farmers and planters. It is said that these Jewish orchard keepers and planters brought the culture of the date palm to Arabia. Jewish settlers had helped found the cities which lay along this strip of oases, through which the merchant caravans traveled east and west. Along these roads the precious loads of Arabian incense and spices were carried to Egypt, Palestine, Syria and Babylonia. Jewish merchants and artisans sold their wares in the cities of Yathrib and Mecca. There the people lived in sturdy houses of stone. The Bedouins visiting these cities marveled at the beauty and comfort which they saw there.

Not all Arabian Jews lived in cities, however. Many lived in tribes in the desert, like the Bedouins, wandering from waterhole to waterhole with their herds, just as Abraham, Isaac and Jacob had done many centuries before.

The Jews of Arabia could hardly be distinguished from their Arab neighbors, for they wore the same kind of clothing and spoke the same Arabian dialect. But there was one important difference: the Jews upheld the laws of the Torah and believed in one God, while the Arab tribes had many different idols, each tribe praying and sacrificing to its own separate deity. As the Arab tribes met their Jewish neighbors along the desert routes and traded with Jewish merchants and artisans in the cities, they learned of the religion of the one

Spout of a fourth century Yemenite lamp.

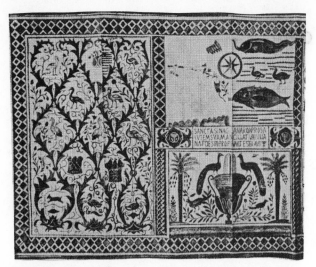

Mosaic floor in the fourth century synagogue in the city of Naro, Tunisia. The inscription reads, "Thy maid servant, the maiden Julia of Naro, installed this mosaic out of her funds for the welfare of the synagogue at Naro."

God. They heard stories from the Aggadah and the Midrashim, and came to know something about the laws by which their Jewish neighbors lived. The ways of Judaism interested and fascinated the Arabs, and Arab converts were added to the Jewish communities.

THE KINGDOM OF YEMEN

In Yemen, in the southwest of the Arabian pen-

These caves in the mountains of Tunisia and Tripolitania are inhabited by "Jewish cave dwellers." Their synagogue is also underground.

insula, Jewish planters and artisans had helped to bring wealth and prosperity to the land. In the fifth century, an Arabian king became a convert to Judaism, taking the Jewish name of Joseph. The realm of King Joseph flourished. Its merchants traded goods in many lands, its artisans forged lovely vessels of silver, copper and gold, and its poets wrote beautiful songs. The Jewish kingdom of Yemen was destroyed by the Byzantines and the Abyssinians in 525 C.E. Although many Jews left the land, there remained a Jewish community in Yemen.

In 575, Yemen became part of the Persian Empire, but the Jewish community never regained its former splendor. Often there was bitter poverty and persecution. In spite of these hardships, the Yemenite Jews held fast to their beliefs and pre-

Modern day Yemenite Jews.

served their skills. They continued to do their fine metal work, and to plant and trade.

The Jews of the northwestern Arabian peninsula had fared better. They had flourished and prospered and were active, respected members of their communities.

THE BEGINNING OF MOHAMMEDANISM (570-632)

In the beginning of the seventh century, a poor, illiterate young Arab camel driver, named Mohammed, was profoundly influenced by the concepts of Judaism. Although young Mohammed was poor and uneducated, he possessed extraordinary intelligence and energy. He worked his way up untiringly until he became a caravan driver, and eventually one of the wealthy merchants and importers of the city of Mecca.

Mohammed's caravan journeys took him through the lands of the Fertile Crescent, through Palestine, Egypt, and through Syria and the Babylonian plains. He came in contact with many educated Jews and developed an interest in the ideas of Judaism.

Like other Arabs, Mohammed believed himself to be a descendant of Ishmael, and also of Abraham, the Patriarch of the Jews. Deeply occupied with the problems of religion, Mohammed began to develop his own new ideas. Finally he came to look upon himself as a great prophet, like Moses. Mohammed affirmed the belief in the one God, whom he called Allah. "There is no god but Allah, and Mohammed is his prophet" he declared. He uttered prophecies which he believed he had received through divine inspiration from Allah himself. He proclaimed a new religion, and devoted all his intelligence and energy to the task of spreading it. He sought to understand the nature of God and to construct a code of ethics. Mohammed called his new religion "Islam"—meaning "submission to the will of God."

The new religion of Islam was founded on the basic principles of Judaism. Mohammed's prophecies contain pronouncements against idol worship and sacrifice, and uphold the worship of one God. Mohammed admonished his followers to live justly by the great basic laws which he had learned from his contact with Jews and Christians. He promised his followers that if they followed the commandments of Islam they would be rewarded with eternal bliss in an "afterlife" in heaven.

The old saying that a prophet is without honor in his own country seemed to be true in Mohammed's case, for he won no following in his own city of Mecca. The people there were enraged at Mohammed's attempt to convert them to Islam and considered him a fanatical rabble-rouser. In the year 622 C.E.—which is the year 1 in the Islamic calendar—Mohammed was forced to flee from his home.

MOHAMMEDANISM SPREADS

Undaunted by the opposition in Mecca, Mohammed continued to preach his faith and seek followers among the Arab tribes. Mohammed's dedication to his faith and his personal magnetism won him many followers. Gradually the new religion of Islam took root and spread over the vast Arabian desert lands and Mohammed became the great prophet of Arabia. The many tribes that had warred and quarreled for centuries among themselves now became united, regarding themselves as one people—the people of Islam, united under the guidance of

In the year 750 Joseph Rabban, a Yemenite Jew, led an expedition to Cochin, India. The king of Malabar, Cheramal Perumal, granted them a charter of privilege. The charter is engraved on two bronze tablets known as "Sasanam."

171

View of the holy city of Mecca and its mosque. Mohammedan pilgrims come from great distances to kiss a black stone called the Kaaba which is enclosed in the square shelter in the middle of the mosque court. Mohammed claimed that the Kaaba was sanctified by Abraham and Ishmael.

Mohammed. The city of Yathrib, the home of the prophet, became a holy city and was renamed Medina (*Medinat-en-Navi,* "City of the Prophet") and Mecca, his birthplace, also became a shrine for his followers.

Mohammed expected the Jews of Arabia to accept his new religion. After all, had it not been founded on the principles of Judaism and was not he, Mohammed, a prophet in the great tradition of the prophets of Israel? The Jews were indeed glad to see idol worship replaced by a religion that proclaimed the one, invisible God—but they could not accept the ideas of Mohammed. They had their own ancient tradition, their own civilization, their laws and religion, all built securely upon the Torah and the Talmud.

When they saw that the Jews would not join their ranks. Mohammed and his followers began to persecute them. They attacked the Jews of Medina and forced them to flee from the city. Many of the Jewish desert tribes were also attacked and a number were conquered and annihilated. Those who survived, together with the Jews of Yemen, were taxed excessively and forced to obey humiliating laws. The freedom and security of the Jewish communities of Arabia had come to an end.

THE CALIPHATE

Mohammed died in the year 632. He was succeeded by the Caliph Abu Bakr who died two years later and was followed by the Caliph Omar. Omar, who had been converted by Mohammed himself, had been the prophet's advisor, and the leader of Mohammed's military campaigns throughout Ara-

A page from the Koran.

The ascension of Mohammed.

quest and conversion. The Moslem empire was spreading over all the Fertile Crescent, from the Nile delta to the Persian Gulf.

It was during the reign of Omar's successor, the Caliph Othman, a son-in-law of Mohammed, that the *Koran,* the holy book of Islam, was put together in written form. At Othman's command all the prophecies of Mohammed were arranged and written down, based on the notes taken by Mohammed's own secretary at his master's dictation.

The Koran is divided into chapters arranged in order of length. Written in beautiful, classical Arabic, the Koran begins with a short passage in praise of Allah. To this day, Moslems study and cherish the Koran, just as the Jews cherish the Torah and the Christians their version of the Bible and their New Testament.

As the new Arabian empire grew and absorbed more and more lands, it became inadvisable to continue the persecution of peoples of different faiths within the empire. Forced conversions came to an end and Christians and Jews could now live in

bia. Caliph Omar was now the princely ruler of Arabia, and the religious leader of all the Moslems. (Moslem, derived from the root of the word *Islam,* means "a follower of Islam.")

Omar declared a holy war. The Caliph and his followers rode across the desert on their swift steeds into the lands of the Fertile Crescent. Omar was a great conqueror, commanding many able generals and a large, zealous army of expert horsemen. The fighters were recruited from all over Arabia. United in their faith, they blindly followed the Caliph, with "Allah" and "Mohammed" as their battle cries.

Omar and his generals conquered Egypt, Palestine, Syria and Persia, spreading the faith of Islam in those lands. The Persians were driven out of the plains of Mesopotamia, back into Iran, the land of their origin. In 641, Iran itself was conquered and the once mighty Persian Empire was brought to its knees by the new power of Arabia.

Omar laid the foundation of a vast Arabian empire, which is often referred to as the Caliphate. Omar's successors continued the campaigns of con-

Page from an illuminated Yemenite Bible signed by the copyist Moses ben Amram, 1409.

peace again. However, the rights and liberties of "non-believers," as the non-Mohammedans would be called, were still severely reduced. All non-believers were forced to pay a humiliating poll tax; they were not allowed to ride on horseback; they were forced to wear clothes that would make them conspicuous and set them apart from the Mohammedans and they were not permitted to bear arms. But they were not forbidden to observe their own religion. As time passed, the Arabian conquerors proved increasingly tolerant. The Jews of the Arabian Empire could follow their religion and way of life. Eventually, in many parts of the empire, they were freed from many of the restrictions that had been imposed upon them on account of their religion.

As the Arabian Empire expanded, the Arabs gradually created a new culture. The Arabian nobles and leaders delighted in poetry and song. Many of them were occupied with the pursuit of the sciences, mathematics and medicine. Talented Arab architects created beautiful monuments and palaces.

The Jews under Arab rule found their place in this new civilization and generously contributed of

Chinese statue of a Jew dressed in Persian costume, seventh to tenth century C.E.

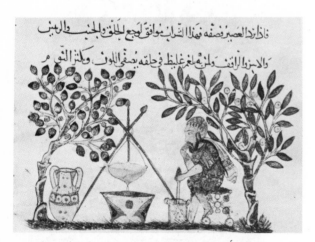

Arab physician preparing cough medicine, thirteenth century.

their own talents. Jewish poets wrote Arabic verses and Jewish physicians, mathematicians and astronomers contributed to the growth of the sciences. Jewish merchants helped establish the trade routes of the new nation throughout the lands of the Mediterranean. Soon these Jewish traders were to follow the Arabian conquerors into the lands of North Africa, and eventually across the Mediterranean to far-off Spain in the southwest of Europe.

PALESTINE UNDER THE CALIPHATE

After Omar's conquest of Palestine, conditions there improved. The Arabs established a Moslem sanctuary in Jerusalem, which had now become the holy city of three religions. Once again the Jews were permitted to enter the city and pray before the ruined western wall of the Temple. Soon a little Jewish community was formed in Jerusalem.

The Arab sanctuary, Dome of the Rock, built by Abd el Malik in 691 C.E., covers the sacred rock of Solomon's Temple.

In Galilee, Jewish communities began to flourish, and an academy in Tiberias became a center of study. Just as the scholars of Babylonia were especially noted for their knowledge of law, so the scholars in Palestine excelled in their talent for poetry. The land of their fathers filled them with inspiration and with a deep reverence for their history. Many of their beautiful hymns were preserved and later became part of the Jewish Prayer Book.

THE MASORAH

An absorbing task that now occupied the scholars of Tiberias was the establishment of the Masorah. "Masorah" means "handing down," or more specifically, the establishment of the correct, standard text of the Holy Scriptures: the correct way of writing down the *Torah* scrolls and other Biblical books for "handing down" to future generations. The scholars who performed this task are called the Masoretes and the authentic text which they determined is known as the Masoretic text. This is the text followed by the Soferim (Scribes) to this day when they copy Scrolls of the Law.

The Masoretes, concerned with preserving the true text and the true meaning of the Scriptures, laid down the text of the Bible word for word, letter for letter. Many non-Jews had translated the Bible during previous centuries; many of these translations had been inaccurate. Even among

Jews, not all the scrolls which were in use preserved the same text. The Masoretes carefully compared different versions of the Scriptures and decided which version corresponded to the pure, original form. Other Masoretes worked in the Babylonian schools, but eventually the authentic, acknowledged Masorah was the text established by the scholars of Palestine.

The Masoretes worked out a system of punctuation to provide the Hebrew script with clear marks for its vowels. The basis of Hebrew consists of consonants, the vowels being understood according to certain rules. In addition the Scriptures were provided with a system of accentuation that serves also as a system of musical notation for the cantillation of the public readings from the Torah and other parts of the Scriptures.

The Masoretes were active from the 7th through the 10th centuries (890-940). Their most outstanding scholars were Ben Asher and Ben Naphtali.

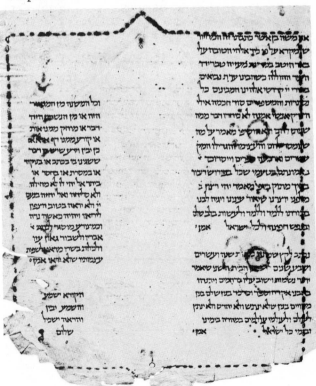

Colophon of the masoretic codex of Moses Ben Asher (897 C.E.)

GLOSSARY OF HEBREW TERMINOLOGY
AND NAMES

Arabs	Ahrvim	עַרְבִים
Bedouins	Beydoo-eem	בֶּידוּאִים
Yemen	Teymahn	תֵּימָן
Mohammed	Moohahmahd	מוּחָמָד
Allah	Ahlah	אַלַאה (אֱלֹהַ)
Islam	Islahm	אִסְלַאם
Moslem	Mooslahmee	מָסְלָמִי
Koran	Kohrahn	קוֹרַאן
Masorah	Mahsohrah	מָסוֹרָה
Scribes	Sohfreem	סוֹפְרִים
Ben Asher	Ben Ahsheyr	בֶּן אָשֵׁר
Ben Naphtali	Ben Nahftahlee	בֶּן נַפְתָּלִי

CHANGES IN BABYLONIA

Although there was a Jewish community in Jerusalem once again, the center of Jewish life was still in Babylonia. The Moslems, led by the Caliph Omar, had conquered Babylonia and changed its name to Iraq. With the Arab conquest, the condition of the Babylonian Jews improved. Once more the schools of Sura and Pumpeditha functioned, presided over by the Geonim. Again the Jewish community was led by an Exilarch, a "Prince of the Exile," who represented the highest official authority among them. The Exilarchs were now appointed by the Caliphs and were authorized to collect the taxes both for the Caliphate and for the Jewish community.

THE EXILARCH BUSTANAI

The first Exilarch appointed by the Caliph Omar was Bustanai, a wise and beloved leader. Many legends were told of Bustanai's birth and personality. The Exilarchs who followed him through many generations looked back to him as their spiritual ancestor. However, these later leaders were often dependent appointees of the Geonim of Sura and Pumpeditha and did not exercise the

The Caliph's guard. From a Moslem manuscript of 1237.

same power as had Bustanai. As heads of the two academies, the Geonim gained in importance and often acted as advisors to the Exilarchs who fre-

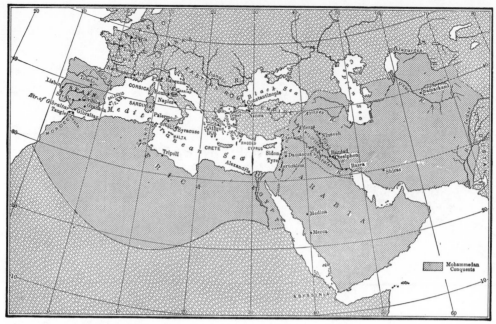

The Mohammedan conquest at its greatest extent, about 750 C.E.

quently depended on the Geonim for guidance in problems of law and scholarship. Even far-off communities would turn to the Geonim for advice.

THE RESPONSA

Wherever Jews were in doubt on questions of Jewish law, they would send their messengers to the Geonim and their colleagues in Babylonia. The Babylonian scholars composed their answers clearly and concisely. The letters in which the Geonim would set forth their answers and decisions were known as *Responsa* (*Teshuvot* in Hebrew). Ever since the time of the Geonim, the decisions made by scholars the world over on matters of Jewish law have been set down according to the form used in the Gaonic Responsa. However, in time these responsa became more elaborate and discursive. A study of the collections of responsa that have come down to us through the centuries from many lands provides the reader with a highly informative survey of Jewish history.

Many of the messengers who came to the Geonim brought gifts and money from distant communities to help preserve the academies and their work. The schools of Babylonia flourished in the days of the Geonim.

Eventually, the system of sending messengers back and forth between the various far-flung communities and the Geonim became too cumbersome. The Geonim then evolved a new plan: they sent out their own messengers—scholars from the academies—to acquaint Jews everywhere with the activities of the schools of Sura and Pumpeditha and to explain the nature of the Talmud and Talmudic studies. On their journeys these scholar-messengers would also collect funds to support the academies. Thus the Jews of many lands acquired a knowledge of the Law and the skill to study, interpret and use the Talmudic text, and the Talmudic tradition became a strong, unifying bond between the many scattered Jewish settlements.

However, not all the Jews in the new Arabian Empire looked to the Geonim for leadership and not all of them lived according to the Talmudic traditions.

FALSE MESSIAHS

The longing to return to the Land of Israel and rebuild the Temple in Jerusalem was strong in the hearts of the Jews. They remembered the words of their own great prophets, predicting the coming of a Messiah, an "anointed one," who would usher in

[Hebrew manuscript text]

An original document letter of the pseudo-messiah Judah ben Shalom of Yemen, known as Mari Shooker Kahail. He succeeded in persuading many Jews and Arabs to follow him. Eventually he was killed by the Arabs.

a new era of peace and justice. Thus from time to time a leader would gain power and influence by pretending he was the long-awaited Messiah. The

The "Coming of the Messiah" to the gates of Jerusalem. From a Haggadah printed in Venice in 1609.

people still remembered Bar Kokhba, who had led the last insurrection against the Romans, and whom many had thought to be the Messiah. Many of these "false Messiahs" were poor and illiterate, but driven by burning zeal. Several such leaders attempted to lead armed bands of Jews to the Land of Israel. Many of these bands were wiped out by Arabian armies. Some of the false Messiahs were put to death; others died in battle, and one took his own life.

THE KARAITES

There was in Babylonia a group which opposed the Geonim and became a powerful threat to the unity of the Jews in that country. The ideas of this

Karaites living in the Crimea, Russia. They were treated by the czarist government as being of a different religion than the Jews.

group greatly resembled those of the Sadducees of old. This new movement maintained that it was not necessary to study the Talmud and the Oral

179

Abraham Firkovich (1728-1812), famous Karaite scholar. He held various posts in the Crimea and owned a collection of ancient Biblical manuscripts. These are now in the Leningrad Library.

Tradition, believing that the Written Law was the only valid Jewish Law and that the Talmud was only an obstruction to its study.

Among the leaders of this movement was Anan ben David. The nephew of a childless, aging exilarch, Anan hoped to succeed his uncle in office. But after the death of the exilarch the Geonim of Pumpeditha and Sura chose Anan's younger brother Hananiah to become the next exilarch. Bitterly disappointed, Anan summoned his supporters to revolt and contested his brother's right to the high office.

The Geonim had the power to choose the exilarchs, but they had to have their choice approved by the Caliph. The Caliph gave his official approval to Hananiah and, fearing unrest, had the rebellious Anan put into prison.

Anan had to stand trial. On the advice of an able Arab lawyer, Anan testified that he did not care about whether or not he would become the exilarch but that he was merely the founder of a new Jewish sect. As a result of this testimony, he was acquitted.

Anan and his followers spoke out sharply against the Talmud. "Forsake the words of the Talmud and I will make unto you a Talmud of my own!" Anan said, evidently ignoring the fact that the Talmud was not the work of one man but an unbroken chain of great ideas and ideals which

had stemmed from many great leaders through many generations, reaching back a thousand years to the time of Ezra the Scribe.

Anan tried to combat the Talmud with laws of his own making and with those laws which the scholars who had compiled the Talmud had rejected. For instance, Anan forbade the use of heat and light on the Sabbath, even if the heat and light had been initiated before the Sabbath. His followers had to sit in the dark and eat cold food on the day of rest, for Anan forbade them to make arrangements to have ovens preheated to provide for Sabbath comfort and joy. The followers of Anan led a grim life in a bleak world of inflexible law. They considered it forbidden to reinterpret the laws and passages of the Torah or to search for the spirit behind them. Under Anan's sucessors, his movement took for itself the name *Bnai Mikra* (Sons of the Scriptures). They were also called the *Karaites* (Scripturists), for they believed only in the literal meaning of the Scriptures, rejecting all Talmudic tradition.

Actually, the Karaites were inconsistent. While they rejected the traditions that had developed in the Talmud, they developed traditions of their own —traditions which in time became very rigid.

In the 9th and 10th centuries the Karaite sect was an active, growing movement, a challenge to Jewish thought. Its leaders wrote eloquent treatises on the subject of Karaism versus Talmudic tradition. There were Karaites in Babylonia, in Pales-

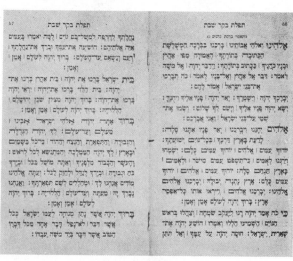

A page from a Karaite prayer book. These prayers consist primarily of verses from the Bible.

Synagogue of the Karaites in Jerusalem.

tine, in Egypt and in North Africa; the sect and its ideas had become a threat to the unity of the Jew-ish people.

AARON BEN MEIR SPITES THE GEONIM

The division caused by the Karaite movement was not the only problem that weakened Jewish unity. Even among the rabbinical scholars, disagreement and struggles for power threatened to disrupt the creative life of Judaism.

In Palestine the new Arab rulers had established peace, and the Jewish academies again became important. Aaron Ben Meir, a Palestinian scholar, who traced his descent back to the great Hillel, was determined to wrest the leadership of the Jewish communities from the Geonim. But Aaron Ben Meir was unable to compete with the brilliant Talmudic scholarship of the Geonim of Babylonia and their colleagues. He decided, therefore, on another plan, caring little what danger it might hold for Jewish unity.

Aaron Ben Meir remembered how for centuries Jews of every land had accepted the annual ruling of the Nasi and the Sanhedrin concerning the dates on which the high holidays were to be celebrated each year. Then in 425 C.E., the Nasi Hillel II had published a permanent calendar with directions for calculating the holiday dates. Based on this calendar, Jews everywhere could make their own

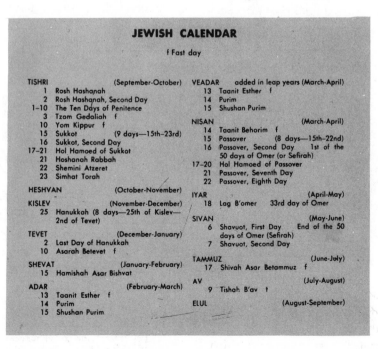

JEWISH CALENDAR

f Fast day

TISHRI (September–October)
1 Rosh Hashanah
2 Rosh Hashanah, Second Day
1–10 The Ten Days of Penitence
3 Tzom Gedaliah f
10 Yom Kippur f
15 Sukkot (9 days—15th–23rd)
16 Sukkot, Second Day
17–21 Hol Hamoed of Sukkot
21 Hoshanah Rabbah
22 Shemini Atzeret
23 Simhat Torah

HESHVAN (October–November)

KISLEV (November–December)
25 Hanukkah (8 days—25th of Kislev—2nd of Tevet)

TEVET (December–January)
2 Last Day of Hanukkah
10 Asarah Betevet f

SHEVAT (January–February)
15 Hamishah Asar Bishvat

ADAR (February–March)
13 Taanit Esther f
14 Purim
15 Shushan Purim

VEADAR added in leap years (March–April)
13 Taanit Esther f
14 Purim
15 Shushan Purim

NISAN (March–April)
14 Taanit Behorim f
15 Passover (8 days—15th–22nd)
16 Passover, Second Day 1st of the 50 days of Omer (or Sefirah)
17–20 Hol Hamoed of Passover
21 Passover, Seventh Day
22 Passover, Eighth Day

IYAR (April–May)
18 Lag B'omer 33rd day of Omer

SIVAN (May–June)
6 Shavuot, First Day End of the 50 days of Omer (Sefirah)
7 Shavuot, Second Day

TAMMUZ (June–July)
17 Shivah Asar Betammuz f

AV (July–August)
9 Tishah B'av f

ELUL (August–September)

calculations and all could celebrate the holidays at the same time. As the Babylonian Geonim gained in importance, they took over the task of calculating the calendar and would announce the dates of the holidays each year.

Aaron published a new calendar, based on his own calculations and different from that devised by the Geonim. Ben Meir's calendar created havoc. Jewish holidays would be celebrated on different days in different cities and sometimes even on different days by different groups of people in the same community. In this manner did Aaron Ben Meir seek to break the power of the Geonim, believing himself to be as powerful an authority in Palestine as were the Geonim in Babylonia. The people took sides heatedly in the struggle between these two sides.

SAADIA GAON

At that time a great scholar arose. Saadia Ben Joseph, an Egyptian Jew, whose brilliant treatises against Karaism helped many people to understand the issues of the conflict between the new sect and Talmudic tradition. Saadia defended the calendar of the Babylonian Geonim with great skill. In a polite but clear letter, he expained to Aaron Ben Meir the faults in his calculations and appealed to all the Jewish world to uphold the calendar devised by the Geonim.

ספר
האמונות והדעות

הוא כולל עשרה מאמרים, מדבר מעניני האמונני האמיתית, והדעות הישרות, שיבור לד הארם, ע״פ התורה והחכמה והמוסר. ונספלו עוד אמונות כוזבות ורעות נסהרות, וההתירה עליהם, ותשובות על שאלות הפונים והכופרים.

חברו כלשון ערב
הנאון רבינו סעדיה ז"ל הפיומי,
ראש ישיבה במתא מחסיא

והעתיקו
ר יהודה ן' תיבון דיין מרמן ספרד ללשון הקדש.

A title page of Sefer Emunot v'Deot.

Soon thereafter, Saadia published his "Book of the Seasons," a beautifully written work, composed in biblical style, and written out with accent and vowel marks so that any Jew who knew Hebrew could read Saadia's book. In it the calculations of the Jewish calendar were made understandable to any one who had mastered the fundamentals of mathematics and who was familiar with the Jewish holidays and the regulations of Hillel II. "The Book of the Seasons" was widely read and put an end to the calendar controversy and restored unity.

The Exilarch summoned Saadia to become the Gaon of the academy at Sura, although it was not customary for anyone but a native Babylonian to hold that high office. Saadia proved the greatest, most capable of all the Geonim. He succeeded in exposing the weaknesses of the Karaite beliefs and restored the community's faith in the Talmudic tradition.

Saadia, who was familiar with both Arabic and Greek, made an excellent Arabic translation of the Bible. This translation was used for centuries afterward by Jews throughout the Arabic-speaking world. He also compiled a Hebrew grammar and was one of the first scholars to attempt to codify the Talmud.

Moreover, Saadia was a poet. Like many Arabic poets of his time he frequently wrote acrostics— that is, using the letters of the Hebrew alphabet in a given order as the beginning of verses in a long or short poem. Indeed, Saadia became so intrested in the art of poetry that he composed a Hebrew rhyming dictionary.

In the days of Saadia, the synagogue services had no fixed order. Saadia composed an order for prayers and rituals, one of the first Jewish prayerbooks, which was called the *Siddur,* meaning "order," as our prayer books are called today.

Saadia's main duties had to do with his position as head of the academy of Sura. He taught a new generation of scholars and composed a great number of Responsa in answer to the many legal questions which Jewish communities of many lands sent to the scholars of Sura.

Saadia was a profound thinker. His greatest philosophical work, "Beliefs and Opinions," explains the fundamental beliefs and ideas of Juda-

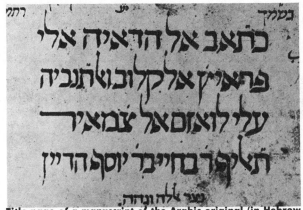

Title page of a manuscript of the Arabic original (in Hebrew characters) of *Hobot Halevavot* by Bahya.

ism. In this work Saadia arranged his subject matter by a new and logical method which he had learned from his study of science. "Beliefs and Opinions" was written in Arabic and gave many non-Jews a clearer picture of Judaism. It is a book which still fascinates many readers of the present day.

The Exilarch opposed Saadia's opinions in an important lawsuit and tried unsuccessfully to persuade Saadia to agree with him. So bitter was the fight over the decision that the Exilarch deposed Saadia from the office of Gaon. For seven years Saadia lived in Baghdad, far from his beloved academy, before he was finally recalled by the Exilarch.

Soon thereafter the Exilarch died. Saadia proved his great sense of fairness by supporting the choice of the Exilarch's son as successor to the office against another contender.

In the days of Saadia, the prestige and power of the Geonim of Sura and Pumpeditha reached their high point. But after the death of the great master the importance of the Babylonian schools slowly diminished, and with it the influence of the Geonim.

THE END OF THE BABYLONIAN ERA

Great changes were taking place in the Moslem Empire, with far-reaching effects on the Jewish community of Babylonia.

The Arabian Empire of the early Caliphate had been divided into separate Caliphates: the Eastern Caliphate, with its capital in Damascus, and later in Baghdad; and the North African or Egyptian Caliphate.

In the year 711, Arab conquerors had crossed the Mediterranean and founded a Western Caliphate in Spain. The Moslem conquerors of Spain encouraged Jewish merchants to settle in Spain and soon the new Spanish Caliphate began to flourish. Jews participated freely, without restrictions, in the building of the new settlements. Eventually the Spanish Caliphs encouraged the Jews in Spain to become an independent community, separating their institutions from the Jewish institutions in the lands of the Eastern Calpihate.

The Jews of Spain, North Africa and Egypt had begun to found their own schools. As other new centers gained in importance, the old academies no longer attracted all the great minds throughout the Jewish world.

The position of the Baylonian Jewish community deteriorated under the rulers of the Eastern Caliphate, who were not as tolerant and enterprising as the Moslem conquerors of Spain. Restrictive laws were restored in the eastern Caliphate and non-Moslems were burdened with exorbitant taxes. To escape these conditions, many Jews emigrated to Egypt and North Africa; others went to Spain or Italy.

The soil of Mesopotamia, like the other lands of the Fertile Crescent with the exception of Egypt, was becoming less and less productive. This increasing barrenness had been the cause of emigration toward the west.

By the beginning of the 12th century, Jews no longer looked to the Babylonian centers for leadership. Although there were Geonim and exilarchs in Babylonia for another two centuries, they were now merely regarded as local dignitaries and their schools only as local academies.

The Jewish community of Babylonia had made lasting and significant contributions to Jewish life: the Babylonian Talmud; the tradition of the Responsa; the first Hebrew grammar, and the first Siddur. The Babylonian community had taught Jews in many lands how to live in the Diaspora and had set an example of greatness, scholarship, unity and dignity. Now, with the decline of the Babylonian community, a great era of Jewish history had come to an end.

183

GLOSSARY OF HEBREW TERMINOLOGY AND NAMES

Exilarch	Reysh Gahloo-tah	רֵישׁ גָּלוּתָא
Bustanai	Boostnahy	בֻּסְתְּנַאי
Geonim	G'ohneem	גְּאוֹנִים
Responsa	Tshoovoht	תְּשׁוּבוֹת
Karaites	Kahrah-eem or Bney Mik-rah	קָרָאִים, בְּנֵי מִקְרָא
Anan ben David	Ahnahn ben Dahveed	עָנָן בֶּן דָּוִד
Aaron ben Meir	Ahahrohn ben Mey-eer	אַהֲרֹן בֶּן מֵאִיר
Saadia Gaon	S'ahdyah	סְעַדְיָה
Diaspora	Gahloot or Gohlah	גָּלוּת, גּוֹלָה

THE POWER OF THE CHURCH

THE JEWS IN ROME

Since the days of Alexander the Great, and increasingly so since the early days of the Roman. Empire, Jewish traders had been in contact with European trade centers. Beginning with the time of Judah Maccabee, Judea had had diplomatic contact with Rome, and Jews had gone to Italy on political missions and to engage in trade. In the days of Pompey's conquests, the first Jewish prisoners had been brought captive to Rome to serve the conquerors as slaves. Soon thereafter, Jewish traders had come bringing spices, dyes and silks to the great city to exchange for Roman arms and leather goods.

The Jews did not make good slaves. They refused to work on the Sabbath. They also refused to eat certain foods, holding fast to the laws of the Torah. They would not bow to the Roman gods, but insisted on worshipping their own invisible God. The Roman masters were annoyed by these stubborn Jewish slaves and were anxious to be rid of them, so Jewish settlers who came to Rome as free men found it easy to ransom their enslaved fellow-Jews for gifts of money.

In the days of Herod many Judean aristocrats had been educated in Rome. Jewish catacombs have been discovered by modern archaeologists, marked with Hebrew inscriptions which date back to that period. By the second century of the Common Era, a Jewish community existed in Rome. Though its membership consisted mostly of poor laborers, it also had some wealthy merchants and even descendants of noble families that had been taken captive.

After the Romans had conquered Gaul and the Germanic lands, they founded Roman settlements in these territories. Jewish traders followed the Roman settlers and established trade routes in Gaul and along great rivers such as the Rhine and the Danube. These Jewish traders traveled back

Fresco in the Jewish catacombs at Villa Torlonia, Rome.

Relief from the column of Antonnia in Rome showing the sack of a Roman village.

Certificate showing that a roman citizen had sacrificed to the emperor as a god.

and forth, bringing new products to Rome and supplying the settlers in the new lands with needed goods. Jewish vintners and farmers who had lost their lands in Judea came to settle in the new Roman colonies, using their skills to cultivate the fertile lands.

Under the Roman rulers, Jewish settlers and traders enjoyed great freedom of movement. In 212 C.E. the emperor Caracalla decreed that all free persons living in the Roman Empire would henceforth be Roman citizens and so the rights and duties of Roman citizenship were conferred also upon the Jews.

However, the Jewish citizens of Rome were set apart by a special tax called the *Fiscus Judaicus.* Instead of sending half a shekel every year to Jerusalem for the Temple, the Jews now had to pay this sum as a tax to Rome to commemorate Rome's victory over Judea.

Many pagans were deeply impressed by the religion and customs of their Jewish neighbors, and visited the Jewish synagogues. Many Romans from all walks of life embraced Judaism. But with the rise of Christianity all this changed; conditions became less favorable for the Jews.

CHRISTIANITY BECOMES THE OFFICIAL RELIGION OF ROME

Until the year 325, the Christians had been only a minor sect, often suffering persecution at the hands of the Romans. Then in the year 325, the Emperor Constantine convened the Council of Nicaea and Christianity became the official religion of the Roman Empire. Soon after the death of Constantine the Empire split into two states: the Byzantine Eastern Empire with its capital at Constantinople, a city built on the ruins of the ancient city Byzantium—and the Western Empire, with Rome as its capital.

Each Empire had its own emperor and church organization. Eventually these two branches of Christianity developed different ways. They differed in their rituals, their music and art and also in the structure of their clergy. The church organization of

Bust of Emperor Carcalla.

The extent of the Kingdom of the Goths. All that remained of the once mighty Roman kingdom is the area marked "Eastern Empire."

the Byzantine Empire became known as the Greek Orthodox Church; that of the Western Empire was known as the Roman Catholic Church.

ROME IS CONQUERED

In the fifth century the pagan Goths captured Rome. The Goths were Germanic tribes from the north of Europe who had moved southward in search of new lands. Beginning with the third century of the Common Era, these barbaric tribes had sought to gain a foothold in Italy and the Roman legions had been occupied in holding them back. But the great Roman Empire had been growing steadily weaker. Luxurious living, corruption and immorality, bad government and oppression of the poor had all contributed to bring about the Empire's downfall. In 425 a Gothic leader captured and sacked the city of Rome and the once mighty empire fell to the new conquerors.

The Goths were divided into several tribes. Some of these tribes conquered Italy; others invaded Spain and Gaul and still another Gothic tribe took the lands which lay along the Danube. These barbarian conquerors were strongly attracted to the civilization of Rome. They accepted the

language and legal system of the Romans and even converted to Christianity, the new religion of Rome. Under Gothic rule the power of the Roman Catholic Church spread to other lands. The early bishops of the Church were diligently engaged in spreading the new religion. Missionaries went out to convert all the peoples of the empire.

As the Church grew in power, the status of the Jews changed, for the young Church feared their religious influence. Under new laws, conversion to Judaism was forbidden and Jews were not allowed to intermarry with Christians. Jews, however, were still allowed to live peacefully in Roman lands. Most of them lived in their own communities, their lives centering around their synagogues and schools.

The Jews tenaciously refused to be converted to Christianity and because heretics, or people who differed from the Church in their beliefs, were considered a danger to the religious unity of the Empire, the early bishops tried to influence rulers to pass harsh laws against the Jews.

By the end of the fifth century, the western part of the Roman Empire had fallen apart. The various lands that had been part of that Empire were now under barbarian kings. These kings and the Church waged a deep and bitter struggle for power and the Jews became pawns in this constant battle. Some kings, in defiance of the wishes of the bishops, refused to pass the harsh laws against the Jews which the Church desired. The kings often saw great advantage in protecting their Jewish subjects, for the Jews brought valuable skills to their lands. They were responsible, tax-paying subjects. They knew many languages and were not

Copy of a relief showing the triumphant parade of Gothic warriors with their spoils of war.

Synagogue in Rome, fifth century, C.E. (Note the Eternal Light.)

Relief of a mounted German warrior, about 700 C.E.

afraid to travel to distant lands. They had good trade connections in many countries and were skilled in the art of acquiring and exchanging goods.

As the Roman Catholic Church developed, the bishops, the princes of the Church, gained more and more importance. The Bishop of Rome, the head of the whole Church of Rome, assumed the title of Pope and eventually claimed the right to crown the emperors of the Christian Roman Empire. As time passed, both the religious and political

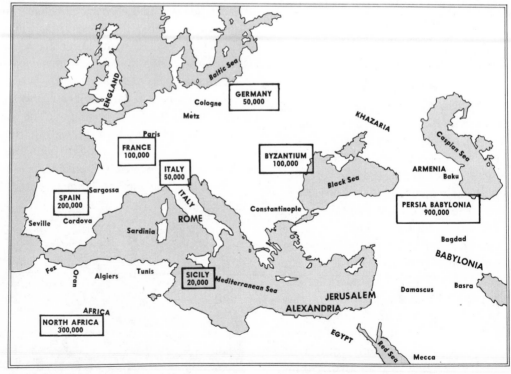

Centers of Jewish population in Christian and Moslem countries in the years 640 to 1100. The largest number, 900,000, lived in Persia-Babylonia, to the east, which after 640 came under Moslem rule. The large communities of Spain (200,000) and North Africa (300,000) were also under Moslem rule. Christian lands shown are France, Germany, Italy, and Byzantium.

power of the popes increased and kings and princes were often dependent on their support and favor.

THE REIGN OF CHARLEMAGNE

In the year 800, Pope Leo III crowned Charlemagne, or Charles the Great, as "Emperor of the Romans." Charlemagne's lands were later called the Holy Roman Empire, to show they were Christian and that the rulers of these lands recognized the authority of the Pope.

Charlemagne was a Frank by nationality. The Franks were a Germanic people, related to the Goths. The Frankish civilization had grown and its people had adopted many Roman ways and converted to Christianity. But the city of Rome had ceased to be a capital or the center of imperial power. The capital of Charlemagne's empire was far to the north of Rome in the land named France, after the Franks. The capital was named Aachen; or in its French form—Aix-la-Chapelle.

Charlemagne was a brilliant man and a great ruler. His kingdom consisted of the lands that lay east and west of the Rhine River, lands that eventually were to become known as France and Germany. Charlemagne was concerned with the welfare of his empire and with the expansion of commerce and communications. He realized that his

Charlemagne being crowned Emperor.

Silver portrait penny of Charlemagne minted in the last year of his reign.

Jewish subjects could contribute much to the growth of trade. Ignoring the advice of the bishops, Charlemagne protected the Jews in his empire and put no restrictions on them.

Charlemagne organized an efficient government and civil service, with himself as chief administrator; all officials had to report to him and all the nobles owed him allegiance and military service. Considering himself to be the highest authority in his own dominions, Charlemagne also managed church affairs by himself and reserved the right to appoint bishops and other church officials independently of Rome. But Charlemagne's system was not to endure. After his death there were long and bitter struggles for power between the popes and the emperors.

A document from the Bet Din in Kairouan, 977-978 B.C.E.

Charlemagne's descendants, known as the Carolingians, were all crowned at Aachen. Under the rule of the Carolingians, the people lived in peace. During the reign of Louis the Pious, the son of Charlemagne who adhered to his father's policies, the Jewish communities prospered. The bishops tried in vain to influence the new emperor to re-

Frankish warrior.

Tenth century Carolingian script.

Byzantine coin of Emperor Heraclius.

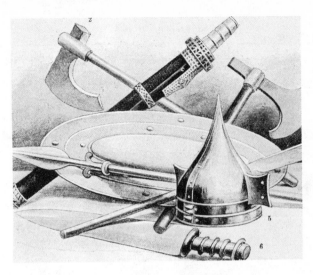

Frankish weapons of war.

strict the rights of the Jews. Louis the Pious continued to protect his Jewish subjects as his father had done before him.

Before the time of Charlemagne many of the kings of Gaul (as the Frankish lands had once been called) had been strongly influenced by the church, which endeavored to bring Christianity to all the pagan peoples conquered by Christian kings. Missionaries were sent to the newly-conquered countries, going as far north as the British Isles and Ireland.

Meanwhile, in the Byzantine Empire, the Christian emperor, Heraclius, who ruled from 610 to 641, feared the rising power of the Mohammedan religion. To safeguard the Christian faith, Heraclius had declared all religions except Christianity forbidden within his dominions. Thus the practice of Judaism too, was outlawed in the Byzantine Empire.

Many kings followed the example of the Byzantine emperor. A king of Gaul had expelled from his domain all Jews who resisted conversion to Christianity. The kings of Burgundy and Lombardy did the same. In Spain, under the Gothic rulers, the Jews fared even worse.

GLOSSARY OF HEBREW TERMINOLOGY AND NAMES

Christianity	Nahtsroot (from Naza-reth)	נַצְרוּת
Shekel	Shehkel	שֶׁקֶל

THE JEWS IN SPAIN

THE VISIGOTHS ENTER SPAIN

It is said that the first Jewish settlers came to Spain in the days of the First Temple. By the fourth century of the Common Era, there were so many Jews in Spain that the Church Council of Elvira found it necessary to pass special laws to check the friendly and peaceful relations between Jews and their Christian neighbors.

At the beginning of the fifth century, the Visigoths, as the Goths of Western Europe were called, invaded and conquered Spain. At first, when they still adhered to their old religion, they were tolerant toward peoples practicing other religions, including their Jewish subjects. But when they converted to Catholicism at the end of the sixth century, the Visigoth rulers came under the influence of the church. At a great Church Council, strict laws were enacted against Jews. Jews could no longer hold public office. They were no longer permitted to sing psalms at their funerals, as had been their custom, but had to bury their dead in silence. Marriages between Jews and Christians were forbidden.

In the year 616, Sisebut, a fanatical Visigoth, became king in Spain. With his rule a century of oppression began for the Jews of Spain. Children were taken away from their parents and forcibly converted. Many Jews, faced with the threat of death, accepted baptism. Until the end of Visigoth rule, Judaism was forbidden in Spain. This was the first time that the Jews in Spain lived as *Mar-*

Ruins of a Christian basilica in Carthage.

Mohammedan warriors.

The everyday language of these Jews of North Africa was Arabic. Learning, science and art flourished in the Arab lands, and many Jews contributed to the study of astronomy, medicine and mathematics. Jewish poets wrote beautiful verses in Arabic.

In 711, the Moorish general Tarik crossed the Straits of Gibraltar and within four years all of Spain was under Arab domination. Many Jews left their communities in North Africa to follow the conquering Moorish armies to Spain. The old Jewish communities of Spain were greatly influenced by these Arab-speaking Jews, who already knew the freedom of the Arab world.

A view of Cordova in the eighth century.

ranos. *Marranos* was the name later given to Jews who had been forced to convert to Christianity but who loyally practiced their religion in secret, although the penalty would be torture and death should they be discovered. But soon this dark period was destined to end. Across the Mediterranean Sea, new conquerors were preparing to invade Spain

THE ARABS CONQUER SPAIN

The Moors, once Arab nomads of North Africa, had been converted to the Mohammedan religion. The teachings of Islam inspired them with the desire to conquer. In the eighth century the Moors prepared to sail across the Mediterranean to conquer Spain. To the Moors, this land of famed beauty just across the sea from their own dry, sandy shores seemed like a rich and fertile paradise.

Under Arab rule, the Jewish communities of North Africa had prospered. Previous to the Arab conquest, they had been under Byzantine rule which kept them in poverty and under great oppression. With the Arab conquest of North Africa this changed. In the city of Kairouan, near the site of ancient Carthage, a Talmudical academy was founded and a center of learning flourished there.

In 755, the city of Cordova, in the south of Spain, became the capital of the Caliphate of Spain. Under its Arabic rulers, Spain became a land of beautiful architecture, a land of learning and science, poetry and music. The cities were graced

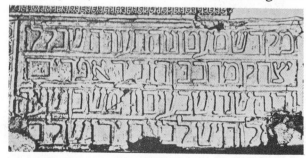

Stone inscription from a fourteenth century synagogue in Cordova, Spain. The inscription identifies the builder of the synagogue as Isaac Maheb and the year 1315.

194

with lovely buildings of Moorish design, with curved roofs and handsome walls, adorned with wooden carvings and wrought-iron gates. Gardens were laid out with winding paths, hedges and bright-colored flowers. With the coming of the Moors, a new era of freedom began in Spain.

The population of Spain now consisted of people from four different groups: the Moorish conquerors, the people of the old Spanish stock who had been in Spain before the coming of the Visigoths, Christian Visigoths, and a small minority of Jews. The north of Spain was still divided into small Christian kingdoms. But the south of Spain, called Andalusia by the Arabs, was in the hands of the Moslems.

The new Moslem rulers were tolerant and wanted all their subjects to participate in the life of the new commonwealth. Although the language of their land was Arabic, and Islam was the religion of the Court and the ruling class, all the people of the land enjoyed equal opportunities regardless of background or religion.

THE GOLDEN AGE

The Jews of Spain entered many professions. They worked as farmers and vintners, goldsmiths, tailors and shoemakers. They were small merchants and large-scale traders. Spanish Jews also entered the sciences, becoming physicians, astronomers and mathematicians. Many Jews were well-traveled, highly educated and achieved high positions in the

Colophon of a Bible manuscript written in Cordova in 1479.

new society. Many were able to speak several languages. Jews acted as ambassadors and interpreters, as men who fulfilled commercial and diplomatic missions in distant lands. Many were respected physicians. A golden age had dawned for the Jews in Spain.

Abraham Zacuto (1450-1515), famous Jewish astronomer and historian, who fled Portugal to escape the Inquisition and settled in Amsterdam.

Dr. Luis Marcado, Jewish physician to the Spanish King Philip II.

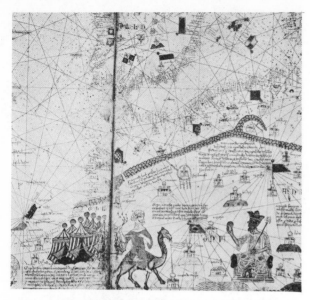

A map from a Catalonian atlas by the Spanish-Jewish cartographer, Abraham Cresques, 1375.

Schools of Jewish learning were founded. The Jews of Cordova had the good fortune to welcome to their midst Babylonian scholars who brought with them copies of the Talmud. The Babylonian teachers familiarized the Jews of Spain with the Babylonian tradition of learning, and interpreting the law. Moses ben Enoch, a wise Babylonian scholar, became head of the new academy of Cordova.

HASDAI IBN SHAPRUT (915-970)

Hasdai Ibn Shaprut, an eminent physician, is one of the best remembered Jewish leaders of Cordova. Among Hasdai's patients was the Cordovan Caliph himself. The Caliph considered Hasdai his friend and advisor. Hasdai Ibn Shaprut knew Latin, the language of Rome and its church, and often acted as the Caliph's interpreter. When ambassadors of distant lands would come to Cordova, Hasdai, speaking for the Caliph, proved a capable diplomat. Occasionally Hasdai would be sent on special diplomatic missions to foreign courts. On one of these missions he healed a king of a serious illness, and as a result the grateful ruler became an enthusiastic ally of the Caliph of Cordova.

As a leading member of the Jewish community of Spain, Hasdai supported the Jewish academies, helped purchase prized copies of the Talmud and gave personal assistance to scholars and students,

Heberw inscription from the year 846 C.E. on a Jewish tombstone in Kerch, Crimea.

poets and writers.

In talking with the foreign ambassadors, Hasdai always asked for news of the Jewish communities in faraway countries and he corresponded with Jews in distant lands.

THE KINGDOM OF THE KHAZARS

An ambassador from Persia once told Hasdai of the Kingdom of the Khazars on the shores of the Black Sea in far-off Russia. This kingdom, ruled by a king named Joseph, stretched to the shores of the Caspian Sea. The Khazars were valiant warriors who had to defend themselves against fierce neighboring tribes. But they lived as Jews, by the

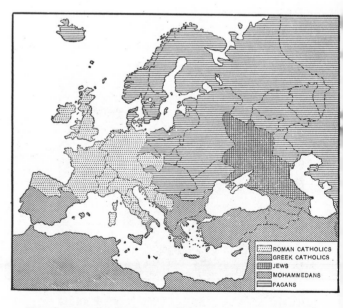

Map showing distribution of religions in Europe in the tenth century. The Jewish population includes the kingdom of the Khazars, which this mapmaker thought was very large.

196

A letter in Hebrew from a Khazar Jew, dated 950 C.E. In this letter are recounted the incidents that led to the conversion of the Khazars to Judaism and events that took place in Khazaria during the tenth century.

laws of the Torah. Hasdai was greatly excited by this news; could these strange Jews be descendants of some of the lost Ten Tribes of Israel?

Hasdai composed a letter which he sent to Joseph, king of the Khazars, by a traveler. The letter passed through many hands, and three years passed before Hasdai received a reply from King Joseph. In this letter the king of the Khazars told Hasdai of his land and his people and of how they had come to accept the Jewish faith. Joseph stated that the Khazars were not part of the Lost Tribes. During the eighth century one of Joseph's ancestors, King Bulan, had decided to abandon his old pagan religion. He had summoned to his court a Christian, a Mohammedan and a Jew, and had listened carefully as each of them presented the ideas of his religion. Bulan chose Judaism and many of the nobles of his court followed his example. Eventually, many more of the Khazar people became Jews.

King Joseph also stated in his letter that he was very happy to have come in contact with other Jews. He told Hasdai that the Khazars read the Bible and that, together with all Jews, they hoped for the days when Jews would live in the Land of Israel again and worship in the Temple in Jerusalem. King Joseph expressed the hope that Hasdai would pay a visit to his court. However, in those days such a journey was a matter of many months, and Hasdai was too busy to undertake it. One of the classics of medieval Jewish philosophy, the *Kuzari,* by Judah Halevi, is based on the tradition of a disputation before the king of the Khazars between the respresentatives of Judaism, Christianity and Islam, as well as a representative of the philosophers.

The kingdom survived until the eleventh or twelfth century, when conquering Russian princes destroyed it and scattered its people over the great steppes of Russia.

SAMUEL IBN NAGRELA (993-1056) THE PRINCE IN ISRAEL

After the fall of the Cordova caliphate, Spain was divided into a number of smaller Moslem kingdoms. New cities gained importance, such as Granada, the capital of the new Caliph of Granada, who also included in his domain the flourishing city of Malaga.

In the city of Malaga there lived a most unusual man—Samuel Ibn Nagrela, a grocer who kept a small spice shop. Samuel had come to Malaga from Cordova. He was a well-educated man—a philosopher, mathematician, and a fine Hebrew scholar. He reportedly knew several languages, including Hebrew, Spanish, Arabic, Greek and Latin. Many nobles of the Caliph's court had discovered how well Samuel read and wrote, and people came to him for advice, or asked him to read or compose letters for them. The Caliph's Grand Vizier, too, heard about Samuel, the scholarly merchant.

The Minister so greatly admired Samuel's handwriting, his learning and his style of composing letters that he called him to his castle in Granada and made him his secretary. When the Grand Vizier died, the Caliph appointed Samuel in his place. Henceforth, Samuel lived in the splendid palace in Granada. Yet he remained modest in demeanor and never denied that he had once been a humble shopkeeper.

A page from the book "Choice of Pearls," a collection of philosophic maxims by Solomon Ibn Gabirol.

SOLOMON IBN GABIROL (1021-1058)

Among the many writers whom Samuel Ha-Nagid encouraged and supported was the poet and philosopher, Solomon Ibn Gabirol. During his short life Solomon wrote many beautiful poems in Hebrew and Arabic, as well as philosophical works that were widely read by both Jews and non-Jews. He wrote hymns for the Sabbath, festivals and fast days, many of which found their way into the *mahzor*. Many of his poems bespeak his passionate love of God and his hope for the coming of the Messiah. His most celebrated poem is the ethico-philosophic hymn *Keter Malkhut* (Royal Crown), which became part of the liturgy of the Day of Atonement.

Ibn Gabirol's philosophical work called *Mekor Hayyim* or "Fountain of Life" was translated into Latin by Franciscan monks. For centuries it was believed that this work, called *Fons Vitae* in Latin, was written by a Christian philosopher. Not until 1846, when a Jewish scholar discovered in a Paris library excerpts in Hebrew from Solomon Ibn

The poem Grief And Desire from the collection of poems by Solomon Ibn Gabirol. The page is from a twelfth century manuscript.

Like Hasdai Ibn Shaprut before him, Samuel, despite his many public duties, always took a deep interest in the intellectual life of the Jewish community. He had the most complete and valuable Hebrew library in Spain. Samuel Ibn Nagrela wrote articles on the Talmud, composed poems about secular subjects and for the synagogue services, and even worked on a Hebrew grammar.

Also like Hasdai, Samuel helped many poets and writers, students and scholars to find work and to support themselves. He aided the charitable collections that supported the poor Jews of Malaga and he collected funds for the Talmudical academies in Spain and for those in Babylonia and in Palestine. The Jews of Malaga considered Samuel Ibn Nagrela, the head of the Jewish community, and the title Samuel HaNagid, meaning "Samuel the Prince in Israel," was conferred upon him.

The Court of Lions in the Alahambra of Granada, Spain. This fountain is mentioned in one of the poems of Solomon ibn Gabirol.

Gabirol's work, originally written in Arabic, did it become clear that *Fons Vitae* was a translation of Ibn Gabirol's *Mekor Hayyim.* In this work the poet explains his own philosophy and faith, and how he viewed the relationship of God to the physical world. The book is characterized by its general philosophical approach, without special emphasis on Judaism. It is for this reason that in its Latin version its Jewish origin was not suspected for centuries.

Among his other works are "Improvement of the Moral Qualities," and "Choice of Pearls," both written in Arabic. His life marks a high point in Arabic-Jewish culture—a golden age that began in the tenth century and was to continue until the twelfth. Scholars, poets, scientists, philosophers— all flourished in the Jewish communities of Moslem Spain, despite the political strife which surrounded them.

A GOLDEN AGE

The various Moslem kings in Spain fought for power and engaged in petty wars. Meanwhile, in the north of Spain, the Christian kings, who still ruled their small kingdoms, prepared to drive the Moslems out of Spain. They made war on the Arab princes and seized the city of Toledo. The Jews suffered greatly during those stormy times— frequently intolerant Arab rulers would drive them from their homes. Yet this was the time when the greatest Jewish poets and philosophers made their contributions to Arabic-Jewish life and created a golden age.

There were many Jewish scholars, writers and poets in the cities of Andalusia, the name which the Arabs gave to southern Spain. Here the Jews excelled as doctors, astronomers and mathematicians. Wealthy Jewish traders traveled to distant lands, Jewish architects built handsome dwellings and synagogues, and Jewish gardeners planted and tended lovely gardens.

ISAAC BEN JACOB HAKOHEN ALFASI (1013-1103)

Jewish academies of learning flourished and produced many Talmudic scholars in Spain. The greatest of these scholars, at this time, was Isaac ben

Purim charity box, 1319 C.E., with a Spanish inscription in Hebrew "King Ahasuerus and Queen Esther."

Rabbi Isaac Ben Jacob HaKohen Alfasi.

parts of the Halakhah (the legal portion of the Talmud) which seemed to him most important. Alfasi's purpose was to help and guide the Jewish scholars and judges of his day who had to deal with questions of Jewish law. His brilliant work known as the *RIF* (*Rabbi Isaac Fasi*) has been a valuable digest and guide to codifiers and students of the Talmud to this day.

But Alfasi's original method of codifying the laws did not please everyone, and many scholars criticized his work. Despite his sharp and precise opinions, Alfasi was a mild and forgiving man. When one of his most bitter opponents was about to die he made his peace with Alfasi by sending his son to study with the master. Alfasi took the orphaned boy into his own household and instructed him together with his own sons and favorite students.

Jacob Hakohen Alfasi. Alfasi had come to Spain, at the age of 75, from the city of Fez in North Africa and had studied and worked also at the great academy in Kairouan. He taught at Cordova and later at Granada and eventually settled in Lucena, where he became head of the Jewish community. Here he established a great academy and a center of Talmudic learning which became famous throughout Spain.

Isaac Alfasi wrote a great code and commentary on the Talmud. In this book he reorganized the material in the Talmud, concentrating on those

Interior view of the church of Santa Maria La Blanca, formerly a synagogue, Toledo, Spain.

Alfasi's academy in Lucena was attended not only by Talmudic scholars. His many brilliant students included writers and leaders of the community. Moses Ibn Ezra and Judah Halevi, the great poets, were students of Alfasi.

MOSES IBN EZRA (1055-1139)

Moses Ibn Ezra wrote many poems, secular as well as religious. He is best remembered for the lovely poems of penitence which he composed and

Part of a letter from Rabbi Hananel, 1057 C.E., in which he describes the destruction of the synagogue in Kairouan, Africa, and the expulsion of the Jews from the city.

Page from the first edition of Abraham Ibn Ezra's commentary to the Pentateuch, Naples, 1488 C.E.

which are still chanted today during the High Holiday season as *Selihot* (penitential) prayers. Like all the great poets of his day, Moses also wrote philosophical works.

ABRAHAM IBN EZRA (1092-1167)

Abraham Ibn Ezra, a younger contemporary of Moses Ibn Ezra, left his family, which was held in high esteem in Toledo, and traveled to many distant places. He visited Jewish communities in North Africa and Babylonia. He even reached the shores of distant England. Wherever Abraham Ibn Ezra wandered, he always found students to listen to his teachings, and scholars with whom he could discuss his work. Despite his restless wanderings, he never gave up his writing. He wrote many commentaries on the Bible and was considered one of the greatest Biblical scholars and commentators of his time. He also wrote extensively on Hebrew grammar and he figures prominently in medieval

Hebrew poetry. The Jewish community of Italy was overjoyed when the brilliant Abraham Ibn Ezra settled there, and scholars and students flocked to his school in Rome.

JUDAH HALEVI (1075-1141)

Most beloved among the Jewish poets of Spain, to this day, is Judah Halevi, a friend of the poet Moses Ibn Ezra. Judah Halevi was born in Toledo, and, like Moses Ibn Ezra, studied at Alfasi's academy in Lucena where he received an intensive Hebrew education. A scholar of Arabic literature, he was learned in many subjects, including astronomy and mathematics, and was an eminent physician.

Judah Halevi's poems dealt with many subjects. He studied the Bible closely and his poetry is saturated with Biblical imagery. As he grew older, Judah developed a passionate longing for the Land of Israel and wrote a number of beautiful poems famed as the "Songs of Zion."

Like most of the other poets of Spain, Judah Halevi was interested in philosophy. He wrote a book in Arabic called *Kuzari* (The Khazar). The title was based on the letter which King Joseph of the Khazars had written about two hundred years before to Hasdai Ibn Shaprut. The subtitle of the *Kuzari* is "The Book of Proof and Argument in Defense of a Despised Religion." It is a work that ex-

Opening lines of the "Ode to Zion" by Judah Ha-Levi. From a fifteenth century manuscript.

Home of Samuel Ha-Levi in Toledo, Spain.

traditions of Israel, with special emphasis on the election of Israel and the covenant between God and His people. Judaism is based on the Revelation of God as recorded in the Torah and the Prophets, rather than on philosophical speculation. At the end of the book, the rabbi bids farewell to the Khazar king, and sets out on a journey to Palestine which he longs to see.

In his old age, Judah Halevi, much like the rabbi of *Kuzari,* set out to see the Land of Israel. His friends tried to dissuade him from this plan for the journey was long and dangerous; ships were often raided by pirates and the roads were made unsafe by warring tribes. But the poet would not change his mind. He crossed the Mediterranean Sea and traveled through North Africa, visiting the Jewish communities along his route. In Fostat (the old city of Cairo) he found a great friend in the *Nagid,* the head of the Jewish community, and in

plains the profound meaning of Judaism. The arguments are presented in the form of a discussion between a scholarly rabbi and the King of the Khazars, who is eager for knowledge and searching for the true religion. They discuss the ideas of Judaism and compare them with those of Greek philosophers and of the Christian and Moslem religious thinkers, whose representatives are also taking part in the discussion. The author stresses the importance of faith and trust in God and in the

Arms or insignia of the Ha-Levi family.

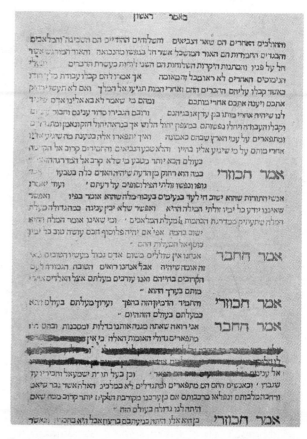

A page from the first edition of the Kuzari. The dialogue form of the writing can be seen. On the side of the page stand the words: "Said the Kuzari," and "Said the Haver" (meaning rabbi), introducing their statements.

the learned head of Fostat's academy. The Jews of Fostat, too, tried to persuade Judah Halevi to give up the idea of traveling on to Israel, warning him of the many possible dangers. But the old man was determined to see his dream fulfilled.

Judah Halevi never returned from his journey. Legend tells us that, as he reached the gates of Jerusalem, he fell upon his knees and, while kissing the holy ground, was trodden to death by the horse of a hostile Arab rider. And so the poet Judah Halevi died—standing at last on the soil of the Land of Israel, in sight of Mount Zion, of which he had sung so often with such deep love and longing. Latest researches tend to indicate that Judah Halevi may have died in Egypt in the year 1141.

BENJAMIN OF TUDELA, THE TRAVELER (12TH CENTURY)

In those days many Jewish traders and messengers often traveled to distant lands. The most famous among these Jewish travelers of this golden age of Spain was Benjamin of Tudela. Wherever Benjamin went he would visit the Jewish communities. He kept a diary of his travels, in which he described in detail the many places where Jews lived in his time, the number of Jews in each place visited, and their professions, customs and ways.

Benjamin, the traveler from Tudela, must have been a courageous, enterprising man indeed. Braving storms at sea, pirates and shipwreck, bandits and illness, he continued on his way, traveling from Spain to France, from France to Italy—and on to Greece. He went to Syria and to Palestine. He traveled on to Babylonia, where he saw Baghdad, the city of the powerful eastern Caliphs. He also visited the Jews of distant Yemen, Egypt and North Africa. His

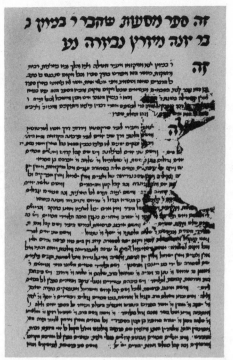

Page from a manuscript of Benjamin of Tudela's itinerary.

last stop before returning home to Spain was the island of Sicily.

Benjamin of Tudela's detailed report includes an account of a bitter disappointment that came to the Babylonian Jews, the story of David Alroy, a learned young man, who had pretended to be the Messiah, but had turned out to be an impostor. Benjamin also told of the fine Jewish goldsmiths of Yemen, of the silk weavers of Greece, the wealthy shipowners in Syria and of the skilled dyers in Palestine.

The diaries of the traveler Benjamin of Tudela give a fascinating picture of the Jewish communities of his day. They were translated into several languages.

GLOSSARY OF HEBREW TERMINOLOGY
AND NAMES

Fountain of Life	Mkohr Ḥayeem	מְקוֹר חַיִּים
Isaac ben Jacob Ha-kohen Alfasi	Ahlfahsi, or Reef, for short (*R*abbi *Y*itzḥak *F*ahsi)	אַלְפַסִי, רִי"ף
Halakhah	Hahlaḥa	הֲלָכָה
Moses ibn Ezra	Mohsheh ibn Ezrah	מֹשֶׁה אִבְּן עֶזְרָא
Selihot	Sleeḥoht	סְלִיחוֹת
Abraham ibn Ezra	Ahvrahahm ibn Ezrah	אַבְרָהָם אִבְּן עֶזְרָא
Mount Zion	Hahr Tsee-yohn	הַר צִיּוֹן
Benjamin of Tudela	Binyahmeen Meetoodey-lah	בִּנְיָמִין מִטּוּדֵילָא

Marranos	Ahnooseem	אֲנוּסִים
Moses ben Enoch	Mohshe ben Ḥahnoḥ	מֹשֶׁה בֶּן חֲנוֹךְ
Hasdai ibn Shaprut	Ḥasdai ibn Shahproot	חַסְדַּאי אִבְּן שַׁפְרוּט
Kuzari	Koozahree	כּוּזָרִי
Judah Halevi	Yhoodah Hahleyvee	יְהוּדָה הַלֵּוִי
Samuel ibn Nagrela	Shmoo-eyl ibn Nahgreylah	שְׁמוּאֵל אִבְּן נַגְרֵילָה
Samuel the Prince	Shmoo-eyl Hahnahgeed	שְׁמוּאֵל הַנָּגִיד
Solomon ibn Gabirol	Shlohmoh ibn Gahbeerohl	שְׁלֹמֹה אִבְּן גַּבִּירוֹל

THINKERS, TRANSLATORS, GRAMMARIANS, AND COMMENTATORS

MOSES BEN MAIMON (MAIMONIDES) (1135-1204)

The golden age for the Jews of Spain was nearing an end. The Almohades, a fanatical Moslem sect from North Africa, invaded Andalusia, and the Arab princes were too disunited to offer resistance. Cordova fell in 1149 and the Almohades became the rulers of Moslem Spain.

The Almohades sought to convert everyone to the faith of Islam. They persecuted Jews and Christians alike, forcing them to become Moslems or to leave the land. But where could the Jews of Spain go? In the north of Spain the Christian kings ruled. The Crusades, the march of the Christians to rescue the Holy Land from the Moslems had begun, and the Jews in Christian lands now faced new dangers. Many Spanish Jews set out by ship for North Africa. Among these emigrants was a young boy of thirteen, the son of a scholar, who had fled with his family from Cordova. The boy's name was Moses, the son of Maimon. Today he is known as Maimonides—or RaMBaM, the abbreviation for the Hebrew words "Rabbenu Moshe Ben Maimon" (our Rabbi Moses ben Maimon). Maimonides was to become the most outstanding figure of the golden age of Spanish Jewry.

The family of Maimon settled in Morocco, where Rabbi Maimon continued to teach his sons. Moses and his brother David were eager students. Despite the hardships under which they lived, they managed to learn and to study. Moses became well-

Portrait of Maimonides.

The autograph of Maimonides.

Battle between Crusaders and Moslems near Ashkelon, 1250 C.E. From a stained glass window in a church in Paris.

frankly. He and his family tried to settle in Palestine, but they could not do this, for the wars of the Crusades left their impact on the Holy Land and conditions were very unstable there. Therefore the family of Maimon settled in Egypt, in the city of Fostat. Maimonides set up a practice of medicine in his new home. His fame as a physician spread through the city and he became the personal doctor of the viceroy of Egypt. Maimonides' reputation as a Jewish scholar brought the people of the Jewish community to him. The *Nagid,* head of the Jewish community of Egypt, asked him to help guide them.

The life of Maimonides was filled with work and with labors of love and devotion. When his medical duties at court were done, he would go home and see the many patients who were waiting for him there. Rich and poor, Jew and Moslem alike would come to see Maimonides, the great physician —and he saw them all. The wealthy paid for his services but the poor were treated free of charge. Somehow, he also found time to write books on medical subjects.

Maimonides was a greatly beloved teacher. After Sabbath services, he would give instruction to

versed in Hebrew, in the wisdom of the Bible, the Talmud and other Jewish writings. He also studied mathematics and astronomy, Arabic literature and the philosophy of the ancient Greeks. Moses had an exceptional mind and an incredible store of energy. Although he had to go to work at an early age to earn money to help support his family, yet he managed to study medicine and become a famous physician.

While still a very young man, Maimonides wrote brilliant books and articles. When the Jews of Morocco were hard-pressed by the Almohades to forsake their religion and become Mohammedans, they asked Maimonides what they should do. He advised them to repeat the words which the Moslem oppressors would want them to utter when this became absolutely necessary. Maimonides explained to them that the words would be meaningless so long as they remained at heart faithful to Judaism. The Jews of Morocco heeded the advice of Maimonides and continued to practice their own religion in their secret synagogues. Maimonides, however, believed that the most desirable solution for these people would be to leave Morocco and settle in a place where Jews would be free to observe their laws.

Maimonides himself was forced to leave Morocco after he had spoken out so courageously and

A Hebrew document from Fostat (Cairo), 750 C.E.

Page of the first edition of the *Aphorisms of Maimonides.*

Calle de Maimonides, Cordova, Spain.

members of the Jewish community in the Talmud
and the Torah. He would spend the entire Sabbath
in study and prayer, together with those who came
to seek instruction and inspiration from him.

The fame of Maimonides spread far and wide.
Letters asking for advice came to him from many
distant places, for times were hard and many Jews
were oppressed and threatened by persecutions.

While conditions in Mohammedan Spain were
improving — the Almohades, realizing that they
needed help in ruling the land, had become more
tolerant. The Jews in Yemen, where they had lived
for so many centuries among the Arab tribes of the
desert, were suffering from cruel persecution. To
add to their sorrows, a man who had claimed to be
the Messiah had been exposed as an impostor. Maimonides wrote a famous letter of consolation to the
Jews of Yemen, urging them to be brave and to
cling to their beliefs.

THE MISHNEH TORAH AND THE "GUIDE FOR THE PERPLEXED"

Despite his many duties, Maimonides managed
also to write brilliant philosophical works, and the
most important code of Jewish law since the completion of the Talmud. This great code is called the
Mishneh Torah (Repetition of the Torah) or *Yad
Hahazakah* (The Strong Hand).

The *Mishneh Torah* codifies all the laws of the
Mishnah and the Talmud, and the commentaries of
the *Geonim* and the generations following them,
down to the interpretations of Maimonides' day,
including those of Maimonides himself. This encyclopedic work has been a great help to Talmudic
scholars and students to this day. Maimonides
wrote it in the beautiful style of the pure Hebrew
used long ago by Judah HaNasi in the editing of
the Mishnah.

The *Mishneh Torah* was accepted by scholars
not as a substitute for the Talmud but only as an
encyclopedic guide to the many legal discussions
and decisions found in the Talmud. In the introduc-
tory chapters of the *Mishneh Torah,* Maimonides

Holograph (a page written in the original handwriting of the author), of Maimonides. This is a page of the *Guide to the Perplexed*, written in Arabic in Hebrew letters by the Rambam himself.

ately translated into Hebrew and later into Latin and many other languages as well. Today, *Moreh Nevukhim* is still considered one of the clearest, most profound philosophical works on Judaism ever written.

Many Jewish thinkers in North Africa, Spain and France were greatly impressed by Maimonides' work and corresponded with him. However, there were some who asserted that his works were not in harmony with the spirit of accepted Jewish tradition and, like the great Saadia before him, and many others who had contributed original works to the treasury of Jewish thought, Maimonides had to defend himself against many attacks by ultraconservatives. But he was beloved by many scholars and leaders of the Jewish community, and by the many simple people for whom he had pleaded and to whom he had written letters of encouragement and advice. When he died in Fostat in 1204, he was mourned throughout the Jewish world and the people said of him: "From Moses to Moses,

explains the philosophy of Judaism as he saw it. In his youthful work, the commentary on the Mishnah, we find his famous "Thirteen Articles of Faith," which have often been quoted and have been rephrased in the declaration of the Jewish creed *"Ani Ma'amin."* They were also put into verse in the hymn "Yigdal," which is included in all Jewish prayer books.

Maimonides' best-known philosophical work is called *Moreh Nevukhim* (Guide For the Perplexed), in which he clearly explains the principles and ideas of Judaism in terms of the principles of logic and philosophical reasoning. Although Maimonides believed that only accomplished scholars would read his book, it found a wide audience among philosophically minded readers. This great classic, originally written in Arabic, was immedi-

Facsimile of Maimonides' Dalalat Al Hairin, the original for the book Moreh Nevukhim.

The gravestone of a grandson of Moses Maimonides, found in Cairo, Egypt. Because of the greatness of the Rambam, the inscription reads: "This is the grave of David, grandson of Rabbenu the Gaon Moses ben Maimon, Light of the Exile."

Conference of Franco-Jewish Rabbis, thirteenth century.

there was none like unto Moses."

Many of the Arabic works of Maimonides were translated into Hebrew by Samuel Ibn Tibbon (born about 1150), scholar, physician and translator, who lived in Lunel and other cities in the South of France.

Many Spanish Jews had fled from the persecutions of the Almohades and had sought refuge in the Provence, in the French lands north of the Pyrenees Mountains, where bishops and princes were tolerant and allowed the Jews to live in peace. Talmudic academies were flourishing in the cities of Lunel and Narbonne. Many Jews of Provence earned their livelihood as vintners and farmers; others studied at the medical school of Montpellier and became physicians. Still others were merchants and ship-builders who did brisk business in the port of Marseilles.

JUDAH IBN TIBBON (1120-1190)

Among the Jews from Spain who settled in southern France were the Ibn Tibbon and Kimhi families who were dedicated to the task of translating the Arabic works of great Jewish scholars into Hebrew, thus making them available to the Jews of Europe who did not know Arabic.

Judah Ibn Tibbon, a physician and translator, had come to the Provence with his family from Granada. They settled in Lunel, a city known for its Jewish intellectual life, and its excellent Talmudic academy. The Jews of southern France were very anxious to read the works of Saadia, Maimonides, and the Jewish writers and poets of Spain. The family of Ibn Tibbon had been fortunate enough to have been able to bring their excellent library with them. They set to work and translated the works of the great Jewish scholars of the Moslem world from Arabic into Hebrew. Judah Ibn Tibbon translated the works of Ibn Gabirol, Judah Halevi, Saadia, and others. His son, Samuel Ibn Tibbon, undertook the translation of the writings of Maimonides. He wrote to Maimonides, asking to

Page from the first Hebrew edition of the Psalms, with commentary by David Kimhi, printed in 1477.

The earliest inscription concerning Jews in France, a gravestone from the city of Narbonne dated 688. For some time, Narbonne was a center of Jewish learning.

came interested in Hebrew, the language of the Bible, they used the grammar and commentaries of David Kimhi.

Largely due to the efforts of these translators, Jewish scholars from Germany and France became familiar with the works of Jewish scholars in the Arab world.

Part of a page from David Kimhi's commentary on the Prophets, Guadalajara, Spain, 1481.

be allowed to visit and to study with him. Maimonides' letter, inviting him to come, is also interesting as a document relating some details of the daily life of this great scholar.

THE KIMHIS

The Kimhis settled in Narbonne. Both Joseph Kimhi and his son Moses Kimhi were well learned in the Bible, the Biblical commentaries, and in Hebrew grammar. Both produced many original works as well as translations. Moses Kimhi arranged a grammar and devised rules for the conjugation of Hebrew verbs.

The most famous of the Kimhis was Moses' younger brother, known as RaDaK (from *Rabbi David Kihmi*), who wrote a masterly Hebrew grammar and dictionary. RaDaK's commentaries on the Bible were second in popularity only to those of Rashi. Later, when Christian scholars be-

GLOSSARY OF HEBREW TERMINOLOGY
AND NAMES

Maimonides	Rahbee Moh-sheh ben Maimon, or Rambam	רַבִּי מֹשֶׁה בֶּן מַיְמוֹן (רַמְבַּ"ם)
Letter to the Jews of Yemen	Eegehret Tay-mahn	אִגֶּרֶת תֵּימָן
Maimonides' Code of Law	Mishnay To-rah or Yahd Haḥazakah	מִשְׁנֵה תּוֹרָה, יַ"ד הַחֲזָקָה
Geonim	G'ohneem	גְּאוֹנִים
Thirteen Articles of Faith	Shlohshah Asahr Ee-kahreem, or Ahnee Mah-ahmeen	שְׁלֹשָׁה עָשָׂר עִקָּרִים אֲנִי מַאֲמִין
Yigdal	Yigdahl	יִגְדַּל
Guide for the Perplexed	Mohrey Ne-vooḥeem	מוֹרֵה נְבוּכִים
Samuel ibn Tibbon	Shmoo-eyl ibn Teebohn	שְׁמוּאֵל אִבְּן תִּבּוֹן
Judah ibn Tibbon	Yhoodah ibn Teebohn	יְהוּדָה אִבְּן תִּבּוֹן
Joseph Kimhi	Yohseyf Kim-ḥee	יוֹסֵף קִמְחִי
Moses Kimhi	Mohsheh Kim-ḥee	מֹשֶׁה קִמְחִי
David Kimhi	Rahbee Dah-veed Kimḥee (Rahdahk)	רַבִּי דָוִד קִמְחִי (רַדָ"ק)

FEUDALISM, THE CRUSADES AND THE GHETTOS

FEUDALISM

While the arts and sciences flourished, and commerce and civic life prospered in Moorish Spain, cultural life in the rest of western Europe had come to a standstill. A feudal system existed under which the powerful churchmen and nobles rigidly controlled the lives of the serfs who tilled their fields. The freedom of the common people was greatly curtailed.

The serfs, who were considered attached to the noble landowners, toiled for their masters and could neither work nor live where they pleased. The burghers of the cities were less restricted. They could change their occupation or move freely from place to place. The nobles in turn were responsible to their own overlords and subject to their commands and often had to join them when they went to battle.

Outside the Jewish community, only the monks and scholars were able to read and write. Very few people could speak more than one language.

Although the people of medieval Europe were no longer pagans, many of the fears and supersti-

Costumes of German Jews in the thirteenth century. Jews were required by law to wear pointed hats.

Kneeling Jews reciting the humiliating "More Judaica," the Jew's Oath, before a Christian judge in Augsburg, Germany, 1509.

tions surviving from paganism still haunted their minds.

Frequently, intolerant princes and churchmen would attack the Jews. Obviously, the Jew was a good target for superstitious slander, a scapegoat whom the nobles and more often the burghers, could easily brand as the cause of all the people's woes.

During the Middle Ages, the pagan peoples of Europe were gradually converted to Christianity. However, it was difficult for men brought up in a world of wars, in which the warrior alone was a hero, to grasp the prophetic ideals of love and peace incorporated by the new church. The pagan traditions of Europe were replete with superstition, with beliefs in witchcraft and magic and in the strange, mysterious power of wicked gods and spirits. The new religion had to struggle against these old attitudes, and often its missionaries them-

selves became confused and bewildered in the process.

The Catholic Church of Rome was the bulwark of Christianity in western Europe. At its head was the Pope, the highest dignitary among the princes of the church.

The church was a strong organization and the Pope and his cardinals and bishops were frequently more powerful than kings. They regarded the kings as the servants of the church and for centuries the princes of the church were engaged in a struggle for power with kings and emperors.

The basic principles of Christianity had been taken over from Judaism. But the people who now groped for these principles and ideals had to rid themselves of the old traditions of their pagan forefathers, so different from the ones of the Hebrew tradition now propagated by Christianity. For many centuries the peoples of Europe were to waver between two powerful influences: the drive for power and the heritage of superstition—and the ideals of a new religion.

A medieval anti-Semitic drawing, depicting Jews taking blood from Christian children for their "mystic ceremonies."

213

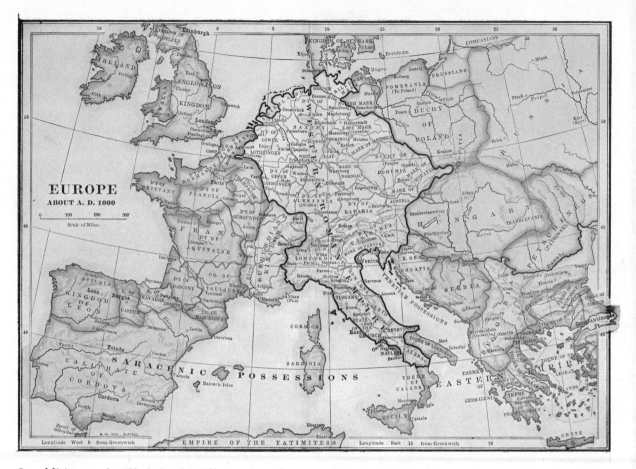

EUROPE
ABOUT A. D. 1000

In addition to the Christian hostility against the Jews, for their rejection of Jesus, the church also regarded the Jewish community as a threat. The Jews persistently clung to their faith. They lived outside the strong organization of the church. It seemed necessary to the popes and bishops that the church should control the beliefs of everyone, for they feared that otherwise many people would simply break away from their new found Christian faith and revert to paganism.

Severe restrictions were imposed on the Jews. They were kept apart from new converts, whose faith might be weak and who might become interested in Judaism. Nor could the Jews enjoy complete independence from control by the church authorities in many other aspects of social and religious life.

THE CRUSADES

The great threat to the early Christian world was the rise of Mohammedanism, or Islam. The church lent its support to any effort to drive the Mohammedans out of Europe and especially out of Spain, which had been their stronghold. Palestine, the ancient Land of Israel, was then also in Mohammedan hands. To the Christians, as to the Jews, Palestine was the Holy Land. The Christians considered it holy because it was the land where the founder of their faith had been born and Christianity founded. It was therefore important to the Church that the Holy Land be wrested from the Mohammedan "unbelievers."

Seal of Baldwin, first crusader king of Jerusalem. In 1059, C.E., the crusaders succeeded in capturing Jerusalem and holding it for eighty-eight years.

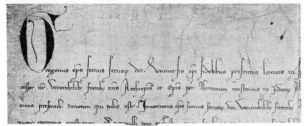

Facsimile of the Bull (1245), of Pope Innocent IV against the Blood Libel of the Jews.

In 1095—when Rashi, Nathan of Rome, and Alfasi of Spain were all old men—a Church Council met in the South of France, and proclaimed the First Crusade, a Holy War against the Moslem "unbelievers." Bands of knights and their followers assembled, accompanied by monks, to march to the Holy Land and recapture it. All sorts of people, including adventurers, attached themselves to the crusaders.

The sentiment against all non-believers (people outside the church) grew stronger. Zealous monks would arouse the people to fever-pitch against the non-believers by their inflammatory sermons. Soon after the First Crusade was proclaimed, a bitter period began for the Jews of Europe. In the great cities of France and Germany, and especially in the centers along the Rhine, the Jews experienced harsh and bloody persecutions.

Occasionally a tolerant bishop, believing that such cruelty was not in keeping with Christian ideals, tried to shield the Jews in his domain, but usually to no avail. The mobs of crusaders were too strong and too fanatical. The Jews were forced to accept baptism and those who refused were massacred. Many Jews—men, women and children— showed great heroism during this difficult period. Accounts have come down of defenseless people offering courageous resistance, of brave men facing death, of whole communities preferring mass suicide, rather than yield to the hordes of attackers or renounce their religion.

Page from the autobiography of Obadiah, the Proselyte. Towards the end of the eleventh century, a young Catholic priest, called John, became a Jew and assumed the name of Obadiah. He was imprisoned but managed to escape to a Moslem country.

A crusader knight.

A TOLERANT EMPEROR

At the end of the First Crusade, Henry IV, ruler of the Holy Roman Empire, pronounced a decree that released all Jews who had been baptized by

Seal of William the Conqueror.

The Jews of England fared as badly as those on the European continent. The courage of the Jews of York is still remembered. They took refuge in a tower, and were besieged by a fanatical mob. Under the guidance of their rabbi, Yomtov Ben Isaac of Joigny, the beleaguered Jews of York all chose to take their own lives rather than submit to the indignities which the mob had in store for them.

THE END OF THE CRUSADES (1189-1192)

In 1187, the crusaders were defeated by Saladin, the Sultan of Egypt, whose court physician was the great Maimonides. In contrast to the Christian crusaders Saladin was a tolerant, moderate ruler.

Two more Crusades followed. But by this time the secular rulers were gaining in power and the kings were no longer afraid to oppose the wishes

force from their vows. The Emperor allowed these Jews to return to Judaism, and even restored their property to them wherever possible. The Jews in turn were of great help to Henry in his commercial enterprises.

THE SECOND CRUSADE (1146-1147)

But then the Second Crusade began. The situation of the Jews in France became unendurable. Peter of Cluny, a monk, preached to excited mobs, urging them to kill the unbelievers in their midst. The king tried to protect the Jews; but could do little to prevent forced mass conversions and massacres. In Germany there was less violence against the Jews during these years; but in England the Jews felt the force of the Crusades.

A caricature of Saladin, the sultan of Egypt, from the Lutterall Psalter, 1340 C.E.

of the Pope. The Emperor Frederick II, who ruled over the Holy Roman Empire from 1212 to 1250, strongly upheld the power of the State. He supported the Crusades but not at the expense of the welfare of his subjects. Frederick therefore protected the Jews in his realm from the crusader mobs.

The Crusades had serious consequences for the Jews of Europe. Even though the Holy Land remained under Moslem domination, life in Europe changed when the crusaders returned. On their journeys, they had learned about distant lands. Many became traders and travelers, taking advantage of the valuable contacts they had established in other lands.

An engraving of Clifford's Tower in York, England. Here, in 1190, the entire Jewish population of York committed suicide rather than fall into the hands of the mob.

Crusader wall in Acre, Israel.

Formerly, most of the trading between various cities and countries had been carried out by Jews. But now more non-Jews entered the field which for so long had been closely associated with the Jews.

NEW RESTRICTIONS

During the time of hatred and massacre, the Jews had drawn closer together as a people. A wall of distrust had risen between Christians and Jews. This wall was to grow, until it would rise some centuries later as a physical barrier, enclosing the Jews of Europe in cramped, restricted quarters known as ghettos.

No longer permitted to engage in large-scale commerce, the Jews were forced to become traders in secondhand wares. They were forced into a new field—that of money and banking—an occupation forbidden to Christians by the church. The Jews became bankers and money-lenders. A few managed the financial affairs of princes, bishops, nobles and kings. But most of the Jews now had to make

their livelihood by keeping pawnshops, lending small amounts of money to the peasants and townsfolk, or trading in secondhand goods.

No longer could Jews be craftsmen. The world of medieval Europe had become highly organized and restricted. All craftsmen were organized into guilds, and only a special group of qualified people could be received into a guild. The applicant had to be of the Christian faith, usually the son of a guild member.

No Jew could own land or vineyards any longer. A farmer in those times was a peasant, or rather, a serf owned by his lord who also owned the land he tilled.

Nobles and princes were the "protectors" of the Jews, whom they regarded as "royal serfs"—that is, subjects under the personal domination of the king or prince of the realm. The ruler would collect high taxes from his Jews, who thus were a steady source of income for him. Sometimes a prince would "sell" his Jews to another prince to meet a debt. Frequently he would not repay loans he had taken from the Jews so that lending money in itself represented a great risk to the Jews. Whatever the rate of interest would be, most of the profit would go to pay the high taxes which the prince exacted from them.

Engraving of a Jewish moneylender, Augsburg, Germany, 1531.

An anti-Semitic caricature of Aaron of Lincoln, an English financier. On his death, in 1185, his property was confiscated by the crown. Notice the Two Tablets of the Law embroidered on his tunic.

Occasionally, debtors would organize a mob and plunder the Jewish quarter. The position of the Jew in Europe became increasingly dependent, humiliating and confining. Often an entire community would be expelled and forced to leave all its belongings behind. Whole communities had to wander through Europe in search of a new home.

In 1290, all the sixteen thousand Jews of Eng-

land were expelled. They were forced to board ships and seek new homes in France, in Flanders and elsewhere on the European continent. Over three hundred years were to pass before a Jewish community would exist again in England.

JEWISH CULTURE SURVIVES

But even at this time of anguish the Jews of

Susskind Trimberg before church dignitaries.

Europe managed to lead an active civic and religious life. Jewish scholars wrote on questions of Jewish law and composed commentaries on the Bible. A singer of ballads or *Minnesinger,* Susskind of Trimberg, appeared at the royal courts of Germany, singing his ballads before the lords and ladies. Then, embittered by the persecution of the

Map of England showing towns where Jews lived before the expulsion in 1200.

Jews, he gave up his career and in 1215 retired to the Jewish community to share the life of his own people. Inside the Jewish community another Jewish poet, Ephraim Ben Jacob of Bonn, was writing heartrending Hebrew elegies commemorating the bravery and suffering of the Jews of his time and a chronicle recording the history of the Jews of the Rhineland during the Second and Third Crusades.

A medieval drawing of a Hebrew teacher and his young pupil (Germany, thirteenth century).

CENTERS OF LEARNING IN NORTHERN FRANCE AND IN GERMANY

While Spain and the Provence were flourishing centers of Jewish learning integrated with the scientific and literary culture of the time, a more conservative spirit pervaded the Jewish communities of Northern France and the lands of the Rhine. There the general population was underdeveloped culturally and intellectually. The Jews therefore had no reasons to emulate the ways of their neighbors. Instead they concentrated on their own heritage and intensified the study of the Torah and the

A Hebrew and German alphabet chart from 1477.

observance of the Mitzvot. Schools for the young and Torah academies for the adults were established everywhere and rabbinic scholars taught and led the people.

RABBENU GERSHOM BEN JUDAH— MEOR HAGOLAH (960-1040).

The most notable rabbinic scholar at the turn of

Alsatian Jews of the twelfth century.

219

The Rashi chapel in the city of Worms, the synagogue where the great commentator worshipped.

the millenium was Rabbi Gershom ben Judah who is more popularly known as Rabbenu Gershom Meor HaGolah (Our Teacher Gershom, the Light of the Exile). Besides his Biblical and Talmudic erudition as shown in his commentaries, he was also endowed with great capacities for spiritual leadership. Scholars from various countries flocked to the Talmudic academy he founded at Mayence. These disciples in turn became the spiritual leaders in the communities they hailed from. Scholars from far and wide directed queries to him and many of his answers were preserved for posterity. He is noted

Facsimile of a woodcut printed in Troyes, France, picturing a ceremony before the Ark.

for his remarkable regulations known as the *Takkanot Rabbenu Gershom Meor HaGolah* that are binding on all Ashkenazic Jews. The most important of these legal innovations are:

1) A ban on polygamy. A Jewish man is not allowed to marry more than one wife. While monogamy, being married to one wife only, was generally the rule, the Biblical and Talmudic laws did not specifically prohibit polygamy.

2) Requiring the consent of the wife in the procurement of a divorce.

RABBI SOLOMON BEN ITZHAK— RASHI (1040-1105)

While many of the disciples of Rabbenu Gershom were prominent rabbis who zealously devoted themselves to the teaching of Torah and the ideals of Judaism, they never reached the stature of their master. In the same year that Rabbenu Gershom died, the continuity of Jewish scholarship

Title-page of Rashi's commentary on the Pentateuch, published by Elijah Aboab, (Amsterdam, 17th century).

was assured by the birth of a Jewish child in the year 1040 in the French city of Troyes. This child was destined to bcome the most popular figure of rabbinical Judaism—Rabbi Solomon ben Itzhak, universally known by his abreviated name *Rashi* (*R*abbenu *Sh*lomo *Itzhak*i). His early youth is shrouded in obscurity. However, the dearth of facts is amply made up by a series of wondrous legends. It is told that Rashi's father was offered a large

1 הַשֵּׁנִית צִלָּה: כ וַתֵּלֶד עָדָה אֶת־יָבָל הוּא הָיָה
2 אֲבִי יֹשֵׁב אֹהֶל וּמִקְנֶה: כא וְשֵׁם אָחִיו יוּבָל הוּא
3 הָיָה אֲבִי כָּל־תֹּפֵשׂ כִּנּוֹר וְעוּגָב: כב וְצִלָּה גַם־הִוא
4 יָלְדָה אֶת־תּוּבַל קַיִן לֹטֵשׁ כָּל־חֹרֵשׁ נְחֹשֶׁת וּבַרְזֶל
5 וַאֲחוֹת תּוּבַל־קַיִן נַעֲמָה: ששי כג וַיֹּאמֶר לֶמֶךְ לְנָשָׁיו
6 עָדָה וְצִלָּה שְׁמַעַן קוֹלִי נְשֵׁי לֶמֶךְ הַאְזֵנָּה אִמְרָתִי
7 כִּי אִישׁ הָרַגְתִּי לְפִצְעִי וְיֶלֶד לְחַבֻּרָתִי: כד כִּי

[Rashi commentary block]

A page with Rashi's commentary.

text as well as on the poetical and legendary interpretations of the ancient rabbis as incorporated in the Talmudic and Midrashic literature. Rashi's commentary and the text of the Torah became inseparable and to this day every Jewish student from his earliest youth will continually consult Rashi in his daily study of the Torah, whether in the form of the weekly portion or in the regular perusal of the Torah. The same applies to the study of the Talmud which cannot be pursued without constant referral to Rashi's commentary on most of the Tractates of the Talmud. The work of Rashi was continued by his grandsons, the most prominent of whom were Rabbi Shemuel ben Meir, also known for his commentaries in Bible and Talmud, and Rabbi Jacob ben Meir, the great Talmudist known as Rabbenu Tam.

THE TOSAFISTS

Despite the difficulties they had to face, the generations following that of Rashi continued to study the Talmud and the Torah, and to add to the commentaries of Rashi. These scholars are called "Tosafists," writers of "Tosafot"—additions, supplements, because they added to Rashi's commentaries.

RABBENU TAM (1100-1171)

Best known among the Tosafists of the 12th and 13th centuries was Jacob ben Meir, a grandson of Rashi, who was called Rabbenu Tam, a name which means "Our Perfect Master." Like many of the scholars of his day, Rabbenu Tam lost all his belongings in the dark days of the Crusades. Undaunted, he continued with his studies and gave advice and leadership to his fellow Jews. Rabbenu Tam called together a synod or council of rabbis at which rules of conduct and questions of internal government were discussed. The purpose of the synod was to find ways to protect the Jewish community, especially those Jews who were poor and who suffered most from the persecutions at the time.

This first synod was followed by other assemblies. The Jews of the Rhineland arranged their communal life as best they could. They helped one another, so that their religious and communal life

sum of money for a rare gem in his possession that was to be used for the embellishment of a non-Jewish figure of worship. He refused the offer and in order to make sure that the gem would not be obtained by force he threw it into the sea. It was for this deed of loyalty to his faith that he was rewarded with a son who would brighten the light of the Torah. When he grew up, Rashi indeed contributed greatly to the perpetuation of the Torah in his own time as well as in ages to come.

After a short period of apprenticeship at the academy of Jacob ben Yakar at Worms (according to some, also at Mayence and other centers of learning that he visited during his alleged wanderings throughout Europe) he returned to his birthplace, Troyes. It was from there that his influence radiated throughout the various Jewish communities. While he had to attend to his vineyards for a living, he found time for his rabbinical studies and writings.

His commentary to the Torah is based on a sound understanding of the plain meaning of the

Jew's hat, compulsory for the Jews by the decree of the Lateran Council of 1215.

could continue and those in need could receive help.

THE YELLOW BADGE

In 1215 a Pope decreed at a Church Council that Jews had to wear a special sort of dress in order to distinguish them from the Christians. From then on, each Jew wore a yellow badge upon his breast, a mark of difference, to label him as an outcast. In addition to the yellow badge, Jews in some localities were also ordered to wear pointed hats.

In 1242, the ancient Jewish community of France was forced to witness the burning of the Talmud. Nicholas Donin, a converted Jew who had become a monk, had charged that the Talmud contained anti-Christian writings. Many wagonloads of the sacred books were collected throughout the land and burned in Paris.

Fifty years later, the Jews of France were expelled by King Philip the Fair, who requisitioned their money and real estate. But the Christian moneylenders who replaced the banished Jews were so greedy and pitiless that the King preferred the Jews and recalled them to his realm.

The king, however, had profited financially by expelling the Jews. They were expelled twice more from France. After the second time, in 1394, they were not allowed to return. For a thousand years

Jews had lived in France—indeed, they had been among the first colonists there. But from 1394 on, until the time of the French Revolution, France had only a handful of Jews—those few who continued to reside in Avignon, Carpentras and Cavaillon, districts which were under the direct rule of the Pope, and some Jews in Bordeaux and Alsace.

THE BLACK DEATH (1348-1349)

In the middle of the 14th century, a terrible plague befell Europe, killing millions. The people called it the Black Death. A rumor began to circulate among the people that as so few Jews were dying of the plague, it was reasonable to assume that the Jews had poisoned the wells and brought about this disaster! Today it is believed that if the Jews indeed enjoyed some measure of immunity to the disease, it was probably due to the ritual laws of purity and cleanliness which they observed.

But in those days scientific knowledge among the people was very limited—and so the rumor spread. The terrified people became convinced that

Map of France showing the towns where the Jews resided before the expulsion of 1394.

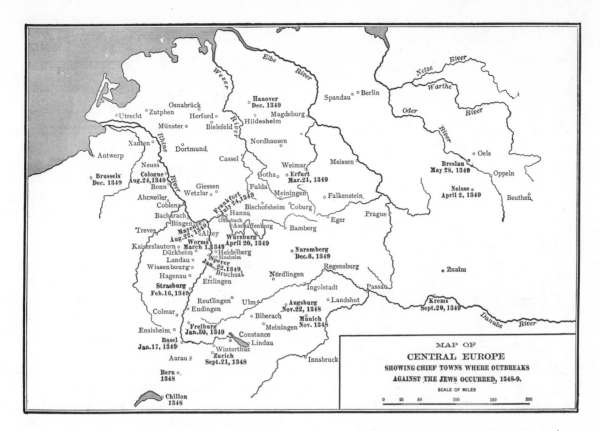

MAP OF
CENTRAL EUROPE
SHOWING CHIEF TOWNS WHERE OUTBREAKS
AGAINST THE JEWS OCCURRED, 1348-9.

SCALE OF MILES

0   25   50   100   150   200

the Jews had joined in a great conspiracy to destroy all Christians. Soon terrible persecutions were under way; Jews were murdered and their homes plundered.

THE GHETTO

After the Black Death epidemic, or from about 1350 on, Jews were allowed to live only in specifically designated neighborhoods of a city. In time this quarter was enclosed by walls and towers. This street or quarter where the Jews lived was called the ghetto.

The ghetto was a crowded section, with housing almost always inadequate. The houses had to be built high and close together in order to accommodate as many people as possible. The ghetto was enclosed inside the oldest part of the cities so that the Jews had to live away from the woods, the fields and fresh, clean air. A Jew had to return to his ghetto at a certain hour and was not free to leave it at night. On many days, such as Sundays and Christian holidays, he was not allowed to leave the ghetto at all.

The position of the Jew is only one example which shows how little human life and dignity counted in medieval Europe; but it is one of the most glaring and disgraceful of examples. In medieval society, everyone was expected to remain in

Black Plague burial scene at Tournoi in 1349.

223

Gate leading to the Jewish ghetto at Vienna.

Old Nuremberg synagogue.

his own station in life. Everyone had to hold the beliefs and practice the way of life acceptable to the king and the church or suffer the consequences. He might find himself excluded from a guild or, if he were a town burgher, from the merchants' league.

The Jews were intended to serve as an object lesson, an example of how men would suffer if they should decide to live independently of the church and outside Christian society. Like the Jews, such men would be treated as despised outcasts.

Yet all the restrictions and humiliating laws could not change the vigorous Jewish life that unfolded inside the ghetto walls. Occasional plunderers and aggressors might enter the ghetto from outside, but the rules of life that guided the community and the synagogue remained intact.

The medieval Jews cherished their heritage. The rabbi and the scholars usually were the leaders of the community. They led the people in prayer and communal affairs and organized the schools.

The heart of life for the medieval Jew was his home. In the home the father, the mother and

their children celebrated Sabbaths and holidays. The Jewish family worked together to uphold the traditions of Judaism. Beginning at the age of five, Jewish boys started the study of Hebrew, then went on to the study of the Torah, the Prophets and other books of the Bible, the Talmud and the great works of the later scholars. The girls were instructed at home to become good Jewish women, to uphold the Jewish traditions and to keep the home pleasant and neat. Some girls were also

A medieval school for Jewish children.

Theological disputation between Jews and Christians.

taught at home by their mothers to read and write.

Outside the ghetto walls in the medieval cities, only a few people had the chance to acquire learning. Only monks, a few noblemen and some burghers had schooling. Many centuries were to elapse before an education was to be regarded by the people of Europe as a right rather than a special privilege.

THE SHTADLAN

The Jews of the Middle Ages managed to develop a well-organized system of internal self-government, much the same as the Jewish communities of ancient Babylonia. Rabbis, scholars and "dayanim" (rabbinical "judges") were the leaders of the communities. Grievances and legal cases of all kinds were taken to the Jewish court of law, the Bet Din—or, in a small town, to the rabbi. Often, all the communities of a realm or a land would choose one learned and righteous man, to represent them at the court of the prince; or, when the cities grew more powerful, before the city councils. Such a representative was called a Shtadlan (advocate, or representative, of the town communities). One such famous Shtadlan was Yosel of Rosheim in Alsace.

RABBI MEIR OF ROTHENBURG (1215-1293)

One of the great German rabbis of the Middle Ages was Rabbi Meir ben Baruch of Rothenburg. He was born in 1215 in the city of Worms, where Rashi once had studied. As a young man, Meir had been taught by the great rabbis of France. It was there that he had witnessed the burning of the Talmud in Paris in 1242. Returning to Germany, he established a Talmudic academy. The great Talmudic schools of northern France had come to a sad end, but Rabbi Meir carried their heritage with him to his new home in Rothenburg where he was soon surrounded by many scholars who were eager to gain all they could from their brilliant teacher. Many of Meir's students actually lived in his house and shared his life.

Rabbi Meir had a vast knowledge of Jewish law, and people came from near and far to consult him about difficult legal problems. His kindly manner endeared him to everyone.

In the days of Rabbi Meir, Rudolph I of Hapsburg became the emperor of Germany. Rudolph started his reign as a powerful ruler, endeavoring to control the nobles and all the subjects in his lands with an iron hand. The nobles had enjoyed com-

Tombstone of Rabbi Meir of Rothenburg in the old Jewish cemetery of Worms.

225

Portrait of King Rudolph of Hapsburg.

these outrageous sums for he knew that this would place an even heavier financial burden on the entire Jewish community. Besides, if they were to submit to the emperor's demand, how were they to know whether he would indeed be satisfied and not ask for more? The rabbi therefore asked his people not to seek his release by ransom. For years he remained in his prison cell, And even as once the students had come to Rabbi Akiba in prison in the days of the Romans, so the students of Rabbi Meir now came to the fortress. Some bore letters asking their teacher for legal advice and decisions to carry back to the courts of Jewish law and to the people of their towns. Rabbi Meir died in prison, a martyr by his own choice; he had put the well-being of the Jewish community above his own.

As intolerance spread, Jews were accused of all sorts of unbelievable acts—of plots to poison people, even of murdering Christian children in order to use their blood in the preparation of the matzah. This superstitious slander became the pretext for bloody attacks on the ghetto and for the torture, burning, plunder and expulsion of thousands of Jews.

plete power over the Jews of these lands; now the Jews became subjects of the Crown and hence responsible to the emperor alone. Rudolph raised their taxes and, whenever he felt that his Jews were guilty of a misdemeanor, took all their property away from them and gave them little protection when they were attacked.

Many Jews decided to emigrate. A large group, led by Rabbi Meir, set out for Palestine. On their journey they traveled through France, where, on a highway, they passed the Bishop of Basle, one of whose companions recognized Rabbi Meir. Now the Emperor Rudolph had given orders that Rabbi Meir be captured and imprisoned. He felt that the Jews had no right to leave the country without his explicit permission, which he had no intention of giving, because the Jews were valuable subjects. The high taxes imposed upon them greatly helped to swell the funds of Rudolph's royal treasury.

Rabbi Meir was arrested and taken in chains back to Germany, where he was imprisoned in a fortress. The Jews appealed to the emperor, asking the rabbi's release. Emperor Rudolph asked them for a large ransom as well as even higher taxes. Rabbi Meir implored his people not to agree to pay

Broadsheet describing the host desecration of Passau, Germany in 1478. Jews who did not accept forced baptism were burnt or expelled. The synagogue was destroyed and the church of Saint Salvador was built over the ruins.

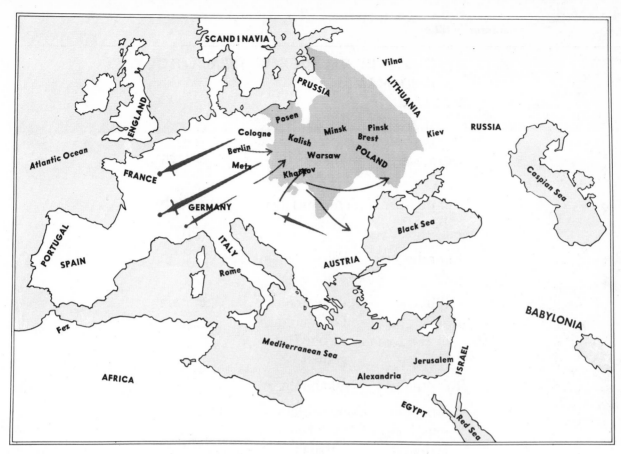

Persecutions and expulsions from German states (1350 to 1648). The many expulsions sent Jews eastward to Poland, where they were welcomed, and where they helped build up industry and trade.

The Jews were the scapegoats of medieval society. Often when war, poverty or disease struck, the Jews would be blamed for all the troubles. The people would then have an object on which to vent their dissatisfaction and disappointment often in rebellion against the rulers themselves.

FLIGHT TO THE EAST

The Jews of Germany somehow managed to survive these dark days. Temporary expulsions occurred but in many instances the Jewish community would eventually be able to return to its home. Impoverished, diminished in numbers though they were, the Jews would come back, their spirit unbowed. Doggedly they would set about to rebuild their homes, their synagogues and their schools and to resume their pattern of study, work, and Sabbath and festival observance.

By the end of the 15th century, new territories in the East of Europe opened to new immigrants—countries, which are today Russia, Poland, Czechoslovakia and Hungary, accepted those who were forced to flee their own countries. Jewish settlers came to these lands, bringing with them their heritage, their institutions of learning and self-government, their love of home and their will to survive. Strong in spirit, these refugees knew how to make a meaningful life for themselves, for even within the walls of the ghetto a wide world lay open to the Jews. It was a world illumined by the Bible and the Talmud, by the writing of Maimonides, Rashi and the Tosafists—and by the wisdom of many generations of scholars.

GLOSSARY OF HEBREW TERMINOLOGY AND NAMES

Crusades	Mahs'ey Hah-tslahv	מַסְעֵי הַצְּלָב
Yomtov ben Isaac	Yohmtohv ben Yitzḥak	יוֹם טוֹב בֶּן יִצְחָק
Ephraim ben Jacob	Efrahyeem ben Yah-akohv	אֶפְרַיִם בֶּן יַעֲקֹב
Rabbi Gershom, Light of the Exile	Rahbeynoo Geyrshohm, M'ohr Hah-gohlah	רַבֵּנוּ גֵרְשֹׁם מְאוֹר הַגּוֹלָה
Takkanot	Tahkahnoht	תַּקָנוֹת
Rabbi Solomon ben Itzhak (Rashi)	Rahbee Shlohmoh ben Yitzḥak (Rahshee)	רַבִּי שְׁלֹמֹה בֶּן יִצְחָק (רַשִׁ"י)
Rabbi Shemuel ben Meir	Rahbee Shmoo-eyl ben Mey-eer (Rahshbahm)	רַבִּי שְׁמוּאֵל בֶּן מֵאִיר (רַשְׁבַּ"ם)
Rabbi Jacob ben Meir	Rahbee Yah-akohv ben Mey-eer (Rahbeynoo Tahm)	רַבִּי יַעֲקֹב בֶּן מֵאִיר (רַבֵּנוּ תָם)
Tosafists	Bah-ahley Ha-tohsahfot	בַּעֲלֵי הַתּוֹסָפוֹת
Dayanim	Dahyahneem	דַּיָנִים
Bet Din	Beyt Deen	בֵּית דִּין
Shtadlan	Shtahdlahn	שְׁתַדְלָן

SPAIN UNDER CHRISTIAN RULE

THE CHRISTIANS GAIN CONTROL OF SPAIN

Meanwhile, in the north of Spain, the Christian kings slowly regained control of the land. Alfonso VI, king of Leon and Castile, was strong enough to unite the three Christian kingdoms of the north. Gradually the Moslem princes were defeated and in 1085 King Alfonso took possession of the Moslem stronghold Toledo.

King Alfonso VI ruled his realm with foresight and tolerance equal to that of the Moslem rulers of an earlier day. He ignored the warning of the Pope to deal harshly with his non-Christian subjects and force their conversion. Many of his subjects were not Christians and Alfonso gained their confidence by granting them religious freedom. His tolerance helped Christian Spain recover from the damage done through years of war and strife. Cities again began to flourish. Traders could bring goods from distant lands and artisans could fashion their wares. Farmers could till their lands and shepherds could tend their flocks. The Jewish community of Spain benefited from these improved conditions and lived freely and prosperously.

The Moslem rulers were gone, but for some time to come Christian Spain was to be a land of many religions and many different peoples: Moslems, Christians, Jews, Moors and Berbers. The wise King Alfonso succeeded in sparing this many-peopled land the great turmoil in which the rest of Europe was embroiled. He realized that to do otherwise might well bring on a long civil war.

The great conflicts between Moslems and Christians, between the church and the kings, had not yet touched the sunny land of Spain that seemed so safely isolated behind the high mountains of the Pyrenees. The rest of Europe and many of the Arab countries were ravaged by the wars of the Crusades. In the meantime the rest of Spain was continually wrested from the Moslems and by the first decades of the 13th century the Christian reconquest of Spain was practically complete. The church now exerted its influence throughout the whole of Spain and its efforts to convert the Jews were intensified.

Public execution by the Inquisition.

In Aragon and Castile the Dominican Friars had charge of the Inquisition, an institution established in 1233 to seek out and punish heretics. Among these friars was Pablo Christiani, a convert from Judaism who was eager to convert other Jews. In an attempt to convince Jews that Christianity was the true religion, he instituted seminars on Christianity, which Jews were forced to attend. Disappointed with the results of his efforts, Pablo persuaded King James I of Spain to hold a public debate at Barcelona in which the friar himself would pit his arguments for Christianity against the arguments of a learned rabbi in behalf of Judaism. Pablo wanted to prove that Jesus was the Messiah and he felt confident that the rabbi would accept his arguments.

NAHMANIDES (1194-1270)

The rabbi chosen to stand up in the debate before the king's court and before many high dignitaries of the church was Rabbi Moses ben Nahman, or Nahmanides. Nahmanides was the most important scholar and rabbi in the Spanish-Jewish community of his day and also its revered and beloved leader.

Nahmanides or RaMBaN, as he was known from his initials, was born in Gerona, Spain, in 1194. As a youth of sixteen he had already begun his first work—a brilliant defense of the Halakhic commentaries of the great Alfasi. Nahmanides was a versatile and open-minded man. Although he himself had criticized some of the ideas advanced by Maimonides, he worked ingeniously to reconcile the opinions of Maimonides with those of other Jewish thinkers. In addition to his many scholarly interests, Nahmanides was deeply influenced by the Kabbalah—the teachings of the Jewish mystics.

Nahmanides, who earned his living as a physician, was the rabbi of Gerona. Eventually he became known as the chief rabbi of all Catalonia. From far and wide, letters and questions would come to him. Such questions addressed to erudite rabbis by letter, and the rabbi's replies, are known as Responsa. The Hebrew name for such literature is *She'elot Uteshuvot* (questions and answers). Nahmanides is particularly known through his exegetical and mystical commentary to the Torah.

A man of great dignity and advanced age, Nahmanides now stood undaunted as he faced the court and the king, before the fanatical Pablo and the

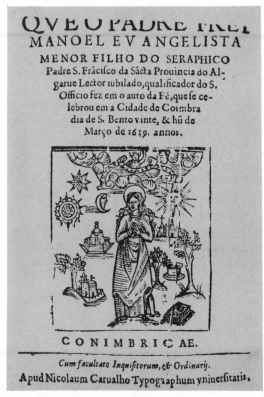

QVE O PADRE FREI
MANOEL EV ANGELISTA
MENOR FILHO DO SERAPHICO
Padre S. Frácifco da Sácta Prouincia do Algarue Lector iubilado, qualificador do S.
Officio fez em o auto da Fé, que fe celebrou em a Cidade de Coimbra
dia de S. Bento vinte, & hú de
Março de 1619. annos.

CONIMBRICAE.

Cum facultate Inquifitorum, & Ordinarij.
Apud Nicolaum Carualho Typographum vniuerfitatis.

Title page of a sermon preached on the occasion of the auto-da-fe of March 21, 1619, at Cordova, Spain.

A medieval artist's idea of a discussion between Christians and Jews.

other Dominican friars. In the debate Pablo tried to prove that Jesus was the Messiah. For proof, he recited Aggadic portions of the Talmud—legends and stories which, he maintained, really referred to Jesus.

Nahmanides gave his reply clearly and brilliantly. He explained to the king that the Aggadic portions of the Talmud contained only legends and stories. The more important part was the Halakhah, the legal portion of the Talmud, and he pointed out that there was nothing in the Halakhah to support the arguments of Pablo.

Nahmanides also asked one very important question. How, he inquired, could Jesus have been the Messiah if wars were still being waged between nations? The coming of the Messiah was supposed to usher in an era of peace and goodwill, but this had still not come to pass. If the Messiah had really appeared, should not all the kings and princes have put away their swords and made peace among men?

The wisdom of the aged Nahmanides impressed

the Spanish king, who adjourned the debate without conceding the victory to Pablo. In parting with Nahmanides, the king gave him a generous gift. Nahmanides published the text of the debate for his congregation. When Pablo heard of this he reported it to the king. Again Nahmanides was summoned. This time he was not received so kindly as before, but was sentenced to two years of exile.

Nahmanides went to Palestine. He was deeply grieved by the state of the Jewish communities there. Wars and invasions had impoverished the Jews in the Holy Land. Schools no longer existed and only a very few synagogues still stood intact. The aged scholar devoted the last years of his life to the Jewish community in Palestine. He built a synagogue in Jerusalem and opened a school. Scholars and students gathered around him. Before his death, Nahmanides could see the results of his work. The spiritual life of the Jews in Palestine had been enriched and rejuvenated through his efforts. Within the next two hundred years other great scholars would follow his path, and once again the Holy Land would become known as a center of Jewish learning. Nahmanides' pupil Solomon Ibn Adret, known as the *Rashba* (1233-1310), carried on his work in Spain.

At the time of Nahmanides, Jews of Spain were already suffering from considerable restrictions, but Jewish scholarship continued active. Scholars still came across the Pyrenees from France and Germany as refugees. Rabbis who had fled to Spain from Ger-

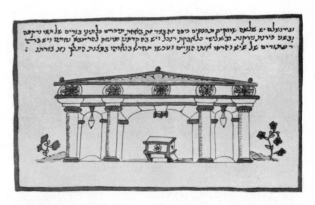

Nahmanides' synagogue in Jerusalem. From the *Casale Pilgrim*, a sixteenth century guide to the holy places of Palestine.

The Bodleian Bowl, early thirteenth century, cast in France. The bowl was used to collect funds for Palestine.

ligious thinkers of Spain. Eventually, it was to spread to the rest of Europe and to the new schools in Palestine. This system, known as Kabbalah, is the basis of the tradition of Jewish mysticism. Students of Kabbalah sought hidden meanings in the passages of the Torah in order to explain the difficult problems of the creation of the world out of absolute nothingness, relation of God to man, and the manisfestation of the spiritual and the divine in the material world. The Kabbalists saw special meanings in the Hebrew alphabet and in the numerical values of the various letters. Seeking to come close to the *Shekhina,* or Holy Presence of God, the Kabbalists added many hours of intense contemplation to the usual religious services to bring them nearer to the spirit of God.

In a time so full of suffering and seemingly insurmountable problems, the Kabbalists found a world apart from the woe and strife of their surroundings—a world filled with beauty, mysterious

many opened a school in Toledo. Among these refugee scholars was Asher ben Yehiel, known by his abbreviated name *Rosh* (1250-1327), the chief disciple of Rabbi Meir of Rothenburg. Rabbi Asher fled to Spain from Germany in the year 1303. He was the greatest rabbinical authority of his day and he is the author of collections of Responsa, decisions and Tosafot. He served as the rabbi of Toledo and was highly regarded throughout the whole of Spain. His work was continued by his son, Jacob Ben Asher, who is also known as *Baal Ha-Turim* for his work, *Turim,* in which he had arranged a code of law designed to help every Jew to understand the basic laws of Judaism as expounded in the Talmud and in later writings. The title of his work, *Turim,* means "Rows," recalling the four rows of precious stones that gleamed on the breast-plate of the High Priest in the Temple and which symbolized the Twelve Tribes of Israel. Jacob also wrote commentaries on the Pentateuch.

THE KABBALAH

A different system of thought, not based on the hitherto prevalent principles of philosophical reasoning, now gained ground among the Jewish re-

Page from the first edition of Jacob Ben Asher's "Arba Turim," Italy, 1478.

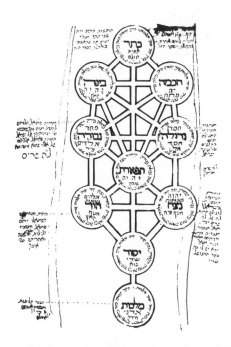

The ten mystic spheres of God. From a book of Kabalah printed in Mantua, Italy, 1562.

meanings and a strange daring of the soul. Beside the lofty contemplative Kabbalah there developed a variant form known as the "Practical Kabbalah" whose exponents were influenced by many of the superstitious and strange magical practices of their day. Most of the traditional rabbis and scholars frowned on the pursuit of Kabbalah. They believed that it would distract its followers from sound scholarship and deprive them of the mental clarity needed to understand the tradition of the Talmud. The unguided pursuit of the Kabbalah led some of its followers along strange paths, where they seemed to be living in a trance, lost to their surroundings. Among the visionaries of that time was Abraham Abulafia who traveled extensively, proclaiming himself prophet and Messiah.

MOSES DE LEON (1250-1305)

The teachings of Kabbalah spread and grew. Eventually they were collected by Moses Ben Shemtov de Leon into a major book called the *Zohar,* which literally means "Brilliant Light." It was said that the true author of the *Zohar* was not Moses de Leon but the saintly Rabbi Simeon Bar

Yohai, who had lived during the reign of the Roman Emperor Hadrian. However, many passages in the book refer to events that happened long after Simeon was dead. Still, Rabbi Simeon's teachings, too, had had a mystical bent and the Kabbalists looked upon him as the founder of their movement so that his name added to the attraction of the *Zohar.*

THE MARRANOS

Christian Spain was divided into two separate kingdoms, Aragon and Castile. Under King Pedro, who ruled in Castile, a Jew became the king's financier and treasurer. He was Samuel Abulafia, who helped build a beautiful synagogue in Toledo which stands to this day. When Henry of Trastamara, Pedro's half-brother, revolted against Pedro, the Jews of Castile fought valiantly for their king. However, King Pedro was defeated and his half-brother became Henry II, king of Castile and Leon.

Title page of the first edition of the *Zohar,* Mantua, 1558.

233

A Sanbenito, a victim of the Inquisition, who is shown as being sorry for his heresy.

The new king hated the Jews, who had fought against him. Under Henry's rule, zealous monks incited the mobs to sack Jewish homes in all the towns of Castile. For the first time, the Jews in Spain were obliged by law to wear the yellow badge—and the once proud Spanish Jews came to experience some of the humiliation suffered by the Jews in the rest of Europe. A wave of anti-Jewish feeling and riots swept through Spain. The Jews were given a choice—baptism or death. The Jews of Spain were not accustomed to such hardships. Many of them, unlike their fellow Jews in northern Europe, chose baptism. Some of the most respected members of the Jewish communities were baptized. Frequently entire communities converted together. These baptized Jews were never fully accepted into the society of Christian Spain. The name "Marranos" by which they became known in Spain, actually means "swine."

Many of the Marranos remained Jews at heart. They attended church, and they had their children baptized—but secretly, and at the grave risk of being denounced to the Inquisition and turned over to the Inquisitors for torture and death, many of them practiced their old faith. They met in secret places to hold services. They observed the festivals and the Sabbath, and studied the Torah.

In Christian Spain the Jews increasingly suffered from the new spirit of intolerance which was felt in many ways. The study of mathematics, medicine and astronomy no longer held a high place in learning as it had in the time of the Moslems. Science no longer flourished in the land. The condition of the Jews in Spain continued to deteriorate until the end of the 15th century.

FERDINAND AND ISABELLA

When Isabella of Castile and Ferdinand II of Aragon married, the two great kingdoms of Spain were united. At that time three different religions were still practiced in the land. There were Christians, Jews and Moslems. But Queen Isabella yearned to make Spain an all-Christian land. She delegated great powers to the dreaded Spanish Inquisition (not to be confused with the much milder Medieval Inquisition) and many unbelievers were burned at the stake.

The largest group of unbelievers happened to

Section of a wall in Samuel Abulafia's synagogue at Toledo.

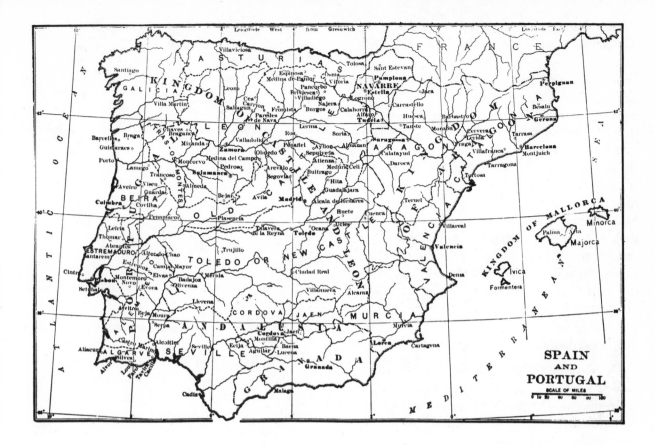

be the baptized Jews. The Marranos who were suspected of secretly practicing their old faith were singled out for special treatment by the Inquisition. Thouasnds of these secret Jews were summoned to the Inquisition. Besides the Jews, many others suffered at the hands of the Inquisition during the reign of Ferdinand and Isabella. Many died for upholding their own faith and opinions. Spain was no longer a land of broad culture and learning. The shadow of the Inquisition darkened every aspect of life in Spain.

At the time of the Inquisition the old witchcraft charges were again revived throughout all Europe. Men and women who seemed in any way strange or unusual, were accused of witchcraft, of brewing strange, destructive potions, of having sold their souls to the devil. The root of these superstitions lay in the old pagan cults of Europe which had prevailed before the rise of Christianity. Thousands of innocent people were tortured and burned at the stake, condemned by the Inquisition and sometimes by civil courts for the crime of witchcraft. The most

Illuminated Hebrew Bible written in Spain, 1476.

235

fanatic Inquisitor was the infamous Torquemada The Spanish Inquisition was not under the jurisdiction of the pope, and many popes disapproved of its sinister methods. Still, the Inquisition was not entirely abolished until the year 1820.

Many Marranos who were brought before the Inquisition "repented." Many others, however, died bravely at the stake, unwilling to relinquish the religion of their fathers even at the cost of their lives. It gradually became clear to the Spanish rulers that if the Jews were to be allowed to stay in Spain unmolested, they would set a bad example for the rest of the population and would prove that it was not necessary to give allegiance to the church. Ferdinand and Isabella decided, therefore, to give the Jews of Spain an alternative—either to accept Christianity or to leave the country.

THE EXPULSION OF THE JEWS FROM SPAIN

Despite all these strict measures, one of the most trusted advisors of the king and queen, the treasurer of the royal household, was a Jew, Isaac Abrabanel. Abrabanel was not only an excellent financier but a wise man whose opinion was valued

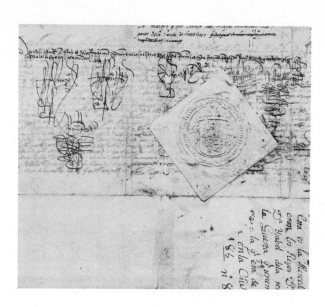

Grant of property, confiscated by the Inquisition, to a Cordovan monastery, by Ferdinand and Isabella (autographed).

at court. In addition, he was a scholar, philosopher and author and a leading member of the Jewish community. After the publication of the order of expulsion, Isaac Abrabanel approached the king and queen and, offering them a large sum of gold

The infamous Torquemada.

An astrolobe, with Jewish writing, constructed by a Jewish astronomer for Alfonso the Wise, king of Castile.

Isaac Abrabanel.

Page from the "Polyglot Psalms," Genoa, 1516. The Psalms are printed in Latin, Hebrew and Arabic. The Latin commentary mentions the discovery of America by Columbus.

and silver, asked them to recall the order of expulsion. But his plea was in vain. The power of the Inquisition was too great—even over the king and queen. Had he chosen, Abrabanel could have stayed at court as an exception to the royal edict, a man whose services were appreciated and needed. He chose instead to leave Spain, casting his lot with his friends and brethren, the Jewish community.

On August 2, 1492, all the Jews of Spain were forced to leave their homes. Fifteen hundred years before, Jews had been among the first colonists and pioneers in Spain, having arrived there with the Roman settlers.

The Jews prepared for the ordeal of departure. For generations, Spain had inspired them to write poetry, to help create a wonderful new style of architecture, to study the sciences and to contribute to the wisdom and growth of Judaism. Now the Jews had to turn their backs on the cities they had helped to build, the fields and forests they had loved, and the possessions they had gathered. Everything had to be left behind. Those Jews who had riches traded them for sturdy traveling clothes. Precious jewels were exchanged for food to take on the journey.

There was still one treasure left them, however —the comfort of companionship. The Spanish Jews, as Jews had always done, rallied together in this calamity and helped one another like broth-

ers. Rich and poor, young and old—all assisted in the preparations for the sad leavetaking.

It is said that as they boarded the ships that were to take them far from their beloved homeland, the Jews of Spain sang songs and psalms, and the hymns of their great poets: Judah Halevi, Solomon Ibn Gabirol and Moses Ibn Ezra.

A scene in a Spanish synagogue, from the *Sarajevo Haggadah.*

A model of the *Santa Maria*.

Just one day after the expulsion of the Jews, Ferdinand and Isabella were instrumental in the sailing of another expedition. On August 3, 1492, the *Nina,* the *Pinta,* and the *Santa Maria,* under the command of Christopher Columbus, set sail westward across the Atlantic in search of a sea route to India. Columbus had received much of the money needed to finance his expedition from Marranos. Many of his maps were made by Jews who knew the art of map making and the routes of the great seas. It is said that some members of his crew were Marranos. There is some speculation that the famous navigator himself was of Jewish origin.

As his three ships hoisted anchor on that day in early August, little did Christopher Columbus dream that between him and the shores of India lay a whole new continent! Columbus made a note in his log of the Jewish refugee ships which he sighted as he began the journey which was to change the course of history and alter the maps of the world.

The expulsion of the Jews from Spain marked the end of a memorable epoch. The journey of Columbus, however, was to signify a beginning—for it set the stage for the birth, centuries later, of

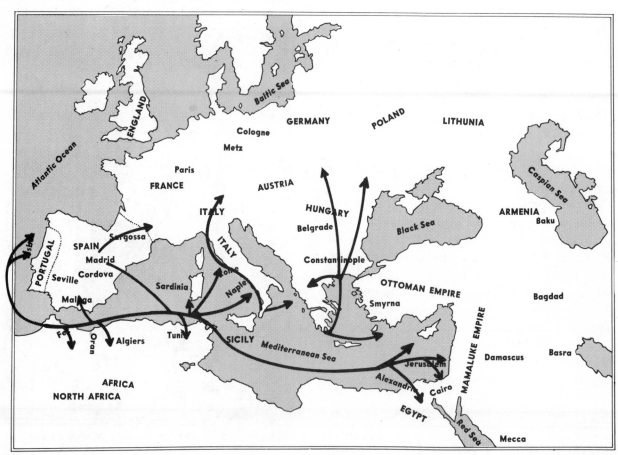

The expulsion from Spain in 1492. The map shows how the first exiles went to Portugal and to southern Italy; persecution followed and many fled eastward to countries of the Ottaman Empire.

a new government in a faraway land, where Jews and men of all beliefs would live in freedom.

WHERE DID THE SPANISH JEWS GO?

But where were the Spanish refugees to turn? England had expelled her Jews; so had France. In German lands Jews fared badly, subject to suspicion, persecution and occasional expulsions. Many Jews from Germany sought new homes in the East, in Poland and Lithuania. Some of these German Jews, especially those who were scholars and successful traders, went to Italy, where Jewish communities were said to prosper under the influence of a freer spirit of new learning.

Many Spanish Jews went to North Africa. Some found new homes in the great cities of Cairo and Alexandria in Egypt—and in Fez, Tunisia and Algiers. Many suffered poverty and found it hard to earn a living. But some among the refugees eventually became great merchants, scholars and physicians. In North Africa, under the rule of tolerant sultans, they could live in peace. Many found refuge in Turkey.

Some of the unfortunate refugees, alas, were robbed and killed by greedy ship captains before they could reach port. Many others, unable to find new homes, died in the sun-baked open fields of North Africa.

HOW DID THE JEWS FARE IN PORTUGAL?

Closest to Spain was the kingdom of Portugal.

A procession of officials and victims of the Inquisition in Goa, in an auto-da-fe.

Abrabanel coat of arms.

Here, for a short span of time, many of the refugees found a haven. Many wealthy Jewish families of Spain went to Portugal. A hundred thousand Jews found new homes there. They had to pay a poll tax but they were permitted to practice their trades and crafts. Their new home was of short duration however. The King of Portugal had married princess Isabella of Spain, the daughter of Ferdinand and Isabella. The Spanish princess had agreed to the marriage only on the condition that Portugal become a Christian country free of all heretics and Jews.

As a result, the Jews of Portugal faced much the same fate as had their brethren in Spain. Many were baptized by force; all those who would not submit to baptism risked expulsion. By October of 1497, the Jews of Portugal were also faced with the choice between conversion and leaving the country. Many submitted to baptism, but most of the Portuguese Jews went forth on the perilous journey in search of new homes. The lot of the Portuguese Marranos was much the same as that of the Marranos of Spain. Despite their official conversion to Christianity, they were constantly suspected of practicing their Judaism in secret. Many were brought before the Inquisition, which now existed in Portugal also, since that country had come into close union with Spain. Many Portuguese Marranos were burned in the public *autos-da fé,* or "acts of the faith" as these executions of heretics were known. Many were tortured and many others faced the threat of denunciation. Still, many among these newly-converted "Christians" practiced their Jewish faith in secret, reciting the Jewish prayers and reading from the Torah. As time passed, however, their contacts with Judaism diminished.

Yet, for centuries, Marranos survived in Portugal as they did in Spain, dimly conscious of their Jewish heritage and, in secret, still proudly considering themselves Jews. At the age of thirteen, Marranos told their children about their heritage, for this is the age when a Jewish boy usually becomes a Bar Mitzvah and joins the community of Israel as a responsible young person. The Marrano communities felt that this was also the age when a young person could realize the gravity and danger of the precarious position of the Marranos and the necessity for absolute secrecy.

Some of the most important and respected Jewish families of Spain and Portugal had become Marranos, hoping that they might eventually be able to make their way to another country where they would have an opportunity to return to Judaism. Many of the Marranos in Spain and Portugal rose to high positions in banking and political life. Their ambition and their abilities often aroused the envy of others, and their enemies sought to oust them from their high positions.

A prominent figure among the Jews of Portugal was Don Isaac Abrabanel, treasurer of the Royal Household (before he fled to Spain to escape false charges in 1483). For centuries the Abrabanel family gave many teachers, rabbis and physicians to the Jewish communities in which they lived.

THE SEPHARDIM

The descendants of the Spanish Jews, now scattered over the world, are known as Sephardim—Sepharad being the Hebrew word for Spain. The Sephardim still preserve the synagogue ritual of Spain and Portugal. And to this day many of them still speak *Ladino,* a mixture of Spanish and Hebrew. They pronounce Hebrew in a way called the Sephardic. As distinct from the Sephardim, the Jews of Central and Eastern European background are called Ashkenazim, the Hebrew for "German,"

since the forefathers of most Ashkenazic Jews once resided in Germany. The Ashkenazim pronounce Hebrew in their own way and have their own traditions. Their everyday language was a mixture of old German and Hebrew. Those of them who settled in eastern Europe brought this language with them. This is how the Yiddish language developed. The Yiddish language grew out of medieval German, combined with Hebrew words and words from the language of the countries in which the Jews lived.

Spanish Jews found refuge in many lands. Some of them traveled with letters of safe conduct in the form of baptismal certificates. But the Marranos were closely watched, especially when they sought to go to countries where it was suspected that they would have a chance to return to Judaism openly.

Title page of the commentary of Don Isaac Abrabanel to the Later Prophets.

Spanish in Hebrew characters (Ladino). Title page of Bahya ibn Pakudah's *Duties of the Heart*.

The Bevis Marks, oldest synagogue in London (1698) has a beam in its roof from a ship given by Queen Anne.

Spain was once a powerful nation. It had taken over the industrious, seafaring Netherlands. Soon after the discovery of America, Spain began to enjoy the fruits of the discoveries of Columbus. Riches from South America and Mexico poured into Spain and were traded in other lands, making Spain the wealthiest country in Europe. But Spain was soon to meet a major defeat. The Spanish Armada, a mighty fleet of armed ships, would be destroyed by bad weather and the fleet of England. Then the Dutch, the French and the English would also take possession of parts of the New World. Only then did Spain and Portugal realize that the expulsion of the Moors and the Jews had brought serious consequences. Through these expulsions, these two countries had deprived themselves of their middle class—the class between the peasants and serfs on the one hand, and the nobility, landowners, soldiers and clergy on the other. The old city dwellers and their traditions had departed with the Jews. In the centuries that followed, Spain and Portugal could no longer keep in step with much of the progress that was made in the rest of Europe.

A Dutch merchant fleet.

GLOSSARY OF HEBREW TERMINOLOGY AND NAMES

Nachmanides	Rahbee Moh-sheh ben Naḥmahn (Rahmban)	רַבִּי מֹשֶׁה בֶּן נַחְמָן (רַמְבַּ"ן)
Kabbalah	Kahbahlah	קַבָּלָה
Messiah	Mahshee-aḥ	מָשִׁיחַ
Halakhah	Hahlaḥah	הֲלָכָה
Solomon Adret	Rahbee Shlohmoh ben Ahdret (Rahshbah)	רַבִּי שְׁלֹמֹה בֶּן אַדְרֶת (רַשְׁבַּ"א)
Asher ben Jehiel (Rohsh)	Ahsher ben Yeḥee-eyl (Rahsh)	אָשֵׁר בֶּן יְחִיאֵל (רָא"שׁ)
Jacob ben Asher (Baal Haturim)	Yah-akohv ben Ahsher (Bah-ahl Hahtooreem)	יַעֲקֹב בֶּן אָשֵׁר, בַּעַל הַטּוּרִים
Turim	Tooreem	טוּרִים
Shekhina	Sheḥeenah	שְׁכִינָה
Zohar	Zoh-hahr	זֹהַר
Simeon Bar Yohai	Rahbee Shi-mohn bar Yoḥai	רַבִּי שִׁמְעוֹן בַּר יוֹחַאי
Marranos	Ahnooseem	אֲנוּסִים
Expulsion from Spain	Geyroosh Sfahrahd	גֵּרוּשׁ סְפָרַד
Sephardim	Sfahrahdeem	סְפָרַדִים
Ashkenazim	Ahshkenah-zeem	אַשְׁכְּנַזִּים
Ladino	Lahdeenoh	לַדִינוֹ

THE RENAISSANCE

THE COMING OF A NEW AGE

The 15th and 16th centuries—the period during which the tragic expulsion of the Jews from Spain and Portugal took place—witnessed great changes in Europe.

The educated nobility and burghers of the cities were growing in numbers and were gaining wealth and influence. In Italy, a new spirit was stirring. As scholars turned their attention to the history of their countries, they rediscovered the heritage of Greek art and thought. The ideas of the scholars and dramatists of ancient Greece differed radically from those of the church. They were more concerned with the individual, his physical life and well-being, than the Christians were. Even as the thinking of scholars and artists was changing, princes became more independent and worldly, increased their wealth through trade, and began to break away from the power of the church. Art was now influenced by two styles: that of the Middle Ages, which centered around the church and religious subjects, and that of ancient Greece and Rome which dealt with things of this world.

As artists became more interested in portraying the physical world, they sought patrons for their work among the princes rather than among the high church officials.

New inventions were made which radically changed the life of men everywhere. One of these was the printing press in Germany. With this simplified method of printing, more books were made available for study. Men became more interested in learning and many people were eager to read the Bible. Scholars became interested in the

A sixteenth century French library.

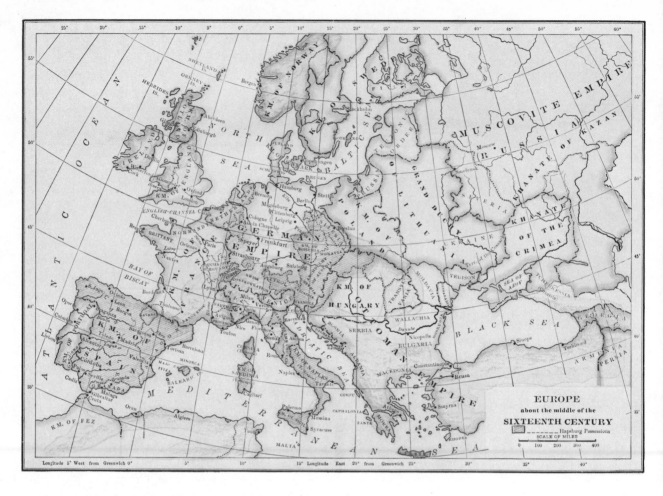

EUROPE
about the middle of the
SIXTEENTH CENTURY
- - - - - - - - Hapsburg Possessions
SCALE OF MILES
0   100   200   300   400

study of Hebrew, and Jews taught Christians the language of the Bible. Indeed, the first book to be printed *was* the Bible (in Latin). In 1456 the German printer, Johann Gutenberg, produced this revolutionary first printed edition in the city of Mayence

Printing was enthusiastically taken up by Jews. Jewish immigrants from Germany brought this new craft to Italy, and soon Hebrew works were being printed in the flourishing Jewish communities of that country.

Italy was filled with an air of freedom and with hope for a new, freer world. This new age which had its beginnings in Italy became known in history as the *Renaissance,* the French for "rebirth." However, the new spirit was confined to the nobles, the princes and the wealthiest among the merchants. Thus the world of the Renaissance was still dominated by the power of the church.

The Jews of Italy were greatly stimulated by the free spirit of the Renaissance. Just as the Christian writers, poets, composers, artists and scientists expressed new ideas and a new view of the world, many Jewish artists and scientists also became

An old-fashioned printing shop.

A street in the Jewish ghetto in Venice.

active. New music was composed, and new poetry was written. The Talmud, Rashi's commentaries, later writings and prayer books, all appeared in printed editions. Despite the restrictive laws still in force against the Jews during the early Renaissance, many of the Jewish communities of Italy flourished, and many Jews were active in trade, banking, science and scholarship.

Coat of arms of the Italian doctor and Rabbi, Abraham Menachem Rapoport.

In the Netherlands, then still struggling against the Spanish overlords, and in Germany, France and eventually in England, the spirit of the Renaissance stimulated the growth of new life. All over Europe the misty Middle Ages were coming to an end.

THE REFORMATION

In Germany the new learning gave rise to a movement known as the Reformation. Martin Luther, the first to translate the Bible into German, and others, opposed the power of the Catholic Church of Rome and strove to replace it with a new and different sort of Christianity. These reformers were the founders of the Protestant denominations which believed that each individual had a personal relationship with God and could find his way to Him without the help of inter-

Martin Luther, leader of the Protestant Reformation.

mediaries. Martin Luther was in close contact with Jews, from whom he learned the Hebrew language in order to be able to translate the Bible into German. Until that time, the Bible had existed only in the original Hebrew and in the Latin and Greek versions which could be read only by the educated and the clergy. By translating it into a modern language, Luther wanted to make it possible for each

Title page of the "Luther Tract to the Christian Nobility of the German Nation," 1520.

among many Christian scholars concerning the true character of the Talmud. The Jews of Germany and France hoped that this new interest in Judaism would lead to a better understanding between them and their neighbors. But despite the prestige which some of the Jewish scholars enjoyed in France and Germany, the position of the Jewish communities behind the ghetto walls did not change for the better.

YOSEL OF ROSHEIM, ADVOCATE OF THE JEWISH COMMUNITY (1480-1554)

The Jewish communities of Germany, Bohemia, and later of Poland, chose *Shtadlanim* to represent them before the government authorities. The outstanding *Shtadlan* of 16th century German Jewry was Yosel (Josel or Joselman) of Rosheim.

Yosel came from Rosheim, a town in Alsace. When still a young boy, he had seen all the members of his family perish as martyrs. Yosel devoted his life to lessening the sufferings of Jews wherever and whenever he could. He traveled throughout the German empire to carry out the task entrusted to him—the defense of the Jewish communities

and every man to read the Bible for himself.

Luther was anxious to convert the Jews to his new way of Christianity. When he realized that the Jews refused his new approach to Christianity, just as firmly as they had refused the older church, he was greatly disappointed. Once friendly toward the Jews, he now became their enemy, expressing his hostile attitude in articles and speeches. His followers soon adopted the same attitude toward the Jews of Germany as that held by their Catholic opponents. The German Jews were bitterly disappointed for they had hoped that the rise of the new Christianity would bring about an improvement in their position.

During the time of the Reformation, many Christians became interested in the literature of Judaism. Christian printers even published the Talmud. At about that time Johann Pfefferkorn, a Jewish convert to Christianity, denounced the Talmud as an anti-Christian work and demanded that it be banned and burned. Johann Reuchlin, an outstanding Christian Hebrew scholar refuted Pfefferkorn's accusation. This dispute set off arguments

Title page of a polemic by the anti-Semite, Joseph Pfefferkorn.

Anti-Semitic picture of Yosel of Rosheim, the "Court Jew" of the Emperor Charles V. In one hand is the Hebrew Bible and in the other a bag of money.

against attack.

Yosel was an active and talented financier, with an excellent background of Jewish learning. In addition to his practical work on behalf of his people, he managed to write two scholarly works, and in the course of his many diplomatic missions he engaged in debate with princes and priests who attacked the Talmud and other Jewish writings.

During the reign of Charles V, ruler of the Holy Roman Empire, when the Jewish communities were threatened with persecution and expulsion by both the Catholic Church and the Protestant forces, Yosel traveled hundreds of miles on his diplomatic missions. He was not always successful but many communities owed their peace and indeed their very life to his efforts. The great community

Jews praying in a medieval synagogue. From a fifteenth century illuminated *mahzor*.

of Prague, in Bohemia, was saved from expulsion by Yosel. He kept a diary in which he recorded many of his experiences during his forty years as *Shtadlan* of the Jews of Germany. These notes have been preserved to this day.

The lives of Yosel of Rosheim, the Jewish *Shtadlan,* and Martin Luther, the leader of the German Protestant Reformation, covered almost the same span of time: Luther's from 1483 to 1546 and Yosel's from 1480 to 1554.

These were stormy times, during which the lands of western Europe were faced with a challenging

Bull of Pope John, May 29, 1554, ordering the burning of the Talmud.

crisis—the struggle between the Roman Catholic Church and the Reformation.

Yet, behind their ghetto walls, following their own traditions and their own way of life, the Jews weathered the storms of the centuries that followed, the struggles between the Christian groups, between church and princes, and the wars and revolutions set off by the new conditions and new ideas.

THE STRUGGLE BETWEEN TWO RELIGIONS

The Protestant groups of the Reformation had

Bull of Pope Leo X against the errors of Luther and his followers.

separated themselves from the Roman Catholic Church and now represented a grave threat to its unity. As a result, stern measures were adopted by the church to guard against the spread of such dangerous influences as the Reformation. The princes of Europe also were concerned about the obedience of their subjects. Many people in the Protestant countries had begun to read the Bible and many accepted the new notion that all men were equal, created by God for the same purpose. Many of the princes, bent on stifling this new spirit of freedom lest it incite rebellion, now joined in the fight of the church for their own purposes. Again "heretics" were persecuted and "non-believers" outlawed.

A Protestant poster ridiculing the selling of "indulgences" by the Catholics. By paying a fee, the peasant could buy forgiveness for his sins.

The free spirit of the Renaissance seemed forgotten. Protestants and Catholics had become involved in a bitter struggle. Each group was bent on proving itself more truly Christian than the other and each vied with the other in performing pious acts. A period of harsh intolerance resulted. Both Catholic and Protestant rulers persecuted the heretics within their ranks and imposed new restrictions on the Jews in their lands.

The struggle between the Protestants and the Catholics was a bloody one. In this medieval engraving of 1525, we see the German peasants plundering a monastery.

All over Europe—except in the tolerant Netherlands—there were ghettos. Again the Jew was set apart, crowded into the ghetto, restricted in his freedom, demeaned to a humiliating status. Of course, the bait of conversion was always held out to all who would accept it. For all Jews willing to convert, the gates of the ghetto were open. But the Jews disregarded this alternative and steadfastly clung to the heritage of their fathers.

THE GHETTO IN ITALY

Although ghetto walls had been erected in Italy, the Italian Jews lived under far better conditions than did their brothers in the rest of Europe. However, they seldom became important traders or bankers. Their activities were restricted, as in all Europe, to the unsavory occupation of moneylending and dealing in secondhand wares. Ironically enough, the secondhand goods often turned out to

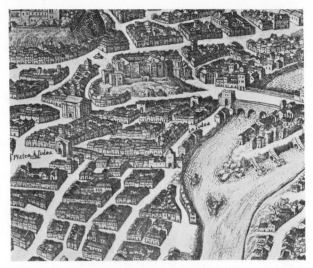

Plan of the ghetto in Rome, 1640.

be valuable antiques and art objects, and the moneylending trade expanded until it was actually a banking business. Italy attracted the persecuted Jews of both Spain and Germany. Jewish traders, seafarers, map makers, doctors, bankers and scholars from Spain, all came to Italy. Jewish printers came from Germany and printed editions of the Talmud, the Bible and the prayer books. Most famous among these printers was the Soncino family, whose name was revived by a group of Jewish bibliophiles in Germany before World War II, and adopted by a publishing house which still prints Jewish books in London, among others,

A costume of an Italian Jew in the seventeenth century.

the complete translation of the Talmud in English.

The Jews fared best in the Kingdom of Naples, where Don Isaac Abrabanel and many other Spanish Jews had found a new home.

THE JEWISH COMMUNITY OF TURKEY

The expulsions from Spain and Portugal led to the founding of a flourishing Jewish community in Turkey, the new Moslem power of the East.

The Turks had conquered many Christian lands. In 1453 they had taken Constantinople, thus ending the long history of the Byzantine Empire. They conquered also the lands of the Fertile Crescent

Printer's mark of the Soncino family.

and Greece. Thus the Moslem Empire of the Turks, known as the Ottoman Empire, was growing in power and influence.

German Jews had emigrated to Turkey even before the Spanish and Portuguese Jews arrived there. Salonica, in the north of Greece, was under Turkish rule and became a center of Jewish life and active trading.

The Turkish sultans welcomed the Jewish traders, bankers and physicians from Spain, and put the talents of the immigrants to good use in the building of their new empire. Jews rose to high positions at the court of the Ottoman sultans in the

249

First page of the Bible printed by Joshua Solomon ben Israel Nathan Soncino in Naples, (1492).

16th century, serving as ambassadors and advisors. Their connections and their knowledge of financial matters helped foster Turkish trade.

It was as if the golden days of Spain under Moslem rule had returned once more in the lands of the East. Jewish ambassadors were sent from Constantinople to the courts of Europe. Solomon Ashkenazi, a learned Jewish physician, became ambassador for Turkey and helped negotiate peace with Venice in 1574. Later, he offered Turkey's help to Venice in case of war with Spain.

At this time the Jews of Venice were being threatened with expulsion. Solomon Ashkenazi, as the Turkish ambassador, put pressure on the Venetian government to revoke the expulsion order. It was due to his efforts that the Jewish community in Venice was saved.

THE MENDES FAMILY

Gracia Mendes was among the Portuguese Marranos who eventually sought refuge in Italy. Gracia Mendes, the beautiful widow of a wealthy and famous banker, had taken over her husband's business after his death. She had left Portugal accompanied by her daughter Reyna and her nephew and business advisor, Joseph Nasi. They had settled first in the great port of Antwerp, in the Netherlands, which was then under Spanish rule. But when they were denounced to the Inquisition as heretics, Gracia Mendes and her family fled from Antwerp. They had found refuge in Venice, the great Italian trade center. But there again Gracia Mendes was denounced as a heretic who had abandoned the Catholic Church to which she officially belonged. She was imprisoned and all her wealth was confiscated. Many of her debtors cancelled their obligations. Even the king of France, who owed the Mendes family great sums of money, declared he would not pay his debt.

Prospects looked bleak for the unfortunate woman. Most probably she had hoped to join the Jewish community in Italy. Instead she was now in prison, poor and in danger of her life, and separated from her daughter Reyna and her nephew Joseph Nasi. But Joseph Nasi was determined to rescue his aunt and his cousin. He left Venice to seek a new life in the Turkish Empire. Arriving in Constantinople, Joseph Nasi enlisted the help of Sultan Suleiman for his relatives. The Sultan, impressed by Joseph Nasi's abilities and business connections, sent a letter to Venice demanding the release of Gracia Mendes. He also had sent a letter to her debtor, the king of France, demanding that he respect the rights of the Mendes firm.

After the sultan's intervention, Gracia Mendes was released from prison and went to the Italian city of Ferrara to wait for the restitution of her

A 1495 artist's conception of the city of Constantinople.

Portrait medal of Dona Gracia Nasi, 1556.

properties. In Ferrara she openly rejoined the Jewish community. Gracia Mendes proved to be a generous and compassionate woman, giving much of her time and fortune to aid troubled Jews and Marranos who were returning to Judaism.

One of Gracia Mendes' business associates in Ferrara was Solomon Usque, a poet, writer and printer. Solomon issued many Hebrew books from his printing press, as well as translations from classical writers and a Spanish translation of the Bible (1553).

Finally, accompanied by her daughter Reyna, Gracia Mendes journeyed to Turkey to join her nephew, Joseph, who then married his cousin Reyna.

Joseph Nasi became the financial advisor to the sultan. The young man's intelligence, his tactful counsel and charming manner made him one of the most respected personalities at the sultan's court. He became a skilled diplomat. His knowledge of languages, and his connections in many lands made him an ideal diplomat, so that Joseph Nasi was appointed to represent Turkey in conferences with many foreign ambassadors.

After the death of Suleiman, Joseph served Suleiman's son, Selim II. This ruler heaped many honors upon his friend Joseph. He made him Duke of Naxos, a beautiful island in the Aegean Sea. Still another gift was the ancient city of Tiberias, in Palestine, where once the rabbis of the Mishnah had taught. Joseph hoped to help many Jews and Marranos to get to Tiberias where they would be free of fear and oppression and build a new life in the land of their fathers.

The vision of Joseph Nasi had a practical side too. In Tiberias he hoped to found a new industry which would bring profit to the new immigrants as well as the Turkish empire—the manufacture of silk. He had the houses and streets of Tiberias rebuilt and had mulberry trees planted for the silk worms to feed upon. However, his plans were not realized. Only a few Jews were able to reach the Holy Land, for a war had broken out between Venice and Turkey and ships could not sail the Mediterranean safely. Yet Joseph Nasi was not discouraged. At a time when few wealthy men put the ideals of charity into action, he continued to devote much of his wealth and energy to the service of his suffering brethren.

Title page of a book showing the Usque printer's mark.

GLOSSARY OF HEBREW TERMINOLOGY AND NAMES

Talmud	Tahlmood	תַּלְמוּד
Shtadlanim	Shtahdlah-neem	שְׁתַדְלָנִים

MYSTICS, SCHOLARS, PHILOSOPHERS AND PIONEERS

PALESTINE

Some of the Spanish and Portuguese refugees managed to reach Palestine. The dream of a return to the Land of Israel was ever present in the hearts of all Jews. It was expressed in many of the holiday prayers. On the ninth of Ab, Jews everywhere still wept and fasted in mourning for the destruction of the Temple. Throughout the centuries a trickle of Jewish emigrants would come into Palestine from Germany, France, Italy and Turkey.

In the period following the expulsion of the Jews from Spain, new blood came to the ancient communities of Galilee in the north of Palestine. A few of the refugees had managed to reach Tiberias. Others had gone to Jerusalem, most beloved of the cities of the Holy Land. But a new community had grown and was now flourishing in the town of Safed, in the mountains of Galilee.

SAFED—COMMUNITY OF THE KABBALAH

In this poor little town, a new type of learning was blossoming. Before, Safed had been a sleepy town populated mainly by simple shepherds and tillers of the soil. Now schools arose there and rabbis passed through the ancient streets dis-

A pilgrim's caravan on the road to Jerusalem. A German artist's conception, 1608.

cussing the deeper meaning of passages from the Bible and problems of Talmudic law. The most active schools of Safed were those engaged in the study of Kabbalah—the teachings of Jewish mysticism. The Kabbalists of Safed were concerned primarily with questions relating to the coming of the Messiah. When would the Messiah appear? When would the sufferings of war and persecution end and the spirit of peace and God's kingdom triumph throughout the world?

Most important among the mystical books

"How awesome is this place," reads the inscription over the entrance to the synagogue of the ARI.

voted bridegroom.

Greatest among the teachers of Kabbalah at Safed was the brilliant young Rabbi Isaac Luria (1534-1572). Born in Jerusalem, he lost his father when he was a young child. He was brought to Cairo, where he was educated under the care of his uncle. He made rapid progress in his rabbinic studies and had become acquainted with the Kabbalah to which he applied himself fervently.

When Rabbi Isaac Luria came to Safed he found many devoted, enthusiastic students there. They lived together, close to their beloved rabbi, seeking to emulate his way of life and his purity of thought. By thus devoting themselves to the joys of mystical speculation, prayer and concentration, they hoped to hasten the coming of the Messiah and the time of eternal peace.

To many Jews it seemed as if the spirit of the early prophets had been revived in the ancient hills of the Land of Israel.

Students would refer to Ashkenazi Rabbi Isaac or "Rabbi Isaac The German" as he was known, (referring to the German origin of his parents), by his Hebrew initials, ARI (the initials ARI, also read Adonenu Rabbi Isaac). ARI is a Hebrew

which the Kabbalists studied was the Zohar. To the Kabbalists of Safed, Simeon Bar Yohai, to whom the book was attributed, was a beloved figure in Jewish lore. On Lag Ba-Omer, said to be the day of his death, the Jews of Safed would make pilgrimages to his grave in Meron to honor his memory with prayer, song and dance. This practice is still followed in modern Israel.

The Kabbalists of Safed sought to compensate for the miseries of this world with the joys of deep contemplation and a pure life. On the Sabbath, they would dress in special garments and devote themselves to the joyous celebration of the day of rest. The famous hymn *Lekha Dodi* "Come My Beloved," which is still chanted in the synagogue on Friday nights, was composed by Solomon Alkabetz, one of the great Kabbalist teachers of Safed. In this poem he compared the Sabbath to a beautiful bride, and the people of Israel to her de-

The Synagogue of the ARI, in Safed, Israel.

word meaning "lion," and indeed, the disciples of Rabbi Isaac considered him as courageous, strong and mighty as the lion, ancient symbol of the Tribe of Judah.

After Rabbi Isaac Luria died at the early age of thirty-eight, his devoted students continued to follow and develop his thoughts, his Kabbalistic teachings and his way of living. For generations his name was a byword in Safed and in ghettos throughout the world, wherever learned Jews studied the Kabbalah and endeavored to unravel the mysteries of creation and the manifestation of God in the universe.

Many of the Talmudic scholars regarded the teachings and the ways of the Kabbalists as dangerous. The Kabbalists, they pointed out, did not show much interest in legal problems. Their ways differed from the rigorous, disciplined life of the scholars. As time went on, the conflict between these two ways of living became more intense. But in Safed, in the days of Rabbi Isaac Luria, the two approaches to Judaism existed peacefully side by side.

THE SHULHAN ARUKH

Safed was also the home of Rabbi Joseph Caro, who was born in Spain in 1488. Rabbi Joseph had wandered through many lands before he found peace at Safed. He had fled from Portugal to Turkey, where he had been the head of an academy of Jewish learning. After settling in Safed, he undertook a gigantic task—the compilation of an encyclopedic code of Talmudic law which would be easier for Jews everywhere to use and follow than the original books of the Talmud and previous codes.

He based his commentaries and explanations of Talmudic laws on the *Turim,* the work composed by Jacob Ben Asher in Spain in 1340. Caro brought the *Turim* up to date by adding the decisions of the rabbis of the last two hundred years and codifying many more aspects of Jewish law. For thirty years Joseph Caro worked on this new code. He then prepared a shorter, well-defined version in which he discussed every aspect of Jewish life and all its rituals. The work of Joseph Caro

Title page of an early edition of the *Shulhan Arukh,* first published in 1564.

is called the *Shulhan Arukh* ("The Prepared Table"). It proved a handy reference work for those seeking guidance on specific details of Jewish law and custom. In spite of initial opposition among Ashkenazic rabbis, particularly in Poland, it finally won full recognition after the glosses of Rabbi Moses Isserles were added to it.

The *Shulhan Arukh* was used by Jews in many lands to help them observe the law even in small communities where there was no scholar to turn to for advice.

THE DECLINE OF SAFED

Unfortunately the attitude of the Sultans toward their non-Moslem subjects took a turn for the

255

אני דויד בן המלך שלמה

A letter of David Reubini, claiming that he represented a Jewish kingdom in the desert.

bia. Many, awed by his strangely fascinating appearance, believed him. Reubeni proposed to Pope Clement VII that he equip an army which he Reubeni, would lead to Jerusalem. He promised to muster men from the tribe of Reuben to assist the Pope's soldiers.

The Pope was impressed by Reubeni. Times were difficult for the Catholic Church. The Reformation was taking hold in many lands and curbing the power of Rome. A new Crusade that would take the Holy Land from the Turks seemed a worthwhile project. The Pope arranged for him to visit the king of Portugal, who was expected to aid in this ambitious plan. In Portugal Reubeni was received with honors and the king gave serious consideration to his plan.

The Marranos of Portugal derived some benefit from Reubeni's arrival, for in his honor the Inquisition seemed to have suspended its persecutions—a sign that they considered his mission authentic. Diego Pires, a young Marrano of a prominent family, was deeply moved by Reubeni. Openly returning to Judaism, Diego left Portugal and went to Palestine to study the Kabbalah. He

worse. Many of the old restrictions which previously had been enforced on Jews in the Moslem world were revived, and the schools in Turkey and Palestine suffered. Safed once again became a poor, small mountain town. But the work of the "ARI," of Joseph Caro and the many other scholars and Kabbalists who flourished in Safed had a profound influence on the Jewish people the world over.

SELF-APPOINTED HERALDS OF THE MESSIAH— DAVID REUBENI AND SOLOMON MOLKO

One day in the year 1524, a strange, dark man rode into the city of Rome on a white Arabian steed. Jews and Christians alike gaped in amazement and ran after him as he went to the palace of the Pope for an audience. This man claimed to be the son of the king of the ancient Israelite tribe of Reuben and called himself David Reubeni. In a strange Hebrew dialect which was difficult for Jews of Rome to understand, Reubeni told tales of the tribe of Reuben, deep in the lands of Ara-

Turkish passport of a pilgrim to Palestine, 1581. On top, the royal mark of the Turkish sultan.

Turkish governor of Jerusalem, 1565.

The battle between the Spanish Armada and the English fleet.

changed his name to Solomon Molko. A zealous man of fiery temperament, he devoted himself wholly to his new life. In time he became convinced that he was meant to be a messenger of God on earth, sent to proclaim the coming of the Messiah. Solomon Molko captured the imagination of many Jews, traveled to many lands, and finally appeared in Rome. There Molko and Reubeni met. Reubeni, for reasons of his own, did not want to speak to Molko, who was convinced of the righteousness of the cause he had embraced. Although these two had little to say to one another, both were to share the same harsh fate.

By this time, the powerful Emperor, Charles V of Spain, felt that both men represented a danger to him since they incited both Christians and Jews to rebellion. Reubeni and Molko were imprisoned by the Inquisition and put to death. Many Jews were shocked by their tragic fate for it spelled an end to their hopes.

THE NETHERLANDS

In the 15th and early 16th centuries, the Netherlands were under the dominion of Spain. The people of that little land by the sea hated the Spanish rulers and their ways. The Spanish rulers were determined to suppress any stirrings of revolt, primarily the Protestant Reformation, which threatened to undermine the unity of the Catholic Church. Charles V, the Spanish Emperor, who ruled over the Holy Roman Empire, wanted his far-flung domains united in loyalty to church and crown. Protestants and Marranos in the Netherlands were suspect of disloyalty to the church and many were denounced and persecuted.

But Spanish rule could not maintain its grip on the freedom-loving Dutch. The people of the Netherlands fought Spain bitterly, and in 1581 they declared their independence. Soon the Dutch proved to be formidable competitors to the Spanish on the high seas. They were to wrest much of the power from Spain, even in the colonies of the New World.

Meanwhile, the English, also wary of Spain, were on the way to becoming a mighty nation of seafarers, merchants and colonists. In 1588, under Queen Elizabeth I, the British navy defeated and

Contemporary engraving of the port of Antwerp.

destroyed the mighty Spanish fleet, or "Armada" as it was called.

After the Netherlands had won their independence, many Marranos from Portugal and Spain joined their fellow Marranos in Amsterdam and Antwerp, where they returned to Judaism. At first they did so only in secret, for they did not know how the people of the new republic of the Netherlands would accept them. But almost everywhere they were met with friendliness and tolerance, and soon the Sephardic communities, descended from the Jews of Spain and Portugal, flourished in the great trading centers of the Netherlands.

Portuguese Jews who had settled in Amsterdam had connections with the traders in the German city of Hamburg and its port on the North Sea. Portuguese Marranos eventually went to live in that city, bringing to it their trade connections with the Netherlands, Spain and Portugal. At first these Marranos were simply known as Portuguese but after a time they openly professed their Judaism. They had already become very useful to the merchant city, so that though they had to accept the restrictions imposed on all Jews in Germany, they were permitted to remain in Hamburg. Under the influence of the immigrants from Portugal, Hamburg's Jewish community became a center of active Jewish life. When the king of neighboring Denmark heard of the industry and excellent trade connections of the newcomers from Portugal and Spain, he invited a number of them to settle in his own country.

The city of Amsterdam was often called the "Dutch Jerusalem." This name had been coined in 1596, when a group of Portuguese Marranos there had returned to Judaism in a solemn, public ceremony. From that time on, Amsterdam was fast becoming the great center of European Jewry. Not only did Marranos come there to return openly to the faith of their fathers but Jews came also from Germany to the free land of the Dutch Protestants, who understood the meaning of persecution, and who extended tolerance and opportunity to the Jews. Jewish communities grew in the large cities of the Netherlands. Many Portuguese and Spanish Marranos had come with no earthly possessions

Title page to Abraham Zacuto's first publication "Index Dioscoridis," published in Amsterdam in 1575. Abraham Zacuto was a Jewish doctor and astronomer who escaped the Inquisition in Portugal and settled in Amsterdam.

other than their excellent trade connections, their language ability and their education. They became successful and respected traders in their new homes and contributed to the growing power of the Netherlands.

JEWS IN THE DUTCH COLONIES OF THE NEW WORLD

Holland eventually gained a foothold in the New World. Eventually too, she attacked Brazil, then a possession of Portugal, and acquired a section of this rich land, including the city of Recife. The many Marranos who had settled there, and had to observe their Judaism in secret, could now openly return to their Jewish faith. They dedicated a synagogue where they proudly worshiped in the Sephardic tradition.

When Portugal sent her armed forces to recapture her valuable colonies in Brazil, the Jewish settlers fought side by side with their Dutch neighbors and many of them died in battle.

Drawing of Manasseh Ben Israel.

RABBI MANASSEH BEN ISRAEL (1604-1657)

One of the most important rabbis of the "Dutch Jerusalem" was Manasseh ben Israel. The son of Spanish Jews, he was steeped in Jewish learning. Since many Christians those days were interested in learning more about the Bible and in the language in which the Bible originally had been written, many prominent Christians turned to Manasseh ben Israel. Kings and queens, scholars and merchants corresponded with the Rabbi of Amsterdam, asking for information and advice.

Among Rabbi Manasseh's many Christian friends was the great Dutch painter, Rembrandt van Ryn. Rembrandt was fascinated by the strong facial types and by the Mediterranean appearance of the Dutch Jews of Spanish and Portuguese descent, so different from the fair, northern Dutch-

men. As a result, Rembrandt asked many Jews to pose for his paintings, among them his friend Rabbi Manasseh ben Israel.

Manasseh ben Israel was a student of the Kabbalah. Like many Jews of his day, he believed that the coming of the Messiah was near. He also believed that to prepare for the Golden Age of peace it was necessary for the Jews to be scattered to all parts of the earth. Some travelers returning from the New World had recently told a strange story in Amsterdam. They believed that they had seen, on the American continent, members of the lost Ten Tribes of Israel! Many Jews were highly excited by this news. Actually, of course, the men of whom the returning travelers told were not Jews but American Indians.

Rabbi Manasseh was a keen observer of all the political developments of his time. He noted the great change that had come over England when it broke away from Catholicism and established the Protestant Church of England. No Jews had lived in England since their expulsion in 1290. In 1649, Oliver Cromwell and the Protestant Puritan party had come into power and deposed the king.

Declaration of privileges granted to the Jews of Altona in 1641 by the King of Denmark, Christian IV.

Title page of an address delivered by Manasseh Ben Israel in a synagogue in Amsterdam, 1642.

Many of England's political leaders looked to the Bible for inspiration. They seriously studied the workings of the Sanhedrin for guidance in conducting their own Parliament. In fact, some of England's parliamentary leaders contemplated making the Biblical code the law of the land. Certainly, Rabbi Manasseh ben Israel thought, such a nation might well be ready to permit Jews to reenter. He therefore decided to appear before the English Parliament, to make a personal plea for the readmission of Jews to England.

In 1655, after a difficult journey, Rabbi Manasseh arrived in London. Cromwell, the Protestant Lord Protector of England, was inclined to grant the rabbi's request. But not all those in power were thus favorably disposed. Some of England's merchants and some of its church groups opposed the readmission of the Jews, and the rabbi's plea was rejected. Still, his journey had not been wholly in vain. By 1656 Marranos who had been in England many years before, returned to the religion of their fathers openly and were granted the right to worship as they pleased. Eventually they were joined by other Jewish immigrants, and Jewish communities arose again all over England.

BARUCH SPINOZA (1632-1677)
LENS GRINDER AND PHILOSOPHER

Among the Jewish merchants and craftsmen of Amsterdam there were many brilliant and unusual people. Some were learned in the Talmud; others were immersed in the study of the Kabbalah. One of them was Baruch (Benedict) Spinoza, an extraordinary man, whose talents grew in isolation from the main stream of Jewish life and learning. The son of immigrants from Spain, Spinoza had studied the Torah and the Talmud like all the other Jewish boys of his day. He had also studied not only the great philosophers of Judaism but also the secular works of the philosophers of ancient Greece and Rome. Spinoza was a brilliant young man and his teachers, the rabbis of Amsterdam, hoped he would become their brightest disciple and successor.

But Spinoza gradually isolated himself from Jewish life. He did not follow all the law of the *Shulhan Arukh,* and some of his ideas seemed shocking and sacrilegious to his teachers. Spinoza

Portrait of Oliver Cromwell.

wrote brilliant philosophical works, in which he stated that God was present in all things and that men could serve Him by being just and righteous to their fellowmen.

Many of Spinoza's ideas were really not so different from some of those held by Maimonides and Saadia Gaon. Spinoza, however, had questioned the validity of certain points of Jewish law, and that was considered shocking by the hard pressed Jewish community of the 17th century. Spinoza's ideas seemed to threaten Jewish unity and survival. Hence he had to be rejected.

In 1656 the rabbis excommunicated him and Spinoza was soon regarded as an outsider by the official Jewish community.

Spinoza was a lens grinder, making lenses for spectacles. He liked this work by which he earned his living. After his excommunication he took his tools and moved to the little village of Rijnsberg

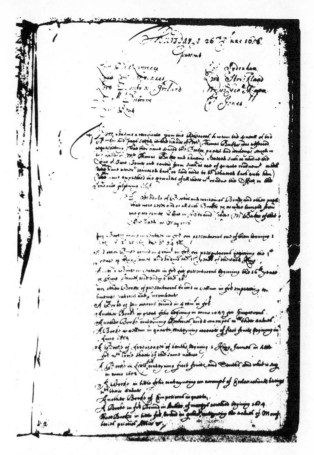

The Marranos were allowed, by the Council of State of England, to establish a synagogue and a cemetery. Above is a page from the minute book in which the permission was entered.

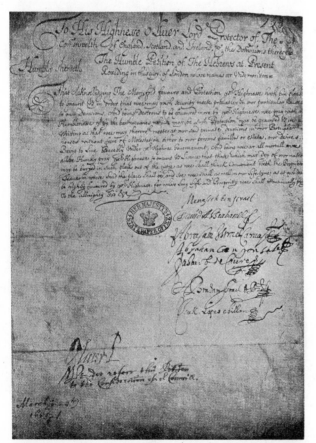

A letter from the Jews of London to Oliver Cromwell, dated March 24, 1655, pleading that "we may with security meet privately in our particular houses for our devotions."

on the outskirts of Amsterdam. Here he continued his quiet life, devoted to his studies and writings. Many of the great scholars of the time came to visit the humble lens grinder. But Spinoza's lot was a lonely one. He was cut off from the Jewish community and estranged from his own family. He died at the age of forty-five, a lonely man, tragically lost to the Jewish community. In later years Spinoza came to be universally recognized as one of the greatest philosophic minds.

MOSES HAYIM LUZZATTO (1707-1747)

Another unusual personality who caused a stir in the Jewish community of Amsterdam some years later was the poet and mystic, Moses Hayim Luzzatto, who like Spinoza, earned his livelihood as a lens grinder. They were however, different types of personalities. Luzzatto had been born in the Italian

Drawing of Baruch Spinoza in a contemplative mood.

the poet further ignored their warnings and wrote a book which he entitled "The Second Zohar." As a result Luzzatto was compelled to leave the Jewish community of Italy in 1733. He went to Amsterdam to begin a new life, grinding lenses for a living.

As Luzzatto grew older he became interested in the works of Judah Halevi. Like that great poet of Spain's Golden Age, Luzzatto longed to see the Holy Land. He and his family managed to translate their yearning for the Land of Israel into reality and after an arduous journey, settled in Tiberias. Unfortunately, however, soon after their arrival the entire family was wiped out by an epidemic of the plague that ravaged Palestine.

Spinoza's house in Amsterdam.

city of Padua. At the age of twenty, Luzzatto already had made a name for himself with a book of poetry patterned on the Psalms of the Bible. Inspired by the spirit of the Renaissance, he wrote plays on Biblical themes, which had a lasting influence on the development of modern Hebrew literature. As he grew older, Luzzatto turned with great interest to Kabbalah and the study of the *Zohar*.

In the days of Luzzatto, the rabbis of Italy forbade young Jewish scholars to engage in the study of Kabbalah, because they considered that only a mature man would be able to do so without falling victim to confusion and doubt. The rabbis therefore strongly disapproved of Luzzatto's interest in mystical writings. They were shocked when

GLOSSARY OF HEBREW TERMINOLOGY
AND NAMES

Ninth of Ab	Teeshah B'ahv	תִּשְׁעָה בְּאָב
Safed	Ts'faht	צְפָת
Galilee	Gahleel	גָּלִיל
Lag Ba-Omer	Lahg Bah'oh-mehr	לַ"ג בָּעֹמֶר
Lekha Dodi	L'ḥa Dohdee	לְכָה דוֹדִי
Solomon Al-kabez	Shlohmoh Ahl-kahbeyts	שְׁלֹמֹה אַלְקַבֵּץ
Rabbi Isaac Luria	Rahbee Yitz-ḥak Loorya (Ha-ahree)	רַבִּי יִצְחָק לוּרְיָא (הָאַרִ"י)
Shulhan Arukh	Shoolḥahn Ahrooḥ	שֻׁלְחָן עָרוּךְ
Rabbi Joseph Caro	Rahbee Yoh-seyf Kahroh	רַבִּי יוֹסֵף קָארוֹ
David Reubeni	Dahveed R'ooveynee	דָּוִד רְאוּבֵנִי
Solomon Molko	Shlohmoh Mohlḥoh	שְׁלֹמֹה מוֹלְכוֹ
Manasseh ben Israel	Menahsheh ben Yisrah-eyl	מְנַשֶּׁה בֶּן יִשְׂרָאֵל
Benedict Spinoza	Bahrooḥ Spee-nohzah	בָּרוּךְ שְׁפִּינוֹזָה
Moses Hayim Luzzatto	Mohsheh Ḥa-yeem Loo-tsahtoh (Rahmḥahl)	משֶׁה חַיִּים לוּצַטוֹ (רַמְחַ"ל)

THE JEWS IN EASTERN EUROPE

EARLY BEGINNINGS

A sprinkling of Jewish settlers had already come to Eastern Europe in Roman days, when Jewish traders had traveled along the great rivers and had brought their wares to many distant lands. Others had followed from Persia and Arabia across the Black Sea. In fact, the Khazars, a Turkish people who lived along the shores of the Black Sea in the South of Russia, accepted Judaism around 800 C.E. and observed the Jewish religion until they were overrun by the Russians in the middle of the 10th century. Karaites had come from far-off Babylonia and traveled on to Lithuania on the shores of the Baltic, and to the Crimea where their descendants still live.

Most of the Eastern European Jews, however, came from Germany. Many of the Jews of Germany who had suffered under persecutions, and many who had lost their homes during the Crusades and the time of the Black Death, had wandered east to Poland. The Polish kings eagerly welcomed able traders to their lands for they were eager to become independent of the nobility. The population of Poland at the time consisted of just two classes—nobles who owned the farmlands and their serfs, the peasants who worked their lands and were little more than slaves. The kings of Poland hoped to attract people who would build cities and bring trade and crafts to their realm. They therefore, made their new Jewish subjects directly subordinate to the crown rather than to the nobles.

Drawn by the opportunities offered by the Po-

Khazar meeeting in a tent *(kibetka).*

lish kings, Christians as well as Jews from Germany wandered eastward. As cities grew, Jewish communities sprang up in them. In time, large and prospering Jewish communities flourished in Warsaw, Vilna, Lublin, Posen, and Cracow. One of Poland's rulers issued a charter promising the Jews of Poland, Bohemia and Lithuania freedom to travel, to trade and most important, freedom to observe their religion.

This charter was renewed by King Casimir the Great. Casimir, who reigned from 1333 to 1370, built many cities in his land. The people said of him that he found a Poland made of wood and left one built of stone. They would refer to him as Casimir, king of the serfs and the Jews, for he was a very tolerant ruler who was genuinely concerned about the welfare of the serfs and his Jewish subjects.

With the arrival of the skilled immigrants from the west, Poland experienced an era of rapid prog-

Exterior of a fifteenth century Russian synagogue.

ress and development. The German craftsmen who had come to live in its new cities organized into guilds, as they had done in their former home. The merchants also formed organizations of their own.

The non-Jewish emigrants from the west had brought to their new homes not only their skills

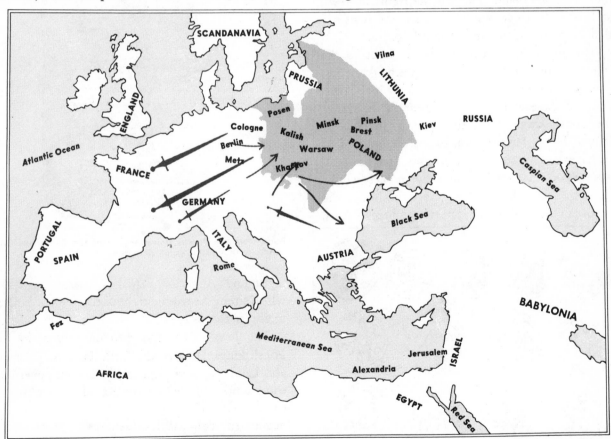

Persecutions and expulsions from German states 1350 to 1648. The many expulsions sent Jews eastward to Poland, where they were welcomed, and where they helped build up industry and trade.

Polish bishop throwing confiscated Hebrew books into the flames. From Jacob Emden's *Sefer Shimmush*, 1762.

but also their traditional prejudices. Thus, they were eager to restrict their Jewish neighbors whom they regarded as their rivals, just as they had done in their former homeland. They often found allies in the representatives of the church. But many of the kings of Poland defended the rights of Jews, and for some three hundred years many Jews settled in Poland to find peace and freedom.

The Jews truly proved to be an asset to the country. They proceeded to set up a banking system and printed the first paper money in Poland. Some of these early banknotes bear the names of the Polish kings of the time printed in Hebrew letters. Many Jews in Poland were employed as managers of estates, tax collectors and financial advisors to the nobility, and the nobles valued their services. The Jews were active also in the export of Poland's many natural resources—corn,

Polish coins with Hebrew inscriptions.

salt and timber—in exchange for goods needed from abroad.

HOW WERE THE JEWISH COMMUNITIES IN POLAND GOVERNED?

The Jews in Poland formed a social class of their own. They did not belong to any one of the four "estates" of medieval Poland. They were neither nobles nor peasants, nor were they city-dwelling burghers like the Christian merchants and artisans. And of course, they did not belong to the clergy. In recognition of their status, King

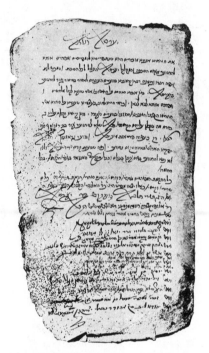

Page from the *Pinkas* (minutebook) of the Council of Four Lands, with signatures of delegates.

Sigismund Augustus issued a charter in 1551 which strengthened the right of the Jews of Poland to govern themselves.

The Jews in the four provinces ruled by the Polish kings, Greater and Little Poland, Volhynia and Lemberg, were organized into self-governing communities headed by the Kahal (assembly), a council elected by the community. The Kahal negotiated with the representatives of the king, and collected taxes. The Kahal was also in charge of the Jewish courts of law, the schools and syn-

Stately house, in Lvov, of Simha Menahem, Jewish physician to John III Sobiesky (1624-1696), king of Poland.

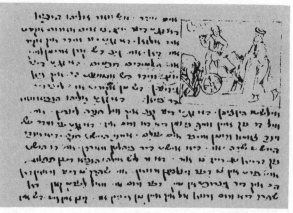

Page from a sixteenth century collection of Yiddish tales.

agogues, the Jewish trade guilds and community charities. The Kahal was not ruled by one individual such as an Exilarch, but was an elected body of representatives of the community meeting in council called *Va'ad Arba Aratzot* or "Council of the Four Lands" (Lithuania was originally a member of the Va'ad, but later established its own Va'ad). The Va'ad of the Kahal would frequently appoint

The meeting place of the Council of Four Lands in Lublin in the sixteenth and seventeenth centuries.

a *Shtadlan* or advocate, a single spokesman for the Jewish community before princes and Christian town councils. The *Shtadlan* sought to prevent persecution and the promulgation of new restrictive laws and in general defended the interests of the community. Some of the *Shtadlanim* were learned rabbis, others spoke many languages and possessed diplomatic talents. Some, too, were financiers or wealthy bankers, who had connections with princes and rich burghers.

Although the Jews in Poland were restricted to certain areas in the choice of a home, they managed to build up an active and independent communal life. They had their own bankers and merchants, farmers and laborers and their own craft guilds of butchers, bakers, printers and locksmiths.

The Jewish merchants of Poland organized great open-air markets, and fairs—much like the country fairs of today. These fairs were visited not only by local farmers and traders but also by merchants and traders from far-off places. In fact, everyone in the district would come to these fairs. The people looked forward to them, for the fairs gave them an opportunity not only to do business but also to exchange news and ideas.

THE YIDDISH LANGUAGE

Gradually, the Jews of Poland even evolved a language of their own. To the medieval German they had spoken in Germany, mixed with some Hebrew words, there were added Polish words and expressions. This developed into what we know today as Yiddish.

267

Woodcut of an assembly in the synagogue to hear a maggid, a traveling preacher.

JEWISH EDUCATION

The Jewish communities organized their own system of elementary and advanced schools. Young boys from four to thirteen years of age went to the "Heder" or elementary school. Older students went to the *Yeshiva,* an advanced institution of Talmudic studies. Indeed, many communities had more then one Yeshiva, each headed by a learned rabbi. Great care was taken to provide boys with a thorough Jewish education. Many studied on for years and some devoted their whole lives to the

The interior of the Rema Synagogue. Rema is the abbreviated name of Rabbi Moses Isserles.

Law. Others who had neither the time nor the money for such advanced learning became workers or craftsmen.

THE CODE OF RABBI MOSES ISSERLES (1520-1572)

As we have already learned, Rabbi Joseph Caro's *Shulhan Arukh* had gained universal acceptance among the Sephardic Jews. However, it lacked information on the customs and ways of observance evolved by the Ashkenazim. Rabbi

Young Yeshiva students.

Bogdan Chmielnicki.

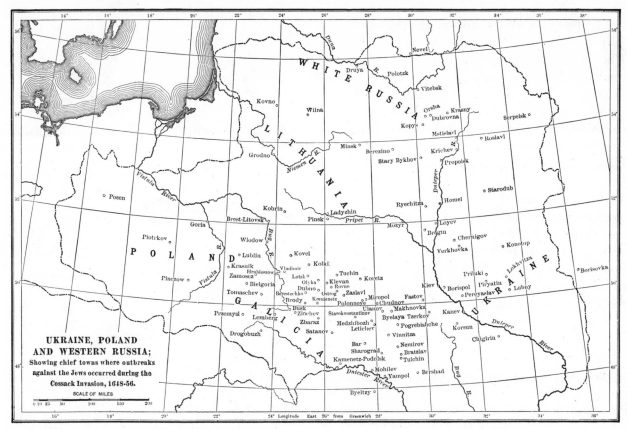

Map of the area where the Cossack invaders under Chmelnitzki destroyed many Jewish communities, in the years 1648 to 1656.

Moses Isserles, a saintly scholar who lived in Cracow, set about to remedy this lack. He compiled all the decisions handed down by Ashkenazic rabbis and scholars into a supplement to the *Shulhan Arukh,* "The Prepared Table," which he entitled *Mappah* or "tablecloth." With these additions the *Shulhan Arukh* became universally accepted.

REVOLT AND WAR

The 17th century was a time of unrest all over Europe. The Reformation had brought dissent into the various Christian groups. The revived interest in learning, coupled with the spirit of the Reformation, had given rise to new thoughts and new demands. The burghers of the cities wanted more freedom. The serfs—the poor, dependent peasants—developed a sense of self-respect and struggled to break loose from the bondage in which they were held by the nobility.

The Ukrainian peasants hated their Polish landlords. The peasants were Russians and belonged to the Russian Orthodox Church, which had originated in the church of the old Byzantine Empire, but the Polish lords were Roman Catholics. As in all Europe, various religious and national groups fought each other for power, both spiritual and secular. The unfortunate Jews were caught in the middle of this struggle. The peasants of Poland rebelled against their lords, the Polish nobles. But most of the contact the serfs had with their masters was through tax-collectors and estate managers, many of whom were Jews. Thus, to the mind of the simple peasant, the Jew was identified with the hated landlord. When the peasants of the Ukraine revolted, they launched an attack against the Jews, some of whom managed the estates on which they worked.

The Ukrainian peasants had organized into groups of fighters, fierce peasant-soldiers known as Cossacks. The Cossacks had defended their lands along the Dnieper and on the frontiers against the Tartars and the Turks. Their commander, Bogdan Chmielnicki, led his Cossacks against the hated Polish landlords and against the Jews of the Ukraine and Poland. When the Cossacks came, the terrified Poles forsook the Jews and left them to their own fate. In spite of the bravery shown by the Jewish communities in trying to defend themselves and to protect one another, many thousands of Jews were killed within a few months. In some instances, Poles and Jews would unite in defense of their towns. However it was to no avail, for the Cossacks swept through the land like a wild hurricane, spreading death and destruction wherever they struck. The Jewish communities of Poland were brutally destroyed by the Cossacks. More Jews perished in the Cossack raids than in the persecutions which had taken place during and after the Black Death epidemic.

The king of Poland, desiring to make a peace treaty with Chmielnicki, named him prince of the

A fight between a mounted and a foot soldier in the Thirty Years War.

Ukraine. One of the conditions stipulated by Chmielnicki was that the Jews of the Ukraine should be expelled from his country. But peace did not come to the torn country even then, for the Cossacks were still not satisfied. They received aid from hordes of Russians who rode through the land, leaving death and ruin in their wake.

Soldiers from Protestant Sweden marched into Catholic Poland. The Swedes were in the midst of fighting a bloody war, which became known as the Thirty Years' War. This conflict involved all the German lands as well as Bohemia. The Protestant states of Northern Europe and their princes were trying to shake off the power of the church of Rome and the Holy Roman Empire.

By the time the Cossacks and the Poles finally signed peace terms in 1654, seven hundred Jewish communities had been destroyed and more than one hundred thousand Jews killed. The Council of the Four Lands had disintegrated. The surviving Jews were left impoverished and scattered. In order to forget their troubles, many of them turned to the study of the Kabbalah, for according to the calculations of some of the Kabbalists, the time was nearly ripe for the Messiah to appear and put an end to war and hatred.

Seventeenth century engraving of a Cossack.

Sabbatai Zevi

SABBATAI ZEVI: THE MAN WHO CLAIMED TO BE THE MESSIAH (1626-1676)

The Kabbalists had calculated that the year of the Chmielnicki uprising would see the coming of the Messiah. The longing for a Messiah during those difficult days was constantly affecting the everyday life of Jews. Mystics and scholars, merchants, craftsmen and physicians, the entire Jewish community, began to prepare for the moment when the Messiah would sound the call for their return to Palestine.

In the Turkish town of Smyrna lived Sabbatai Zevi, the son of Spanish refugees. Sabbatai was a handsome young man of commanding appearance. As a young boy he had studied the Kabbalah and became deeply involved in its intricacies and calculations. He fasted and afflicted himself and bathed in the ice-cold sea, believing that such a stern regime would put him into a state where he would be able to delve into the mysteries of the Kabbalah.

In 1648, the year that supposedly was to bring the Messiah, Sabbatai, who was then only twenty-two years old, stood up in the synagogues of Smyrna and pronounced the Ineffable Name of God which was permissible only to the High Priest on the Day of Atonement. By this revolutionary act Sabbatai had clearly declared himself to be the Messiah. The Congregation was awed and stunned. Shocked by what Sabbatai had done, his former teacher excommunicated him and he was forced to leave Smyrna. However, he had gained some loyal disciples and accompanied by these followers, Sabbatai set out for Jerusalem. After winning the support of the Jewish community of the Holy City, the group journeyed on to Cairo. There they heard of a beautiful Jewish maiden from Poland named Sarah who had lost her parents in the Cossack uprisings and who claimed that, according to a vision she had beheld, she was destined to be the bride of the Messiah. Sabbatai sent for Sarah and made her his wife.

To many Jews, Sarah's visions seemed a clear indication that Sabbatai was indeed the Messiah. Even rabbis and scholars came under the spell of Sabbatai Zevi. New prayer books with prayers for Sabbatai, the Messiah, were printed in Amsterdam. Many Jews wound up their affairs and prepared themselves so that they might be able to leave for Palestine on Sabbatai's command. Jewish communities everywhere were in a state of high excitement. Even the Christian world was watching

Jews of Salonika, Turkey, doing penance during the Sabbatai Zevi agitation.

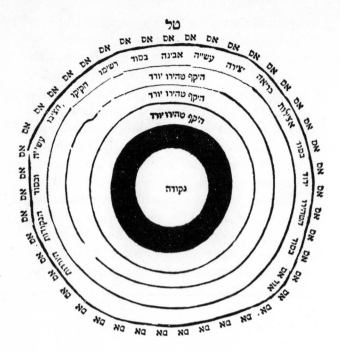

טל

A drawing of the Kabbalistic spheres.

Sabbatai.

Sabbatai went to Constantinople and it was whispered that the Sultan himself was about to receive him. The Sultan, however, ordered Sabbatai put into prison, for he believed him to be a dangerous man. But so many sumptuous gifts poured into Sabbatai's prison cell that it became almost like a palace. Since the Sultan had no desire to make a martyr of this man who called himself the Messiah, Sabbatai was allowed to receive visitors. These visitors brought him still more gifts and addressed him reverently as "The Messiah." Unfortunately Sabbatai Zevi, like all his previous counterparts, turned out to be a fraud. The Sultan chose a most effective way of dealing with him. He gave Sabbatai the choice between death and conversion. To everyone's amazement the would-be Messiah, who had sparked a fire of hope in Jewish hearts throughout the world, accepted conversion and became a Moslem!

Jewish communities everywhere were dumbfounded. Many found it impossible to believe that Sabbatai Zevi had really been nothing but an impostor. Others chose to believe that he had been killed and that another man had become a Moslem in his stead.

For years, small groups in many countries continued to believe in Sabbatai Zevi. But eventually all had to face the fact that Sabbatai had not been the true Messiah.

After this, the teachings of the Kabbalah lost much of their appeal for most Jews. The scholars and rabbis, who had always disapproved of the study of Kabbalah, concentrated on the teachings of the Talmud and urged the people to do likewise.

There were still some extremists, however, who clung to the Messianic hopes which Sabbatai Zevi had aroused. They gathered around a leader who proclaimed that he was possessed by the spirit of the dead Sabbatai. One of these groups was led by Jacob Frank (1726-1791) who, a hundred years after the appearance of Sabbatai Zevi, declared himself to be the latter's successor. To the scholars of the time the Frankists seemed merely another example of the detrimental effects of the study of the Kabbalah in the superstitious atmosphere then prevailing. A council of rabbis excommunicated this extreme group and declared that henceforth only masters of Talmudic wisdom or mature students over the age of thirty or forty might engage in the study of the Zohar.

Jacob Frank, a false Messiah.

Catherine the Great.

BELIEFS AND SUPERSTITIONS

During the days of Sabbatai Zevi, when the Kabbalah was still widely studied, many mystical beliefs and superstitions arose and found their way into Jewish folklore in Poland and elsewhere. One of these strange legends was that of the *dybbuk,* the strange wandering souls that would possess unsuspecting people, just as the spirit of Sabbatai Zevi had once supposedly dwelt within those who had proclaimed themselves his successors.

RUSSIA—THE PALE OF SETTLEMENT

The last half of the 18th century was another stormy era for Poland. Three times the land was invaded and partitioned. By 1796 Poland had lost her independence. Thus hundreds of thousands of Polish Jews became subjects of the mighty Czars of Russia.

At the time of the partition of Poland, the Russian lands were ruled by a Czarina, Catherine the Great. Although the Czarina regarded herself as a progressive and liberal empress, her subjects lived under extremely primitive conditions. Russia had a wealthy nobility and a merchant class composed of immigrants from Germany. The rest of the people were mostly serfs.

Catherine and her successors permitted Jews to live in Russia but only in that province which had once been part of Poland. The district allotted to the Jews came to be known as the "Pale of Settlement." Here, in little towns and villages, in a few crowded cities and in lonely inns along the highway, most of Europe's Jews were to live for two hundred years. Many harsh restrictions were placed upon the Jews of the Pale; they were forced to pay high taxes and could not move or travel without permission. They were not permitted to attend Russian schools or academies of higher learning and were barred from many other public institutions. But within the community of the Pale, life was active and full. While among the Russians all but a few nobles were illiterate, even the humblest Jewish family sent its sons to the *heder* to learn to read and write and engage in the study of the Torah. It seemed as if the very restrictions that had been forced upon them served to knit the Jews of the Pale more closely together, for they evolved a way of life based on brotherhood, neighborliness and genuine affection for one another.

Map of western Russia showing the Jewish Pale of Settlement.

PERCENTAGE OF JEWS
IN GOVERNMENTS

From 4% to 5%   From 8% to 10%   From 10% to 12%

From 12% to 14%   From 14% to 16%   From 17% up

Poltava	4.02%	Podolia	12.15%
Taurida	4.57%	Kherson	12.32%
Yekaterinoslav	4.77%	Wilna	12.90%
Chernigov	4.99%	Volhynia	13.31%
Kalisz	8.59%	Kovno	13.71%
Plock	9.13%	Radom	13.89%
Suwalki	10.09%	Lomza	15.69%
Kielce	10.82%	Minsk	15.77%
Bessarabia	11.65%	Piotrkow	15.83%
Vitebsk	11.80%	Syedlitz	15.84%
Moghilef	11.92%	Grodno	17.28%
Kiev	12.03%	Warsaw	18.12%

GLOSSARY OF HEBREW TERMINOLOGY AND NAMES

Kahal	Kahahl	קָהָל
Va'ad Arba Aratzot	Vah-ahd Arbah Ahratzoht	וַעַד אַרְבַּע אֲרָצוֹת
Yiddish	Yidish	יִדִּישׁ
Yeshiva	Ysheevah	יְשִׁיבָה
Mappah	Mahpah	מַפָּה
Sabbatai Zvi	Shahbtai Tsvee	שַׁבְּתַי צְבִי
Day of Atonement	Yohm Keepoor	יוֹם כִּפּוּר
Dybbuk	Deebook	דִּבּוּק
Pale of Settlement	Ṭhoom Hah-mohshahv	תְּחוּם הַמּוֹשָׁב
Heder	Ḥeyder (in Yiddish) Ḥeder (in Hebrew)	חֶדֶר
Hasidism	Ḥahseedoot	חֲסִידוּת

THE RISE OF HASIDISM

THE DECLINE OF JEWISH LIFE IN POLAND

After the Cossack wars and the general disillusion that set in as a result of the exposure of the messianic pretenders, Jewish life in Poland went into a decline. Many thriving communities had disappeared; others had been greatly reduced in size. Most of the Jews of Poland were impoverished, and only the larger communities were able to maintain Yeshivot. Many of the smaller communities were hard-pressed to maintain even their simple "heder," the elementary religious school for Jewish children. The number of scholars and good teachers had diminished greatly.

Yet this period was to produce two great religious leaders, each very different from the other and each concerned with a different way of life. One was Israel Ben Eliezer, called the Baal Shem Tov; the other was Elijah Ben Solomon, called the Gaon of Vilna.

ISRAEL BEN ELIEZER, THE BAAL SHEM TOV (1700-1760)

Israel Ben Eliezer was born in a small town in the Ukraine about 1700. When still a small child he lost both his parents and was cared for by the community. After graduating from the heder he became the assistant to the teacher. Israel liked children, and they, in turn, loved to listen to his stories. Although he was not known as a Talmudic scholar, Israel was a bright young man with an unusually sweet disposition. He took great delight in roaming the woods around the little town and often would take his small pupils with him. There, amidst the wonders of nature, the teacher and his pupils would chant the psalms and the melodies of the prayers.

Israel married a young woman called Anna and the two went to a small village in the Carpathian mountains, where Israel earned his living as a lime digger. He enjoyed his work, for while it brought

A typical *heder* of the city of Vilna.

him very little money, it still left him time to study and to meditate on God and life.

For seven years Israel and his wife lived in solitude in the mountains. All around him Israel could behold the beauty God had created. The humble lime digger was convinced that the holiness, or *Shekhinah,* of God dwelt within every living thing. Each man, he believed, could see and experience the *Shekhinah* within himself and all around him. Every man, scholar and simple laborer alike, he asserted, can reach spiritual heights by prayer and contemplation and the constant endeavor to ennoble his life by devotion to God and His commandments, the practice of kindness and love for all creatures. The "worship of the heart" through joy and ecstasy, he taught, is of greater importance than dry, routine, ritual observance. He reemphasized in a novel way the ethical values of the Prophets, thereby infusing religious zest and vigor into the hearts of the physically downtrodden and spiritual-

ly impoverished masses.

Israel learned to make healing salves and ointments out of plants and herbs, for he wanted to help the sick and the suffering. He also kept an inn which his wife managed for him while he devoted

The synagogue of the Baal Shem.

277

"Kedushat Levi," a book containing teachings by and about the Baal Shem Tov, printed in 1919.

The synagogue of Baal Shem, interior view.

himself to teaching and healing. After seven years in the mountains they returned to town, where Israel became a beloved and respected teacher. Faithful and inspired students flocked to him.

The teachings of Israel appealed not only to students but also, and particularly, to the humble classes of the Jewish community. Israel ben Eliezer wrote no books; his wisdom was spread by word of mouth among the rabbis and among the tradesmen, artisans and laborers who were his followers. His followers told one another many wonderful stories about the good deeds of Israel, who had become known as the *Baal Shem Tov,* the Master of the Good (holy) Name, for it was said that he could heal people by merely pronouncing the Holy Name of God. The Baal Shem Tov was a kind and humble man. He taught his wisdom in a simple and forthright way, often merely by setting an example of kindness and good cheer, for he believed that man was put upon this earth to discover its beauty and wonders and to "serve the Lord with rejoicing."

The followers of the Baal Shem Tov, who called themselves the *Hasidim* or "pious ones," would dance with joy in their synagogues when they welcomed the Sabbath. Even in the midst of fervent prayers they would dance and sing *niggunim,* wordless melodies in praise of God.

The Hasidim continued to follow the laws of the Talmud, the *Shulhan Arukh* and the *Mappah,* but they were not great Talmudic scholars and they were not engrossed in the legal debates of the rabbis of their day. In a way, they were the spiritual heirs of the students of the Kabbalah, for they placed devotion, prayer, and joyous emotion above dry study and discussion. The scholarly rabbis of Poland became concerned, for it seemed that Hasidism posed a threat to the old tradition of learning, and possibly even to the foundation of Jewish law.

The leaders of the Hasidim came to be known as *Tzaddikim* ("righteous ones"), and their disciples followed them with great fervor. As time passed, some of the Tzaddikim indeed became men of great power and influence.

A view of the town of Miedziboz, where the Baal Shem lived.

278

A Hasidic Rabbi giving his blessings to a young follower, about 1815.

ELIJAH BEN SOLOMON, THE GAON OF VILNA (1720-1797)

The rabbis who fought the influence of the Hasidim were called the *Mitnagdim* (or *Misnagdim*), "the opponents." Their leader was Elijah ben Solomon, the greatest among the many scholars of Vilna, a city known as the "Jerusalem of Lithuania" because of the great schools that flourished there. In time Elijah ben Solomon became known far and wide as the Gaon of Vilna. No one since the days of the great academies at Sura and Pumpeditha had been accorded this honored title. Elijah never accepted an official position as rabbi. He spent many hours in his quiet study at scholarly work and teaching a small circle of disciples—advanced scholars who wanted to acquire his approach to Talmudic study. The Gaon had observed how often scholars of the past had accepted the decisions and commentaries of earlier teachers without really understanding them or agreeing with them in their hearts. His method, therefore, was one of exacting detail. He would first study each passage thoroughly, and then refer to its original sources in the Mishnah and in the Bible itself. This thorough method made for a much clearer understanding of the Law than study by rote.

Like the great scholars of earlier days, the Gaon of Vilna studied not only the works of Jewish philosophy but also mathematics and astronomy. Some of his students encouraged the study of the sciences as bearing upon the proper understanding of Torah. This was unusual, for in those days most of the *Yeshivah* scholars confined themselves strictly to teaching the Babylonian Talmud and the commentaries of Rashi and the Tosafists. This narrowness was due to the fear that any other studies would lead man astray, just as the unauthorized study of the Kabbalah had done.

The Vilna Gaon never held public office but gave his advice freely and helped the community cope with the difficult issues it faced. Unofficially, however, he was recognized as the spiritual head of Lithuanian Jewry. Many people came to the kindly Rabbi Elijah with their personal problems. He wisely arranged that people in need of financial assistance who were ashamed to approach the officers of the Kahal could come to him directly to ask for help.

In the days of the Vilna Gaon the conflict between the Hasidim and the Mitnagdim had become very bitter. The Tzaddikim had become very

The great scholar Elijah, Gaon of Vilna.

A view of the city of Vilna.

powerful, for their followers had come to consider them as intermediaries between themselves and God. The Mitnagdim, on the other hand, believed that each man was directly responsible to God and needed no intermediary. The Gaon of Vilna took up the fight against Hasidism, going so far as to excommunicate the leaders of the Hasidim and forbidding his followers to intermarry with them.

In time, however, this ban was lifted. Though Hasidism had spread in the Ukraine and later in Hungary, Poland and Galicia until it was more popular than Rabbinic Judaism, it had gone no further and remained loyal to all the tenets of traditional Judaism, and with even greater emphasis. Eventually the two ways of Judaism made peace with one another. It became evident that the Hasidim faithfully followed the laws and commandments of the Talmud and of the *Shulhan Arukh*, and were not by any means strangers to the study of the Law. Hasidim and Mitnagdim still persisted in continuing in their different ways, as they do to the present day, but they came to respect one another and to appreciate the contribution made by the other to Judaism.

Hasidism, with its mystical teachings, was to be a small but influential trend in Judaism. The songs and dances of the Hasidim, and their way of serving God with rejoicing, have had a profound influence not only on the simple masses but also on scholars and thinkers.

עליות אליהו

תולדות האדם הגדול בענקים

אלופנו גאון הגאונים, וחסיד כאחד מהראשונים, נכנס לפני ולפנים ופתח גנזי מטמונים, וחכמות ומדעים שונים, סביב לרגלו חונים ראש גולת אריאל, כשם **אליהו גאון וחסיד** מווילנא, נודע בישראל

ונאספו רועי העדרים, גדולי הדור הנודעים בשערים, והעריכו לזה מאמרים ולראשונה יבואו דברים נפלאים, חכמה ודעת קדושים טלאים, נקראים כשם

עלית השער   מעלות הסולם   עלית קיר תכלית יסוד החבור   דרך הגאון והילוכו בקורש   ע"ד חיבוריו וכתביו

A page of one of many learned works about the Vilna Gaon.

GLOSSARY OF HEBREW TERMINOLOGY
AND NAMES

Messiah	Mahshee-aḥ	מָשִׁיחַ
Small Jewish school	Ḥeyder Ḥeder, Ḥeyder	חֶדֶר
Israel ben Eliezer	Yisrah-eyl ben Elee-ezer	יִשְׂרָאֵל בֶּן אֱלִיעֶזֶר
Master of the Good Name	Bah-ahl Shem Tohv	בַּעַל שֵׁם טוֹב (בעש״ט)
Elijah ben Solomon	Eyleeyahoo ben Shloh-moh	אֵלִיָּהוּ בֶּן שְׁלֹמֹה
Gaon of Vilna	Hahgah-ohn Meevilnah or Hagrah	הַגָּאוֹן מִוִּילְנָה (הגר״א)
Shekhinah (God's Presence)	Sheḥeenah	שְׁכִינָה
Niggunim (Hasidic melodies)	Neegooneem	נִגּוּנִים
Code of Jewish Law	Shoolḥan Arooḥ	שֻׁלְחָן עָרוּךְ
Commentary on Code of Law	Mahpah	מַפָּה
Kabbalah	Kahbahlah	קַבָּלָה
Tzaddikim (Hasidic leaders)	Tsahdeekeem	צַדִּיקִים
Mitnagdim (Opponents of Hasidism)	Mitnahgdeem	מִתְנַגְּדִים
Yeshiva	Ysheevah	יְשִׁיבָה

NEW HORIZONS

FIRST STIRRINGS OF DEMOCRACY

During the 18th century the ideas first advanced in the days of the Renaissance took on new life. Scholars and thinkers everywhere had become deeply concerned with the rights and needs of mankind. First in the British colonies of North America, and then across the sea in France, men proclaimed thoughts that seemed nothing less than revolutionary. "Were not all men created by God?" they pondered, "and if so were not all men, kings, nobles and serfs alike, entitled to freedom and equal rights?"

This was an entirely new concept, frightening to some because of its implications. But as the world grew wider and the economic needs of men changed, the new ideas steadily gained ground.

Europe was slowly outgrowing the old forms of absolute monarchy in which the noble classes had the right to subject their inferiors. A new class of citizens had arisen—burghers who lived in the cities. Many of the burghers were dignified tradesmen or powerful merchants, who helped build connections with other countries and with the faraway colonies of the New World. Also among the burghers were doctors, teachers and men of science.

Painting by M. Oppenheim of a Sabbath evening in a Jewish home.

Universities began to rise in the European cities, attended by sons of nobles and wealthy burghers.

Writers and poets put forth new and stimulating ideas.

But despite the interest in the Bible which had developed during the Reformation, and the awareness of the Christians that the Bible was part of their religious heritage, the Jews of Europe whose ancestors gave the Bible to the world were among the lowest and most despised class of people in Europe.

Occasionally an individual Jew would rise to high honor. At many of the large and small courts of Europe, a Jewish banker—often referred to as a "court Jew," would manage the financial and business affairs of a prince. Many a court Jew enjoyed respect and prestige but his position was precarious, for in many instances the kindness of the prince would turn to wrath.

Frequently a court Jew would speak to his prince in behalf of his community. Sometimes Jewish traders who had helped a free city in times of war would be invited to settle in the city with their families and friends. In this way some Jewish communities had increased in size. But there also

An old Hanukah menorah from Frankfurt.

were small communities, surrounded by the high walls of the ghetto from which a Jew could go forth only when he had to do business. No social relations existed between the world outside and the ghetto Jews.

Developments outside the ghetto had become foreign to the Jews of the 17th and 18th centuries; except insofar as they affected their lives directly in the form of persecution or wars.

So isolated was the life of the Jews in Germany that the language they spoke was not the German of their day but Judeo-German, medieval German closely interwoven with Hebrew words, the same dialect which in Eastern Europe had evolved into Yiddish.

The writers and poets of Germany had little occasion to meet Jews. But as they became increasingly interested in the theories of man's equality and natural rights, they turned their attention to

Joseph Suss Oppenheimer (1698-1738), financial advisor to the Duke of Wurtenberg. When the Duke died "Jew Suss" was arrested and sentenced to death.

283

The old synagogue in Berlin.

MOSES MENDELSSOHN (1729-1786) AND HIS ERA

Moses Mendelssohn was a small hunchbacked man, who spoke with a slight stammer. But in this warped physical shell there dwelt a vigorous spirit and a brilliant mind. The son of a Torah scribe, Moses Mendelssohn had been born in the German town of Dessau and had studied with the rabbi there. When Moses was a boy of fourteen his beloved teacher moved to Berlin. The boy followed his teacher and on paying the tax required of Jews, he succeeded in gaining entrance into the city.

Mendelssohn found a new world in Berlin. Even though most of the Jews there lived much as their brethren in other German communities, there were quite a few enterprising Jewish merchants and financiers in Berlin who enjoyed special privileges and who were in contact with the world outside the ghetto. Young Mendelssohn continued his Jewish studies with his old master, but broadened his education by taking up a variety of other sub-

the minority that suffered so much discrimination in their country.

THE PLAYWRIGHT WHO BEFRIENDED THE JEWS: GOTTHOLD EPHRAIM LESSING (1729-1781)

In Berlin, the capital of the German kingdom of Prussia, lived Gotthold Ephraim Lessing, a Christian writer who never really had been in contact with Jews, having seen the ghetto only from the outside. But Lessing was bent upon making his contemporaries understand that the Jews were human like other men and that they were the bearers of the heritage of the Biblical Prophets.

Lessing had written many successful plays including a highly controversial one entitled "The Jews." The hero of the play is a Jew who saves the life of a baron and then refuses to accept a reward. One day a friend of Lessing's, who knew of his intense preoccupation with the lot of the Jews, brought him into contact with a most interesting Jew—the talented Moses Mendelssohn.

Moses Mendelssohn, cultural leader in Berlin in the eighteenth century, who wished to educate his fellow Jews so that they might be accepted as German citizens.

jects as well. He found willing teachers; a merchant's son taught him English and French, and a mathematician instructed him in mathematics. Mendelssohn studied the writings of the philosophers, Latin, and particularly German, which he longed to speak beautifully and well.

Mendelssohn found employment as tutor to the children of a wealthy silk manufacturer. In time he became the bookkeeper in his employer's firm, and later his business manager. In his spare time, however, he soon began to write critical essays on philosophy and current ideas. These essays were written in a beautiful style, in pure, flowing German.

At that time many of Germany's nobles, still influenced by the court of Louis XIV of France, spoke French in preference to their own language. But German writers and intellectuals like Lessing and his friends wrote and spoke in clear, flawless German, and were anxious to influence other educated Germans to follow their example.

Moses Mendelssohn was the first German Jew of his day whose writings and intellectual interests transcended the ghetto walls. The educated people of Berlin became very much interested in this unusual man. Thus it came about that he was introduced to the celebrated Lessing over a game of chess. The two men took a great liking to each other and became close friends. Lessing discussed his ideas of tolerance and freedom of thought with Mendelssohn. Lessing had also read and admired the works of Spinoza.

Influenced by Mendelssohn and by his admiration for Spinoza, Lessing wrote another play about Jews. The hero of this play, Nathan, was a kind, intelligent and tolerant Jew who believed in the rights of all men. The play, entitled "Nathan the Wise," was a great success. Wherever it was presented, audiences began to see Jews in a different light. Lessing had succeeded in showing them that the Jew was not a strange and alien creature lacking the assumed morality of the Christian world, but that he was human and strove to be kind, just and compassionate.

All through the German lands Jews still were enclosed in ghettos. In the great and ancient communities of Frankfurt, Mayence, Worms and Hamburg as well as in the new community of Berlin, Jews lived under severely confining restrictions. Usually only the eldest son of a Jewish family was permitted to marry, and then only after a special tax had been paid. Jews had to pay taxes for such acts as entering a walled city. Often families would be separated by these cruel restrictions, as in cases when daughters and sons had to go to distant communities in order to be able to marry and have families of their own.

It was difficult for the Jews to make a living, for most Jews were only permitted to engage in small trades such as money lending and dealing in secondhand goods. They were not allowed to own land or real estate outside their crowded ghettos.

In many German towns and cities where there were not enough Jews to warrant a ghetto, Jews would live in special streets set aside for them. These streets, like the ghettos, had gates that were closed at night.

Moses Mendelssohn became a privileged or "protected" Jew, like some of the influential Jewish merchants and financiers and a few Jewish physicians who were permitted more freedom than the rest of the community. Mendelssohn met many of the writers and scholars of his day. It is said that he even met Frederick the Great, the king of Prussia, who was very much interested in philosophy and the arts.

Memorial book of the Frankfurt ghetto, 1626 to 1900, bearing the names of departed members of the community.

The synagogue in the Frankfurt ghetto.

world around them.

At that time few children in Germany went to school. Most of the country's common people were still illiterate. But the Jews all knew how to read and write—at least in Hebrew. Under Mendelssohns' influence, new schools were founded in Berlin where Jewish children were given their Jewish education and secular training under one roof. He insisted, too, that the children receive thorough trade and vocational training to prepare themselves adequately for life as free citizens among their non-Jewish neighbors.

Mendelssohn undertook to translate the Five Books of Moses into German. The translation was printed in Hebrew characters—so that every Jew might be able to read it. To this work he added a Hebrew commentary which he prepared in collaboration with a Biblical scholar.

Mendelssohn's main concern, however, was the Jewish community. He devoted his efforts to the task of helping his brethren break down the ghetto walls from within by bringing to them the learning and culture of the world outside. Like his friend Lessing, he believed that a new era of universal freedom was about to dawn. Mendelssohn knew that in order to participate fully in life outside the ghetto the German Jews would first have to learn to speak the German language. Mendelssohn had no intention of sacrificing Jewish education for this purpose. As a matter of fact, he participated in the publishing of a Hebrew magazine which carried articles, poems and commentaries in the Hebrew language. But he insisted that in addition to traditional Jewish studies, Jews must learn German and become acquainted with the

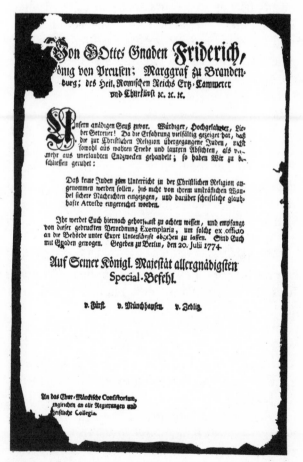

Edict of Frederick the Great, ruler of Prussia in the time of Moses Mendelssohn. The decree concerns the conversion of Jews to Christianity, demanding proof of true belief rather than self-seeking motives.

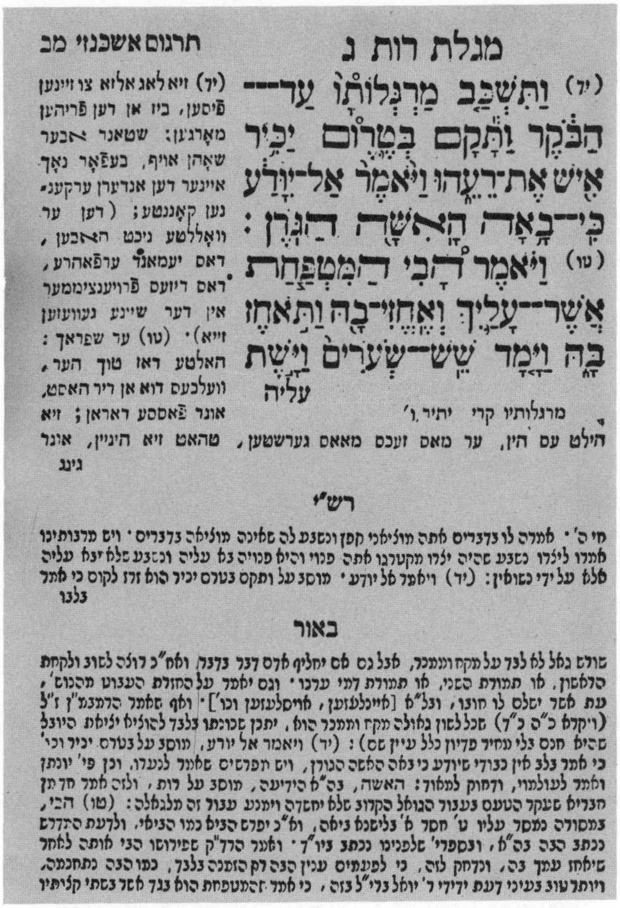

מגלת רות ג

תרגום אשכנזי מב

(יד) ותשכב מרגלותו עד־הבקר ותקם בטרום יכיר איש את־רעהו ויאמר אל־יודע כי־באה האשה הגרן: (טו) ויאמר הבי המטפחת אשר־עליך ואחזי־בה ותאחז בה וימד שש־שערים וישת עליה

מרגלותיו קרי יתיר ו׳

(יד) זיא לאג אלזא צו זיינען פֿיסען, ביז אן דען פֿריהען מארגען; שטאנד אבער שאהן אויף, בעפֿאר נאך איינער דען אנדערן ערקענ־נען קאננטע; (דען ער וואללטע ניכט האבען, דאס יעמאנד ערפֿאהרע, דאס דיזעס פֿרויענצימער אין דער שייגע געוועזען זייא)· (טו) ער שפראך: האלטע דאז טוך הער, וועלכעס דוא אן דיר האסט, אונד פֿאססע דאראן; זיא טהאט זיא היניין, אונד הילט עס הין, ער מאס זעכס מאאס גערשטען, גינג

רש"י

באור

A page from the Book of Ruth, with Moses Mendelssohn's translation in the upper left column. Written in German, printed in Hebrew letters.

The new translation caused a great stir. It had been prepared with the permission of the rabbis of Germany and at first it was accepted and read in many circles. Most Jews knew and had read the Bible in the original Hebrew for it was read regularly in every synagogue. Thus Mendelssohn's German Bible became a primer for many who wanted to learn German and in this manner introduced to the Jews a whole new world beyond the ghetto walls. Indeed, the translation was used by students in Polish-speaking villages in far-off Russia who wanted to acquire a mastery of pure German as the first step on their way to "enlightenment." The rabbis soon considered Mendelssohn's German Bible and his commentary a dangerous innovation and they felt that the old, traditional way of teaching was safer and more desirable. However, this did not deter those who were eager to learn German from continuing to rely on Mendelssohn's Bible. The disciples of Mendelssohn continued to publish translations of the other books of the Bible, the Prophets and the Writings.

No explicit laws were passed in the German states during Mendelssohn's lifetime to better the lot of the Jews. But new ideas had paved a path for new hopes and attitudes. Both within and beyond the ghetto walls, Christians and Jews met on common ground. Many Jews now spoke German, and a number of German intellectuals developed and spread new concepts of tolerance, equality and freedom.

THE EDICT OF TOLERANCE (1782)

Among Mendelssohn's many Christian friends who were favorably disposed toward the new concepts of liberty and tolerance was Christian Wilhelm Dohm, a Prussian lawyer. When Mendelssohn was asked by the Jews of Alsace to write a petition for them requesting the authorities to remove some of the heavy restrictions placed upon them, it was to Dohm that Mendelssohn turned, asking him to draft the text of the memorandum. Dohm not only complied with his friend's request, but also wrote a plea for freedom and equality for all the Jews of Western Europe.

It was Dohm's plea that brought Joseph II, the emperor of Austria, to proclaim the famous Edict of Tolerance. While this law did not lift all restrictions from the Jews of Austria, it eased their burden considerably and opened doors hitherto closed to them. They no longer had to pay the special poll taxes; they were allowed to engage in trade and

Tzedakah box, for money to help fellow Jews. The words read "For the sake of Zion I will not be silent."

manufacturing and to become apprenticed to Christian mastercraftsmen. However, when the emperor died in 1790, most of the old restrictions were revived.

OTHER PROCLAMATIONS OF FREEDOM

Meanwhile, in the New World across the ocean, the American colonies had revolted against England. Their Declaration of Independence and the draft of their new Constitution undoubtedly stimulated much discussion among thinking people throughout Europe. The ideas which Moses Mendelssohn and his friends had helped formulate in Berlin had been incorporated into the law of a new land.

FREEDOM AND ASSIMILATION

Moses Mendelssohn not only fought for enlightenment and religious freedom but also wanted to assure the survival of Judaism and its traditions. He was by no means an assimilationist. He did not feel that it would be good for the Jewish people to merge into the other nations of the world. All he hoped for was that his brethren would be able to

Medal struck in commemoration of the erection of the Frankfurt synagogue in 1852.

make a contribution to civilization outside the ghetto and to live in peace and harmony side by side with their Gentile neighbors.

That some of his own children and grandchildren—including the composer Felix Mendelssohn-Bartholdy—left the Jewish faith by way of the baptismal font was anything but in accordance with his wishes. Conversion to Christianity due to the wish to assimilate was to become a problem with which generations after Moses Mendelssohn had to grapple and which to some degree is still with us today.

Der Jude. Front page of a German-Jewish weekly.

GLOSSARY OF HEBREW TERMINOLOGY
AND NAMES

Yiddish	Yidish	יִדִּישׁ
Enlighten-ment	Hahskahlah	הַשְׂכָּלָה

REVOLUTION, REACTION AND REFORM

THE FRENCH REVOLUTION

For a hundred years France had set the style for all of Europe. The elegant dress and manners of the court of Louis XIV were imitated in many countries. Princes built their palaces in the style of the beautiful French palace at Versailles. In Germany, Poland and Austria, and even in Russia, French was the language of the nobility, the educated and the wealthy. The works of French architects and artists, French philosophers, poets and dramatists, were admired and widely imitated throughout Europe.

When French philosophers, writers and poets first began to speak out for religious and political freedom, the rulers of France were greatly disturbed, for in order to continue their policies they needed obedient subjects who would willingly supply the immense sums of money necessary to support the elegant French court.

The people of France, however, were weary of

A lavish theatre presentation at the palace of Louis XIV in Versailles.

the increasingly high taxes they were forced to pay in order to keep the nobles in luxury and indulge their every fancy. They felt the desire for liberty and for relief from the burdens imposed upon them by their ruling class.

French soldiers from Marseilles marching to Paris in 1792.

On July 14, 1789, the people of Paris stormed the Bastille, a fortress in which many people who had been unable to pay the high taxes, and many others who had shown signs of rebellion, were imprisoned.

This was the start of the French Revolution, an upheaval in which the people came to power, and the King and Queen and many of the nobility were tried and put to death.

In 1789, the year the Revolution began, the French Assembly proclaimed a "Declaration of the Rights of Man." This document, which is similar to the American Declaration of Independence, declared that all men were born free and entitled to equal rights.

In 1790, the naturalized Jews of Bordeaux were granted equality, and a decree passed in 1791 gave the Jews the rights and privileges of full citizenship.

But then the new republic became involved in war. First, it had to defend itself against the monarchs of Europe, who were afraid that the spirit of revolt would spread to their lands. But only a short time later, the French armies themselves became armies of conquest. They were led by one of the Consuls of the Republic—a young general named Napoleon Bonaparte.

THE REIGN OF NAPOLEON

Napoleon was a brilliant strategist. A highly ambitious man, he had dreams of great conquest. He hoped to carry the ideals and the new freedom of the young republic of France to every country in Europe. Wherever his conquering armies took over, serfs and Jews were freed. The ghetto walls of Germany, Austria and Italy fell.

Many Europeans regarded Napoleon as a great liberator. His Code of Laws, which became known as the Napoleonic Code, lent legal force to his concepts of freedom and civil liberties.

However, Napoleon was not satisfied to be a mere general and Consul of the Republic. His ambition was to become the undisputed ruler of the French state, the crowned conqueror of Europe. In 1804 he had himself crowned Emperor of France. Many freedom-loving people in Europe were bitterly disappointed at this turn of events for they regarded it as a threat to their own newly-won freedom. Napoleon deposed the kings he had defeated, replacing them with rulers of his own choosing. He made his brother, Joseph, king of Spain, and his brother, Jerome, king of Westphalia in the conquered lands of Germany.

NAPOLEON CONVENES A SANHEDRIN (1806)

Napoleon had advanced ideas and great ambitions, but he often showed a lack of the understanding necessary to solve the problems of his

Decree of the French National Assembly, granting equal rights to Jews, September 27, 1791.

The meeting of Napoleon's Sanhedrin.

Illustration in French pamphlet urges Jews to give up the practice of moneylending and engage in farming and manufacturing.

subjects. Eager to gain the loyalty of the Jews, as well as to exercise a measure of control over his Jewish subjects, he called together an assembly of prominent French Jews (the Assembly of Notables) and questioned them closely concerning the nature of Jewish law and the attitudes of French Jews toward France. Soon after, Napoleon called a new assembly which was patterned on the ancient Sanhedrin of Palestine. Seventy-one representatives, forty-six rabbis and twenty-five laymen, were chosen to settle legal and religious questions and to demonstrate their loyalty to Napoleon's France. Napoleon and his officers knew next to nothing about the customs and ways of the Jews. He therefore addressed to the Sanhedrin twelve questions about their religion and their attitude toward non-Jews and France.

The Sanhedrin was soon dissolved but it served to emphasize to the non-Jewish world some of the fundamentals of Judaism as, for instance, that Jews regarded their Gentile neighbors as their brothers; that Jews were loyal to the country in which they lived; and that there was nothing in Jewish law forbidding them to enter into all kinds of trades and professions, crafts and agriculture. This short-lived Sanhedrin had no lasting effect on Jewry. To some it was a source of pride and hope but in general it was rightly looked upon as a spectacular display of the emperor's grandiose aspirations.

REACTION

Eventually the allied countries of Europe defeated Napoleon. In many of those countries the Jews had fought side by side with their Gentile fellow-citizens for the independence of their fatherlands. With Napoleon defeated and banished to Elba, a small island off the coast of Italy, they lost

Title page of the prayers recited at the meeting of Napoleon's Sanhedrin.

many of their freedoms. In many German and Austrian cities and towns the Jews had to return to the ghettos, and many of the peasants were forced to revert to serfdom.

Having had a taste of freedom, the Jews found it difficult to readjust to the old restrictions. Some Jews in Germany and Austria had attained high positions; had attended universities and had embarked upon brilliant careers; many were now respected bankers and merchants. They realized that they would gain definite advantages from conversion to Christianity and a number of wealthy and educated Jews in Austria and Germany became Christians. Some underwent baptism merely in order to be able to keep their positions, planning to bide their time until freedom of religion would again be established. Others, motivated by intense frustration, turned to Christianity permanently as a new way of life.

In their hearts many of these new Christians still regarded themselves as Jews and found it difficult to accept the thought that intolerance and bigotry should have taken root again among the people in whose midst they lived.

HEINRICH HEINE (1797-1856)

Among the German Jews who had undergone baptism was the poet Heinrich Heine. His conversion notwithstanding, Heine was deeply intereseted in Jewish history, particularly in the Spanish Golden Age and the fate of the Marranos. One of Heine's most beautiful poems is dedicated to Judah Halevi, the poet-philosopher of Spain (1075-1140).

Comparing his own era with the end of the Middle Ages that had seen the Golden Age of Spanish Jewry, Heine must have deplored his own lack of courage and steadfastness. His writings reflected his love and understanding for the Jewish people and their faith. One of Heine's well-known poems, "Princess Sabbath" describes the life of the Jew and his devotion to the Sabbath. In the poem, Heine likens the Jew during the workaday week to an enchanted prince who was transformed into a dog. When the prince greets the Princess Sabbath on Friday evening, he is magically transfigured into his own self, but when the Princess Sabbath de-

Heinrich Heine.

parts, the spell returns.

CHANGES WITHIN

However, not many Jews abandoned their faith. Most of the Jews of Germany and Austria continued to follow the ways of their fathers. But, like all men living in the 19th century, the Jews, too, had to adjust to the radical changes which occurred in their time. The face of Europe had been changed by the fight for freedom. The invention of various machines had brought about an "industrial revolution" which gradually was to change the economy of the entire world. Tillers of the soil left the countryside by the thousands to become workers in the growing urban industrial centers.

Patriotism and nationalism reached new heights. The Jews, too, were proud of their newly-won citizenship of the countries in which they lived. And this brought them face to face with a new problem. How would they be able to remain faithful to the traditions of Judaism and still be loyal and active citizens of the countries that had accorded them a measure of freedom and equality.

Impelled by a desire to eliminate all differences between themselves and the people in whose midst they lived, many Jews were anxious to make

293

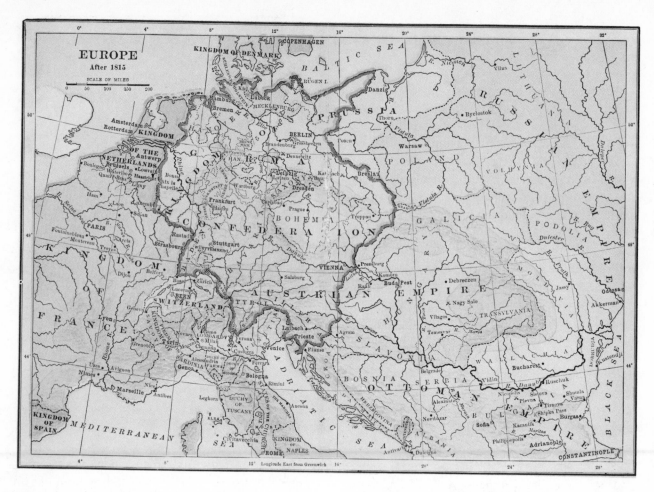

changes in Judaism itself, and the Jews of 19th century Western Europe hotly debated the issue of the desirability of such changes. Leaders arose to champion both positions: eagerness for change on the one hand, and resistance to change on the other.

REFORM JUDAISM

Those calling for radical changes in the observance of Judaism founded the Reform movement. They felt that if Judaism was to have a meaningful function in the modern world, many of the old ceremonies which they claimed had grown out of the many years of ghetto life had to be eliminated from the synagogue ritual. The leaders of Reform in Germany, headed by Rabbi Abraham Geiger (1810-1874), proposed a different form of service. They introduced many German prayers, and shortened those Hebrew prayers which seemed too long or which seemed to have lost their meaning. The

prayers which referred to the return to Zion and the coming of the Messiah were omitted. Believing that a "reformed" Judaism would attract more Jews and would adjust Jewish life to the demands of the times, they set aside the authority of the Talmud and the *Shulhan Arukh*. The Reform movement took root in some of the larger German cities. The first Reform temple was dedicated in Hamburg in 1818.

ORTHODOXY

Those who steadfastly resisted all changes in Jewish law and ritual, maintaining that any break in the chain of tradition would endanger the very foundations of Judaism, became known as the "Orthodox." Orthodoxy, which still held the loyalties of most German Jews, had a number of brilliant spokesmen. Most prominent among them was Rabbi Samson Raphael Hirsch (1808-1888) who defended his position in brilliant essays and com-

Abraham Geiger.

of the evolving tradition of Judaism. The Historical School was a forerunner of what is known today as the Conservative movement in Judaism.

THE "SCIENCE OF JUDAISM"

A group of young German Jewish university graduates believed that the best way of ensuring the survival of Judaism was to make the history and values of Judaism better known to Jews and Gentiles alike. To this end, they sought to apply scientific methods to the study of the Jewish heritage. This group, headed by Leopold Zunz (1794-1886), called itself "The Society for the Scientific Study of Jewish Culture" or "The Science of Judaism."

HEINRICH GRAETZ (1817-1891), HISTORIAN

Among the adherents of Zunz' school was Heinrich Graetz, a man of great talent and imagination. Graetz, a professor at the rabbinical seminary of Breslau, devoted seventeen years of his life to the task of writing a well-documented history of the Jews. The first work of its kind, it is still widely read to this day.

mentaries written in a classic, eloquent German style. Hirsch was convinced that a Jew could be a good citizen, steeped in the culture and learning of his country, and still remain loyal to all the laws that had come down through the ages in the Bible and Talmud.

THE HISTORICAL SCHOOL

Still another group took a midway position between Reform and Orthodoxy. Led by Zechariah Frankel (1801-1875), the president of the rabbinical seminary in Breslau, this movement, which took the name of "the Historical School" of Judaism, emphasized the importance of the historical continuity of the Jewish heritage. While pointing out that Judaism had undergone changes throughout its history and believing change to be inevitable, the adherents of the Historical School insisted that such changes as were made had to be within the framework of Jewish tradition. Radical reform, they felt, was not in keeping with the spirit

Samson Raphael Hirsch.

Rabbi Zechariah Frankel.

THE STRUGGLE FOR DEMOCRACY
IN CENTRAL EUROPE

In the second half of the 19th century, Europe was shaken by uprisings and revolts. When the revolt of 1848 in Germany was crushed, many of the disappointed freedom fighters left their homeland. Some of them crossed the Atlantic to settle in the United States of America, and the wave of immigration which landed on the shores of America during that period included thousands of German Jews as well.

The cause of civil liberties in Germany was greatly advanced by the unification in 1871 of all the German lands and provinces into one nation, under the leadership of Prussia. All Germans were recognized as free citizens with equal rights and liberties, including the freedom to worship as they chose. At last the Jews of Germany were free men. True, in seeking to enter new professions or applying for certain positions, they often encountered the old prejudices, but at least they no longer had to contend with restrictions enforced by law.

Heinrich Graetz.

GLOSSARY OF HEBREW TERMINOLOGY AND NAMES

Sanhedrin	Sahnhedreen	סַנְהֶדְרִין
Marranos	Ahnooseem	אֲנוּסִים
Princess Sabbath	Shahbaht Ha-Mahlkah	שַׁבָּת הַמַּלְכָּה

ENGLAND—THE ROTHSCHILDS AND MOSES MONTEFIORE

THE JEWS RESETTLE IN ENGLAND

Across the Channel from France, England had been developing into a modern power. This land of seafarers and merchants had attracted many Jewish immigrants since the days when Rabbi Manasseh Ben Israel had first come from Holland to plead for the readmission of Jews to England. The first Jews to settle in England in the 17th century were Marranos. These were followed by Sephardic Jews from Italy and Ashkenazim from Germany and Poland. By the 19th century a sizable Jewish community existed in England.

TWO FAMOUS BROTHERS-IN-LAW

Among the leading members of Britain's Jewish community was the banker Nathan Mayer Rothschild (1776-1836). His father, Meyer Amschel Rothschild (1743-1812), had built up a banking business in the German city of Frankfurt, and established contacts with banks in all the capitals of Europe. Of Meyer Amschel's five sons, the oldest remained in the family business in Frankfurt, while the other four established branches in four different European cities—Paris, Vienna, Naples and London. Nathan Rothschild settled in London and was an agent of the British government during the Napoleonic wars.

The Rothschild family's original house in the ghetto of Frankfurt-am-Main.

Mayer Amschel Rothschild.

Another prominent British Jew serving in the war against Napoleon was Nathan Mayer Rothschild's brother-in-law, Moses Montefiore, whose family had come to England from Italy. After his discharge from the British army, Montefiore returned to his business. At the time of the battle of Waterloo, he was a successful stockbroker. Through some of their agents on the continent, Rothschild and Montefiore heard of Napoleon's defeat at Waterloo before this good news reached England. The two men jubilantly rushed to the Prime Minister, informing him of this decisive victory.

Both Rothschild and Montefiore were farsighted financiers. When the British stock exchange threatened to collapse during the wartime crisis they helped stabilize the market with their wealth and financial talents.

CHAMPIONS OF FREEDOM AND CIVIL LIBERTIES

Both men were ardent champions of freedom. When England considered passing a law abolishing slavery, they assisted the British government with a large loan to make the enforcement of the new law possible.

In 1835, David Salomons was elected Sheriff of London and two years later the same post was occupied by Montefiore. At that time Jews in England still could not receive an academic degree and were barred from most public offices because—with the exception of the office of Sheriff of London—they entailed an oath of office requiring an affirmation of the "true faith of a Christian."

Neither Montefiore nor Rothschild and the other Jewish leaders were satisfied with these conditions. They wanted no special place for themselves in British society but only hoped to obtain a better position for all British Jews. Montefiore and Rothschild fought for the elimination of the old public oath and for the right of British Jews to hold public office.

THE FIRST JEW ENTERS PARLIAMENT

Eventually a special oath was devised so that Jews could be sworn into public office and accept professional positions. The son of Nathan Rothschild, Baron Lionel de Rothschild, was elected to Parliament four times in a period of ten years, resigning each time because the required oath of office was still Christian in form. Finally in 1858 the rules were changed so that Rothschild could take the oath of office on a Hebrew Bible on the faith of a Jew. He was the first Jew to become a member

Sir Moses Montefiore.

Coat of arms adopted by the Rothschild family in 1817.

MOSES MONTEFIORE

The year when Montefiore became Sheriff of London he was knighted by young Queen Victoria, who had just ascended the British throne. Although Sir Moses was prominent in British public life, he devoted much time and effort to the Board of Deputies of British Jews, of which he was president. In that capacity he represented the Jewish community in its pleas for the removal of the restrictions under which the Jews of England still suffered. One by one, during his long lifetime, the humiliating restrictions were abolished.

THE DAMASCUS LIBEL—1840

Interior of the sukkah of the Montefiores.

of Britain's House of Commons.

When Prime Minister Benjamin Disraeli was negotiating for control of the Suez Canal, it was Lionel de Rothschild who provided him with the necessary funds to make the purchase possible.

Benjamin Disraeli (1804-1881) was himself a symbol of the new position of the Jew in England, for although he had been baptized a Christian at an early age, he never denied his Jewish descent, believing that he was a descendant of Spanish Jews who had fled from Spain in 1492. A brilliant statesman and trusted advisor to Queen Victoria, Disraeli still found time to write novels and political essays. Many of his books deal with Jewish subjects. During his periods of office as Prime Minister (1867; 1874-1880) Britain gained control of the Suez Canal, annexed various territories and proclaimed the British Queen, Empress of India.

Baron Lionel de Rothschild, in top hat, takes his seat in the House of Commons, 1858, as shown in a magazine drawing of the time.

In 1840, news came to Sir Moses Montefiore that the Jews of Damascus in Syria had been falsely accused of the murder of a monk. Jews there were being arrested and tortured and Jewish children imprisoned, to compel their parents to confess guilt to a crime they had never committed. Since Syria was under the jurisdiction of Egypt, Montefiore, supported by the British government, went to Egypt to press for the release of the prisoners and for an official acknowledgement of their innocence. In this journey he was accompanied by his wife, Judith, and by a committee which he had organized, including the statesman Isaac Adolphe Crémieux (1796-1880), a French Jew who had fought successfully for the civil rights of the Jews of France.

Drawing by Moritz Oppenheim of the kidnapping of Edgar Mortara.

The incident in Damascus had aroused indignation all over the world. The Egyptian government bowed to public pressure. The prisoners were released and the innocence of the Jews of Damascus was publicly proclaimed.

SIR MOSES AND THE CZAR

In the east of Europe, in the vast, isolated land

Isaac Adolphe Cremieux

of Russia, the Jews still had no rights. While restrictions against Jews were lifted throughout the rest of Europe, the situation of Russian Jewry was deteriorating. The Jews were still forced to live in special districts and under humiliating restraints. For centuries they had lived as craftsmen and innkeepers in the Pale of Settlement near the borders of Germany and Austria. Now the Czar wanted to force them to leave their homes and settle as farmers in the far-off province of Astrakhan and in the region of the Caucasus.

Moses Montefiore hoped to prevent this cruel decree from being put into effect. He and his wife made the long journey to Russia, bearing with them a letter of introduction from Queen Victoria. They made two such visits, one in 1846 and again in 1872, and each time they were received with

Moses Montefiore speaking to Czar Nicholas I in St. Petersburg.

great courtesy at the court of the Czar. Montefiore asked for mercy for the Russian Jews, pointing out to the Czar that they were industrious people who would make good citizens. The Czar listened politely and permitted the Jews to remain in the Pale of Settlement—but nothing was done to alleviate the hardships under which they had to live.

Soon after his return home, Montefiore was given the added title of baronet by Queen Victoria, who desired to honor him for his courageous efforts in behalf of Jews everywhere.

SIR MOSES AND PALESTINE

Realizing that there was little he could do to

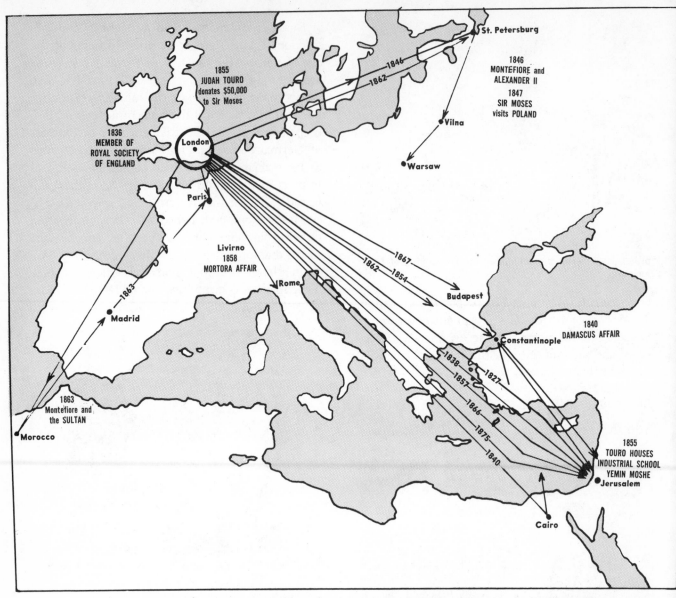

The travels of Moses Montefiore to protect the rights of the Jews. Note the seven trips to the Holy Land.

better the position of his brethren in the lands of the Czar, Montefiore cast about for another solution.

Like Joseph Nasi, the statesman and philanthropist who lived three hundred years before him, Sir Moses dreamed of the return of the Jews to the Land of Israel. He visited Palestine six times, and each time brought assistance and support to the Jews there, helping them to build hospitals, schools and synagogues. To attract immigrants, he planted vineyards and olive groves and opened the first experimental agricultural school in the land. On

The windmill in Yemin Moshe named after Moses Montefiore in modern Jerusalem. Much new building has taken place since the time of this photograph.

the outskirts of the old city of Jerusalem, Montefiore built a group of homes which eventually was to form the nucleus of what is called the New City today and is the present capital of the State of Israel.

Sir Moses Montefiore lived to the prodigious age of one hundred and one. His one hundredth birthday in 1884 was marked by elaborate celebrations and parades, for his name had come to be known far and wide as a symbol of charity, progress and the love of liberty.

GLOSSARY OF HEBREW TERMINOLOGY AND NAMES

Blood Accusation	Ahleelaht Dahm	עֲלִילַת דָּם
Pale of Settlement	Teḥoom Ha-mohshahv	תְּחוּם הַמּוֹשָׁב
Old City (of Jerusalem)	Ha-eer Ha-ahteekah	הָעִיר הָעַתִּיקָה

JEWS SETTLE IN AMERICA

JEWS SETTLE IN AMERICA

The expulsion from Spain in 1492 had begun a long period of wandering for many thousands of Jews. Some found comparative safety and were able to remain in various cities of North Africa, Syria, and the Turkish Empire. Others found further oppression and hardship; and, all too often, another decree of expulsion.

Those exiles who went to Portugal found themselves betrayed by King Manuel. Thousands were forced to convert to Christianity. Pretending to adopt the new religion in order to save their lives, they remained secret Jews (*Marranos*), living under the threat of the Inquisition and in constant danger of discovery.

Marranos who were able to leave Portugal often sought refuge in free countries such as Holland. Even after generations had passed, some still longed to return to open practice of their religion. Small numbers of these devoted secret Jews managed during the sixteenth and seventeenth centuries to travel to various colonies in the New World, including Brazil, the West Indies and Mexico.

Recife in the 1600's

THE COLONY OF RECIFE

When the Dutch conquered the Portuguese colony of Recife in Brazil in 1630, the community of Marranos living there joyfully resumed the faith of their fathers. They were able to join in public worship and in observance of the Sabbath, and openly to teach their children Torah.

To serve as their religious leader and teacher they invited Rabbi Isaac de Fonseca Aboab of Amsterdam. Born to Marrano parents in Portugal,

Rabbi Isaac de Fonseco Aboab

Aboab had escaped with his family to Holland and had there studied for the rabbinate. In 1642 he came to Recife, becoming the first rabbi in the Western Hemisphere.

The freedom of the new Jewish community did not last long. In 1654 the Portuguese reconquered Recife, and reintroduced the court of the Inquisition. The Jews, who now were considered heretics, or traitors to the Christian faith, were forced once more to flee for their lives. Isaac Aboab and some others returned to Amsterdam. Other refugees were able to sail to the Caribbean colonies of Surinam and Curacao.

FIRST JEWS IN NORTH AMERICA

Twenty-three of the exiles traveled first to the West Indies, and then in a small boat, the *Saint Charles,* up the North American coast to the Dutch colony of New Amsterdam. Robbed on the way by pirates, the penniless group arrived in September of 1654 at the port that was later to be named New York.

Peter Stuyvesant, the director appointed by the Dutch West India Company, let the arrivals know they were not welcome. He "required them in a friendly way to depart," allowing them tempor-

arily to remain while he awaited instructions from Amsterdam. After some months, a letter came from the Dutch West India Company, saying that because the Jews had fought for Holland and because there were Jews among the Company's shareholders, the newcomers were to be permitted to remain, "provided the poor among them shall not become a burden to the company or to the community, but be supported by their own nation."

The instructions by the Company that the Jews be allowed to travel and trade like other settlers did not find favor in the eyes of Stuyvesant and his Council. Jacob Barsimson and Asser Levy had to request permission to stand guard as citizens of the colony, instead of paying a special tax; Abraham de Lucena, Salvador Dandrada and other Jews signed petitions asking for the right to buy homes, to trade, and finally to enjoy full "burgher rights."

Three years after they had first landed, the Jews of New Amsterdam were granted citizenship. This did not mean that they enjoyed every civil right. They were not permitted to build a synagogue,

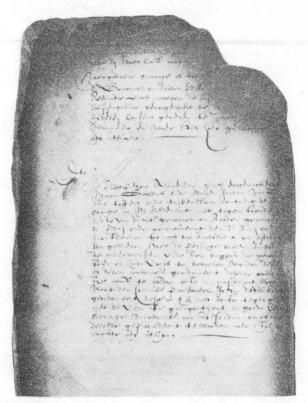

First entry in the Dutch records of New York City relating to the Jews, Sept. 7, 1654.

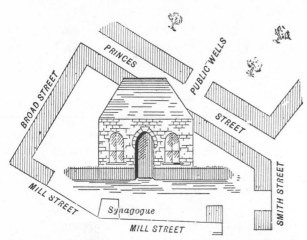

Sketch and site of the Old Mill Street Synagogue, New York.

being required to "exercise in all quietness their religion within their houses." They still had to petition the Dutch Council and later the British governor—for the British conquered the colony and renamed it New York in 1664—when they were

Interior of the Touro Synagogue, Newport, R.I., showing the southwest corner. The colonial architecture blends with the style of Sephardic synagogues in this house of worship which is now a U.S. National Shrine.

faced with restrictions in trade or professions. Through their outspoken demands for justice and freedom, this small group of Jews proved themselves worthy ancestors of the American Jewish community.

JEWS IN THE COLONIES

The earliest Jewish settlers were Sephardim, or, as they called themselves, "of the Portuguese nation." The first synagogue to be founded in

Benjamin Nones, Jeffersonian Democrat, answers an antisemitic attack in the Philadelphia Aurora by a Federalist editor in the Presidential campaign of 1800.

North America, the Shearith Israel congregation of New York, follows to this day the Spanish and Portuguese *minhag,* the Sephardic order of prayer. By 1750, however, half of the three hundred Jewish settlers in New York were Ashkenazim from Central or Eastern Europe.

During the eighteenth century, small numbers of Jews came, like other pioneers, from all countries of Europe, to make their home in the cities of the eastern seaboard, such as Philadelphia, Charleston and Savannah.

Rhode Island, the state founded on a declaration of religious freedom by Roger Williams, was a

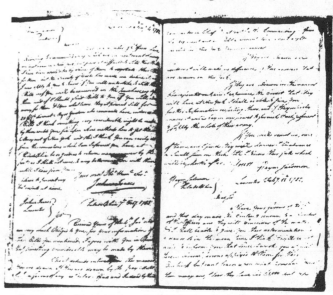

On October 30, 1761 Aaron Lopez and Isaac Eliezer, both of Newport, R.I., were granted the right to be naturalized, to buy land and to transmit inheritance by the General Assembly of Rhode Island. However, they were not granted the right to vote or to hold office since they were Jews.

a Trustee of Columbia College.

Isaac Touro, similarly, accompanied by many members of his congregation, fled from Newport when the British occupied it. Aaron Lopez, rather than collaborate with the British, left his wealth and holdings and settled in a small town in Massachusetts until the patriot forces were victorious.

Service beyond the call of duty was rendered by Haym Salomon (1740-1785), a Jewish broker who came to New York from Poland in 1772. Imprisoned for his support of the revolutionary cause, he managed to escape to Philadelphia. There he worked with Robert Morris, superintendent of finance, extending loans and arranging credit for the conduct of the war. Though in America only a few years, he was an ardent patriot, never hesitating to risk all his own funds to bring about victory for the cause of right.

WORDS OF GEORGE WASHINGTON

When the new nation came into being, and George Washington became the first President, the Jews of Newport were one of the many groups to send a message of good wishes. They expressed their appreciation for "a Government which to bigotry gives no sanction, to persecution no assistance," and their thanks to God for "all the blessings of civil and religious liberty."

In answer, President Washington stated, "The

favorite destination. Aaron Lopez, son of an old Marrano family in Lisbon, became a wealthy trader in Newport, where Isaac Touro was the acting rabbi. The Newport synagogue building, one of the earliest to be erected in America, is now a national shrine.

About three thousand Jews lived in the British colonies at the time of the American Revolution. Many were fighters for the patriot cause. Francis Salvador, a Jewish planter born in England, was chosen a member of the provincial congress in South Carolina in 1774. Two years later, he gave his life in one of the first skirmishes of the Revolution.

Among other Jewish soldiers was Benjamin Nones, who came from France in order to participate in the battle for freedom and human rights which he felt the Revolution represented. He rose to the rank of major, and afterwards served the new country as legislator.

Supporters of the American cause were in danger of imprisonment when British forces temporarily took over the cities of New York and Newport. Gershom Mendez Seixas (1745-1816), minister of Shearith Israel, had been so outspoken a patriot that he had to flee from his city when the British army entered. Having taken the Torah scrolls with him, he was able to reestablish his congregation in Stratford, Connecticut, and then to set up a new congregation, Mikveh Israel, in Philadelphia. In New York after the war, he was honored as a leading religious figure, taking part in George Washington's inauguration and serving as

Haym Salomon's letter book, 1782, showing correspondence.

citizens of the United States of America have a right to applaud themselves for having given to mankind examples of an enlarged and liberal policy. All possess alike liberty of conscience and immunities of citizenship." He continued with a clear statement of the position of the new nation on human liberty.

It is now no more that toleration is spoken of, as if it was by the indulgence of one class of people, that another enjoyed the exercise of their inherent natural rights. For happily the government of the United States, which gives to bigotry no sanction, to persecution no assistance, requires only that they who live under its protection should demean themselves as good citizens, in giving it on all occasions their effectual support.

FREEDOM OF RELIGION

The United States was the first country in the world to guarantee full freedom of religion. The first amendment to the Constitution begins:

A page from a speech delivered December 6, 1809 to the House of Commons of North Carolina by Jacob Henry, arguing against a move to unseat him because he was a Jew.

George Washington's letter to the Jews of Newport.

"Congress shall make no law respecting the establishment of religion, or prohibiting the free exercise thereof." Laws restricting the right of holding office to those of recognized Christian faith still remained in some states. Gradually all these laws were challenged and removed. Jews were able to take their place as active citizens in the new democracy.

IMMIGRATION AND WESTWARD EXPANSION

Encouraged by the promise of liberty and opportunity, great numbers of Europeans migrated to America during the nineteenth century. The Industrial Revolution was changing the ways of life in Europe, and many displaced workmen and farmers sought new homes in the New World. The reaction following the wars of Napoleon in 1815, and the failure of the revolutions of the 1840's in Central Europe, caused those who longed for freedom to turn their eyes to the New World.

Between 1820 and 1870, the population of the United States rose from ten million to forty million. Among the newcomers were hundreds of thousands of Jews. Many of them came from German states, particularly the province of Bavaria; and many others from Bohemia and other Central European areas.

It was the great period of Westward expansion. Jews were among those who explored and pio-

A license issued to Solomon Raphael, a Jewish peddler, by Benjamin Franklin on March 23, 1787.

neered. Many became traveling peddlers and traders, some exchanging goods with Indian trappers, some helping to bring needed supplies to far-flung farms and outpost settlements.

Often, a pioneering Jew would settle down in a Midwestern or Western community, perhaps to set up a printing press and newspaper, or to establish a small general store. In five or ten years, enough of his fellow Jews might arrive to form a religious community and build a synagogue.

Jews made their homes in many cities as new

Aaron Lopez

territories opened. A good number crossed the continent to join the first settlers in California in 1849. Within the first five years after the Gold Rush, there were Jewish congregations in a dozen California towns.

SOME MEN OF PROMINENCE

Ezra Stiles, distinguished president of Yale, had found much to praise in his Jewish fellow citizens.

Judah Touro

Speaking of Aaron Lopez, he had said, "His beneficence to his family, to his nation, and to all the world is without a parallel." Other Jews in early America also displayed the philanthropy and the desire to serve their fellow men that characterize the American Jewish community to this day.

One of the many public spirited Jews was Judah Touro (1775-1854) of New Orleans, son of the acting rabbi of Newport, Rhode Island, who willed his entire fortune to synagogues, schools, hospitals and orphan homes in eighteen cities. A patriotic soldier who had barely escaped death in the Battle

The Touro Infirmary, endowed by Judah Touro, New Orleans.

of New Orleans, he gave the largest contribution, ten thousand dollars, for the building of the Bunker Hill Monument. A large portion of his estate went to build homes for the poor in Jerusalem, under the direction of Sir Moses Montefiore.

A quite different public figure was Mordecai Manuel Noah (1785-1851), well-known as a politician, playwright, and newspaper editor. For a short time he was American consul at Tunis, there learning about the poverty and persecution suffered by Jews of North Africa. In a grand gesture, Noah rallied support and proclaimed the establishment of "Ararat," a settlement on Grand Island in the Niagara River, as a "city of refuge" for the oppressed Jews of the world. He felt that, until the

Mordecai Manuel Noah

ancient homeland in Palestine was restored, this free nation would be the proper host for the persecuted of Israel.

A top-ranking officer in the United States Navy, Uriah Philips Levy (1792-1862), showed courage both in his naval career and in his fight against discrimination and abuses in the service. He asked

A portrait of Uriah Phillips Levy

that these words be inscribed on his tombstone: "He was the father of the law for abolition of the barbarous practice of corporal punishment in the United States Navy."

WOMEN OF VALOR

Jewish women in this country were active in the fields of education and good deeds. Lovely Rebecca Gratz (1781-1869), of a distinguished Philadelphia family, founded the first Jewish Sunday School in America, and worked for orphanages and other welfare institutions. It is thought that she was the inspiration for the virtuous heroine who bears her name in Scott's *Ivanhoe*.

Penina Moise (1797-1880), an educator and writer, supervised the Jewish Sunday School of Charleston and composed poems and hymns throughout her life, even though she became blind in middle age.

The outstanding Jewish writer of this period was Emma Lazarus (1849-1887), whose early poetry on themes of nature and mythology won praise from Ralph Waldo Emerson. Czarist persecutions of the Jews of Russia, and the increasing immigration of refugees from Eastern Europe, made the young woman more aware of her people and faith. She studied Hebrew and Jewish history, gaining new pride and loyalty and a powerful theme for her later writings.

Songs of a Semite and *By the Waters of Babylon* are collections of poems expressing sympathy for her people's past, and hope for their rebuilding. "Let but an Ezra rise anew," she wrote, "to lift the banner of the Jew!" Her best-known poem is *The New Colossus,* inscribed on a plaque in the base of the Statue of Liberty in New York harbor.

THE CIVIL WAR

The Civil War found Jews remaining loyal to the sections of the country in which they lived.

Emma Lazarus

Jews were officers and fighting men on both sides. The Confederate Secretary of War in 1864 estimated that there were ten to twelve thousand Jews in the Confederate armies. Seven Jewish soldiers in the Union ranks were awarded the Congressional Medal of Honor. Judah P. Benjamin (1811-1884), Senator from Louisiana, was Secretary of State for the Confederacy.

In the years of controversy before the war, many Jews were active in the anti-slavery movement. Three Kansas Jews joined John Brown's special army leading the fight against slavery. Newspaper editors like Moritz Pinner in Kansas wrote editorials in favor of abolition.

Two outspoken rabbis, Sabato Morais (1832-1897) of Philadelphia, and David Einhorn (1809-1879) of Baltimore, met strong opposition when they preached against slavery. Rabbi Einhorn, in fact, had to flee from his community at the time of the secessionist riots of 1861.

EARLY RELIGIOUS ORGANIZATION

In every city where the Jews settled, they established synagogues as soon as possible. The first

Rebecca Gratz, a painting by Scully.

Army News.

The following co-religionists were either killed or wounded at the battle of Fredericksburg:

T. J. Heffernam, A, 163 N. Y., hip and arm.
Serg. F. Herrfukneckt, 7 " head.
M. Ellis, 23 N. J., hand.
Moses Steinburg, 142 Penn., legs bruised.
A. Newman, A, 72 " ankle.
Lt. H. T. Davis, 81 " arm.
J. Killenback, 4 N. J., head.
S. S. Vanuess, 15 " leg.
W. Truax, 23 " back.
J. Hirsh, 4 " "
Jacob Schmidt, 19 Penn., left arm.
Jos. Osback, 19 " wounded.
W. Jabob, 19 " left arm.
Lieut. Simpson, 19 " left leg.
Capt. Schuh, 19 " wounded.
C. M. Phillips, 16 Maine, cheek.
Lieut. S. Simpson, 99 Penn., leg.
R. Harris, 107 " thigh.

A partial list of Jewish Union Soldiers killed in the Battle of Fredericksburg, December 13, 1862. In this battle the Union Army was defeated and suffered over 10,000 casualties in killed and wounded.

congregations in the cities of the eastern seaboard all followed the Sephardic *minhag,* preserving the customs, the pronunciation, and the prayer melodies which had been handed down by Spanish and Portuguese ancestors. The Sephardic ritual was retained even after Jews of Central and Eastern Europe outnumbered the Sephardim in these congregations.

There were no skilled teachers or ordained rabbis for the early congregations, and no system of higher Jewish education in the new land for the training of native-born leaders. Men who had received some Jewish religious education in their youth in the lands of their birth were called upon to head congregations and to perform ritual services. Some of these acting rabbis, such as Isaac Touro and Gershom Mendez Seixas, gave strong spiritual leadership to their people and gained much respect from the general community. In many of the scattered communities of the nineteenth century, there was a lack of deep Jewish knowledge and very little religious education.

ISAAC LEESER

Isaac Leeser (1806-1868), most zealous of the acting rabbis of his day, set about almost single-handed to try to remedy all the lacks in Jewish life and education in America. He published textbooks, and translations of the Bible and the prayerbook. In his Philadelphia congregation, Mikveh Israel, he delivered vigorous sermons in English, advocating intensified education and Jewish unity. With the help of Sabato Morais he was able to establish Maimonides College for formal Jewish studies in 1867, but the number of supporters was few, and it soon closed its doors.

Leeser's greatest contribution was the editorship of *The Occident,* which appeared monthly from 1843 to 1869. Its pages tell of the interests and problems of the Jews in America in those years, including items ranging from the arrival of a new Hebrew teacher in New York to protests against

A letter from President Abraham Lincoln dated May 13, 1862 acknowledging the prayers of the Congregation Mikveh Israel in Philadelphia for the victory of the Union cause.

313

Brigadier General Frederick Knefler (1833-1901), highest ranking Jewish officer in the Union Army.

the kidnapping of an Italian Jewish boy, Edgar Mortara, by the Catholic church in 1858. At such times of crisis as the Mortara case, magazines such as *The Occident,* David Einhorn's *Sinai,* and Isaac Mayer Wise's *Israelite* served to inform and in some measure to unite the Jews of America.

EARLY ATTEMPTS AT REFORM

The free atmosphere and the lack of central authority in pioneer America encouraged changes and reforms in religion. In 1824, a group called the Reformed Society of Israelites broke away from Congregation Beth Elohim in Charleston. Led by Isaac Harby (1788-1828), a young writer, the Society issued its own prayerbook, and for several years conducted services, largely in English.

The Reform movement became stronger in the United States with the arrival in the 1840's of many Central European Jews, including a number of rabbis who agreed with the teachings of Abraham Geiger in Germany. They wished, while upholding the ethics and "moral law" of Judaism, to

adapt to modern times by abolishing rituals and ideals which they felt no longer had meaning.

Rabbi David Einhorn came to Baltimore and Rabbi Samuel Hirsch to Philadelphia with radical Reform ideas. They wished no longer to consider ritual laws binding. They felt that the age-old hopes for the coming of the Messiah and the return to Zion had no meaning for the American Jew. They dropped much of the use of Hebrew in the prayers, substituting German readings and hymns.

Other Reform rabbis who had more moderate views, wishing to continue more of the traditions of Judaism, were Bernhard Felsenthal of Chicago and Max Lilienthal of Cincinnati.

ISAAC MAYER WISE, FATHER OF REFORM

The leading organizer of Reform Judaism was Isaac Mayer Wise (1819-1900), who introduced such changes as English readings and sermons, instrumental music, Confirmation for both boys and girls, and the one day observance of holidays instead of two in his congregations in Albany and Cincinnati. For years he edited the weekly *Israelite,* advocating in its pages that American Jewry unite.

Sabato Morais (1823-1897) one of the founders of the Conservative movement.

Isaac Leeser (1806-1868)

He hoped for a minhag America, one form of Jewish observance and worship, in which both traditional and Reform Jews could join.

Calling together congregational leaders from twenty-eight cities, Rabbi Wise was able in 1873 to found the Union of American Hebrew Congregations. The next year he established and became the head of the Hebrew Union College in Cincinnati, the first abiding institution for higher Jewish education and the training of rabbis in America.

Rabbi Wise was not able to unite American Jewry to follow one pattern of belief and worship. The Radical Reformers of the eastern cities believed he did not go far enough; they did not agree with his devotion to the use of Hebrew in the service and his insistence that the Sabbath be ob-

Title page of one of the early issues of "The Israelite."

served on Saturday instead of being transferred to the commonly accepted American day of rest, Sunday.

On the other hand, Orthodox or traditional Jews could not accept his reforms in the service, his abolition of many rituals, and his denial of basic ideals such as the return to Zion.

American Jewry, though it did not unite under his leadership, learned from Rabbi Wise how to organize and strengthen its religious life.

IN THE YEAR 1880

The Jews of the United States in 1880 numbered 250,000. In many communities, they had established synagogues, Young Men's Hebrew Associations, orphan homes, old-age homes, hospitals, and fraternal lodges, including the nation-wide

This Torah Ark of Cong. Beth Elohim, Charleston, S.C., is a replica of the one destroyed by fire in 1838. The original Ark was built in 1799.

315

Isaac Mayer Wise

B'nai B'rith. They were vocal in their own press and in the general press, speaking out when Jewish rights were abused abroad or threatened at home.

A very early photograph of Hebrew Union College, Cincinnati, Ohio.

In the growing country they had taken their place as workers, professional men, merchants and even as manufacturers in new industries such as the production of ready-to-wear clothing, then developing in the larger cities.

In the setting up of national religious institutions and in the education of their children for Jewish life in the New World, they had just begun. The great majority of Jewish children growing up in America received very little Jewish learning. While many synagogues, such as Rabbi Wise's in Albany, conducted day schools in which

Facsimile of first Hebrew periodical in America.

both general and Jewish subjects were taught, the rise of public schools was making such enterprises less necessary. Jewish education was generally confined to one or two hours a week. Teachers and rabbis with a profound knowledge of the three-thousand year old Jewish tradition could come only from the European centers of learning.

Indeed, immigration of Jews from the most learned communities, those of Eastern Europe, had been increasing each decade. Many of the Jews under Russian rule, promised liberty and receiving instead more and more measures of persecution,

Title page of the first Reform prayer book to appear in America. It was prepared by a commission consisting of Rabbis Kalish, Wise and Rothenheim, and was issued in English, German and Hebrew.

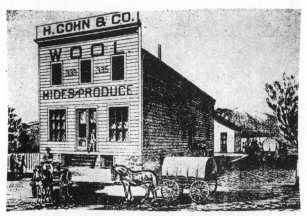

Cohn's Hides and Produce in Salt Lake City, Utah in the 1870's

looked westward to America.

The next fifty years were to see a great influx of Jewish immigration that was to establish the Jewish community of America as we know it today, along lines that had already been drawn.

Julius Meyer (1851-1909) of Omaha, Nebraska, an Indian trader in the 1870's, with some of his Indian friends.

GLOSSARY OF HEBREW TERMINOLOGY AND NAMES

Minhag	Min-hahg	מִנְהָג
Hazzan	Ḥah-zahn	חַזָּן
Rabbi	Rahv	רַב
Ararat	Ah-rah-raht	אֲרָרָט
Nusah	Noo-saḥ	נוּסָח

THE HASKALAH: ENLIGHTENMENT IN EASTERN EUROPE

CZAR NICHOLAS I AND THE JEWS

Not even the intervention of so prominent a personality as Sir Moses Montefiore could bring about an improvement in the situation of the Jews of Russia. Czar Nicholas I, who came to the throne of Russia in 1825, was bent upon unifying his land and assimilating all groups into one vast Russian nation. During the reign of his brother, Alexander I (1777-1825) Napoleon's soldiers had marched east, deep into the very heart of Russia. Russia had defended herself well and the French armies had retreated, severely beaten and

Napoleon meets Alexander in 1807 on a raft in the Nieman River. An alliance was concluded by the two rulers. In the not too distant future this treaty of peace would prove to be of no value to the power hungry Napoleon.

defeated. But the new ideas of freedom and equality that had arisen in France had been carried by her soldiers into the lands of the Czar. Poland, which never had accepted Russia's rule gracefully, now chafed under her reins.

To gain greater control over the minorities in his realm, Nicholas I instituted a double administrative policy. On the one hand he lifted some of the restrictions that had been imposed upon them, but at the same time he wanted to divest them of

Medal commemorating the emancipation of the Jews by Alexander I.

Gustave Dore pictures the plight of the Russian peasants who were treated as slaves.

their identity as separate nationality groups. He dealt a severe blow to the Jewish community of the Pale of Settlement when he ordered the Kahal, the time-honored instrument of Jewish communal self-government, to disband.

The Czar wanted the Jews to give up their Yiddish language, their religion and their traditions. He wanted to convert them by force, if necessary. He also wanted a large and powerful army, and to realize this aim he instituted a draft of boys at the age of eighteen, for a term of twenty-five years. Jewish boys, however, were already drafted at the age of twelve and had to serve for a period of thirty-one years. Recruiters would come and take them from their homes by force. Once they were in the army, pressure would be brought on them to convert. Frequently they would be beaten and

Caricature by Daumier showing Czar Nicholas I extracting money from his Jewish subjects.

starved in an effort to persuade them to renounce their faith. Parents in the Pale of Settlement lived in constant fear for their sons.

As another means of hastening the disappearance of the Jews as a separate minority group, Czar Nicholas I set up special schools in the Pale of Settlement, called Crown schools. In these government schools, Jewish children were to learn Russian, receive an education that would wean them away from their traditional way of life, lead them to assimilation and possible conversion to Christianity.

Despite all the pressure brought upon them, the Jews of Russia remained loyal to Judaism and

Russian peasants.

to one another, helping each other and supporting their many poor as well as possible. The community was hard-pressed. Many had been forced out of the villages of the Pale into the cities and could not find a way to earn a living. When the Czar realized that his policy toward the Jews did not bring about the hoped-for wholesale conversions, he invoked sterner restrictions to make their life more difficult.

ALEXANDER II, A LIBERAL RULER

Nicholas I died in 1855 and was succeeded by his son, Alexander II (1818-1881), a man of liberal leanings. When in 1861, Alexander abolished serfdom, the Jews in the Pale of Settlement took heart and hoped that soon their lot too, would

Yitzhak Ber Levinson.

given also in the Hebrew language and Hebrew grammar. Needless to say, however, that the Jewish masses stood by their rabbis and opposed these schools. The Haskalah made rapid progress nevertheless.

In the western part of Europe "enlightenment" had tempted many Jews away from their heritage —but not so in the East. There "Haskalah," as enlightenment was called in Hebrew, took the direction not of assimiliation but of a more intense cultivation of the Hebrew language and modern Hebrew literature along with knowledge of the western world. Thus began the rebirth of Hebrew as a living language. Hebrew and Yiddish writers both applied their talents to immortalize the folkways and customs of the Jews of the Pale, their ideals and their daily lives. In their works, both prose and poetry, they described the negative as well as the positive aspects of life in the ghetto, thereby stimulating their readers to social and intellectual adjustment.

Among the great exponents of Russian Haskalah were the following Hebrew authors whose works have left an indelible mark in the annals of modern Hebrew literature and culture: Abraham Mapu (1808-1867), pioneer Hebrew novelist famed for "Ahavath Zion" a biblical romance written in a superb biblical Hebrew style; Judah Leib

be improved.

Their hopes were realized in great measure. Alexander abolished the draft of Jewish boys at the age of twelve so that they did not have to join the army at all, until the general draft was applied to them in 1874 and they were inducted into the army when they reached the age of eighteen, like other Russian youths.

The coming of the Machine Age had wrought great changes everywhere and Alexander wanted to keep pace with developments in the west of Europe by furthering the growth of Russia's factories and industrial centers. He therefore permitted Jews to move to Russia's large cities and encouraged them to go into manufacturing, to learn trades, become merchants and to take professional training at the universities.

No longer did all Jews have to live in the Pale of Settlement. Some became respected and successful merchants and manufacturers; others practiced law and medicine in the large cities. Still others became skilled workers in the new industrial centers.

HASKALAH

As early as the days of Nicholas I, the new ideas that had risen in the West had managed to find their way into the Pale of Settlement, and some Jews of Russia became interested in learning about the world around them. Some of the Jewish schools founded with government support, began to teach history, Russian, and the new sciences in addition to religious subjects. Systematic instruction was

Judah Leib Gordon.

Sholem Yaakov Abramovich

Gordon (1830-1892), greatest of 19th century Hebrew poets who fought valiantly against some harsh survivals of manners and customs, while remaining loyal to Jewish tradition as a whole; Yitzhak Ber Levinsohn (1788-1860), erudite author of works demonstrating the complete harmony of Torah and the scientific spirit and advocating the return to handicrafts, agricultural and other practical pursuits.

THE DEVELOPMENT OF YIDDISH LITERATURE

Many authors wrote in Yiddish, the everyday language of the Jewish people of Russia and Poland. One of the best-loved Yiddish writers was Sholem Yaakov Abramovich (1836-1917), or Mendele Mokher Sefarim—"Mendele the Bookseller"—as he was known. He started his career as a Hebrew author, in fact, he is also considered as one of the founders of modern Hebrew prose. It is, however, as a Yiddish writer that he gained special fame. He painted a vivid picture of life in the towns of the Pale and his books were read with great enthusiasm. The writings of Mendele and others of his day revealed Yiddish for the first time as an expressive language, capable of reflecting the thought and character of the Jews of eastern Europe. Among the other great luminaries of Yiddish literature were Sholem Aleichem (Sholem or- Shalom- Rabinowitz), and Isaac Leibusch Peretz who was also creative as a Hebrew writer.

REVOLUTIONARY MOVEMENTS

Most of the Russian Jews were still following much the same way of life as their fathers. They were dedicated to the study of the Torah, and derived strength from their loyalty to Jewish tradition. But some of the pioneers of Haskalah went beyond the movement's original educational and cultural aims and became interested in problems of human welfare in general and the welfare of the Jewish working masses in particular. People all over Russia had begun to resent the arbitrary rule of the Czars. They felt that the reforms of Alexander II were not enough. Students contemplated revolution, and workers in the new industrial centers began to compare their own rights with the rights of the workers in other countries.

Some Jews joined the revolutionary groups, believing that the Jews, too, would benefit from bringing equality to all the minorities in Russia. They worked with high hopes and deep devotion alongside like-minded non-Jews to bring about a better way of life for all Russia. The difficult years when revolutionaries were exiled to Siberia or imprisoned and shot seemed to them only an unavoidable period of suffering that would inevitably lead to an era of universal freedom.

Some of the liberal Russian leaders agitated for a democratic constitution that would make the peo-

Sholom Aleichem.

A Russian police raid on a revolutionary organization. From a French illustrated weekly, 1881.

ple's rights secure. Alexander II and his government aides began to fear revolt. People were arrested and sent to Siberia on the slightest suspicion. University students in St. Petersburg and Moscow formed secret terrorist organizations aimed at undermining the power of the Czar and his government. Frequently bombs were thrown and acts of sabotage committed. In 1881 Alexander himself was assassinated by terrorists in the streets of St. Petersburg.

ARRESTS AND POGROMS

Alexander II was succeeded by his son Alex-

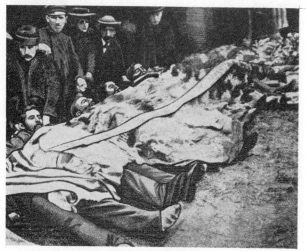

Jewish victims of the Russian pogroms.

ander III (1845-1894). Determined to establish his rule securely at all costs, he was coldly indifferent to the well-being of his people. His main concern was to ward off revolution and to make certain that the people would submit to his power.

Like the rulers of the Middle Ages, Alexander III looked for a defenseless minority group on whom the people would be able to place the blame for their troubles. Naturally, the choice fell on the Jews. Alexander accused the Jews of fomenting revolt in Russia and of having had a part in the assassination of his father. He also persecuted students and workers, writers and merchants, and anyone else whom he suspected of inciting rebellion. Many were arrested and shot; others were sent for long prison terms to the freezing wastelands of Siberia.

Mendel Beilis on trial.

For the Jews the Czar had a special punishment in store. Officers and agents in the service of the government stirred up the Russian people with speeches against the Jews, inciting them to attack the Jewish community. Jewish homes were broken into and plundered; Jews were brutally beaten and many lost their lives.

These terrible pogroms—a Russian word for "destruction"—shocked and saddened Jews the world over. But there was nothing they could do for their brethren in Russia except to give them some material aid and help those who left the country. As new laws were passed, forcing the Jews back into the towns of the Pale, many Russian Jews decided to emigrate.

Tablet with poem by Emma Lazarus affixed to the Statue of Liberty.

AMERICA BECKONS

One country in particular opened her doors to the poor and the wronged of all nations and creeds. Indeed, at the very gateway to this land stood a statue, the symbol of liberty, on which were engraved words written by Emma Lazarus (1849-1887), a compassionate and gifted Jewess.

Give me your tired, your poor,
Your huddled masses yearning to breathe free,
The wretched refuse of your teeming shore,
Send these, the homeless, tempest-tost to me.
I lift my lamp beside the golden door.

In the latter part of the 19th century and in the beginning of the 20th, hundreds of thousands of Russian Jews left their homes and sailed for America. Most of them had to make the long journey under difficult conditions, crowded together in the ship's steerage. But they were glad to leave Russia for the land of promise across the Atlantic.

In 1905 a revolution took place in Russia. It was brutally crushed. Again, bloody pogroms against the Jewish communities followed.

Jews in Europe and America held out a helping hand to the emigrants who poured out of Russia. Jewish philanthropists donated generous sums of money, and organizations were formed in many countries to aid the immigrants in establishing new

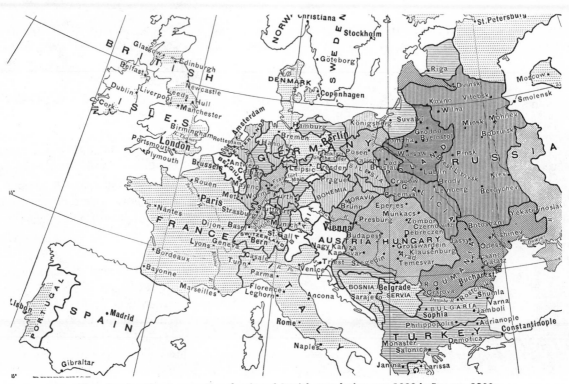

Map showing the comparative density of Jewish population per 1000 in Europe, 1900.

Early *halutzim* ploughing in a Palestinian farm settlement.

homes. Some of the emigrants settled in England, Germany, France and Holland. But most of them went on from there to America.

THE "LOVERS OF ZION"

A small group of Russian Jews went to Palestine. The spirit of nationalism that had spread through the whole world had caused many to see the Jewish problem in a new light. In 1881 Leon Pinsker, a physician, excited Russian Jewry with a pamphlet entitled *Auto-Emancipation,* which caused a great stir, particularly among Jewish high school students. Pinsker maintained that no one could really emancipate the Jews except the Jews themselves. And the only way in which the Jews

Members of a Zionist group preparing to go to Palestine. In the center is young David Ben-Gurion.

could secure their freedom and self-respect, Pinsker declared, was by returning to their ancient homeland. Pinsker's call gave rise to a society which took the name of Hovevei Zion, "Lovers of Zion."

The "Lovers of Zion" helped some of their members to settle in Palestine, where they founded, under the most adverse conditions, new agricultural colonies. They also joined some of the already existing colonies founded with the aid of Moses Montefiore, and the French-Jewish organization, Alliance Israélite Universelle, which had founded the agricultural training school Mikveh Yisrael in Petah Tikvah.

Conference of the Hovevei Zion in Odessa, 1890.

THE BILU GROUPS

The early colonists from Russia found a barren land—dry, rocky and sandy, with many swampy areas. They saw that the desert areas would have to be irrigated and swamps filled in before it would be possible to plant vegetables and trees. Most of the colonists were students and townspeople. What they lacked in knowledge of farming they made up in enthusiasm. They stood upon the soil which their ancestors had tilled centuries before, and they resolved that with the same unswerving faith which had inspired the Israelites of old, they would make the land of their fathers bloom again.

The first groups of high school students from Russia which landed in Palestine in 1882 were known as "Bilu," the Hebrew initials for "Bet

325

The original group of Bilu pioneers in their later years.

Members of *Hashomer* (watchmen), the first Jewish defense organization in Palestine.

Yaakov, Lekhu V'nelkha!"—House of Jacob, let us arise and go forth!

The "Lovers of Zion" and the Biluim founded the first agricultural settlement in the Land of Israel—Rishon Le-Zion ("First in Zion") and Petah Tikvah ("Gate of Hope") also *Nes Tziyyonah* and *Zikhron Yaakov*, followed by others.

The pioneers had set themselves a mighty task —but their idealism and their comradeship carried them through the arduous beginnings, through hunger and malaria, lack of water during the dry season, and attacks by raiding Bedouins. Their task of course, was infinitely more difficult than had been that of their ancestors, for the soil they found was much less fertile and hence harder to

cultivate than it had been when the Children of Israel first took possession of it.

The Jews of Europe followed the progress of the new settlements in Israel with keen interest. Wealthy men extended financial aid. Baron Edmond de Rothschild (1845-1934) the French financier and philanthropist, contributed generously until the new settlements could support themselves.

The settlers worked during the day and stood guard at night with their guns, ready to defend their land. Eventually they made a safe and good place for themselves. Their orange groves and their olive trees attested to their labors as did the towns of Rishon Le-Zion and Petah Tikvah which are still the pride of Israel today.

GLOSSARY OF HEBREW TERMINOLOGY
AND NAMES

Kahal (Jewish self-government)	Kah-hahl	קָהָל
Haskalah (Enlightenment)	Hahskahlah	הַשְׂכָּלָה
Ahavath Zion	Ahah-vaht Tseeyohn	אַהֲבַת צִיּוֹן
Mendele the Bookseller	Mehndehleh Moh-ḥeyr Sfahreem	מֶנְדֶּלֶה מוֹכֵר סְפָרִים
Pogrom	Pohgrohm	פּׁגְרוֹם
Lovers of Zion	Ḥohvevey Tseeyohn	חוֹבְבֵי צִיּוֹן
Mikveh Yisrael	Mikvey Yisrah-eyl	מִקְוֵה יִשְׂרָאֵל
Petah Tikvah	Petaḥ Tikvah	פֶּתַח תִּקְוָה
Bilu	Beeloo	בִּיל"וּ
House of Jacob, let us arise and go forth	Beyt Ya-ahkohv Lḥoo Ve-neylḥah	בֵּית יַעֲקֹב לְכוּ וְנֵלְכָה
Rishon Le-Zion	Reeshohn Letseeyohn	רִאשׁוֹן לְצִיּוֹן
Bedouins	Beydoo-eem	בֵּידוּאִים

THE CAPTAIN AND THE JOURNALIST: BEGINNINGS OF POLITICAL ZIONISM

THE DREYFUS AFFAIR (1894-1906)

The situation of French Jewry in the late 19th century was in many ways similar to that of the German Jews. Even though full civil rights had been extended to them by law, the French Jews often found themselves face to face with old prejudices when they sought to enter certain professions. The old picture of the Jew as a convenient scapegoat could not be wiped out by the mere passing of liberal legislation. It was easier to pass laws proclaiming freedom and tolerance than to educate people to abide not only by their letter but also by their spirit.

In October of 1894, Captain Alfred Dreyfus, a Jew on the General Staff of the French Army, was arrested on a charge of espionage. More specifically, he was accused of giving away French military secrets to Germany. Captain Dreyfus was tried and convicted of high treason. He was sent to imprisonment and exile on Devil's Island. To the last, Dreyfus insisted that he was innocent. Even while he was stripped of his military rank and honor he had cried "Long live France! Long live the army!"

Many people believed that Captain Dreyfus had been a victim of anti-Jewish discrimination, and were convinced of his innocence. There was a suspicion that the document which Dreyfus was supposed to have written and which was submitted as evidence of his guilt, was the work of someone else. Among the non-Jews who championed the captain's cause was Émile Zola (1840-1902), the French novelist who fought passionately to have justice done to the unfortunate officer. To Zola, as to many others, the way in which the French au-

The degradation of Captain Dreyfus.

Photograph of part of a letter Dreyfus sent to the Grand Rabbi of France from prison, the day after he was found guilty.

thorities had handled the case was a crass example of injustice, intolerance and corruption.

It was not until 1899 that Dreyfus was recalled from Devil's Island and granted a pardon. It had come to light that many of his superiors had been involved in espionage and that the real culprit was one Major Ferdinand Esterhazy, who had sold information to the Germans.

Freedom loving people in many lands had taken part in the fight to have Captain Dreyfus freed and to have his innocence established. His fate had become a test case in the much larger struggle then taking place in all Europe—the struggle between those who clung to old prejudices and those who demanded civil rights and equality for all men. Finally, in the year 1906 the innocence of Captain Dreyfus was openly proclaimed and he was reinstated as an officer in the French army.

THE JOURNALIST AT THE TRIAL

Among the journalists present at the trial of Dreyfus in 1894 was Theodor Herzl, a young newspaperman from Vienna. The miscarriage of justice and the prejudiced, degrading treatment to which Dreyfus was subjected, made a lasting impression on young Herzl. Up to that time he had had little contact with Jewish life and Jewish traditions. But when he saw what damage hatred could do even in a civilized nation such as France, he felt himself united with Dreyfus, the French Jew, in a bond of shared suffering.

The reinstatement of Captain Dreyfus.

Theodor Herzl

Herzl and the Zionist delagation to Kaiser Wilhelm returning from Palestine.

A letter, written by Herzl in 1897 about the proposed Jewish state.

"THE JEWISH STATE"

The patriotism and nationalism that were so strong in the 19th century had worked their influence on Theodor Herzl. These ideas caused him to conceive a new solution for the problems the Jews faced in their quest for equal rights. Why, he declared, should not the Jews establish a state of their own? This would give them a place of their own to stand on, as a nation among other nations. In 1896 Herzl wrote a brochure entitled *The Jewish State,* in which he explained his ideas.

As Herzl met other like-minded Jews it became increasingly clear to him that the land where the Jews should establish their state could be none other but Palestine. He set forth his vision of the return to Zion in a novel, *Altneuland, (Old-New Land),* which was published in 1902. He and his associates, who called themselves "Zionists," published a periodical, "Die Welt" ("The World") in which they expounded their point of view.

THE ZIONIST MOVEMENT

In 1897 Herzl called the first Zionist Congress in Basel, Switzerland. At this Congress the Zionist movement was officially founded and its basic platform proclaimed—namely, the establishment of a legally secure Jewish homeland in Palestine. Theodore Herzl dedicated his whole life and energy to the realization of this ideal. Since Palestine was then part of the Turkish Empire, he sought audiences with the Sultan of Turkey, to secure permits for Jews to enter the Holy Land. How-

ever, the Sultan refused to grant such permission and only a few Jews were allowed to enter Palestine. In despair, Herzl then approached authorities in Egypt and England to see whether he could not obtain as an alternative to Palestine, some territory in East Africa for a Jewish homeland (which was bitterly opposed by the ardent Zionists). Herzl's original Zionist project aroused interest in many circles but he did not live to see even the beginnings of the realization of his plans. He died in 1904 at the age of forty-four, leaving his associates to continue the work he had begun.

Herzl's most enthusiastic followers did not live in Austria, Germany or France. Most of the men who carried on his work at that time lived in Russia, the land where Czar and nobles still ruled with a heavy hand and where Jews lived under the most difficult conditions. Herzl's ideas had helped to open a gate of hope for many young Jewish stu-

The meeting place of the Zionist Congress.

Bronze medal struck in honor of the second Zionist Congress at Basel. The quotation, from the book of Ezekiel, tells of God's promise to bring the Children of Israel from among the nations to their own land.

dents in Russia, who looked to Palestine for a life of dignity and freedom.

THE FIRST ALIYAH (1880-1905)

After the death of Theodore Herzl, David Wolffsohn, one of his close co-workers, took over the leadership of the Zionist Organization. These were stormy days. New and terrible pogroms were taking place in Russia and many thousands of Jews had fled. Most of them courageously made the long journey across the Atlantic and found new homes in the United States. Others went to the western countries of the European continent and to England. Only a few were permitted entry into Palestine. Yet Jewish immigration into Palestine continued steadily and a number of new settlements were founded.

Ever since the days of Ezra, the Hebrew word *aliyah* (literally "going up" or "ascent") has been

Zionist leaders: Dr. Bodenheimer, Herzl, Max Nordau, and David Wolfssohn.

used to refer to the return of Jews to the Land of Israel. The term *aliyah* refers also to the "ascent" to the reader's desk of a person who is called upon to participate in the reading of the Torah. Basically the connotation in either case is the same. The Jew who is honored by an *aliyah* in the synagogue feels a sense of dedication and inspiration. So too, did the men and women who "went up" to Palestine to settle and rebuild the Jewish homeland.

By the time Herzl died, a whole generation of *olim* (from "aliyah") had already grown up in Palestine. This group of immigrants, which had come to the land during the period from 1880 to 1905, has become known as the First Aliyah or the

Halutzim reaping a harvest.

first immigration wave.

The men and women of the First Aliyah had found an enormous task awaiting them. For centuries the soil of Palestine had lain neglected and uncultivated. The settlers of the First Aliyah literally had to make the desert bloom again. They first filled in the malarial swamps and irrigated the parched, sandy soil. Then they proceeded to plant vineyards and fields, where nothing but wilderness had been before. They founded the first agricultural settlements in Palestine where they lived and worked together—the forerunners of the kibbutz-

Eliezer Ben Yehudah, father of modern spoken Hebrew.

im of later decades.

The settlers brought with them the heritage of the Enlightenment. Many of them had studied the sciences, literature and languages at Russia's universities. They began to create new literary works, and most important, made Hebrew—so long the language of prayer and study—come alive again as a spoken, everyday language.

THE REVIVAL OF HEBREW

The two most ardent champions of the revival of Hebrew were Eliezer Ben Yehudah (1858-1927) and the essayist Asher Ginzberg, (1856-1927) who called himself Ahad Ha-Am ("One of the People"). Eliezer Ben Yehudah was a talented linguist and educator who foresaw the creative role that the Hebrew language could play in everyday life in the new Jewish homeland. Ben Yehudah allowed only Hebrew to be spoken in his home,

and his family and friends followed his example. He coined new words for tools and ideas which were unknown to ancient Hebrew. Prior to the outbreak of World War I, he embarked on the monumental task of compiling an unabridged dictionary of the Hebrew language which included the new expressions he had created.

Ahad Ha-Am was the leading essayist in modern Hebrew literature. He fashioned the Hebrew language into an instrument of precise and articulate expression. In his essays he expounded the philosophy that the Land of Israel must again become the spiritual and cultural center of the Jewish people. In this effort he had clashes with the Zionist ideology of Theodor Herzl where the emphasis was almost exclusively on political statehood. His work inspired a whole generation of creative Hebrew writers, chief among whom was his close disciple, the poet of the Hebrew national renaissance, Hayyim Nahman Bialik.

THE SECOND ALIYAH (1905-1914)

The Second *Aliyah* took place from 1905 until the outbreak of World War I. This new immigration wave marked the development of a new type of agricultural settlement in Palestine—the Kibbutz or cooperative. In the Kibbutz the pioneers not only worked and lived together, but actually owned all the property jointly, with the kibbutz supplying its members with food, clothing and other necessities, paying for these goods with the proceeds from the sale of its agricultural products.

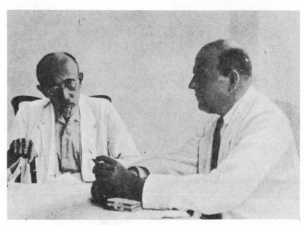

Hayyim Nahman Bialik with the famous Hebrew writer, Ahad Ha-am.

THE JEWISH NATIONAL FUND

The land for the settlements was purchased by the *Keren Kayemeth Le-Yisrael* or Jewish National Fund, which was established in 1907 as the land purchasing agency of the Zionist movement. The Fund is supported by contributions from Jews the world over.

THE HISTADRUT

The pioneers organized into a strong federation of labor unions known as the *Histadrut Ha-Ovdim* ("Federation of Workers"). Eventually the Histadrut evolved into a powerful organization which included all Jewish working people in the country.

GLOSSARY OF HEBREW TERMINOLOGY
AND NAMES

Theodor Herzl	Binyahmeen Ze-eyv Hertzl	בִּנְיָמִין זְאֵב הֶרְצְל
The Jewish State	Mdeenaht Hayehoo-deem	מְדִינַת הַיְהוּדִים
Zionism	Tseeyohnoot	צִיּוֹנוּת
Aliyah	Ahleeyah	עֲלִיָּה
Olim	Ohleem	עוֹלִים
Eliezer ben Yehudah	Elee-ezer ben Yhoodah	אֱלִיעֶזֶר בֶּן יְהוּדָה
Ahad Ha-Am	Ah-ḥahd Ha-ahm	אַחַד הָעָם
Hayyim Nah-man Bialik	Ḥahyeem Naḥ-mahn B'yahleek	חַיִּים נַחְמָן בְּיַאלִיק
Jewish National Fund	Kehren Kah-yehmet Le-yisrah-eyl	קֶרֶן קַיֶּמֶת לְיִשְׂרָאֵל
Federation of Workers	Histahdroot Ha-ohvdeem	הִסְתַּדְרוּת הָעוֹבְדִים

THE RISE OF THE AMERICAN JEWISH COMMUNITY

About a quarter of a million Jews lived in America in the year 1880. In the next fifty years, two and a half million more came to these shores.

The great majority of this vast influx of immigrants came from Eastern Europe, from lands, including the former Poland and Lithuania, which were now under Russian rule. Large numbers also came from Rumania and from the province of Galicia in Austria-Hungary.

Jews suffered harsh oppression under the government of the Czars. The assassination in 1881 of Czar Alexander II, who had attempted some reforms, brought on a rapid worsening of their condition. Government-inspired pogroms were followed by the May laws of 1882, which expelled the Jews from many towns and many professions, forbade them to buy or own property, and made their already hard lives even more difficult.

THE GREAT EXODUS

As hopes for living a good life or improving the lot of their children faded for the Jews of Eastern Europe, a great exodus began. Without funds and with few skills for living in the industrialized western world, hundreds of thousands crossed the western borders of their homelands, seeking new lands and new opportunities.

Some went to France, Germany and other West European countries; some to England and to South Africa. A small idealistic group went to Palestine, although they knew that Turkish oppression and the hardships of an undeveloped land awaited them. Baron Maurice de Hirsch, the great philanthropist, aided the emigration from Russia, setting up the Jewish Colonization Association to aid resettlement, particularly in Argentina. The Alliance Israelite Universelle in France, and later the Hilfsverein der Deutschen Juden in Germany, furnished some help. The British Mansion House Committee helped those who arrived in England.

The great majority of those fleeing Old World persecution had no other wish than to go to the land of opportunity, the free country of America. After miserable voyages, usually in the crowded steerage or cheapest compartment of the steam-

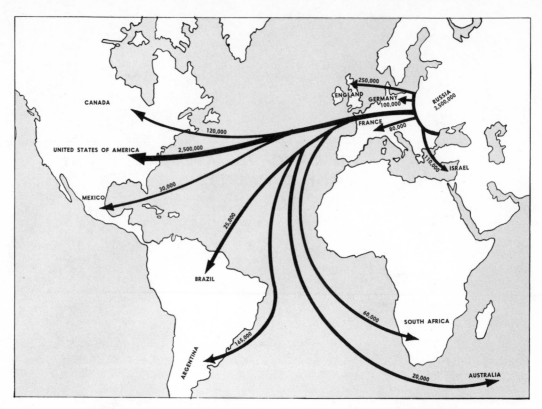

The stream of Jewish immigration from Eastern Europe, 1881-1932.

ships that carried them, these hopeful refugees arrived in the "Golden Land."

Baron Maurice de Hirsch

LIFE IN THE NEW WORLD

For most of them, the promise of America was long delayed in its fulfilment. The majority of the immigrants docked in New York, and great numbers found homes there and in the other large cities of the east. They lived in crowded tenements in neighborhoods, such as the Lower East Side of New York, that could be called ghettos. Unlike the ghettos of Europe, these were social and economic, not legal, but it was only those who gained some measure of success who could afford to move to better areas.

Not knowing English, the immigrants found low-paying jobs, and in these jobs were often exploited. The great new industry in the cities was the manufacture of clothing. Many of the newcomers became workers in this industry, doing simple sewing or tailoring or pressing. Often working hours were twelve or more hours a day, six days a week. Piece work was brought home for the whole family, including the children, to work on till late at night. Even so, the whole family in-

Mauricia, Jewish colony in Argentina founded by the Jewish Colonization Association of Baron de Hirsch.

Yiddish Constitution of the United Cloth Hat and Cap Makers Union of 1921.

come might be ten dollars a week.

Poor conditions at work and at home often led to shortened lives. Tuberculosis claimed many exhausted workers. More dramatically, unsafe conditions led to injuries and to fires which took many lives. The newcomers were willing to submit to all this because of their great need to make a living for themselves and their children.

Jews played a large part in the growth of unions, such as the International Ladies Garment Workers Union, which united the workers in their demands for shorter hours, safe conditions, and steady pay. In advising and cooperating with the manufacturers, the unions ultimately benefited them as well.

THE LOVE OF LEARNING

There were Jews who became farmers, encouraged by the Jewish Agricultural Society and the National Farm School, but they were few. The immigrants for the most part wished to live in cities, in communities where there were many fellow Jews and where there would be synagogues to attend and religious schools for their children. The *schul* and the *heder,* or schoolroom, which they had loved in the old country were transplanted to America.

The Jews of Eastern Europe brought with them their love of learning. They managed to find the few dollars necessary to pay the *melamed* who taught their children Hebrew, *humash* and prayers. They wished in this new country to fashion the

A farmstead of a Jewish settler in the Lasker Colony, Kansas 1885.

337

life of faith and piety that they had known in their small towns in Europe.

Even those who no longer strictly observed Jewish law, those who had devoted themselves to Haskalah or to progressive political movements, had the Jewish love of learning and the printed word. Among the Jewish immigrants there were more periodicals published than among any other immigrant group, before or since. They read Yiddish newspapers and Hebrew magazines, and flocked to the Yiddish theatre and to public lectures and discussions.

After a hard day of work, many of the adults went to night school to learn English and to qualify to become American citizens. They sacrificed to send their children to high school and if possible, to college, so that they could do more in life than their parents had been able to do. The ideal profession they wished for their children was one that combined learning and service, such as medicine, law or teaching.

HELPING EACH OTHER

Poor as most of them were, the immigrant Jews never forgot their responsibility to each other. They set up free loan societies, charities, and organizations for fellowship and mutual help. Those who came from the same European towns had their own society or *landsmannschaft*.

The old tradition of charity and good deeds was continued. No home was too crowded to take in a cousin or other relative who had just arrived from the old country. Jews who had come in earlier immigrations helped the newcomers.

These workers, employed in small factories, had parcels of land on which they raised crops.

Organizations such as B'nai B'rith and the American Jewish Committee, supported largely by "German" Jews who had come a few decades earlier and were now comparatively well-to-do, fought anti-Semitism and protected the rights of the recent immigrants.

Poverty, crowded slum conditions and unfamiliarity with the ways of the new world were all handicaps for the immigrant. To make the younger people feel at home in America courses and group social activities were sponsored by such agencies as the Hebrew Immigrant Aid Society, the Na-

Farmers' Synagogue in Toms River, New Jersey.

קאָנסטיטושאָן

דער

"...קאָמענעץ פּאָדאָלער
"...פּראָג. ליידיעס אַסס'ן

געגרינדעט דעם 16טען סעפטעמבער, 1908

––––––––––––––––––––––
רייטער און רייגער, יוניאָן פּרינטערס, 121 נאָרפאָלק סטריט.

Title page of a landsmanschaft constitution, The Komenets Podolier Progressive Ladies Association, founded 1908.

tional Council of Jewish Women, the Educational Alliance in New York, YMHA's and settlement houses.

THE SECOND GENERATION

The second generation, the children of the immigrants, were able to find better jobs and often to enter professions. In the free atmosphere of the new country, many of the children of the immigrants left the old way of life. They were not willing to be different from their neighbors, or to sacrifice the money they would gain by working on the Sabbath. Many felt that the religion of their parents could not be kept in modern America.

Even the secular culture so dear to some of their parents was often not important to them. They did not attend the Yiddish theatre and lecture hall, or read the Yiddish newspapers and magazines of their parents. Their language was English and they wanted above all to become like other Americans.

Some were even ashamed of their parents because of their foreign accents or old-fashioned ways.

The Reform temples of that time, the end of the nineteenth century and the beginning of the twentieth, were not places where the children of East European immigrants could feel at home. Many temples held their Sabbath services on Sunday. Further, the members of the temples were not pleased with the foreign traits of their East European brethren, and preferred the society of their own group.

Not respecting their parents' ways, and not welcomed in the Reform temples, the young East Europeans were all too often growing up detached from Jewish tradition and from the Jewish community.

THE JEWISH THEOLOGICAL SEMINARY

A group of founders, including Sabato Morais, its first president, set up the Jewish Theological Seminary of America in 1886 in New York. They hoped that the rabbis ordained there, all of whom were to be English speaking college graduates, would be able to keep Jewish youth loyal to their heritage.

Alexander Kohut, Benjamin Szold, and Marcus Jastrow were among the scholars who helped fashion this Conservative movement in American Ju-

The Educational Alliance in New York, 1895.

339

Solomon Schechter

daism. From the start the Conservatives differed with the Reform movement, upholding loyalty to Torah and Talmud, observance of the Sabbath and dietary laws, Hebrew as the language of prayer, and the preservation of hopes for the return to Zion.

From Cambridge University in 1902 came Dr. Solomon Schechter, a dynamic teacher whose great learning combined East European devotion with modern scholarly discipline, to head the Seminary. He had become famous for his discovery of the Cairo *genizah,* a storehouse of discarded ancient manuscripts that shed much light on Jewish history.

Under his leadership, the Seminary became a first-rank scholarly institution with an unsurpassed library. Dr. Schechter and his associates continued the "Historical School" of Judaism, of which Zechariah Frankel had been the leading spokesman in Europe. Their view is that Judaism, like other human institutions, has developed through the ages, not by sudden reforms but in response to the will and needs of its faithful adherents.

OUTSTANDING PUBLIC SERVANTS

By the year 1900 there were a million Jews in America. Many of them, mostly members of the group which arrived in the first part of the nineteenth century, had attained prosperity and status. Among them were well-known public servants and philanthropists, whose activities and charities benefited many others besides their own people.

Oscar Straus was appointed envoy to Turkey by Grover Cleveland and three presidents after him, and was named to the Cabinet of Theodore Roosevelt as Secretary of Commerce and Labor. His brothers Nathan and Isidor Straus, owners of Macy's in New York, were known for their good deeds. Isidor, at one time a Congressman, was president of the Educational Alliance. Nathan brought about the compulsory pasteurization of milk in New York, and gave generously for health clinics in Palestine in response to the appeal of Henrietta Szold.

Julius Rosenwald, of Sears Roebuck, gave tremendous sums for the higher education of Negroes, and other cultural causes. Others who supported learning through their activity and con-

The Jewish Theological Seminary

Jacob Schiff

ment of Jews. Schiff was perhaps the outstanding patron of learning of the time, giving funds to institutions of learning ranging from Harvard and Barnard to the Seminary and the Haifa Technion.

ORTHODOX JEWRY AND YESHIVA

The leading rabbis and congregations at the turn of the century, as well as the leading philanthropists, mostly were in the Reform wing of Judaism. Rabbis Kaufmann Kohler, Emil Hirsch, David Philipson, Henry Berkowitz (who founded the Jewish Chautauqua Society), were among the leaders of Jewish religious life. Conservative and

Main building, Yeshiva University.

tributions were Judge Mayer Sulzberger of the Court of Common Pleas in Philadelphia, who was one of the founders of the Seminary; and his cousin Cyrus L. Sulzberger, president of the Jewish Agricultural Society.

Louis Marshall (1856-1929), outstanding civic leader, founded the American Jewish Committee and worked for Jewish minority rights at the Versailles Conference. Though not a Zionist, he supported the building of Palestine as a Jewish refuge. Jacob H. Schiff (1847-1920), worked with him on many projects, including influencing the United States to censure Russia for its mistreat-

Orthodox rabbis and congregations were not as yet well organized.

The great majority of immigrants from 1881 on were Orthodox in background. They attempted to set up the same type of community as had served them in their former homes. Each congregation, following strict Jewish tradition and the customs of its members, felt it could stand by itself without looking toward a central authority.

Jews of New York made one attempt to find unity under the leadership of Jacob Joseph (1848-1902), whom they brought from Vilna to be chief rabbi. Other Orthodox leaders refused to accept his authority, and he was not able to bring order to the teeming Jewish community of New York. In Chicago a similar attempt failed.

Oscar S. Straus

Bernard Revel

Rabbi H. Pereira Mendes, of the Spanish and Portuguese Synagogue in New York from 1877 to 1937, brought about the organization of the Union of Orthodox Jewish Congregations in 1898. A group of Orthodox rabbis joined in forming Agudas Harabonim in 1902. One of their aims was to aid academies of learning, *yeshivot,* both in America and abroad.

The outstanding Yeshiva of the new world was named after the scholar Isaac Elhanan in 1896. This New York institution, at first a rabbinical seminary for students who had already steeped themselves in Jewish learning in European academies, expanded into a complete university. Under the presidency of Rabbi Bernard Dov Revel (1885-1940), it grew to include a high school, a teachers' institute, and an undergraduate college.

Torah and general studies were to be taught under one roof, fulfilling the doctrine of Samson Raphael Hirsch, that the Jew could be observant of Jewish tradition and at the same time an active and informed member of general society.

PROBLEMS AT HOME AND ABROAD

In the democratic climate of America, Jews were finding themselves accepted as they had never been elsewhere, as first-class citizens and productive members of society. Still, anti-Semitism all too often made itself felt even on these shores. Full legal rights in all states had first to be won; the Know Nothing party and similar movements aroused feeling against all foreigners and minority groups.

"Polite" anti-Semitism, which meant exclusion of Jews from high society and refusal to sell them homes in certain areas, was always known to exist. In a famous case in 1877, a hotel in Saratoga refused to admit a prominent Jewish banker, a former friend of Lincoln and Grant, Joseph Seligman, as a paying guest, informing him bluntly that "no Israelite shall be permitted to stop in the hotel." The public reaction did not stop this common practice, but made hotel managers more careful in their statements.

Meeting at the London Guildhall, 1890, in protest against the persecution of the

The Bishop of Ripon at a meeting at the London Guildhall, 1890, leads a protest against the persecution of the Jews of Russia.

A SENSATION AT SARATOGA.

June 19, 1877 — N Y Times

NEW RULES FOR THE GRAND UNION.

NO JEWS TO BE ADMITTED—MR. SELIGMAN, THE BANKER, AND HIS FAMILY SENT AWAY—HIS LETTER TO MR. HILTON—GATHERING OF MR. SELIGMAN'S FRIENDS—AN INDIGNATION MEETING TO BE HELD.

On Wednesday last Joseph Seligman, the well-known banker of this City, and member of the syndicate to place the Government loan, visited Saratoga with his wife and family. For 10 years past he has spent the Summer at the Grand Union Hotel. His family entered the parlors, and Mr. Seligman went to the manager to make arrangements for rooms. That gentleman seemed somewhat confused, and said: "Mr. Seligman, I am required to inform you that Mr. Hilton has given instructions that no Israelites shall be permitted in future to stop at this hotel."

Mr. Seligman was so astonished that for some time he could make no reply. Then he said: "Do you mean to tell me that you will not entertain Jewish people?" "That is our orders, Sir," was the reply.

Before leaving the banker asked the reason why Jews were thus persecuted. Said he, "Are they dirty, do they misbehave themselves, or have they refused to pay their bills?"

"Oh, no," replied the manager, "there is no fault to be found in that respect. The reason is simply this: Business at the hotel was not good last season, and we had a large number of Jews here. Mr. Hilton came to the conclusion that Christians did not like their company, and for that reason shunned the hotel. He resolved to run the Union on a different principle this season, and gave us instructions to admit no Jew." Personally he [the manager] was very sorry, inasmuch as Mr. Seligman had patronized the hotel for so many years, but the order was imperative.

Mr. Seligman felt outraged and returned to New

The New York Times reports the discrimination against Joseph Seligman.

More seriously, the large number of Jewish immigrants and the growth of European anti-Semitism aroused anti-Jewish sentiments among many Americans around the turn of the century. Jews were accused of controlling governments and of working for revolution; of being wretchedly poor and fabulously rich; of sticking clannishly to themselves and of trying to break into society. The Anti-Defamation League of B'nai B'rith was the first organization specifically founded to combat such libels and protect the civil rights of Jews and other minorities.

Such problems at home did not compare with the false accusations, persecutions and pogroms to which Jews were subjected in various countries of Europe and the Near East. Jews of America, though few in number, had protested and enlisted the good offices of their government at the time of the "blood-accusation of Damascus" in 1840. They appealed to the President when American Jews as well as Swiss were suffering from restrictions imposed by Switzerland. Their outcry was echoed by Protestant leaders at the time of the Mortara case. The Board of Delegates of American Israelites, which lasted from 1859 to 1878, was one of the attempts at a unified authority to speak out and protect Jewish rights.

The Dreyfus Affair of 1894 once more aroused Jewish concern as well as the concern of all justice-loving people. The Kishinev pogrom of 1903 and the wave of pogroms in 1905 were followed by mass demonstrations and protests in all the civilized world. The Congress passed a unanimous resolution expressing American horror at the incidents. Oscar Straus and Jacob Schiff headed a committee which raised a million dollars for relief of the survivors.

Because of the apparent need for a national group to safeguard Jewish rights, the American Jewish Committee came into being in 1906. Leading Jews such as Louis Marshall, the Sulzbergers, Judge Julian Mack, and Rabbi Judah Magnes were among the founders, whose objectives were "to prevent the infraction of the civil and religious rights of the Jews in any part of the world; to render all lawful assistance; to secure for Jews equality of economic, social and educational opportunity; and to afford relief from calamities affecting Jews, wherever they may occur."

The Committee encouraged the organization of the one and a half million Jews of New York in 1909 into a *Kehillah*, or community, which was to regulate religious law, settle disputes, protect civil rights and further education. For ten years, under the chairmanship of Rabbi Magnes, who later became president of the Hebrew University, the

Judah Leib Magnes

Kehillah carried on its activities, including the founding of a Bureau of Jewish Education. This attempt at unity, however, like others, soon came to an end.

The Committee was active in a long campaign to prevent discrimination by Russia against American Jews. Though it spoke for American Jewry, it was strongly anti-Zionist, reflecting the Reform ideology of most of its members.

AMERICAN ZIONISM

Many Americans, Christians as well as Jews, had been interested in the prophetic return of Jews to the land of Israel. In 1852, Warder Cresson of Philadelphia, converted and bearing the new name of Michael Boaz Israel, tried to establish a Jewish colony near Jerusalem. Clorinda S. Minor of Philadelphia led a Christian group to a settlement called Mount Hope near the site where Tel Aviv was later to be built.

Emma Lazarus looked forward to a revival of Jewish national spirit and a rebuilt homeland. Immigrants from Eastern Europe brought with them the Hovevei Zion movement, setting up groups in New York, Boston and other cities during the 1880's.

To the first Zionist Congress called by Theodor Herzl in Basel in 1897 only a token delegation came from America. Yet the Zionist movement had already been growing. In 1898 nearly one hundred small Zionist clubs united into the Federation of American Zionists, which in 1917 became the Zionist Organization of America.

The membership of Zionist groups was largely East European. The leadership included some outstanding Reform rabbis, Bernhard Felsenthal, Gustav Gottheil and Maximilian Heller, who opposed the Reform doctrine that Jews must remain dispersed throughout the world in order to fulfill the "mission of Israel." True fulfilment would come, they felt, when a Jewish model state was

SAYS MASS OF JEWS OPPOSE BOLSHEVIKI

Louis Marshall, Head of American Jewish Committee, Replies to Dr. Simons.

EAST SIDE NOT A HOTBED

Statement Calls Testimony to the Contrary Before Senate Committee "Ridiculous."

Louis Marshall, President of the American Jewish Committee, has given out a statement taking issue with the testimony of Dr George S. Simons ... ... Committee ... quota to our military and ... than any other part of our population ... than any other part of our population ...

Louis Marshall head of the American Jewish Committee reacts to a smear against the Jews, The New York Times, February 15, 1919.

This anti-Semitic cartoon by Harrison Cady, appeared in the center-spread of "Life," May 12, 1910, entitled "The Surrender of New York Town."

Henrietta Szold and other Zionist leaders.

allowed to flourish in Palestine.

First secretary of the Federation was Reform Rabbi Stephen S. Wise (1874-1949), already known for his fiery oratory. It was he who later became the outstanding spokesman for American Jewry to the conscience of the world.

Henrietta Szold (1860-1945), daughter of Rabbi Benjamin S. Szold of Baltimore and a scholar and editor of the Jewish Publication Society, founded Hadassah, the women's Zionist organization, in 1912. Louis Lipsky, also American-born, became the leading figure in early Zionism. He was editor of *The Maccabean,* monthly magazine of the Federation, for many years, and presided at annual conventions.

The twenty thousand active Zionists in America in 1914 grew to 100,000 in 1920. Yet there was much opposition from Jews who felt that loyalty to America required them to forsake all interest in the reconstruction of the Jewish national homeland.

The strongest statement of the compatibility of Zionism with American loyalties came from Louis Dembitz Brandeis (1856-1941), leading lawyer and Zionist, who in 1916 was appointed to the Supreme Court of the United States. "The ideals of the twentieth century," he said, "have been Jewish ideals for twenty centuries. To be good Americans, we must be better Jews, and to be better Jews we must become Zionists."

RESTRICTIONS OF IMMIGRATION

World War I called a halt to the flood of immigration which had increased the number of Jews in the United States to nearly four million. Immigrants who had entered the country during the previous thirty-three years made up most of the Jewish population. They had begun to learn to live in the new land and had established themselves as citizens. Their children were growing up as Americans; religious organizations were trying to improve the education they were receiving, so that they also might grow up as proud Jews.

Following the war, when many displaced persons of Europe wished to come to America, nationalist feelings in the United States were aroused, and resentment grew against foreigners. Bills were introduced into Congress limiting immigration under a quota system. The bill that was passed in 1924 allotted very small quotas to countries of Southern and Eastern Europe, favoring the Germanic countries and England.

After 1924, therefore, with the number of Jewish immigrants coming from Europe curtailed, the problem of the preservation of Jewish identity in America assumed new forms. The problem was not that of integrating the newcomers into America,

Louis D. Brandeis

but that of raising the native-born American Jewish citizen to a higher level of Jewish knowledge and sensitivity.

The new community of American Jews had established its own institutions and was beginning to develop its own leaders and teachers, while the great Jewish communities of Europe faced a period of darkness and destruction.

This prayer room for Congress, the first in congressional history, was opened in 1955. The window's main panel shows George Washington praying for all America. Behind him, a verse from *Psalm 16*.

GLOSSARY OF HEBREW TERMINOLOGY
AND NAMES

Landsmann-schaft	Lahnts-mahn-shahft	לאנדסמאנ־שאפט
Schul	Shool	שׁוּל
Melamed	Mlahmed	מְלַמֵּד
Humash	Ḥoomahsh	חֻמָשׁ
Genizah	Gnee-zah	גְּנִיזָה
Yeshiva	Y'shee-vah	יְשִׁיבָה
Yeshivot	Y'shee-voht	יְשִׁיבוֹת

THE FIRST WORLD WAR

THE FIRST WORLD WAR

In 1914 the "shot that was heard around the world" sparked off the First World War in which the Central Powers (Germany, Austria and Turkey) and the Allies (France, Russia, England and Italy) were pitted against each other in battles fought in Europe, in the African colonies and in the Middle East.

In each belligerent country Jews fought together with their fellow citizens to defend their native land. Many Jews died in the First World War on both sides. The situation of the Jews in Palestine was different in that they found themselves in the center of a battle between both sides.

Most of the major battles of the war were fought in France and Belgium, the western European front—and in Poland and Russia, the eastern front. The eastern front stretched along the borders of Russia and through the Pale of Settlement. The war brought great suffering to the Jews in these territories. Most of the able-bodied men fought in the Russian armies. Many lost their homes. Others were deported because the Russians suspected them of disloyalty. Many Russian Jews were sent deeper into the vast eastern areas of Russia.

In 1917 the Russian people revolted against the Czar. The Czar was deposed and executed. In 1918 Russia, torn by confusion and bloodshed, signed a separate peace treaty with the Central Powers. Civil war broke out in the west of Russia with supporters of the new Communist regime fighting an opposition ranging from moderate Socialists to Czarists.

THE BALFOUR DECLARATION

In England, many Jewish soldiers left their homes for the many fighting fronts. Jewish scien-

Painting by the Russian artist Sokolov-Skalya pictures the November Revolution, 1917, in front of the Czar's winter palace.

Dr. Chaim Weizmann

tists aided the war effort at home. One of England's most brilliant chemists was Dr. Chaim Weizmann who was to become a leader of the World Zionist movement and first President of the State of Israel, Dr. Weizmann, who was born in Russia in 1874, had come to England in 1903 to teach chemistry at the University of Manchester. During World War I England had to cope with a serious shortage of acetone, a material required for the manufacture of explosives. Dr. Weizmann discovered a new for-

The 39th Battalion, in which Jews fought for the liberation of Palestine during World War I, camped outside Jerusalem.

mula for acetone, thus making an invaluable contribution to the Allied war effort. Representatives of the British government expressed their appreciation and, so the story goes, asked Dr. Weizmann to name a price for his discovery—but he refused payment. He only asked that if England should gain control of Palestine after the defeat of the Turks, the Jewish people should be given special consideration.

He proposed that England allow free and unrestricted Jewish immigration into Palestine once the war was won.

General Allenby entering the city of Jerusalem.

In any event, the British government looked with favor on the Jewish settlement of Palestine. They knew that the Jewish settlers, having no bonds with Turkey, could be relied upon to help England in their own interest. In addition, many members of the British government sympathized with the Zionists in their heroic efforts to resettle the Holy Land.

On November 2, 1917, Arthur James Balfour, the British Foreign Secretary sent a letter to Lord Walter Rothschild asking him to inform the Zionist Organization of his Government's favorable attitude toward the proposed Jewish national home in

Lord Balfour, British Foreign Secretary.

Palestine. This letter which became known as the

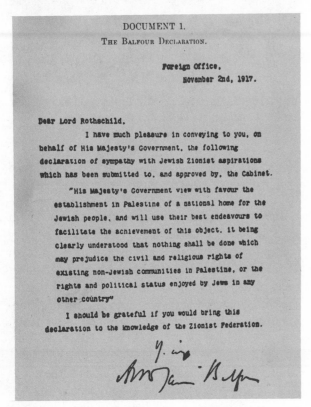

The Balfour Declaration in full.

Balfour Declaration, brought rejoicing to Zionists the world over.

There had been hard fighting in Palestine. Ever since the beginning of the war the Turks had shown a deep distrust of the Jewish settlers. The Allies, on the other hand, had been anxious for Jewish support in Palestine, and held out the promise of better conditions for the settlers there in the event of an Allied victory.

A Jewish Legion, organized in 1917, fought side by side with the British general, Lord Allenby. Among the recruits to that Jewish Legion was a young Jewish immigrant from Russia, David Green—who was to become known to the world as David Ben-Gurion and who was to be the first Prime Minister of the State of Israel.

Allenby and his troops defeated the Turks in 1918. That same year World War I ended with victory for the Allies, who had been greatly assisted by America's entrance into the war in 1917.

THE MANDATE OF PALESTINE

After the war, former Turkish territories and German colonies were given in trusteeship to other countries to be guided and controlled until such time as they would be able to govern themselves. These territories were called mandates. Palestine became a mandate of the British government with three official languages—English, Arabic and Hebrew. The Balfour Declaration was incorporated into the charter which Britain was to follow in guiding its mandate.

The Jewish Legion at the Wailing Wall.

David Ben-Gurion in the Jewish Legion.

But many Arabs in Palestine were opposed to the Balfour Declaration and to Jewish immigration in general. The wealthy Arab landowners were afraid that Jews coming from Europe would bring with them a standard of living much higher than that of the poor Arab peasants who tilled the soil of Palestine with the same primitive tools as their ancestors had used for centuries and that the Arabs would become discontented with their lot. Arabs were incited to raid Jewish settlements in an attempt to force the Jews to leave the land. But the Jews fought back. They worked their land by day

Jewish delegates to the Versailles Peace Conference.

and guarded it at night with their guns.

Those early years of the British Mandate—1919 to 1929—marked the coming of the Third Aliyah. This wave of immigration consisted of Jews who had left Poland and Russia after the Russian revolution.

THE PEACE OF VERSAILLES

After World War I the governments of the victorious nations were anxious to establish a lasting peace and better conditions in the postwar world. The face of the world had changed. Germany and Austria had lost their empires, revolted against their rulers and become republics. Russia had become a Communist dictatorship. France, although a victor in the great conflict, was exhausted, ravaged by the many bloody battles fought on her soil.

During the great Peace Conference which took place at Versailles in 1919, many nations that had once belonged to Czarist Russia, and in part to Germany and Austria, were given independence. Poland, Finland, Estonia, Latvia, Lithuania and Yugoslavia became independent countries, as did Hungary and Czechoslovakia, which had been part of the Austro-Hungarian Empire. Germany had lost her African colonies and in the Middle East, Turkey was defeated. Palestine, along with Syria and Iraq, soon became a British mandate.

Woodrow Wilson, the President of the United States, had been instrumental in creating the

Louis Marshall

351

Julian Mack

quered and the conquering lands but also delegates from the many nations who were about to win their independence, and those who were gaining new mandatory status. Also present were Jewish delegations from many countries. The American Jews were represented by the delegates of the American Jewish Congress, Louis Marshall, Judge Mack and others. Louis Marshall succeeded in uniting all the Jewish delagations from the various countries of the world into one voice in behalf of the rights not only of the Jews but of all minority groups the world over.

The terms of the Versailles Peace Conference provided for equal rights and representation to all minority groups within the various countries, and the League of Nations became the guardian of these rights.

League of Nations, an international organization which was to be responsible for maintaining peace in the world. It was the League of Nations which supervised the administration of the mandates, including Palestine.

Participating in the Versailles Peace Conference were not only representatives from both the con-

The enforcement of these terms, of course, proved difficult in countries where democratic rule did not exist for, unfortunately, the League of Nations did not have any concrete power to guarantee protection to minorities.

Yet many left the Peace Conference with great hopes for a brighter future, certain that the terrible World War had indeed been a war to end all wars.

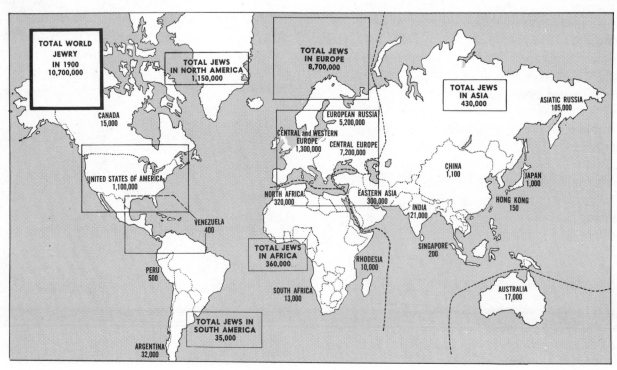

World Jewish population in the year 1900.

JEWISH WAR VICTIMS

The Jews in the countries of western Europe—England, France and Germany—did not regard themselves as minorities, for they had achieved complete emancipation. But the Jews in the many newly created countries of eastern Europe were in need of protection. The Jews of eastern Europe still were the victims of discrimination. The only larger eastern country to recognize their minority rights was the new republic of Czechoslovakia. For a number of years (1918-24), Jews were granted national autonomy in Lithuania.

Among the grave problems of the postwar period was that of the thousands of Jewish war victims on the Russian and Polish borders. They had suffered war, revolution and persecutions—tens of thousands of Jews were killed in the bloody massacres initiated by the Ukrainian Nationalists and the roving bands of White Russian Czarist loyalists—and now many of the survivors were faced with the added problems of poverty and homelessness.

American Jews, aware of the desperate plight of their brethren across the sea, were anxious to help. In 1914 all the charity and relief organizations of American Jews united into one vast organization called the American Joint Distribution Committee. Its aim was to bring quick and effective help to the Jews of Russia and Poland, aiding them wherever possible to emigrate to other European countries or to the United States. American Jews from all walks of life contributed funds to the organization which became known the world over as the "Joint" and has been a source of help to millions of Jews.

Many of the Jews of eastern Europe left their homes and settled in the countries of western Europe, where some of them made important contributions in many fields of endeavor. In spite of the ravages of war and the difficult times, the people of Western Europe were optimistic.

THE JEWS IN SOVIET RUSSIA

Still, about two and a half million Jews remained in the Union of Soviet Socialist Republics. These Jews were faced with a completely new situation. On the one hand, anti-Semitism was officially

Entrance to a collective farm in Biro-Bidjan.

outlawed and punishable in Communist Russia. On the other hand, Jews were required to give up their own religion and culture to become part of the new Communist order. Some of the Russian Jews were able to adjust to the new life but many others found it impossible to abandon their traditional ways of life, language and religion.

An attempt was made by the Soviet authorities to settle the Yiddish-speaking Jews in Biro-Bidjan, a remote area in southeastern Siberia near the Manchurian border where they could engage in farming. But life in Biro-Bidjan turned out to be a very disappointing experience for those Jews who accepted the Russian offer and settled there.

The Jews of Russia hoped that they would eventually be given the rights of full citizenship in the Soviet Republic, including the freedom to preserve their religious and cultural heritage. The Communists, however, were ambitious to forge a new Russia, with only one way of living—the Communist way. And so again the Jews of Russia found themselves outside the accepted order. Many Zionists and religious leaders were accused of being reactionary enemies of the new regime, and were arrested and deported. Many who had fought in the revolution themselves came to view the new system with bitterness and disappointment. Yet for several decades many of the Jews of the Soviet Union continued to hope for a happy adjustment under the new order. Their final disillusionment was not to come until after another world war even more terrible than the first.

GLOSSARY OF HEBREW TERMINOLOGY
AND NAMES

Balfour Declaration	Hahts-hahraht Bahlfoohr	הַצְהָרַת בַּלְפוּר
David Ben Gurion	Dahveed Ben Gooryohn	דָּוִד בֶּן גּוּרְיוֹן

A NEW THREAT AND A NEW REFUGE

THE JEWS IN PRE-NAZI GERMANY

Many Jews played a prominent and active role in the German republic which was created at a national assembly in the city of Weimar. Most prominent among the Jews in the German foreign service was Walter Rathenau (1867-1922), one of the great statesmen of his time. As Minister of Reconstruction, and later Minister of Foreign Affairs, Rathenau made every effort to improve relationships between Germany and France. He had a profound understanding of the political problems of Europe and hoped to help forge a thriving, peaceful new continent. But reactionary German forces disapproved of Rathenau and he was assassinated in 1922.

During the days of the "Weimar Republic," German Jews became prominent also in the arts, sciences, education, banking and business. It seemed to many that a new Golden Age of full emancipation had dawned.

Jewish scholars and philosophers made their contributions to Jewish learning. With the ideas of earlier Jewish scholars and philosophers and the wisdom of the modern world as a foundation, Jewish thinkers expounded new theories on the meaning of God and man.

For a time it seemed as if the forces of progress in western Europe would triumph. Yet there were still many problems that needed solving. The "Weimar Republic" struggled valiantly to solve its problems but it was hampered by old nationalistic military groups, disgruntled men, former army

Walter Rathenau

officers and impoverished aristocrats. These military groups, yearning for the old ways of life they had known in the Germany of the Kaiser, were unable to accept the fact that Germany had lost its glorious empire and many of its territories. They therefore sought to regain their own lost power in the government.

FASCISM IN ITALY

In Italy, too, there were many who dreamed of a powerful military regime. In 1922 the Fascist party headed by Benito Mussolini, who called himself Il Duce (the leader), seized power in Italy. The Fascists had an exaggerated feeling of nationalism. They believed that the young men of a nation should be educated first as soldiers, who would devote their lives solely to the service of the nation. No opposition was tolerated. All those who did not agree with the Fascists were conveniently silenced—by imprisonment; frequently they would be tortured and put to death.

THE RISE OF ADOLF HITLER AND NAZISM

A new kind of fascism now developed in Germany. In addition to the militarists, there were many other groups who disliked the new democracy. Many felt bitter over Germany's defeat in the First World War and over her loss of territories and prestige. These groups, which fought the democratic builders of the New Germany, eventually found a leader in Adolf Hitler.

Adolf Hitler promised all the disappointed groups a different, powerful Germany—a Germany that would conquer the world and become an empire such as it had been under the Kaiser; indeed, he promised that he would make Germany even greater than she had ever been under any previous leader.

Hitler and his followers developed the theory that the German people were a "master race," superior to all other nations. They and other "Nordic" peoples, they declared, were the master race of mankind which would lead and dominate the world and wipe out all inferior peoples.

Hitler announced that the Jews would be the first to be eliminated since they were the lowest on the scale among the inferior races. Choosing the

Adolph Hitler, Herman Goering and Joseph Goebbels, the Nazi triumvirate.

Jews as his scapegoat was neither original nor brave. After all, there were only half a million Jews among the sixty million inhabitants of Germany.

Hitler's theories were not taken seriously in other countries. Even many Germans laughed at them. Nevertheless, Adolf Hitler, the ex-paper-hanger from Austria, succeeded in winning more and more followers who were blindly devoted to their leader and his ideas.

Hitler founded organizations similar to those which Mussolini had founded in Italy. Dressed in military uniforms, trained like soldiers, the members of these organizations of Hitler's party marched through the streets of Germany, shouting, singing and breaking up orderly meetings of democratic groups. They started fights and made trouble. Trying to appeal to ill-informed socialists, Hitler called his party the German National Socialist Workers Party, which became known by its abbreviated name, the Nazi Party.

Meanwhile, the Great Depression of the 1930's began. Germany, like the rest of the western world, suffered severely. Many Germans were unemployed and desperate. During the years of the Depression, Hitler's following increased rapidly. His fanatical manner seemed to have an almost hypnotic effect on many Germans.

In 1933, Adolph Hitler came into power, marking the end of the Weimar Republic. The Nazis (the Nationalist Socialist Party) took over the

Front page of the Nazi newspaper *Der Sturmer* with headline "The Jews are our Misfortune."

country. All democratic organizations in Germany were dissolved systematically. Germany was in the hands of uniformed men. The people were forced to spend their time in military parades and demonstrations to show their loyalty to Hitler, their "Fuehrer" or leader. Behind this masquerade of zeal and devotion the Nazis conducted a reign of terror. Aided by the police, Hitler's Storm Troopers made hundreds of arrests. No man or woman who had a different point of view or who would not support the new Nazi organizations was safe. The people who were arrested were mistreated, tortured, imprisoned. Many were killed.

Germany became a land of fear. People whispered stories of a new kind of prison—the concentration camp. In Hitler's first years of power the Nazi concentration camps were filled mostly with Germans who had dared oppose his regime. But from the very beginning Hitler declared war on the Jews. He used the Jews as a scapegoat and incited latent anti-Semitic prejudices against them. Cruelties against Jews were encouraged, and one humiliating restriction after another was put into force against them.

Hitler's main ambition was to forge a Germany that would follow him blindly into a great, victorious war. All obstacles hindering the unity and mindless obedience of such a Germany had to be removed. The German people became afraid to speak freely, even to think. German history was shamelessly rewritten in accordance with the new Nazi viewpoint. Many respected educators and scientists were removed from their posts and replaced by followers of Hitler. These new replacements did as they were told, and helped fashion a Germany that would follow the Nazis to war. More and more Jews experienced cruelties and restrictions. Jewish lawyers, physicians, teachers, scientists, journalists and actors lost their jobs. Jewish places of business were boycotted by Hitler's party troops and stormed by mobs of hysterical people. In 1935, the infamous Nuremburg Laws were put into effect. The Jews of Germany were suddenly torn out of their equal and useful places in the German nation and became maligned and humiliated outcasts.

WHERE DID THE GERMAN JEWS FLEE?

Many Jews fled from Nazi Germany to other European countries. Among the refugees were prominent bankers and merchants, renowned artists, writers and scientists.

Many other Jews went to the United States, where the first German Jews had settled in the middle of the 19th century. Many German Jews who had formerly ignored or opposed Zionism now contemplated emigration to Palestine. The Fourth Aliyah was composed primarily of Jews from Central Europe.

German community leaders and rabbis expounded the ideas of Zionism and the timeless values of the Jewish tradition. Many young German Jews joined the Zionist organizations and prepared themselves for settlement in the land of their forefathers. Many of them were high school students who had been expelled from school by the Nazis. The Fourth Aliyah included also many of Germany's young Jewish academicians, doctors of

Felix Frankfurter

philosophy, science and medicine. Today many of them still live in Israel's villages and Kibbutzim contented and productive farmers.

There were many Jews, however, who hesitated to leave their homeland, the land where their fathers had lived for hundreds of years. Like many other Germans, they still believed that Hitler's power would soon come to an end.

PALESTINE

Palestine was still under British mandate but, as the Nazis gained in strength and occupied one European country after another, Jewish settlers were arriving there in increasing numbers. Despite considerable Arab opposition, the settlers built strong communities, joining in the efforts of the earlier pioneers. Nothing could stop this new Aliyah. If there was not enough land for planting, the settlers made new land by reclaiming dry areas and swamps. They fought drought and malaria. No hardship or political problem could stop them.

Dr. Chaim Weizmann, who had guided the Zionist organization for many years, was now at its head. He had able helpers in many countries. In America: Louis D. Brandeis, Justice of the United States Supreme Court; Julian Mack, a collaborator of Judge Brandeis; Louis Lipsky, one of the most active leaders of the Zionist Organization of America; Rabbi Stephen S. Wise, one of the most dynamic figures in American Jewish life; Felix Frankfurter, who was later to become a Justice of the United States Supreme Court; Rabbi Abba Hillel Silver, eloquent preacher and author, who was yet to play a decisive role in the subsequent establishment of the State of Israel; and others worked to help finance and increase the growth of communities in Palestine.

Also in America, Zionist women, led by Miss Henrietta Szold (1860-1941) had founded Hadassah in 1912. Under the leadership of Miss Szold and her successors Hadassah has founded hospitals and health and welfare services in Palestine. These services were open to all the people of the country, Jews, Arabs, Moslems and Christians alike.

Also under the leadership of Miss Szold, Youth Aliyah was organized to rescue as many children and adolescents as possible from Nazi Europe. Once the youngsters had arrived in Palestine, Youth Aliyah would place them into homes and plan their further schooling and vocational training. All this work was done with the help of funds raised in America and other free countries. Youth Aliyah saved thousands of children. Their parents, naturally enough, found it difficult to part with

Henrietta Szold

Hadassah Hospital in Jerusalem.

them. Many fathers and mothers did not succeed in leaving Germany, but they were glad that at least their children would be safe.

On the outskirts of the old city of Jerusalem, in the section where once Montefiore had built model houses, a new Jerusalem was growing. In 1925 the Hebrew University had been founded. Many eminent philosophers, scientists, Hebrew scholars and educators now pursued their work at this university. New industrial centers were founded. The all-Jewish settlement of Tel Aviv which had been founded in 1909 as a garden suburb of Jaffa, had grown into a beautiful modern city.

THE ARAB PROBLEM

But the progress which the Jewish settlers had made in Palestine was viewed with great anxiety by the rich Arab landowners. They feared that the fellahin—the Arab peasants—would become discontented. The fellahin lived much as their forefathers had lived thousands of years ago. Uneducated, and possessing only primitive farm tools,

Amin-Al-Husseini, the Grand Mufti of Jerusalem, meets with Hitler during World War II.

they worked hard for a mere pittance. In the cities Arab propagandists stirred up hatred against the Jews, and anti-Jewish riots broke out repeatedly.

In 1936 the Grand Mufti of Jerusalem, head of the Arab population, endorsed the Arab terrorists. The British tried to arrest him but he managed to escape to the state of Lebanon. The situation became constantly more dangerous. A British commission of inquiry proposed that Palestine should be divided into an Arab section and a Jewish section, each independent and separate. This proposal was not acceptable to the Arabs and their anti-Jewish riots increased. But the *Yishuv*—the Jewish community of Palestine—kept right on growing.

Convention which founded the Histadrut, Haifa, Dec. 1920.

THE YISHUV GROWS

In the late 1930's the Yishuv was already composed of Jews from many lands and many walks of life. In it were Jews from Iraq, from Yemen and North Africa, who were very similar in culture to their Arab neighbors. Other Jews had come from eastern Europe. Still others had moved to Palestine, and a few from the United States. Now in the years of Hitler's Nazi empire, most of the new immigration was from Germany, Austria and Czechoslovakia.

As the Nazi terror spread, Jews came to Palestine from Poland, from Rumania and Yugoslavia. A few even managed to leave Russia, despite the danger of being arrested or killed at the guarded borders.

"The Young and the Old." Israeli farmers harvesting watermelons.

increased. The English, unwilling to antagonize the Arabs, could not deal with this friction between Arabs and Jews. The Jews secretly organized their own defense groups of men and women of the Yishuv, farmers and workers, city and country folk. These citizens trained to defend themselves against Arab terrorists who preyed upon isolated settlements. This group of defenders took the name of Haganah ("defense").

In 1939 the British published a document known as "The White Paper" concerning the new administrative policy in their Mandate of Palestine. The British declared their intention to set up after ten years a mixed Jewish-Arab state in Palestine. According to the new rulings, however, Jewish immigration to Palestine would in the meantime be severely restricted. In this, the British were motivated by a desire to win badly needed Arab support in the war which was threatening England. The British knew that Hitler had sent agents to Palestine who were also trying to win the support of the Arabs. The British therefore were faced with the necessity of winning the Arabs away from the Germans. As the British saw it, the only way this could be done was by appeasing the Arabs and restricting Jewish immigration into Palestine. The British had no fear of losing Jewish support, for they knew very well that the Jews would side with Britain in any conflict with Nazi Germany.

The members of this varied community learned to live together and to know each other. They learned to speak Hebrew, which had become a modern language used in everyday life by the Jews in Palestine. Poets and writers composed literary works in Hebrew. Hebrew was the language of the scientists in the university, of the farmers and workers. The newspapers of the Yishuv were published in Hebrew and the *Histadrut,* Palestine's labor federation and the *Vaad Leumi,* the governing body of Palestine's Jewish community conducted their affairs in Hebrew.

In the land which had been the scene of Biblical history, a new Jewish community was building a new life using the language of the Bible in everyday speech for the first time in two thousand years.

THE BRITISH WHITE PAPER

With the growth of the Yishuv, Arab resistance

Arab rioters attacking Jewish shops in Jerusalem.

GLOSSARY OF HEBREW TERMINOLOGY AND NAMES

Israel	Yisrah-eyl	יִשְׂרָאֵל
Kibbutzim	Keebootseem	קִבּוּצִים
Youth Aliyah	Ahleeyaht Ha-noh-ahr	עֲלִיַת הַנּוֹעַר
Hebrew University	Ha-oonee-vehrseetah Ha-ivreet	הָאוּנִיבֶרְסִיטָה הָעִבְרִית
Tel Aviv	Teyl Ahveev	תֵּל אָבִיב
Jaffa	Yahfoh	יָפוֹ
Lebanon	Lvahnohn	לְבָנוֹן
Yishuv	Yeeshoov	יִשׁוּב
Histadrut	Histahdroot	הִסְתַּדְרוּת
Vaad Leumi	Vah-ahd Le-oomee	וַעַד לְאוּמִי
Haganah	Hahgahnah	הַגֲנָה

THE SECOND WORLD WAR

THE DESPERATE SEARCH FOR REFUGE

The publication of the White Paper of 1939 brought consternation to Jews everywhere. What would happen now to the Jews in the lands under Nazi domination? Where would they go? Restrictions on immigration were increasing in every country; even the gates of America were closing, for so many Jews had emigrated there that many of the quotas such as German, Polish, Czech and Austrian were filled.

The Jews of Europe now went wherever they could. However, it became increasingly difficult to find a place of refuge. Some fled to South America, to Africa and even to war-torn Shanghai. But even so, only a few could make their escape at this late date. President Franklin D. Roosevelt called an international conference at Evian-les-Bains, France, to discuss ways and means of saving European Jewry. The conference was a dismal failure. The results of other endeavors were equally meager.

ALIYAH BET

In these dark days a desperate new kind of Aliyah had begun. Operating illegally and in secret, it was called Aliyah Bet—Immigration Wave B. In Palestine and in Hitler's lands, desperate men and women of the Haganah secretly began to buy boats. These were usually old, dilapidated vessels —no other kind could be had under the circum-

stances. An "underground railroad" was organized so that Jews could reach these boats and sail for the Land of Israel. Many such groups were organ-

```
100/1/GS                                    C.I.D.

     SECRET
                                      28th March, 1939.

     C.I.D. Haifa.

     C.I.D. Jaffa

     Port and Marine, Haifa.

     Subject:- Illegal Immigration.

          It is learned on good authority
     that the Greek steamer "COLORADO", sailing
     under the Panama flag, is actively engaged in
     transporting Jewish refugees from Susak to the
     island of Solta where they are transferred to
     smaller ships bound, it is believed, for
     Palestine.
          Early this month the "COLORADO"
     transhipped 350 Jewish refugees from Germany
     to the ss. "ATRATTI" which left for an unknown
     destination.
          It is now understood that the
     "COLORADO" has returned to Susak, where it is
     to embark a considerable further number of Jewish
     refugees from Germany.

                         (Sgd.) W.G. Buttolph.
                              D.I.G.C.I.D.
```

A secret message by a British spy, warns of the activities of two "underground" ships—the Colorado and the Atrato. In 1939, these two so called "illegal" ships crammed with desperate Polish Jewish refugees escaping Hitler's holocaust were intercepted by British warships and turned back.

ized—but only a few ships succeeded in reaching Palestine and landing there. Landings had to be made under cover of the fog of night. In spite of all the precautions, many boats were intercepted by the British guards, and the passengers were forced to turn back to Europe. Some of these ships never completed their journeys, but floundered and sank and their passengers went down with them into the Mediterranean Sea.

THE OUTBREAK OF WAR

Then came September 1, 1939—and the Second World War.

The gates closed on Nazi-occupied lands, trapping millions of Jews. The darkest days for the Jews of Europe—and the blackest hours in Jewish history—were yet to come. Before the war ended, the Nazis would stoop to unthinkable acts. Scorning human dignity and decency, they were to sink to depths of cruelty and depravity that would shock and sicken all mankind. Their concentration camps were to become crematories for innocent victims of their mad desire for world dominion.

In 1939, to the great astonishment of the world, the Nazis made an alliance with Communist Russia, the land they had reviled in all their speeches. For years, Communism and its adherents had been brutally suppressed in Germany. Now Communist Russia and Nazi Germany marched into Polish territory. The Second World War had begun.

In the first years of the war, Hitler managed to conquer all the countries of Europe except Switzerland and Sweden and Spain. Switzerland and Sweden had maintained a position of strict neutrality. Spain was officially neutral, too, but actually was a silent ally of Nazi Germany, for it was ruled by the Fascist leader General Franco, who had come to power in a bloody civil war.

HITLER CONQUERS EUROPE

Early in 1940 Denmark and Norway were invaded and also became part of the Nazi empire. Soon after, Hitler's army marched into neutral Holland, Belgium and from there into France. The Nazis took all these countries by sur-

Jews being rounded up for shipment to the death camps.

prise, swiftly and completely. A sorrowing French nation saw Hitler's soldiers march into their beloved Paris, thus bringing all western Europe under the ruthless Nazi boot.

The Nazis shifted the peoples of Europe around to accommodate their own plans and needs. Frenchmen were deported to Poland as slave laborers; Poles were shipped off to Holland. Like the cruel conquerors of old, the Nazis tried to uproot and utterly subdue their subjects, for according to "der Fuehrer," as Adolph Hitler was now titled, these peoples were all inferior to the "master race." In the few short years of Hitler's rise to power, the men who followed him had forsaken Biblical teachings of centuries and turned their backs on the ideals of mercy and justice.

Under the leadership of Winston Churchill, England doggedly withstood the Nazi efforts to invade her. Even the terrible Nazi air raids did not break the English spirit. England became the gathering place for the various resistance groups of Europe which had organized to fight the Nazis by sabotage and in every way possible.

In 1941 the Nazis did an about-face and turned on the Russians who now became one of the allies of the Western powers. But the Germans had other allies—Italy in Europe and Japan in the Far East. In 1941 Japanese planes bombed the United States' naval fleet at Pearl Harbor in Hawaii in a surprise attack and plunged the United States into the war. American supplies and men began to stream across the ocean. For almost six years nearly

Distributing Yellow Star of David arm bands which, under the Nazi regime, Jews were forced to wear.

all the world was at war. Millions of lives were lost before the conflict came to an end with the defeat of Germany in May 1945 and the surrender of Japan that summer.

THE AFTERMATH

The war left Europe in ruins. The Nazis, who had believed themselves the master race, left behind them a memory that still horrifies men. They are remembered not as a party which led Germany to glory, but as criminals who brought monstrous shame and disgrace upon their fatherland. The record of their crimes stands out on the pages of history in letters of fire and blood—the blood of millions of innocent men, women and children whose lives were snuffed out with systematic cruelty such as the modern world had never seen before.

As soon as the war had begun, the Nazis gathered together the Jews of Germany and the Jews of all the conquered lands, and herded them into ghettos. From there they were deported by the carload to Nazi concentration camps. Six million Jews lost their lives in Hitler's factories of death. The

holocaust is remembered each year on the *Yom Hashoah,* so that future generations should not forget this most horrible manifestation of man's inhumanity to man.

PALESTINE FIGHTS

During World War II the men and women of the Yishuv gave valiant aid to Britain in the fight against Nazi tyranny. At the outset, David Ben-Gurion had spoken for all the Jews of Palestine: "We will fight the war as if there were no White Paper," he said, "and we will fight the White Paper as if there were no war."

Very few Palestinian Arabs fought in the war, but many Jewish settlers volunteered for active service in the British Army. The Nazis, anxious for a foothold in the Middle East, flooded the area with their agents and their propaganda. They found many sympathizers among extreme Arab nationalists who hated the British and who were also opposed to Jewish immigration to Palestine.

Eventually, the British permitted the Jewish soldiers of Palestine to organize their own Jewish Brigade and to fight under their own blue and white flag, the Star of David.

The men and women of the Haganah found another heroic way to fight in order to help the Jews who were trapped in Nazi dominated lands. They accepted dangerous assignments which were to be carried out behind enemy lines. These self-sacrficing men and women were the unsung heroes of the Second World War. They volunteered for

Soldiers of the Jewish Brigade in Italy lend a helping hand to the local populace.

Enzo (Haim) Sereni

special intelligence work and were dropped by parachute into Nazi-occupied territory. Their task was to establish contact with the men and women of the local resistance movements, the fighters who sabotaged the Nazis in factories, fought them in guerilla bands in the mountains and villages, on country roads and city streets. Even though all Europe seemed powerless in the Nazi stranglehold, there were still small, fearless groups who fought constantly, secretly using the radio and other means to keep in contact with the Allies. These courageous underground fighters, who faced torture and death if they were caught, prepared the way for the Nazi defeat.

The Jewish fighters from Palestine who were parachuted behind the enemy lines were part of the British intelligence service. They performed many missions for the Allies, as well as special missions for the Jewish people. They returned to their native lands and, under false names and with false passports, tried to organize underground railways to help Jews escape from the Nazi death camps. Many of these heroic fighters lost their lives. Many more were imprisoned and executed as spies. Among them was Enzo Sereni, a young Italian, whose father had been a physician to the royal family of Italy. Sereni, who had gone to Palestine to live as a pioneer, had worked for the Haganah for years. In an effort to save imprisoned Jews, Sereni returned to his native land. He never returned from his mission. He was killed by the Germans who had by that time occupied Fascist Italy.

Among the best remembered of the Jewish heroes who operated in secret against the Nazis was Hannah Szenesh. She had left a comfortable home and her parents to live the life of a pioneer in Palestine. Miss Szenesh was parachuted into Yugoslavia, where she made contact with the Resistance and aided them in their underground operations. After this mission was accomplished she made her way to Hungary to bring help to the Jews. There she was captured and put to death by the Nazis. Hannah Szenesh was a girl with a strong and dedicated spirit. Before she died she wrote a poem "Blessed is the Match" in which she compares herself to a fiery match, which kindles a flame and is itself consumed in performing this task.

THE HEROES OF THE CONCENTRATION CAMPS AND GHETTOS

There was still another kind of heroism during those trying times—the quiet heroism of the Jews in the German concentration camps. Many of these martyrs preserved a spirit of hope and compassion despite the bestial treatment which they received from the Nazis.

In their crisis, the Jews had elected spiritual leaders to guide them. In Germany, Rabbi Leo Baeck, a brilliant preacher, a leader of liberal Judaism had been the spiritual head of the Berlin Jewish community. Dr. Baeck, an old man of great courage and dignity, devoted himself entirely to the welfare of the Jewish community. He could have left the country, for he was offered many positions abroad, but chose to remain with the Jews of Germany. He was the head of the "Reichsvertretung" the council which represented the German Jews before the Nazi government. Under Dr. Baeck's guidance many brave men and women helped the Jewish community, giving them courage and hope during the dark days of Hitler's power. While synagogues

Dr. Leo Baeck, the heroic rabbi of the death camps.

concentration camps proclaimed their faith, recited their prayers and held fast to their belief in the God of justice and mercy. Many Hasidic rabbis and Talmudic scholars inspired the multitude of devout Jews to cling to their faith under the most unbearable circumstances. Some of the Jewish victims went to their deaths singing psalms and hymns. But there were others—like the heroes of the Warsaw ghetto—who died fighting every inch of the way.

The defense of the Warsaw ghetto is a story of heroism such as the world has rarely known. The ghetto of Warsaw, the capital of Poland, was a small area surrounded by newly-built walls, barbed wire and Nazi guards. In its cramped space lived 450,000 Jews whom the Nazis regarded as prisoners, ready to be slaughtered. They had a systematic plan to kill the whole population of the Warsaw ghetto. After that, the murder action began, wiping out one group in the ghetto after another.

and Jewish communal institutions were destroyed and Jews fled to other countries by the thousands, Dr. Baeck stayed behind. Eventually Dr. Baeck himself was sent to the concentration camp of Theresienstadt. Despite the intolerable conditions there, Dr. Baeck held religious services and encouraged others to do so. Classes were held and lectures were given. Thus, even in concentration camps, a community life of sorts was developed.

In the face of death, many Jews in the Polish

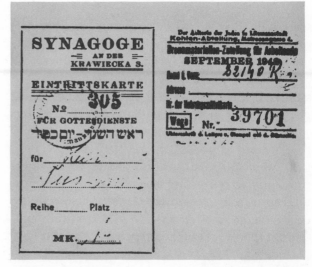

Admission card for the High Holiday services in the German ghetto in Lodz, Poland.

Nazis capturing Jewish combatants in the Warsaw ghetto.

But then, in 1944, something unexpected happened. These prisoners, trapped within their walls, had declared war on their conquerors. Arms had been smuggled to them from the Polish Resistance movement; the Jews had built barricades and underground bunkers. Every Jewish man, woman and child in the ghetto became a fighter in this life or death battle.

Nazis forcing Jews to dig their own grave.

From house to house, from street to street, the Nazis had to fight the Jews of the Warsaw ghetto. Through sewers and underground tunnels the fighters had established contact with the Polish Resistance. A handful of the ghetto fighters escaped by this route. Some of those who escaped joined the Resistance. A few others simply went underground and lived under false names until the war was over. But most of the heroes of the Warsaw ghetto died there, fighting to the end.

HOPE FOR A NEW AND BETTER WORLD

When the Nazis were finally defeated in May, 1945, and the Japanese in September of the same year, the victors were faced with a grave challenge. They tried to learn by the mistakes they had made after the previous World War. The problems of 1918, however, could hardly be compared with those of the new age. In this Second World War,

men all over the world had suffered, and all over the world civilians and soldiers alike had been killed.

Wherever there was life on the face of the globe, that life had been changed by the events of the Second World War. In the final hours of that war an awesome and terrifying new power had been set free—the power of the shattered atom. A new age had dawned for all mankind—an age that would challenge the most brilliant minds—and the most valiant spirits. Ironically enough, the man who had contributed the most toward unleashing the power of the atom was a gentle, peace-loving scientist— Dr. Albert Einstein (1879-1955), a German Jew who had fled Hitler's Germany and found a new home in the United states.

The Warsaw ghetto engulfed in flames.

GLOSSARY OF HEBREW TERMINOLOGY AND NAMES

Aliyah Bet	Ahleeyah Bet	עֲלִיָּה בֵּית
Yom Hashoah	Yohm Ha-shoh-ah	יוֹם הַשּׁוֹאָה
Star of David	Mahgeyn Dahveed	מָגֵן דָּוִד
Blessed is the Match	Ahshrey Hah-gahfroor	אַשְׁרֵי הַגַּפְרוּר
Warsaw Ghetto	Hah-getoh Behvahrshah	הַגֶּטוֹ בְּוַרְשָׁה

AMERICAN JEWRY TAKES THE LEAD
SWORDS INTO PLOWSHARES:

AMERICAN JEWRY TAKES THE LEAD

The Nazi holocaust left the five million Jews living in America as the largest and most important Jewish community in the world. Indeed, it has proved to be the most secure, the most affluent, and the most influential Jewish community ever to exist anywhere outside of Palestine.

Since its beginnings, American Jewry has shown itself concerned when brethren in other countries suffered oppression and wrong. Organizations for charity and relief, and for appeal to the sense of justice of the American people and government, grew and flourished during the twentieth century. The terrible needs brought on by Russian pogroms, revolution, world war and Nazism aroused the Jews of the western world to united protest, and to charitable giving unmatched by any other group in world history.

ORGANIZING FOR RESCUE

By 1914, when World War I began, differences between earlier and later arrivals to America, the so-called "German" and "Russian" Jews, were becoming less important. In their concern for

Anti-Nazi demonstration in New York City on May 10, 1933.

brethren in Europe, faced with the devastation of war and continued anti-Semitism, members of both groups joined to form the American Jewish Joint Distribution Committee.

The work of the J.D.C., or Joint, including finding homes for hundreds of thousands of refugees, providing medical aid in epidemic areas, caring for orphaned children, providing schooling in backward areas, and helping economic rehabilitation, has continued all over the world. In 1917 the

Cyrus Adler

Rabbi Meyer Berlin

Herbert H. Lehman

chairman by Paul Baerwald, and then by Edward Warburg. Men of religious rather than financial standing who were active included Reform Rabbi Jonah B. Wise and Orthodox rabbis Meyer Berlin, Moses Z. Margolies, Leo Jung and Aaron Teitelbaum.

THE AMERICAN JEWISH CONGRESS

Soon after World War I began, there was a strong movement among Jewish organizations and leading writers and educators for a democratically elected Jewish Congress, that would work for minority rights for Jews in Eastern Europe and for the fulfilment of Zionist aims.

amount contributed by American Jews for its operation was $10,000,000.

This responsibility taken upon itself by the comparatively wealthy American Jewish community has been led and supported by many outstanding Jews of differing interests and walks of life. Among its officers have been members of the American Jewish Committee such as Felix M. Warburg, Louis Marshall, Cyrus Adler, Jacob Schiff, Herbert and Arthur Lehman and Cyrus Sulzberger. Felix Warburg was succeeded as

A meeting in Philadelphia in 1916 brought together delegates from hundreds of smaller organizations. It stated as its aim "the attainment of full rights for Jews in all lands, for national autonomy rights wherever such are recognized, and for the furtherance of Jewish interests in Palestine."

Louis D. Brandeis, chairman of the organization committee, was appointed to the Supreme Court by President Woodrow Wilson that same year. When the American Jewish Congress, after much controversy, was actually convened in December of 1918, following the Armistice, Julian W. Mack was chosen president. Harry Friedenwald and Henrietta Szold, ardent Zionists, were among the vice-presidents. Jacob Schiff was treasurer.

Menahem Ussishkin

Different factions in American Jewry thus united to work for the relief and help of fellow Jews after the ravages of war.

The American Jewish Congress sent a delegation to Europe to join with representatives of other countries in demanding recognition of Jewish rights by the Peace Conference. The delegates were instructed also to ask for fulfilment of the Balfour Declaration. Representatives of the World Zionist Organization were Chaim Weizmann, Nahum Sokolow, and Menahem Ussishkin. With the tacit support of the Congress delegation, they urged the appointment of Great Britain as mandatory over Palestine, with the purpose of bringing about a Jewish state. The mandate was agreed to at the San Remo Conference.

In the Treaty of Versailles, minority rights for Jews and other groups in such countries as Poland, Lithuania, and Rumania, were guaranteed and placed under supervision of the League of Nations. Louis Marshall and others who had demanded these provisos were exultant. The promised reforms, however, did not come about.

The American Jewish Congress had been formed as a temporary emergency body. When it met in 1920, however, a group of delegates, of whom the strongest member was Rabbi Stephen S. Wise, remained and voted for its continuation. With Rabbi Wise as president from 1925 till his death in 1949, the Congress remained active in promoting Zionism; fighting anti-Semitism and Nazism; and working for Jewish needs and human rights.

ANTI-SEMITISM AT HOME

After World War I, anti-Semitism became more evident in the United States. The Ku Klux Klan, advocating "native, white Protestant supremacy," gained an estimated four to five million members. Politicians running for office all through the South, and even in Oregon, Indiana and Maine, won elections through Klan backing. Support of the Klan fell off to a large extent in the 1930's, but it did not die out.

A most deplorable attack on the Jews was carried on in Henry Ford's *Dearborn Independent,* which printed in the 1920's libelous material against the Jews based on the famous forgery telling of secret meetings of international Jewry plotting to dominate the world, called *The Protocols of the Elders of Zion.* In 1927 Ford, made to realize his error apologized to Louis Marshall, calling the Jews his "fellow men and brothers," and begging their forgiveness. The damage could not be completely retracted, however; and the *Protocols* and other vicious material have been reprinted since then by anti-Semites.

Social anti-Semitism, the refusal to admit Jews to country clubs, resort hotels, and "restricted" residential areas, was a well known phenomenon

Headline in Henry Ford's newspaper.

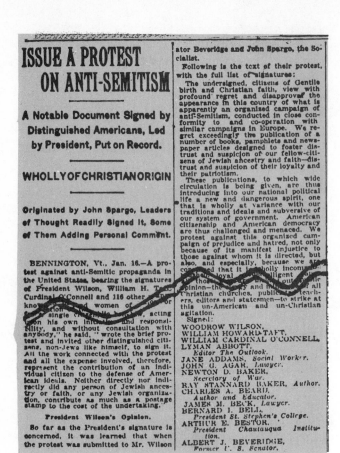

ISSUE A PROTEST ON ANTI-SEMITISM

A Notable Document Signed by Distinguished Americans, Led by President, Put on Record.

WHOLLY OF CHRISTIAN ORIGIN

Originated by John Spargo, Leaders of Thought Readily Signed It, Some of Them Adding Personal Comment.

BENNINGTON, Vt., Jan. 16.—A protest against anti-Semitic propaganda in the United States, bearing the signatures of President Wilson, William H. Taft, Cardinal O'Connell and 116 other well known men and women of the nation...

Article in the New York Times, January 16, 1921, records a protest against anti-Semitism signed by hundreds of distingushed Amercan leaders and the then President of the United States, Woodrow Wilson.

in the 1920's and 30's. More serious was the semi-secret "quota" system, whereby only a certain percentage of Jewish students were admitted to many colleges and most professional schools, no matter how high the qualifications of Jewish candidates might be. Jews knew that they could not expect to be hired in certain jobs. Before World War II there were few Jewish engineers or college professors, to name just two fields.

The American Jewish Congress, the American Jewish Committee, the Anti-Defamation League of B'nai B'rith, and the Jewish Labor Committee all worked to fight false accusations and to protect the rights of fellow Jews. They early lent their efforts to supporting the cause of civil rights for all minorities.

THE ZIONIST CAUSE

Partly as a hope for saving the persecuted Jews of Europe, and partly as a natural fulfilment of the age-old dream of return and rebuilding, Zionism became a cause which attracted more and more American Jews.

Before World War I, there were about twenty thousand active Zionists in the United States. These included members of the Socialist Zionist Party, *Poale Zion,* which had been founded in 1903; the Orthodox Mizrachi party led by Meyer Berlin; women members of the newly formed Hadassah; the fraternal order, Sons of Zion; and the youth group, Young Judea. The last three groups were under General Zionist auspices. They were affiliated with the Federation of American Zionists, which in 1917 took the name Zionist Organization of America.

It was the General Zionist group, whose main concern was education and political action, that was largest in number and put forth the spokesmen who were to appeal to world powers in favor of the formation of a Jewish state. The dynamic oratory of Louis Lipsky, Stephen S. Wise, and Abba Hillel Silver moved thousands of Jews at national Zionist Conventions, and helped persuade the general

Rabbi Stephen S. Wise and Louis Lipsky.

American public of the need for rescue and the justice of the Zionist cause.

The number of active Zionists in the United States rose by 1930 to 150,000. The growth of the Nazi movement in Europe aroused more American Jews to a realization of their Jewish identity and a desire to help their brethren. By 1940 there were 400,000 enrolled Zionists, and at the highest point, following World War II, there may have been twice that many.

During the actual deliberations in the United Nations on the "Partition Plan" for Palestine in 1947, the almost unanimous voice of the Jews of America, and particularly the spokesmanship of Abba Hillel Silver, had some effect. The vote of the American Jewish Conference four years earlier showed that most American Jews, favored a Jewish state. The UN decision of November 29, 1947, establishing Jewish and Arab states in the mandated territory of Palestine, was hailed with joy by American and world Jewry.

American public opinion, the resolutions of the U.S. Congress, and the favorable attitudes of American Presidents all carried weight in persuading the nations of the world to vote for a Jewish State.

AMERICAN JEWRY UNITES TO GIVE

Great sums were donated by American Jewry all through the twentieth century for the relief and rescue of suffering co-religionists. No other group has ever organized itself for voluntary taxation for the help of needy brethren to the same extent.

In 1925 the two funds for Palestine, the *Keren Hayesod* or Foundation Fund started by Judge Brandeis, and the Jewish National Fund for purchase of land and planting of trees, joined forces and became the United Palestine Appeal. When war broke out in 1939, and the need for rescuing the Jews of Europe became desperate, the Joint Distribution Committee combined its efforts with the U.P.A. Thus was formed the United Jewish Appeal, whose purpose has been to help Jews in all countries of the world, and particularly to aid them in reaching Palestine and, after its founding, the State of Israel.

The UJA made a new life in the land of their forefathers possible for them. Here you see new arrivals, young and old, being helped as they disembark at Haifa.

Finally, in almost all cities, the U.J.A., the Joint Defense Appeal, and the local causes (such as hospitals, Jewish centers, homes for the aged and educational institutions), combined their efforts so that there was one major fund drive for the entire community each year.

In giving to welfare and charity funds, the Jews of America have set an example for all other groups. In the first twenty years after World War II, a billion and a half dollars were donated to the United Jewish Appeal. This generosity has not stopped with Jewish causes, for Jews have been among the largest supporters of all types of welfare, educational and cultural projects.

JEWS IN AMERICAN SOCIETY

The Jew as American citizen has seen many changes. Anti-Semitism after World War II, when the terrible results of Nazism were made known, became an underground or fringe activity, and almost disappeared in many areas of life. There

On May 20, 1946 the Marine Flasher arrived in the United States. This was the first ship carrying displaced people to America.

was a dramatic improvement in publicly expressed attitudes towards the Jews. Quotas for Jews in universities and restrictions against Jews in certain jobs have largely ceased. Young people growing up in America today find it hard to believe that their parents met prejudice and had to fight discrimination.

Jews play a prominent role in American art, literature and general culture, as patrons and as creative writers, artists and musicians. They have long contributed to science and medicine, and are giving leadership increasingly in education, industry and government.

OTHER JEWISH COMMUNITIES

Since the State of Israel became a reality in 1948, American Jewry has continued to feel a close kinship with the now two million Jews of that land. They show their interest through membership in organizations such as Hadassah; through contributions to the United Jewish Appeal, which helps new settlers and educates them for citizenship; and through purchase of bonds and other investments for industrial development.

American Jews in increasing numbers are studying Hebrew and Israeli culture, visiting the country, and in many cases spending time in study or service in Israel.

Of the other Jewish communities in the world, the largest is that of three million Jews under Soviet rule. Though identified on their passports

as "Hebrews," they are not permitted to have schools for teaching Hebrew or Jewish tradition to their children. They may not belong to religious or Zionist organizations. Whereas other religious faiths, despite the anti-religious stand of the government, are allowed to exist, there has been a seeming effort to wipe out completely the Jewish knowledge and loyalties, the spiritual heritage of the Jews of the Soviet Union. Few synagogues remain, and religious supplies are unavailable. Protests by American Jews in the 1960's attracted the attention of the world to this situation.

The number of Jews in most other countries of Europe since the Nazi catastrophe has been small. There are, however, half a million in France, augmented by Algerian Jewry who fled when their homes came under Arab rule; and nearly that number in England. South Africa has an active community which has close ties with Israel.

Among the countries of South America, Argentina has the largest Jewish population. Lacking sufficient religious leadership, the communities of South America look to the United States and Israel to provide them with rabbis and teachers.

JUDAISM IN AMERICA

In the early part of the century, many children of immigrants had felt that they ought to stop being distinctively Jewish in order to become "like

Secretary General Trygve Lie of the United Nations (left) checks the vote of the General Assembly delegates on the Palestine Partition question on November 29, 1947. Dr. Oswald Aranha of Brazil, president of the Assembly, awaits their verdict on the crucial vote which was 33 to 13 to set up independent Jewish and Arab states in Palestine. From the Zionist Archives.

This is the nation's first "traveling synagogue." It is sponsored by the North Carolina Association of Jewish Men. Inside the bus are an Ark, Torah, library and other ceremonial objects.

other Americans." It was soon realized, however, that America was made up of many different groups, all of them immigrants, and that each in preserving the best elements of its own heritage might add variety and richness to American life.

Judaism has every opportunity to flourish in America today. Though the Jews are few in number, being only three per cent of the population, Judaism is regarded as one of the three great faiths of the nation.

Interest in Jewish culture and the solutions Judaism can offer to modern problems continues to grow. Jewish education for children and adults has vastly improved. It is no longer felt that the three-thousand-year history and tradition of Judaism can be taught in two hours weekly for a few years.

More intensive and better teaching in religious schools has been extended to include the high school grades.

An increasing percentage of young students are gaining a solid foundation in Jewish learning by attending bi-cultural day schools (Yeshivot), where equal attention is paid to general and Hebraic studies.

In the leading universities of the country, Jewish studies, language, history and philosophy are part of the general curriculum.

Organized into Orthodox, Conservative and Reform movements, the Jews of America continue to unite for purposes of education, social action, and help to the needy.

The Jews of America enjoy freedom, good fortune, and the respect of their neighbors. By learning and practicing Jewish tradition, and by living according to Jewish ideals of justice and love of fellow man, they can begin to write a glorious chapter in the history of their people.

Interior of the Touro Synagogue, Newport, R. I., showing the southwest corner. The colonial architecture blends with the style of Sephardic synagogues in this house of worship which is now a U. S. National Shrine.

Medal issued on the 250th anniversary of the Jewish settlement in America.

GLOSSARY OF HEBREW TERMINOLOGY AND NAMES

Kehillah	K'heelah	קְהִלָּה
Zionism	Tseeyohnoot	צִיּוֹנוּת
Mizrachi	Mizraḥee	מִזְרָחִי
Poale Zion	Poh-ahley Tseeyohn	פּוֹעֲלֵי צִיּוֹן
Hadassah	Hah-dah-sah	הֲדַסָּה

Chapter XL

THE PROMISED LAND

THE DISPLACED PERSONS

In the lands which Hitler's armies had occupied during the war, entire populations had been uprooted. Thousands of people had been transported by the Nazis as prisoners or slave laborers to places distant from their homes. In the liberated concentration camps there were hundreds of thousands who had no homes, families or source of livelihood to which to return. These people were called Displaced Persons or, for short, DP's.

The problem of the Jewish displaced persons was particularly acute. Not many Jews had survived the Nazi death camps. Those who had managed to stay alive no longer had homes or relatives. Many of these survivors wanted to go to Palestine.

ILLEGAL IMMIGRATION TO PALESTINE

But the British White Paper of 1939 was still in effect, a pitiless barrier to further Jewish immigration.

The Haganah, the organization which had aided illegal immigration during the war in spite of the White Paper, again went into action. "Underground railroads" were again organized. The survivors of Hitler's death camps, waiting in detention centers until their problems could be solved, had cause for new hope.

Once again ships were brought and people smuggled across the seas to Palestine. Again, Haganah assumed the perilous task of landing illegal immigrants in secret, under cover of night. Often the passengers, young and old, many of them scarred by years of prison life, had to wade through a stormy surf or row in small boats to elude the British guards.

The Irgun Zvai Leumi, hebrew for National Military Organization, a Palestinian underground movement founded in 1937 by members of the Betar youth organization, and the Zionist-Revisionist movement, was also very active in the organization and success of the "illegal" immigration of Jewish displaced persons.

The British showed little sympathy for the plight of the Jews. Their concern was for good relations with the Arab nations and no trouble in the Middle East. Because of the heavy British guard very few of the Haganah ships succeeded in bringing their illegal passengers to Palestine. Most of the ships were intercepted by British authorities. The passengers were arrested and sent to internment camps especially set up for them on the island of Cyprus. This was done despite the fact that these Jewish immigrants would never have been a burden to the British in Palestine. As always, the Jewish community itself was ready to take care of them. With funds collected by the Zionist Organi-

An escape tunnel in the detention camp at Cyprus.

zation all over the world, these homeless Jews could have been settled on the land. They were turned back, but their spirits were not broken. Now they waited in Cyprus, sure that the moment would come when they would be able to ascend to the Homeland.

THE S.S. "EXODUS"

In 1947 the British policy toward the Jews in Palestine became even more harsh. In order to set an example, they sent back to Germany the S.S. "Exodus," a Haganah boat which had set sail for Palestine with a cargo of illegal immigrants, men, women and children who had survived the Nazi

"The Exodus." A ship filled with immigrants seeking to enter Palestine "illegally."

death camps. These refugees had risked their lives to come to Palestine. Now they were sent back to Germany, where there was no room for them except in the Displaced Persons camps where for all they knew, they might have lived on for years without hope, waiting for a solution to the problem of their homelessness.

The fate of the "Exodus" stirred the Jews of Palestine to open rebellion. New groups formed and resorted to acts of sabotage against the British who seemed willing to appease the hostile Arabs at the expense of the Jews.

The protest against this closed-door policy of the British now became a matter of open discussion. Britain being unable to find a solution for the

Jewish internees on Cyprus protesting their exclusion from Palestine.

"Palestine problem," the United Nations took up the question. In 1947 a new Committee of Inquiry went to Palestine, this time under the auspices of the United Nations. The committee returned with a proposal to partition Palestine into two separate states—one Arab and one Jewish. In this way, the committee believed, peace would be established and the new Jewish State would deal with the problem of Jewish immigration as it saw fit.

THE STATE OF ISRAEL IS BORN

Despite Arab protest, the United Nations on November 29, 1947, passed a resolution in favor of partition. Jews everywhere rejoiced. Although the plan gave the Jews only part of Palestine, the

THE PALESTINE POST

JERUSALEM
SUNDAY, MAY 16, 1948

PRICE: 25 MILS
VOL. XXIII. No. 6714

STATE OF ISRAEL IS BORN

The first independent Jewish State in 19 centuries was born in Tel Aviv as the British Mandate over Palestine came to an end at midnight on Friday, and it was immediately subjected to the test of fire. As "Medinat Yisrael" (State of Israel) was proclaimed, the battle for Jerusalem raged, with most of the city falling to the Jews. At the same time, President Truman announced that the United States would accord recognition to the new State. A few hours later, Palestine was invaded by Moslem armies from the south, east and north, and Tel Aviv was raided from the air. On Friday the United Nations Special Assembly adjourned after adopting a resolution to appoint a mediator but without taking any action on the Partition Resolution of November 29.

Yesterday the battle for the Jerusalem-Tel Aviv road was still under way, and two Arab villages were taken. In the north, Acre town was captured, and the Jewish Army consolidated its positions in Western Galilee.

Most Crowded Hours in Palestine's History

Between Thursday night and this morning Palestine went through what by all standards must be among the most crowded hours in its history.

For the Jewish population there was the anguish over the fate of the few hundred Haganah men and women in the Kfar Etzion bloc of settlements near Hebron. Their surrender to a fully equipped superior foreign force desperately in need of a victory was a foregone conclusion. What could not be known, with no communications since Thursday morning, was whether and to what extent the Red Cross and the Truce Consuls would secure civilised conditions for prisoners and wounded, and proper respect for the dead. Doubts on some of these anxious questions have now been resolved.

On Friday afternoon, from Tel Aviv, came the expected announcement of the Jewish State, and its official naming at birth, "Medinat Yisrael"—State of Israel, with the swearing in of the first Council of Government. The proclamation of the State was made at midnight, coinciding with the sailing from Haifa of Britain's last High Commissioner. Within the hour, President Truman announced in Washington that the Government of the United States had decided to give de facto recognition to the Jewish State, with

JEWS TAKE OVER SECURITY ZONES

The Battle for Jerusalem, which began when the British forces withdrew on Friday morning, continued all day Friday and yesterday. The crackle of small-arms fire and explosions of mortar shells were still being heard in the early hours of this morning as the battle entered its third day.

Repeated efforts on Friday evening and again on Saturday by the U.N. Truce Commission to bring about a "cease fire" were brought to nought when the Arab representatives failed to agree within the specified time limit.

On Friday morning, Jewish forces entered the Russian Compound and Zone C to reoccupy the buildings requisitioned from Jews last year. This operation was almost bloodless, but beyond the western edge of Zone C, Arabs engaged the Jews in Jaffa Road. The Arabs were forced back and the Barclays Bank area was taken.

In other parts of the city fighting flared up. Jews overran one after another the areas evacuated by the British. By last night, the quarters and North-Eastern Galilee.

The Security Council met yesterday in a special session to consider action on the invasion of Palestine by member states of the U.N.

In the afternoon, Jerusalem was subjected to shelling from the northwest.

Haganah forces throughout the country continued mopping up, and Jewish sources claimed most of Western Galilee safe against attack. Naharayim, near Jisr el Majamie, inside Trans-Jordan.

Egyptian Air Force Spitfires Bomb Tel Aviv; One Shot Down

Kol Israel, the Tel Aviv broadcasting station, reported at 2 o'clock yesterday afternoon that Tel Aviv had been bombed three times in the previous evening and morning, and that one plane had been shot down and its Egyptian pilot taken prisoner.

In the first raid, four planes attacked from a height of 300 feet. Two dropped bombs, while the others strafed the city. Little damage was caused. In the second attack two hours later, the airport to the north of the city was bombed, and an Air France plane parked there was damaged. The third raid was launched shortly before midday, but the planes were driven off without causing any damage.

Two settlements in the Negev had also been attacked from the air, the radio reported

A country-wide blackout was ordered by Air Raid Precaution Headquarters in Tel Aviv.

Mr. David Ben Gurion, the Prime Minister, broadcast to the people of America yesterday morning. As he spoke, Egyptian planes were bombing the city.

In the north, the settlements of Ein Gev and Shaar Hagolan and Dan had been shelled, but no further details were available.

Kalandia airfield was taken by the Jewish army on Friday morning, shortly after the High Commissioner had left; there by plane for Haifa. The field was evacuated, together with the neighbouring settlement of Ataroth, on Friday night. The settlement itself was burnt by Arabs yesterday.

2 Columns Cross Southern Border

By WALTER COLLINS
U.P. Correspondent

CAIRO, Saturday. — A com-

Etzion Settlers Taken P.O.W.

Fighting in the Kfar Etzion bloc continued throughout Friday, after Kfar Etzion itself

U.S. RECOGNIZES JEWISH STATE

WASHINGTON, Saturday. —Ten minutes after the termination of the British Mandate on Friday, the White House released a formal statement by President Truman that the U.S. Government intended to recognize the Provisional Jewish Government as the de facto authority representing the Jewish State.

The U.S. is also considering lifting the arms embargo but it is not known whether to Palestine only or the entire Middle East, and the establishment of diplomatic relations with the Jewish Provisional Government.

The White House press secretary, Mr. Charles Ross, told correspondents today that reaction so far to the recognition had been overwhelmingly favourable. He said this step had been discussed with Mr. Marshall and Mr. Lovett before action was taken, and it had their complete support.

Mr. Ross said that the President had decided several days ago to grant American recognition

Proclamation by Head Of Government

The creation of "Medinat Yisrael", the State of Israel, was proclaimed at midnight on Friday by Mr. David Ben Gurion, until then Chairman of the Jewish Agency Executive and now head of the State's Provisional Council of Government.

The first act of the Council of Government, as announced by its head, was to abolish all legislation of the 1939 White Paper of the late Mandatory Power, particularly the Ordinances and Orders relating to immigration and land transfer.

In the declaration of independence, Mr. Ben Gurion called on the Arabs of Palestine to restore peace, assuring them full civic rights and full representation in all governmental organs of the State.

Mr. Ben Gurion prefaced his proclamation with a review of the historic connection of the Jewish people with the Land of Israel and of their efforts to return, which never ceased throughout the generations of their dispersal, until the Nazi holocaust proved anew the urgency of the need for a Jewish State.

The Balfour Declaration of 1917, confirmed by the League of Nations, had given explicit international recognition to the right of the Jewish

Special Assembly Adjourns

FLUSHING MEADOWS, Saturday. — The Special U.N. Assembly, called four weeks ago to discuss the U.S. proposal

A banner headline announces the birth of the new State. Although the State of Israel was proclaimed on Friday afternoon, May 14, 1948, the paper is dated Sunday, May 16, because no papers in Israel are printed on the Jewish Sabbath.

Jewish State of which generations had dreamed had become a reality. In Palestine the Jews danced in the streets in jubilation.

On May 14, 1948, the British gave up their mandate and left Palestine. The Jews at once set up a provisional government headed by David Ben-Gurion, and proclaimed the establishment of a state which was given the name of "Israel."

ISRAEL'S WAR OF INDEPENDENCE

The Arabs, however, were bitterly opposed to the partition plan. The Arab countries refused to recognize the decision of the United Nations. Lebanon, Syria, Saudi Arabia, Jordan, Iraq and Egypt united in a war against the new little State of Israel. The Jews fought valiantly. Under the Haganah, volunteers were trained and men, women and children fought with all their strength and

Abba Eban and Moshe Sharrett, members of the Israeli delegation, help hoist the flag of Israel at the United Nations, May 12, 1949.

Chaim Weizmann, the first President of Israel, addressing the first Knesset of Israel.

State of Israel held elections and formed its first government. Dr. Chaim Weizmann, the revered Zionist leader, became the first President of the new state and David Ben-Gurion its first Prime Minister. In May, 1949, Israel was admitted to the United Nations.

To many who witnessed the birth of Israel it seemed like a miracle. After pain and hopelessness, after the death of six million martyred Jews, the day of liberation had dawned for the survivors.

The State of Israel has its problems. It is a small country and many of the holy places of Jewish tradition are in Arab territory. Hebron, with the cave of Machpelah and the graves of the Patriarchs, is outside Israel. Even the Wailing Wall area where once the Temple stood, and the Old City of Jerusalem, are not in Israeli territory.

But Israel is an energetic young country. Cities and villages are growing. Jews from many walks of life, from many cultures and many different nations, are learning to live together. Some of them are Orthodox, devoted to the old, Talmudic tradition. Others have no religious affiliations but are dedicated to the building and development of the new Homeland. The doors of the new land are open to any Jew who wishes to come and live in the State of Israel. Although the land is small and sacrifices must be made to accommodate the immigrants, all are welcome.

Many Jews who once were displaced persons in Europe are now proud citizens of the State of Israel. Many have come from Arab lands. Almost

courage.

The Jews were victorious and drove out the invaders. Like their forefathers in olden times, the Israelis fought fiercely and victoriously for their freedom and for the right to their land. People who only a few years before had been slaves in the concentration camps now became the heroes of the War of Independence, fighting side by side with the older settlers. The Israeli soldiers drove off the invaders and moved on, carrying the war into enemy territory.

THE FIRST YEARS OF THE NEW STATE

In January 1949 an armistice was declared. Again the problem of Palestine was brought before the United Nations. This time it was agreed that the Jews had won their right to the new State. The

North African immigrants resting by the wheels of a plane which will fly them to freedom in Israel.

immediately after the establishment of the State of Israel, a rescue campaign was organized to bring to Israel all the Jews who were victims of persecution in Arab lands. Jews were evacuated by airplane from Yemen, Iraq and Iran and brought safely to the Land of Israel. This courageous project was known as "Operation Magic Carpet."

THE SINAI CAMPAIGN

In the year 1956 Israel had to face Arab hostility once more—this time from Egypt. Gamal Abdel Nasser, the president of Egypt, had nationalized the Suez Canal and declared the Canal closed to all Israeli shipping. Egypt also attacked the Jewish

A captured Egyptian Mig being repaired by the Israelis.

settlements on the Negev, near the Gaza Strip, which lay along the Egyptian border, and made a pact with Syria and Jordan to attack and destroy their neighbor—the State of Israel.

In October 1956, Israel invaded the Sinai desert in an act of self-defense and again repulsed the enemy. The campaign was terminated by interven-

Morning prayers on the battlefield.

tion on the part of the United Nations. Though Egypt retained her previous boundary after this war, the Israeli settlements of the Negev were safe from that time on.

Nasser then began to persecute the Jews in Egypt. Many Egyptian Jews were forced to leave their homes and found a new home in Israel.

However, for almost a decade, Israel's situation was not affected by problems outside its own borders. As always, there was the problem of irrigation. To meet the need of water, pipes were laid at great cost from the Sea of Galilee up north, all the way down to the Negev, and still there was not enough to make the arid Negev bloom. Israel then wished to draw water from the Jordan, but the Arabs said they would make this impossible by lowering the reserves of Lake Huleh. So tension continued to increase.

In every way it could, Israel developed its physical and cultural resources. Tel Aviv, once a small seashore town, became a humming city of 400,000, boasting two great institutions of learning—Tel Aviv University, and, nearby, Bar-Ilan University. An hour away to the north, the industrial city of Haifa, capped by beautiful Mt. Carmel, was now home to 200,000. Eilat, at the southernmost tip of Israel, no longer consisted of a few shacks, but was a port which, at the head of the Red Sea, loomed in importance for Israeli commerce.

Jerusalem, divided though it was, had expanded to almost 300,000 since Israel had won its independence. Hebrew University, unable to get to its campus on Mt. Scopus, which was in Arab hands, erected a magnificent new home in the western part of the city. Nearby, the Israel Museum was built and, on the other side of the University center, Hadassah created its hospital complex. Crowning the whole area was the spacious new Knesset building, housing the Israeli Parliament. The home of the Knesset was dedicated on August 30, 1966.

As 1967 began, Israel was struggling with such economic difficulties as a high rate of unemployment and an unfavorable balance of trade. In the background, there was the constant gnawing at Israel's borders by its neighbors. Often, Israel was forced to take defensive action.

One such incident, the retaliation at Es Samu, when Israel struck back at Arab terrorists in a pre-dawn raid on this Jordanian village, set off a chain of international firecrackers.

As a result, Israel was harshly criticized by the UN Security Council, an act that could not conceal the fact that the real responsibility rested clearly on the Arab nations that ringed 594 miles of Israel's land border—Lebanon, Jordan, Egypt, and especially Syria.

More important, the Es Samu incident brought into focus the reality of the arms-and-men race in the Middle East. It also taught Israel a bitter lesson: that it was useless for the Jewish State to lodge complaints with the United Nations. Russia would veto any resolution dealing with Israel whenever such a resolution condemned the Arabs, while, behind the UN's back, Soviet guns, planes, and tanks continued to pour into both Syria and Egypt. Thus was the stage set for the Six Day War.

THE SIX DAY WAR

June 1967 will be forever remembered as one of the most fateful periods in the history of our people. For six fantastic days, the Middle East crossroads was torn by gunfire and screaming rockets. Then all was still. On the seventh day, when the smoke had cleared, the map of the world had been altered and the faith of Israel tested and found true in one of the greatest epics of all time. Here is a brief account of the epochal events of that unforgettable week.

The tension was terrific on Sunday, June 4th. Tel Aviv and Cairo buzzed with rumors. Tiny Israel, hemmed in by foes, listened to bulletins coming over Kol Yisrael: Iraq had joined Egypt and Jordan in a defense pact. Nasser had proclaimed that Israel would be driven into the sea. Ahmed Shukairy, head of the Palestine Liberation Organization, arriving in Amman, stated: "When we take Israel, the surviving Jews will be helped to return to their native lands." Then he added: "But I think that none will survive."

The cities of Israel were empty of men—those 18 to 49 had left for the Army. Yet spirits were high in this country of 2½ million people, the size of Massachusetts, all included in one telephone book. Surrounded by 110 million Arab enemies, Israelis dug foxholes and trenches and marked time from Kibbutz Ein Gev, on the Eastern shore of the Sea of Galilee and scarcely more than a mile from the Syrian border, down to Eilat, which looked out upon the Gulf of Aqaba, closed by Egypt in an effort to choke Israel to economic death.

And there was evening and there was morning . . . Monday, June 5. As day broke and the rim of the blazing sun edged up over the distant Moab hills, the orange sky was filled with Israel's air force, and motorized infantry and Israeli armor, in three main columns, had plunged deep into enemy territory. The scales of history were trem-

Israeli tanks firing into the Arab lines.

bling, and shadows of the past—of the brave Hasmoneans, of plucky David facing a giant Goliath, of countless heroes of Jewish history— stirred to life to strengthen the modern Maccabees of Israel, now engaged in a desperate struggle for survival.

ROOTS IN ANCIENT SOIL

The Six Day War had its roots in ancient soil. The Promised Land had become a Jewish kingdom 3,000 years ago, had been ravaged by the Assyrians, Babylonians, Romans, Moslems, Crusaders, and Turks. But the text of the Bible, "If I forget thee, O Jerusalem," was engraved on every Jewish heart, and at Seder tables around the globe the concluding words were always, "Next year in Jerusalem."

It was only after six million of our people were murdered by the Nazis, however, that the 2,000-year-old dream became reality. On November 29, 1947, the United Nations offered the pitiful remnant of European Jewry a plan under which Palestine would be partitioned into two states— one Jewish, one Arab.

The Arabs rejected the idea. On May 14, 1948, when David Ben-Gurion stood up in Tel Aviv and declared the birth of the State of Israel, they attacked in ugly fury. When the War of Independence was over, the Jewish State had gained 2,380 square miles (plus the 5,760 granted by partition), and had lost 700,000 Arabs (who had fled at their leaders' command).

Now began the enormous task of building a new country. But the Arab world refused to admit that Israel even existed. Goaded by their rulers to dedicate themselves to the death of Israel, they sent in guerrilla snipers called *fedayeen,* blocked the Strait of Tiran, forbade Israel to fly over the Gulf of Aqaba or to use the Suez Canal.

Aided by Britain and France, Israel in 1956 overran the Sinai Peninsula and broke the stranglehold.

A decade passed, during which the Arabs plotted revenge. In the spring of 1967, bolstered by a huge supply of Russian armament, Nasser felt the time had come for action. He demanded that the 3,400-man UN force withdraw from buffer positions between Egyptians and Israelis, and then blockaded the Strait of Tiran, shutting off Israeli shipping from the East. This was an act of war.

As June began, statesmen argued and soldiers prepared. Piece by piece, destiny's jigsaw puzzle took form. Jordan's King Hussein flew to Cairo and agreed to put Jordan's army under Egyptian control. In Tel Aviv, the army, under newly appointed Defense Minister Moshe Dayan, was given the authority to decide the time and method

David Ben Gurion, the first Premier of Israel.

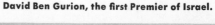

383

Israeli jets defending the Land of Israel.

of response to Arab attack. Everything was ready. The stage was set for the clash of armies that would stun the Arabs, astound the world, and cause Jews everywhere to stand taller and prouder than ever before.

Shortly after dawn on June 5, Egyptian tanks moved toward the border and shelled Israeli positions.

At the same time, Egyptian planes were picked up on radar screens. At 7:55 A.M. there was an air-raid alarm, followed five minutes later by the order to advance on the southern front.

"Kill the Jews" cried the Baghdad radio. "The holy war has started!" blared loudspeakers in Jordan. "The battle will be total," said Nasser. "Our basic aim will be the destruction of Israel."

On the first day the gleaming Israeli jets rained tons of bombs on Arab airfields. Armored columns plunged into the sands of the Sinai Desert. To the east, tanks and half-tracks rolled toward the 329-mile-long border with Jordan.

By sundown Israel had destroyed 410 enemy planes and had total air superiority. The Gaza Strip had been cut off, El Arish taken. Meantime, President Johnson and Premier Kosygin, using the famous "hot line," had assured each other that both super-powers wished only peace in the Middle East, and the UN Security Council had met in New York to hammer out a cease-fire resolution.

By Thursday, Egypt and Jordan had been defeated. The Old City of Jerusalem, liberated at

great sacrifice by the unbelievable bravery of paratroops under Col. "Motke" Gur, was in Jewish hands.

Hardened soldiers, who had wrestled with death in the city streets, on Ammunition Hill, at the Arab-fortified police station, rushed to the Western Wall. There they found an outlet for their emotions. Some kissed the ancient stones. Others wept for friends who had fallen in Jerusalem's streets.

Soldiers cheered as they saw the blue and white flag raised above the wall after an absence of 19 years. Then—a hush as the blast of a shofar pierced the air. Chief Chaplain Shlomo Goren, among the first to enter the Old City, had lifted the ram's horn to his lips for the historic call. Rabbi Goren offered a *Yizkor* prayer for the dead, and then somebody raised his voice in *Hatikvah,* and at once the sound swelled in a thousand throats.

Now, only Syria remained in the field of battle. The entire Israel Air Force—some 400 planes— flew non-stop raids against deeply-dug Syrian gun emplacements on the heights above the Sea of Galilee. The morning sun on Shabbat revealed Syrians running toward Damascus on roads littered with equipment and clothing. Israel's ground forces then conducted a mopping-up operation. At 6:30 P.M. a ceasefire was put into effect. When three stars blinked in the sky at the time for *Havdalah,* a brilliant campaign, one of the most remarkable in military history, was over.

Chief Chaplain Goren blowing the shofar at the Wailing Wall.

The capitals of the world breathed a sigh of relief. The tinderbox had not exploded. What might have spread into a global conflict had been confined, and the flames of war were snuffed out. And, although our hearts were with the Jewish State day and night, it owed its triumph to no outside aid. As its Chief of Staff, Maj. Gen. Itzhak Rabin solemnly declared: "All this has been done by us alone, with what we have, without anybody else."

Said Moshe Dayan: "We have returned to our holiest of places, never to depart again."

A few days later, on a sunlit day, these two great leaders joined the late Levi Eshkol, then Prime Minister of Israel, in a visit to the *Kotel Ma'aravi*—the Western Wall—last remnant of the Second Temple.

Each one, following an old Jewish tradition, had written a prayer to place in a crevice in the wall. "What did you write?" curious reporters inquired. *"Shema Yisrael,"* said Mr. Eshkol. "May peace be upon all Israel," said Gen. Dayan. "This is the Lord's doing; it is marvelous in our eyes," said Gen. Rabin, quoting *Tehillim,* the Book of Psalms. Thus was an element of holiness acknowledged in the return of Jerusalem to the Jewish people.

Chapter XLI

JEWS IN THE WORLD TODAY

THE AFTERMATH OF THE SIX DAY WAR

The State of Israel emerged from the war in an immensely strengthened position. The armed forces of its Arab enemies had been smashed. Even as it fought, it aimed for peace. As Abba Eban, then Foreign Minister, declared, the Six Day War had been the only war in history "where the victors sued for peace and the vanquished demanded unconditional surrender."

The spirit in which *Tzahal*—the Israel Defense Forces—fought, was perhaps best described by Itzhak Rabin, in a speech delivered as he accepted an honorary degree from the Hebrew University in Jerusalem on June 28, 1967. He said:

"The entire nation was exalted and many wept when they heard of the capture of the Old City. Our Sabra youth, and, most certainly our soldiers, do not tend to be sentimental. But the strain of battle and the sense of confrontation with Jewish history cracked the shell and released wellsprings of emotion. The paratroopers who conquered the Wailing Wall leaned on its stones and wept.

"And there is more to be told. The joy of triumph had seized the entire nation. Nevertheless, a strange phenomenon can be observed among our soldiers. Their joy is incomplete, and their celebrations are marred by sorrow and shock. The men in the front lines saw with their own eyes not only the glory of victory, but also the price of victory—their comrades fallen beside them soaked in blood. I know too, that the terrible price paid by our enemies also touched the hearts of many of our men. It may be that the Jewish people has never learned and never accustomed itself to feel the triumph of conquest and victory, with the result that these are accepted with mixed feelings."

Israeli tank soldier guarding the Suez Canal.

Israel's desire for peace was not shared by the governments of the Arab states. No sooner had Israel won the war than it was proclaimed the aggressor by the very nations that had agreed to the blockade of Aqaba and moved armies into Sinai, planning to destroy the Jewish state. It declared repeatedly that it sought peace, but that such peace could only be obtained through a treaty negotiated and signed in a direct meeting of the states involved in the fighting. Except for Old Jerusalem—the most sacred spot in Judaism—from which Jews had been barred since 1948, and where Arabs had committed such shameful desecrations as using the tombstones on the Mount of Olives for paving-stones, all territory could and would be negotiated.

The nation's military victory had given Israelis and their friends overseas renewed confidence in the future. The number of tourists arriving in Israel nearly doubled from 1967, when 328,000 came, to 1970, when 650,000 visited the land.

Table of composition of Jerusalem's population:

Year	Jews	Moslems	Christians	Total
1844	7,120	5,000	3,390	15,510
1905	40,000	7,000	13,000	60,000
1931	51,222	19,894	19,335	90,451
1948	100,000	40,000	25,000	165,000
1967*	195,700	54,963	10,800	261,463
1975*	264,000	81,000	11,000	356,000

*These figures refer to area of Greater Jerusalem

Earlier investments, such as the chemical plants at Arad, or the new harbors at Eilat and Ashdod, began to pay off significantly after 1967. Israeli industry began producing, and exporting, advanced technical products. Exports of Israeli goods and services jumped by about 100% in the four years after the war.

The years after the Six Day War also saw a rising tide of Aliyah, and an unprecedented flow of investments and contributions from Jews abroad for the development of Israel. The tensions of those fearful days in May and June 1967, when Israel's existence hung in the balance, and the victory that followed, jolted many Jews in the Diaspora deeply. It awoke in them a sense of unity with Israel that would never leave them.

World Jewish Population.

U. S. of A. —	6,000,000	
Canada —	300,000	
	6,300,000	Total North American Jewry
Argentina —	450,000	
Brazil —	160,000	
	700,000	Total Latin American Jewry
South Africa —	110,000	
Australia —	70,000	
Israel —	3,000,000	
Iran —	80,000	
Turkey —	30,000	
India —	15,000	
	3,150,000	Total Non-Soviet Asian Jewry
Soviet Union—	3,000,000	
France —	500,000	
Gt. Britain —	400,000	
	4,100,000	Total European & Soviet Jewry
	14,100,000	Total World Jewry

SOVIET REPRESSION AND THE RUSSIAN JEWISH RENAISSANCE

Many Jews in the Soviet Union experienced just such a rediscovery of their identity in the late 1960's. After its Arab clients lost the Six Day War, the Soviet Union launched a vicious propaganda campaign against Israel, Zionism, and Judaism. Thousands of Russian Jews responded to their government's repressive efforts by defiantly asserting more clearly than ever that they were Jews. Throughout the Soviet Union, circles of Jewish activists began organizing illegal courses in Judaism and the Hebrew language. On Simhat Torah, at the Great Synagogue in Moscow, one of the few synagogues still allowed to remain open in the Soviet Union, thousands of young Jews began to gather to dance, sing, and celebrate together their Jewishness.

Russian Jews had been cut off from the rest of World Jewry since the Revolution in 1917. Ever since then the Soviet regime had systematically aimed at destroying all organized Jewish communal life and obliterating Jewishness from Russia. Although anti-Semitism was outlawed after the Revolution, it survived not only among the populace, but even at the highest levels of the Soviet government. Jewish artists and intellectuals, many of whom had devoted their lives to the cause of the Russian Revolution, were accused of being "cosmopolitans," without roots in native Russian culture, and were disgraced, or executed. Over the decades since the Revolution, Jews have also been subjected to growing discrimination in schools and employment. Except for the anti-Semitic tracts that it issues itself, the Soviet government permits hardly anything to be printed in Russia concerning Jewishness or Israel.

Israel's courageous stand in the Middle East sparked hope for escape among some Soviet Jewish activists. They began applying for visas to emigrate to Israel, where they could live freely as Jews. It would be extremely embarrassing for the government to allow these Jews to leave, so their requests were refused. Jews who asked to leave for Israel were thrown out of work, their children denied entry to school. These Jews were threatened, persecuted, often arrested, yet they persisted in seeking to rejoin the Jewish people in Israel.

Protests on behalf of Soviet Jewry mounted during the late 1960's. The Russian government reacted by staging a series of arrests and show trials, starting with the seizure of several Jewish activists at the Leningrad airport on June 15, 1970. The group arrested at the Leningrad airport were accused of attempting to hijack an airplane. During the course of their trial, it became clear that they had been drawn into a trap prepared by the KGB (the Soviet Secret Police). The unfair manner in which the case was conducted, and the harsh sentences given the accused, outraged not only Jews, but just people all over the world. Two of the defendants, Edward Kuznetsov and Mark Dymshitz, were condemned to death by the court. This ignited a world-wide upsurge of denunciation and protests. In Israel, Prime Minister Golda Meir appealed "to parliaments, governments, religious and intellectual leaders, educators and molders of public opinion, to raise their voices and call for the annulment of the sentence." In New York, and other cities throughout America, thousands of Jews demonstrated angrily against the sentences. And the Russian government backed down! The death sentences were commuted to prison terms, and other sentences were lightened.

The concern of Jews throughout the world focused on the Soviet Jewish problem. Jews began organizing protests against the Russian government's restrictions on emigration by Jews. In America, groups of young Jews, such as the Student Struggle for Soviet Jewry (SSSJ), formed to conduct demonstrations and mobilize popular support for the cause of Soviet Jewry.

Under pressure from both within and without, the Russian government loosened up somewhat on its emigration restrictions. In 1971, about 13,000 Jews left for Israel. The next year, 31,000 Jews were allowed to go. In 1973 this wave of Russian Aliyah crested, and 32,000 Jews from the Soviet Union settled in Israel.

For a while it seemed as if the Soviet regime would allow even more Jews to leave for Israel. An American Senator, Henry Jackson, hoped to use an amendment to a law regulating trade between the United States and Russia to pressure the Soviet Union into giving more Jews permission to go to Israel. Other American leaders, such as Henry Kissinger, tried to negotiate informal agreements that would guarantee a freer flow of Jews to Israel. But after the Yom Kippur War the Russian government began to cut back on the number of Jews it would allow to leave.

Picketing the Russian Embassy.

American Jews, in Washington, D.C., protesting Russian immigration policies.

Thousands of Jews have applied and been denied the right to leave. These "refusniks" await the day when they will be able to leave Russia. Many of them have lost their jobs, or the right to go to school. Others have been arrested. Yet courageous young Jews throughout the Soviet Union still go on risking their careers, and, perhaps, even their lives, by participating in secret Hebrew courses, circulating hand-copied, illegal books on Jewish history, and by applying for visas to emigrate to Israel. At the Moscow Book Fair in 1979, an exhibit sponsored by a delegation of American Jewish publishers, led by Bernard Scharfstein of Ktav Publishing House, inspired and encouraged scores of thousands of Russian Jewish visitors to continue their struggle.

AMERICAN JEWRY

Jews in America continue to enjoy every opportunity to pursue their chosen careers, to contribute to American artistic, scientific, and political affairs, and to involve themselves in Jewish religious and cultural life.

Interest in Israel continues to grow among American Jews. Israel's struggle to survive concerns all Jews, and the growing political and economic support for the Jewish state provided by the six-million-strong American Jewish community has been of vital importance. In addition

to raising funds, American Jews have continually rallied to Israel's support in times of need. In 1979, for instance, they protested to the White House when UN Ambassador Andrew Young met with PLO representatives for unauthorized private discussions. In 1980, when the United States inadvertently voted for an anti-Israel UN resolution, Jewish protests led President Jimmy Carter to make a public apology.

Interest in Judaism, in Israel, and in Jewish history is growing among American Jews. Enrollments in Yeshivot and Jewish day schools are rising. Many good colleges and universities now offer a variety of courses in Jewish studies. The widespread interest in Jewish culture was heightened in 1978 when the Nobel Prize for Literature was awarded Isaac Bashevis Singer, the Yiddish novelist whose works have often been best-sellers in English translations. The showing of the multi-part television series *Holocaust,* both in America and throughout the world, also did much to strengthen Jewish identity and self-awareness. The American Jewish community's strong commitment to Jewish causes has been shown not only by its support for Israel and for Russian Jewry but in the assistance it has extended to Jewish refugees who were forced to flee from Iran after the Islamic Revolution in that country.

ISRAEL AND THE ARABS

A few months after the Six Day War, in August 1967, the leaders of the Arab states assembled in Khartoum, the capital of the Sudan, to determine their response to the new situation in the Middle East, and their policy toward the strengthened Jewish state. Nasser, the most important Arab ruler, had good reason to feel his forces stood a chance of tiring out the Israelis dug in on the Suez Canal. The Egyptian army and air force were already being rapidly resupplied by the Russians. In the late 1960's several thousand Russian "advisors" arrived, to train the Egyptians in the use of modern weapons. Exchanges of artillery shells and raids gradually built in intensity from the summer of 1967 on. The Egyptians had many more soldiers, tanks, and cannons than the Israelis. Yet the Israelis held on. They built a system of forts along the canal, and named the line of steel and concrete bunkers after General

Chaim Bar-Lev, then Israel's chief of staff. The Israelis counterattacked too. Israeli jets bombed Egyptian targets across the canal, and even deep inside Egypt. The Egyptians' plans to make defense of the canal and Sinai so costly in men and equipment that the Israelis would be forced to withdraw were foiled.

General Chaim Bar-Lev, eighth Chief-of-Staff of the Israel Defense Forces.

The war of attrition did take a heavy toll. In the three years between the Six Day War and July 1970, the Israelis lost more than 3,000 dead and wounded. The Egyptians suffered more than 10,000 casualties in the four months between April and July 1970 alone.

In order to avoid more casualties, both Israel and Egypt agreed to a cease-fire proposed by the American government in August 1970.

On other fronts, Arab terrorists committed a number of murderous crimes, designed to undermine the morale of Israelis and of their friends abroad. In the Israeli town of Ma'alot in 1974, more than a score of harmless youngsters were murdered. Israeli athletes at the Olympics in Munich in 1972 were also killed.

The question of what Israel is to do with the West Bank and the Gaza Strip territories, with their large Arab population, has been debated by Israelis almost since the end of the Six Day War. Many Israelis, particularly members of the "Gush Emunim" (Mass of the Faithful) movement, feel that these lands, especially the West Bank, are integral parts of the country promised to the patriarchs of the Jewish people. They feel that Jews have a right to settle throughout these territories. They oppose returning the West Bank to Jordan, and, in general, would prefer to incorporate the Arabs living there into Israel. There are some Israelis, however, who hold a very different view. Yigal Allon, a former Foreign Minister and Deputy Prime Minister of Israel, for instance, has long called for Israel to eventually withdraw from most of the territories, including the bulk of the West Bank. Allon argues that Israel should hold on to strategically vital parts of the West Bank, such as a strip of land along the Jordan River. The rest of the West Bank could be organized into a confederation with Jordan. Israelis who advocate these "dovish" solutions are often deeply worried that if the Arabs in the territories, who have a much higher birth-rate than the Jewish population of Israel, were included in the state, there could emerge an Arab majority in Israel within a few decades.

Meanwhile, the Arabs in the territories have prospered under Israeli rule. Their standard of living has risen, and the schools their children attend have improved. Israel has encouraged peaceful contacts between inhabitants of the West Bank and other Arabs by an "open bridges"

Over eighty thousand people gather together for the memorial ceremony in Munich Stadium in honor of the thirteen Israeli sportsmen killed by Palestinian terrorists during the 1972 Olympics.

policy on the Jordan River. Thousands of Jordanian and other Arabs have been able to visit their friends and relatives on the West Bank because of this policy. Arabs from the West Bank and Gaza have also been allowed to find work and visit Israeli Arabs within the pre-1967 borders of the Jewish state. These contacts have helped to improve relations between Arabs and Jews, and to dispel some of the prejudices they held concerning one another.

On one issue there is almost unanimity in Israel—Jerusalem must remain a united city under Jewish control. There is no other city on earth like Jerusalem. It is holy to Christians and Moslems, but has only a secondary order of importance for them. Moslems have Mecca, Catholics have Rome, but only for Jews is Jerusalem the center of their religious world.

For a hundred years before Israel became independent, Jerusalem was a city with a Jewish majority. Between 1948 and 1967, when the Old City was under Jordanian rule, Jews were banned from visiting the Wailing Wall. Synagogues in the ancient Jewish quarter were destroyed, or used as stables or chicken coops. Of some 50,000 Jewish tombstones on the Mount of Olives, 38,000 were torn up to pave a road, and to serve as building material for latrines. All this occurred even though Jordan had signed an Armistice Agreement with Israel, in which "free access to the Holy Places and to cultural institutions, and use of the Jewish cemetery on the Mount of Olives," was guaranteed! By contrast, since 1967, when Israel took control of the Old City with its sites holy to three religions, all sects and their holy places have enjoyed full religious freedom and protection.

Jerusalem today is the capital of Israel. It is a united city, with a band of parks dividing the eastern and western parts of town, instead of barbed wire. The city's population has risen to over 370,000, of whom almost 270,000 are Jews, and over 100,000 Moslems or Christians. It is still growing rapidly.

Jerusalem is a city in which Jews and Arabs have learned to live together in peace. The archaeological excavations near the Temple Mount, and in the Jewish quarter have resulted in many discoveries that have deepened the connection Jews feel for this city.

THE YOM KIPPUR WAR

At precisely 2:00 P.M., on October 6, 1973, Arab shells began crashing down on Israeli positions along the Suez Canal and in the Golan Heights. Thousands of Egyptian and Syrian soldiers poured across the lightly defended 1967 cease-fire lines. Most of the Israeli soldiers were away on holiday leave. It was Yom Kippur, the most sacred day in the Jewish calendar.

The Egyptians attacked with 600,000 men, 2,000 tanks, 2,300 cannons, 160 batteries of anti-aircraft missiles, 550 combat planes, and almost complete surprise. Against this huge force Israel had to depend on 436 soldiers strung out in bunkers all along the 110-mile-long canal, and three tanks plus a few cannons. The Egyptians were across the canal, and by October 9 they were consolidating their forces along a front five to ten miles deep into Sinai.

In the Golan Heights the situation was even more dangerous. The Israelis had, at first, only a few hundred soldiers to hold back the entire

An Egyptian soldier captured behind Israeli lines is brought to an army post for questioning.

Syrian army. The Israelis struggled desperately, but the Syrians forced them slowly back toward the B'not Ya'akov Bridge, which spanned the Jordan River, and marked the boundary between pre-1967 Israel and the Golan Heights. Syrian missiles and shells began falling on Israeli Kibbutzim. The new Israeli settlements on the Golan Heights had to be hurriedly evacuated. By the evening of October 8, the situation of the Israelis was desperate. West of the city of Quneitra, Colonel Avigdor Janos, commander of the Israeli Seventh Armored Brigade, had only a half-dozen tanks left with which to prevent the Syrians from pouring into northern Israel.

The Israeli Air Force was fully mobilized when the war began. The Syrian advance in the north presented the greatest immediate danger to Israel, so it was on this front that Israeli air power at first concentrated. The Arabs were now equipped with the latest Russian antiaircraft and antitank missiles. Many Israeli planes were shot down as they attacked Arab positions. Yet the skill and daring of Israeli pilots, combined with the bravery of Israeli troops on the ground, succeeded in slowing down the Arab advance until a counterattack could be organized.

Syrian guns rained down a murderous stream of shellfire, but Colonel Janos' Seventh Armored Brigade on the Golan Heights made it through the night. By dawn of the next day Israeli reserves were moving up in force. The Syrians had already suffered heavy losses. When Janos now spearheaded the Israeli counterattack, the Arab army broke, and began to retreat toward Damascus. The tide of battle had turned in the north.

With pressure from the Syrians relieved, Israel began shifting forces to deal with the Egyptians in Sinai. Reports indicated that there was a gap in the lines of the Egyptians just north of the Great Bitter Lake, near the center of the Suez Canal. General Arik Sharon was given a crucial, but risky, task. He was to drive a wedge between the two sections of the Egyptian army, cross the canal, and cut them off from the rear. There was no time to lose. The Egyptians had gathered hundreds of tanks to hurl at the Israelis in a new offensive. The Israelis had hastily brought together a very powerful tank force of their own. On the morning of October 14, the Egyptian and Israeli armies tangled in the largest, fiercest

tank battle since World War II. The fighting raged all day, but now the Israelis were ready. The Egyptian attack was smashed, their tank force almost wiped out. In the darkness and confusion that night, Sharon's men pushed through the gap between the Egyptian armies, and crossed the canal. During the next few days they strengthened their bridgehead and began racing to trap the Egyptians in Sinai.

When reports of Syrian reversals and Israeli canal crossings began to come in, the Arabs remained unwilling to halt the bloodshed. Once it had become clear that Israel was winning, the Egyptians began appealing to their Russian backers to force an end to the fighting. On the night of October 18, therefore, Russia invited Henry Kissinger to fly to Moscow in order to discuss cease-fire terms.

Meanwhile a dangerous confrontation was brewing between the United States and Russia. The Soviet Union had not only given the Arabs great amounts of equipment before the war, but had been resupplying them by massive airlifts as they battled with the Israelis. The losses suffered by the Israelis made resupply by America a vital necessity. At first the American government was hesitant to provide Israel the supplies it needed. When the United States learned that the Russians were resupplying Egypt and Syria by means of the largest airlift in history, American planes began flying tons of equipment to Israel.

Henry Kissinger arrived in Moscow on October 20. This first Jewish Secretary of State had come to America as a refugee from Hitler's

Henry Kissinger.

Germany while still a boy. Now he felt that the way in which the war had evolved provided a unique opportunity to settle the Arab-Israeli dispute. He reasoned that the Arabs had fought well enough to recover their "honor," but the Israelis had proven that even with the advantages of more manpower, better equipment, and complete surprise, the Arabs could not defeat them in battle. The war was ending in a draw. In the agreement that Kissinger worked out with the Russians, Israel was to refrain from completing the destruction of the Arab armies, but "immediately and concurrently" with the cease-fire direct talks were to begin between Israel and Egypt aimed at "just and durable peace" in the region. Israel had hoped for just such negotiations since its foundation, so it accepted the proposal, and on October 22 the UN Security Council passed the joint American and Russian cease-fire appeal.

All the while that these cease-fire talks continued, the Israelis kept on advancing. By the time that the cease-fire finally became effective, they had managed to trap over 20,000 men, the entire elite Egyptian Third Army, along the southern part of the canal. The Egyptians feared that the Third Army would have to surrender unless the Israelis pulled back. Such a defeat was unacceptable to the Russian patrons of the Arabs. It would also have upset, in Israel's favor, the battlefield stalemate Kissinger wanted in order to

Yigal Allon.

force the start of peace negotiations.

On October 24 the Russians sent President Nixon a message in which they threatened to take matters into their own hands if America would not cooperate in forcing Israel back from its advanced positions west of Suez, thereby freeing the trapped Egyptian Third Army. The United States could not allow Russian soldiers to intervene directly in the Middle East. President Nixon ordered American nuclear forces around the globe to be placed on the alert. For a few hours a much more destructive type of war seemed to menace the world, but a compromise was reached. Instead of Russian or American troops, a neutral UN force was sent to patrol the cease-fire lines. Israel allowed food and water to reach the Third Army but kept it trapped.

More than 11,000 Arabs died in the Yom Kippur War, but so did over 2,500 Israelis. Israel emerged victorious on the battlefield, but at a bloody price.

ISRAEL AND WORLD JEWRY SINCE THE YOM KIPPUR WAR

The Arabs won their greatest victories in 1973 not on the battlefield, but in the oilfields and at the conference table. In that year the Organization of Petroleum Exporting Countries (OPEC), of which Arab states such as Saudi Arabia, Iraq, and Libya were prominent members, forced an increase in the world price of oil of over 400%. The Arabs' vast oil resources ensure them increasing wealth and political power for years to come. During the Yom Kippur War the effects of this new Arab oil power began to hurt Israel's relations with other nations. Western European nations refused to allow American planes to fly over their territories on the way to resupply Israel. Japan, with no oil of its own, made pro-Arab statements. Even before the war, Black African nations, whose friendship Israel had long cultivated, began breaking off diplomatic relations with Israel and moving to a pro-Arab position.

After the war, Israel found itself increasingly isolated. At the United Nations, the institution in which Jews had placed their hopes for a just and peaceful world after World War II, and which had fostered the creation of the Jewish state, Israel was now subjected to unjust and in-

Arab poster reaffirming the Arab claim to Palestine and "justifying the use of murder."

sulting resolutions forced through the General Assembly by the Arabs and their supporters. Zionism was called "racism." The supposedly non-political United Nations Educational, Scientific, and Cultural Organization (UNESCO) cut off funds for Israel in 1974 because of Arab pressure. One of the saddest incidents at the UN in this period occurred in November 1975, when Yasir Arafat, leader of a coalition of Arab terrorist groups called the "Palestine Liberation Organization," was invited to address the UN General Assembly. Arafat shocked friends of this world organization dedicated to peace by wearing a gun in his belt while making his speech to the General Assembly.

The war itself worked to strengthen the bonds uniting the Jewish communities of the world with Israel. They shared the anguish of the Israelis as casualties mounted, and their relief when the fighting ended with Israel in control of the battlefields. The political and financial support of World Jewry for Israel has increased since 1973. Israelis have become more aware of the need for maintaining the unity of the Jewish people throughout the world. American Jewry especially continues to provide Israel with great contributions of funds. American Jews have worked to counter Arab propaganda, and to guarantee strong American government backing for Israel. Organizations such as the American Jewish Congress and the Anti-Defamation League have been fighting against the Arab boycott of businesses dealing with Israel, and have succeeded in having several states and Congress pass laws designed to block compliance with it.

In spite of Arab oil blackmail, Israel has been recovering from the diplomatic isolation it experienced immediately after the 1973 war. America has remained deeply committed to Israel's survival. Many of the industrialized nations of Europe, and Japan, have recovered some of their courage, and have become somewhat less anxious to appease the Arabs. Several African nations have been disappointed by the manner in which the Arabs have failed to come through with huge amounts of promised aid. Although they pleased the Arabs by breaking relations with Israel, these nations never felt hatred for Israel or Jews. Recently, they have been growing more resistant to Arab pressure to condemn Israel in the United Nations.

When the 1973 war ended, the battlelines between the Arabs and Israelis were very unstable. War threatened to erupt again at any moment. Kissinger hoped to exploit the military deadlock to force peace talks to begin, but the direct negotiations between Arabs and Israelis, in Geneva and at "Kilometer 101" on the front along the Suez-Cairo highway, soon stalled. The Arabs and Israelis had very different ideas of the terms and goals of peace talks. Kissinger stepped in to try to rescue the situation. Instead of an immediate attempt to reach a comprehensive settlement of the Arab-Israeli conflict, he substituted a "step-by-step" approach. Personally involving himself in negotiations, as intermediary between Israeli and Arab leaders, he traveled back and forth between Jerusalem and Cairo, and then Damascus and Jerusalem, so many times that this style of

Menachem Begin.

394

political bargaining became known as "shuttle diplomacy." During the next two years Kissinger managed to arrange a series of disengagement agreements between Egypt and Israel, and also with Syria. In these agreements Israel consented to return thin slices of territory near Suez and in the Golan to the Arabs, and in exchange received guarantees, through Kissinger, that Egypt and Syria would not attack Israel, at least for the duration of the agreements. Israel also was promised billions of dollars worth of military and economic aid from the United States, and the general diplomatic support of the United States in international forums such as the United Nations. Israel and the Arabs would be separated by neutral UN forces. In the last of these agreements, reached in September 1975, Egypt and Israel stated that they would avoid "resort to the threat or use of force or military blockade against each other." Egypt also promised to allow cargos on neutral ships traveling to or from Israel to pass through the reopened Suez Canal. In return, Israel pulled back from a larger section of Sinai, and gave back the Abu Rudeis oil fields to Egypt. America placed itself behind the agreement. Americans were to man an electronic early warning station on behalf of the Israelis in Sinai.

These partial settlements caused considerable criticism in Israel. Israel was being asked to trade away its bargaining chips little by little, without receiving a final peace treaty in return. By the time Kissinger left office early in 1977, he had by no means achieved peace between Israel and the Arabs. However, he had helped create an atmosphere in which peace was spoken of in more realistic terms, and seemed more possible, than ever since Israel's independence.

Within Israeli society the Yom Kippur War produced an earthquake. Itzhak Rabin replaced Golda Meir as Prime Minister. Many Israelis began to reexamine the direction in which their society had been developing. They have been trying to deal with their problems, to restructure their economy, and make it more productive. The Labor Party had ruled Israel ever since independence. In the May 1977 elections the young democratic system of Israel passed a crucial test. The Rabin government was defeated, and another party called Likud, headed by Menachem Begin, won the elections. For the first time in Israeli

Itzhak Rabin

history, political power was transferred from one party to another.

An equally important event soon followed. Begin, publicly invited President Anwar Sadat of Egypt to visit Israel. Sadat accepted, and in November 1977, while the whole world watched in astonishment and other Arab leaders fumed in anger, the two men met in Jerusalem. Sadat made a speech to the Israeli Knesset and visited the Holocaust memorial at Yad Vashem. During the intensive peace negotiations that ensued, Begin visited Sadat in Egypt. The long-awaited peace treaty between the two countries was finally signed after a final negotiating session held at Camp David, Maryland, under the auspices of President Jimmy Carter of the United States. In 1978 Begin and Sadat were jointly awarded the Nobel Peace Prize.

By the terms of the treaty, Israel withdrew from the Sinai in stages and normal relations between the two countries began for the first time, including trade, tourism, and diplomatic representation. Many differences remained to be ironed out, most especially the difficult problem of the territories on the West Bank, but the two countries seemed at last to have entered upon a new era of peace that promised many benefits for both of them. Egypt could devote its resources to modernizing its backward economy and upgrading the living standard of its growing population. Israel could also now concentrate on domestic problems. While it still had to remain militarily alert on all of its frontiers, it was secure in the knowledge that the most powerful of the Arab states was no longer actively hostile.

Syria, Iraq, Libya, and other Arab countries still threatened Israel, however. So did the Palestinian terrorists, operating out of the enclave they control in southern Lebanon, where they have also been fighting against the country's Christian Arabs. PLO terrorist raids in Israel remained a problem. One of the worst occurred in March 1978, when 37 Israeli civilians—men, women, and children—were slaughtered near Tel Aviv while returning from a picnic. Another terrorist attack, in May 1980, resulted in the death of 6 Israeli students in the town of Hebron. Israel responds forcefully to all of these attacks, and on several occasions Israeli military forces retaliated against terrorist bases in Lebanon.

Through their control of a large part of the world's oil resources, the Arabs have worked to isolate Israel among the nations. Many countries fear that their oil will be cut off if they are too friendly to Israel. Even the United States has wavered from time to time, but it continues to be Israel's chief support in the international political arena. Most Americans are very sympathetic to Israel and recognize its importance as the only bastion of democracy in the entire Middle East.

Israel is a unique country, whose survival has special meaning. Perhaps it requires an episode like Entebbe to make clear how important Israel is. On June 27, 1976, an Air France airbus carrying some 300 passengers and crew was hijacked by a fanatic band of Arab and German terrorists. The plane landed at the international airport of Uganda at Entebbe. The hijackers demanded that Israel release several terrorists serving sentences in Israeli prisons. Before long it became clear that the hijacking had taken place with the cooperation of the Ugandan government and its head, Idi Amin. Israel and Jews all over the world were shocked and dismayed when the terrorists released most of their hostages but held on to Israelis and Jews. Bitter memories of Jews selected for death during the Holocaust were revived. The lives of more than a hundred Jews were in the balance. Days passed, and no other agency or government moved to save the Jewish hostages. It seemed as if Israel would be forced to submit to the terrorists' demands. Then, on Sunday, July 4, 1976, miraculous news stunned the world. An Israeli raiding party had flown more than 2,500 miles into the heart of Africa and rescued the hostages! They had taken the

Yonathan Netanyahu.

Ugandan guards and the terrorists by surprise. Israeli transport planes swept into the airport at night. A hundred troops raced off the planes and toward the building in which the hostages were being held. Other Israelis destroyed Ugandan fighters lined up on the runway. For a few minutes a hellstorm of gunfire broke out, then quiet. The terrorists and Ugandans were killed or driven off. A few unlucky hostages were shot in the cross fire, but the great majority were safe. There was one tragic Israeli death—Lt. Col. Yonathan Netanyahu, the young son of an American professor of Jewish history. After less than 90 minutes in Entebbe, the Israelis and the rescued hostages were flying back to Israel.

Indeed, Israel is an inspiring country. Hundreds of thousands of people, many of them Jews from America, visit Israel each year. There is so much to see and do! The range of things to see and do in Israel today is perhaps best symbolized by the fact that you can swim in the salty depths of the Dead Sea or ski on the slopes of Mt. Hermon. And all in the Land of the Bible, whose archaeological riches add meaning to all we've learned in the Torah.

Our Book of Books—in history, in archaeology, in daily practice—is ever present in Israel. That holds true for visitor and resident alike. Any non-Israeli, for example, who celebrates his Bar Mitzvah in Israel has something special in store for him; the thrill of a lifetime in the land of the

Bible, a silk *tallit* presented by the Government, a certificate from the President of Israel, and the chance to plant a tree in B'nai Mitzvah Forest in the Jerusalem hills.

The situation of the State of Israel among the Arab nations is difficult. The Israelis hope that eventually the Arabs will accept them as neighbors, living and working peaceably with them. Meanwhile, the Israelis continue to build a new land; they continue giving a home to the homeless, to all Jews who wish to come and join their community. Agricultural and industrial projects are constantly growing. Beautiful new settlements are being developed. Israeli ships ply the oceans of the world; the planes of an Israeli commercial airline now soar above the ancient routes once traveled by kings and caravans en route to the court of Solomon and far beyond.

The world has watched the birth and growth of this new nation with interest and admiration. Visitors from around the globe now travel to the Land of Israel on business and vacation trips. People from all walks of life—and of many faiths —wend their way to the ancient land—and marvel at the "miracle in the desert" that is the new State of Israel. And the air they breathe as they walk along its lovely streets or roam its quiet hills is the sweet air of freedom.

The search for this freedom has come full circle. It is a never-ending search—for ever greater understanding of man, his destiny and his relationship to God. It is a search that has led the Jewish people across all the lands and oceans of the world—and it has not ended but only begun, with the finding, once more, of the Promised Land.

The faith that is Israel has been forged like an endless chain, generation by generation, across the centuries—of a substance far stronger than the chains of slaves or the gates of ghettos; for this is the substance of the human spirit— indomitable, unbreakable—and infinite.

INDEX

A

PHOTOGRAPHIC CREDITS

Academy of Sciences, Kaufman Collection, Budapest, 215

American Jewish Committee, 352

American Jewish Historical Society, 305, 306, 307, 308, 309, 310, 311, 312, 313, 314, 315, 316, 317, 341, 343, 344, 345, 371, 372, 375

American Society for Oriental Research, 43, 65, 119

Biblical Archaeologist, The, 13

Bodleian Library, Oxford, 232

Boston Museum of Fine Arts, 117

British Museum, Courtesy of the Trustees of the, 2, 9, 14, 17, 23, 58, 60, 67, 69, 70, 71, 72, 73, 74, 80, 87, 90, 96, 109, 111, 126, 127

Brooklyn Museum, 92

Cairo Museum, 6, 9, 209

Cambridge University Library, 135, 197

Cliché des Musées Nationaux, Paris, France, 1, 9, 55, 57, 61, 122, 156, 196, 219, 241, 243, 257, 290, 291, 292

Cordova Museum, Spain, 207

Cyprus Museum, 95, 144

Department of Antiquities, Jerusalem, Israel, 20, 70, 120, 157

Department of Antiquities, Amman, Jordan, 7, 25, 33, 35, 52

Educational Alliance, New York, 339

Fogg Art Museum, The, Harvard University, 81

Hadassah, 345, 358, 359

Haifa Maritime Museum, 108

Hebrew Immigrant Aid Society, 374

Hebrew Union College, Cinn., 316

Israel Exploration Society, 18, 61, 75

Israel Museum, 132, 133

Israel Office of Information, 14, 15, 31, 42, 43, 53, 88, 89, 98, 114, 115, 129, 131, 133, 137, 142, 143, 217, 254, 378, 380, 381, 382

Istanbul Museum of the Ancient Orient, 6, 59

Jewish Agricultural Society, 336, 337, 338

Jewish Historical Society of England, 218, 259, 261, 299, 300, 301, 343

Jewish Museum, New York, 12, 45, 101, 157, 169, 283

Jewish National Fund, 41

Jewish Theological Seminary, New York, 163, 173, 175, 198, 201, 202, 206, 208, 210, 220, 232, 240, 255, 292, 314, 340

Library of Congress, 346

Matson Photo Service, The, Alhambra, Calif., 10, 26, 34, 40, 46, 56, 66, 68, 100, 105, 113, 120, 121, 128, 175

Metropolitan Museum of Art, 8

Morgan Library, The Pierpont, New York, 190

Naples Museum, 92, 97

National Museum, Teheran, 166

Oriental Institute, University of Chicago, 20, 27, 44, 48, 78, 80, 85, 157

Palestine Archaeological Museum, Jerusalem, Israel, 28, 36, 64, 65, 72

Royal Library, Brussels, 223

Scharfstein, Joel, 162, 302

Schloss, Ezekiel, Art Collection, 174

Soncino Press, 164

Staatliche Museen, Berlin, 68, 190

Toledo Museum, Spain, 234, 235, 236

Trans World Air Lines, 199

United Jewish Appeal, New York, 373

University Museum, The, University of Pennsylvania, 2, 68

Vaticani, Mus., Archivio Fotograf Gall., 110, 156, 185, 186

Yale University Art Gallery, 31

YIVO, Yiddish Institute for Jewish Research, 268, 277, 278, 280, 285, 287, 288, 322, 323, 338, 363, 364, 366, 367, 369

Yeshiva University, 341, 342

Zionist Archives, New York, 45, 135, 148, 149, 150, 153, 154, 325, 326, 329, 330, 331, 332, 349, 350, 351, 353, 355, 356, 357, 359, 360, 362, 364, 365, 372, 374, 378, 379, 381, 382

We have made every effort to identify the sources for all the photographs in this book. If anyone has information about any photographs that have not been identified we will be glad to list them in the next edition.